The Nationalist Revolution in China, 1923–1928

The Nationalist Revolution
in China, 1923–1928

C. MARTIN WILBUR

George Sansom Professor Emeritus of Chinese History
Columbia University

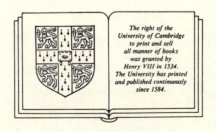

The right of the
University of Cambridge
to print and sell
all manner of books
was granted by
Henry VIII in 1534.
The University has printed
and published continuously
since 1584.

CAMBRIDGE UNIVERSITY PRESS

CAMBRIDGE

LONDON   NEW YORK   NEW ROCHELLE
MELBOURNE   SYDNEY

Published by the Press Syndicate of the University of Cambridge
The Pitt Building, Trumpington Street, Cambridge CB2 1RP
32 East 57th Street, New York, NY 10022, USA
296 Beaconsfield Parade, Middle Park, Melbourne 3206, Australia

First published 1983 as chapter 11 of *The Cambridge History of China*, volume 12
Reprinted 1984 as *The Nationalist Revolution in China, 1923–1928*

Printed in Great Britain at the
University Press, Cambridge

Library of Congress catalogue card number: 84-9588

British Library Cataloguing in Publication Data
Wilbur, C. Martin
The Nationalist Revolution in China, 1923–1928
1. Nationalism – China – History – 20th
century   2. China – History – Warlord period,
1916–1928
I. Title
322.4'2'0951   DS777.36

ISBN 0 521 26780 3 hard covers
ISBN 0 521 31864 5 paperback

CONTENTS

List of maps   vi

Acknowledgements   vii

Creating a revolutionary movement   1

Competition and dissension within   27

The drive to unify China – first phase   49

Conflict over revolutionary goals   77

Mounting problems for the Wuhan regime   113

The communists turn to rebellion   147

The final drive – Peking captured and Nanking the new capital   170

Bibliographical essay   195

Bibliography   199

Index   214

MAPS

1 Kwangtung and Kwangsi in the early 1920s   28
2 The Northern Expedition 1926–28   54
3 Hunan and Kiangsi during the Northern Expedition   56
4 Hupei   58
5 The Lower Yangtze region   89
6 North China about 1928   177

ACKNOWLEDGEMENTS

The footnotes show that I have tried to base my statements on archival and other materials contemporary to the events discussed. In assembling these materials I have become indebted to many institutions and individuals. In 1962, as a Fulbright scholar in the Republic of China, I was privileged, through the help of the late Professors Kuo Ting-yee and Lo Chia-lun, to read in the archives of the Central Committee of the Kuomintang. Two archivists, Professors Chiang Yung-ching and Li Yun-han, helped me greatly. On later visits to Taiwan they helped me to see other important archival material, and I have drawn on their books based upon the Kuomintang's holdings. Professors Chin Hsiao-i and Huang Chi-lu also helped me with such access, while Professors Chang Chi-yun, Chang Peng-yuan, Chiang Fu-tsung, Hsiao Tso-liang, Liu Feng-han, Shen Yun-lung, Sung Shee, Tsao Po-i, Wan Wei-ying, and the late Professor Wang Chien-min helped me with introductions, accompanied me on interviews, procured restricted publications, or provided information that I have absorbed in notes. I am grateful to some participants in the Northern Expedition who granted me interviews and to others interviewed in the oral history project of the East Asian Institute of Columbia University, including the late President Chiang Kai-shek, Generals Chang Fa-k'uei, Li P'in-hsien, Li Tsung-jen, Pai Ch'ung-hsi, and Messrs Chang Kuo-t'ao, Cheng Tien-fong, and Lo Chia-lun.

In London I did research in the Public Record Office on dispatches from HM diplomatic and consular officials in China during the 1920s, made available to me through the good offices of Mr R. W. Mason, then Keeper of the Papers. I also read among the papers of the late Sir Frederick Maze, Inspector General of the Chinese Customs, now held at the School of Oriental and African Studies, University of London. The late Sir Miles Lampson and the late Sir Owen O'Malley graciously permitted me to interview them on events in which they participated in China. Mr Peter Hayman, Director General of the British Information Service in New York, and Mrs Ruth Isaacs arranged for me to read in their office the so-called

'Confidential print', *Further correspondence respecting China*, for the period of my interest. I feel much indebted to many helpful British public servants.

American archives I studied mainly on microfilm, but was assisted on visits to the National Archives in Washington by Dr J. Taylor of the Military Records Division. Mr Philip Jaffe permitted me to read in his extensive private collection on revolutionary China.

Many contemporary Russian and Chinese Communist documents were discovered in a raid on the Soviet Military Attaché's office in Peking on 6 April, 1927. I have used some of the published documents and others sent in translation to London and Washington by the British and American military attachés in Peking. In my use of these materials I am deeply indebted to the late Mrs Julie How Hwa, my collaborator in an earlier publication and in the forthcoming expanded version. For other Russian materials such as reminiscences by participants in the military campaigns or scholarly articles based upon Russian archives, I remember with deep appreciation the translation assistance of my student, the late Mrs Lydia Holubnychy. Mrs Lea Kisselgoff also helped me; I thank her, and Professor Rudolph Viatkin for sending me Russian works on my subject. Others who helped me with scanning or abstracting were Mrs Lillian Chu Chin, Mr Akira Kurihara, Mr Anthony Ma, Mr Ichiro Shirato, and Ms Julie Wei.

Friends who have enriched this book with their knowledge are Dr Dorothy Borg, Professors Carol Corder Andrews, Gilbert Chan, Bernadette Li Gentzler, Donald W. Klein, T. K. Tong, Odoric Wou, Tien-wei Wu, Ka-che Yip, Captain Marvin Williamson, and Dr David C. Wilson. Special thanks should go to Professor John K. Fairbank, the organizing genius and editor of *The Cambridge History of China*, volume 12, in which this book first appeared as an overly long chapter.

April 1984   C. Martin Wilbur

The Nationalist Revolution
in China, 1923–1928

CREATING A REVOLUTIONARY MOVEMENT

The Nationalist Revolution of the 1920s, one of the most interesting episodes in modern Chinese history, succeeded because of a remarkable mobilization of human energy and material resources in the service of patriotic and revolutionary goals. An organizational phase lasted from late 1923 until mid 1926 during which time a group of determined Chinese, starting with very little, created a revolutionary movement aimed at uniting the country, overcoming foreign privilege, and reforming a variety of social inequities. They were advised and aided by a group of Russian experts, who provided revolutionary doctrine, organizational know-how, money, military training and weapons. Next came the conquest phase, lasting until mid 1928, when armies originally based in the extreme south fought their way to Peking in the north. This campaign combined military prowess, effective propaganda, and subversive activity in the enemy's rear. There was also a great tragedy. Part way through the campaign the leadership split over the issue of violent social revolution – inter-class warfare within the revolutionary camp – during the course of a national unification war. In the eight months of internecine struggles thousands of revolutionaries lost their lives. Thereafter the civil war between the more radical and more conservative Chinese nationalists never really ceased.

China's political and social environment provided the revolutionary potential, but this potential had to be converted into a revolutionary situation. The cradle of the revolution was Canton, one of the largest, richest and most progressive Chinese cities, set in a fertile and densely populated delta where three important rivers merge. The chief inspirer of the national revolution was the indomitable Sun Yat-sen. He had devoted most of his adult life to advocating constitutional republicanism and opposing regimes in Peking which obstructed his ideal. Twice he had set up governments in Canton, once in 1917 in opposition to the Peking government dominated by Tuan Ch'i-jui and the Anfu Clique, and again late in 1920 in opposition to the government dominated by the Chihli Clique. During the second regime he arranged for a rump parliament to elect him 'Extraordinary President' of what he proclaimed to be the Chinese Republic. In the spring of 1922, in alliance with several military factions, he attempted a campaign against the Peking government, but Wu P'ei-fu defeated his major ally, Chang Tso-lin, while troops of his own theoretical subordinate, Ch'en Chiung-ming, drove Dr Sun from his presidential residence in Canton on the night of 15/16 June. By mid August 1922 he was back in Shanghai scheming to acquire the presidency in Peking by political means and to recover his base in the south by military force.

Sun Yat-sen's weak position in 1923

Dr Sun was unsuccessful in the first aim, but by 15 January 1923 troops in his pay had driven Ch'en Chiung-ming from Canton, and he returned there in triumph on 21 February. He was then 56 years old, but in less than two years he would be struck down by cancer. In this brief period he launched the organizational phase of the Nationalist Revolution in the face of great initial difficulties.

The difficulties may be summarized as follows. Upon his return to Canton, Sun's hold on the southern base was precarious, for he lacked the substance of power. He was not really master of the armies which had captured the base for him nor did he control the purse strings of its government. His Nationalist Party, the Chung-kuo Kuo-min-tang, had only a few thousand members in China, was loosely organized, and had no well-devised strategy for achieving its reformist goals, which aroused little enthusiasm from the articulate public. The goals were stated in a Kuomintang manifesto on 1 January 1923, which gave some detail to Sun's famous Three People's Principles – nationalism, democracy and people's livelihood.[1] His problem was to create a dynamic revolutionary movement, to gain control over sources of substantial revenue, and to create a subservient and reliable military force that could protect and enlarge the southern base.

The military problem had two aspects, internal and external. A miscellany of essentially autonomous divisions, brigades and regiments had taken Canton when their commanders were bought over by Dr Sun's associates in Hong Kong. Those from Yunnan were headed by General Yang Hsi-min but there were several independent Yunnanese forces,

1 See Milton J. T. Shieh, *The Kuomintang: selected historical documents, 1894–1966*, 65–70.

including one led by Chu P'ei-te, one of Dr Sun's more loyal military followers. Generals Liu Chen-huan and Shen Hung-ying headed the Kwangsi units. There were also divisions and regiments of the politically-divided Kwangtung Army, and several local 'people's corps' which entered the fray at the last moment. On arrival in the delta the commanders of these units scrambled to establish lucrative bases in the cities and towns, seizing most of the revenue-producing agencies. The troops, which numbered some 35,000 (by a well-informed contemporary estimate), were poorly equipped and most of them badly trained. There was rivalry between them, and they faced other military forces associated with Ch'en Chiung-ming that were eager to take Canton. General Ch'en seemed to be in alliance with Dr Sun's foe, Wu P'ei-fu. To get Generalissimo Sun Yat-sen's armies into battle required large amounts of extra cash, most of which was extracted from the Canton population by the municipal government imposing extra tax levies that were collected by the efficient Canton police.

During the spring and summer of 1923 Sun's military supporters defended his base from attacks by General Shen Hung-ying, who had support from Wu P'ei-fu, as well as from armies backing Ch'en Chiung-ming. Through these wars the base area was extended west and north to the borders of Kwangtung, but Canton was still exposed to attack from Ch'en's adherents nearby on the east. By autumn Dr Sun had not been able to bring his forces under more than nominal control, and there was very little improvement in their quality. The 'guest armies' were virtually armies of occupation.[2]

Dr Sun's financial problems were serious. Essentially there were three sources of revenue – contributions, loans and taxes. In the autumn of 1922 his party had raised more than half a million dollars (Shanghai and Hong Kong currency) in gifts and loans from his Chinese supporters to finance the recapture of Canton. Now it was difficult to raise more. In the spring of 1923 he tried unsuccessfully to negotiate a six-million-dollar loan from Hong Kong merchants and a million from the Canton Chamber of Commerce. He also hoped for a large concessionary loan from British business interests, but his precarious military position made this impossible. In order to realize the tax potential of his base it was necessary to get the administrative apparatus under the control of his own appointees.

Sun's government was organized on three levels – the generalissimo's

2 This discussion and what follows in the next few paragraphs is based upon C. Martin Wilbur, 'Problems of starting a revolutionary base: Sun Yat-sen and Canton, 1923', in *Bulletin of the Institute of Modern History, Academia Sinica*, 4.2 (Dec. 1974) 665–727.

headquarters (set up like a national administration), the provincial government and the Canton municipal government, the last mentioned being the most substantial. Canton was a wealthy city. It had a relatively efficient government under Sun Fo, Dr Sun's 31-year-old son, who returned to the job as mayor near the end of February. The city also had a fine police force, and Dr Sun appointed an old associate, Wu T'ieh-ch'eng, as commissioner of public safety for Canton. Mayor Sun and his six Western-educated commissioners pushed forward Canton's modernization during the following months, and also made the city the chief source for military financing.

According to the official municipal report for 1923 the city provided the generalissimo's headquarters with more than six million dollars (Cantonese) for military rations, in addition to the city's operating expenses. By contrast provincial revenues declined by nearly nine million from the previous year because only parts of the province could be tapped by the Provincial Finance Office. Dr Sun was able to seize control of the local salt tax revenues, netting nearly three million from May through December 1923, although the foreign-managed salt gabelle was supposed to be a collecting agency for the Peking government to assure payment of a foreign debt contracted in 1913. The interested powers protested but did not prevent this 'misappropriation'; although when Dr Sun threatened at the end of the year to seize the most stable source of revenue, that collected by the Maritime Customs Service at Canton, they intervened by force to prevent it.

The picture is one of crisis finance, with Sun's government competing with the military to collect tax revenues, and both laying heavy burdens on the populace. Yet during the first eight months after Sun's return the southern government gradually increased its income, which was necessary for its survival, and extended its territorial base.

The Nationalist Party had a history of nearly three decades, counting as its antecedents revolutionary parties organized and headed by Sun Yat-sen. Central headquarters in Shanghai had five bureaus and a small staff engaged in fund-raising and publicity. Apparently in 1923 there were no active branches in other cities except Canton, though there were many lodges among Chinese communities overseas. Total membership was unknown because records of local branches in Kwangtung had been lost as a result of Ch'en Chiung-ming's revolt of June 1922. In any case, membership figures were deceptive because of Dr Sun's practice of enrolling entire organizations such as armies, unions and student organizations – or of claiming them as members.

Nevertheless, the party had a potential for national influence because of its experienced leaders and its reputation for crusading against the Manchus, opposing Yuan Shih-k'ai, denouncing foreign privilege, and advocating governmental reform. The leaders came from various strata of society. Many had a good classical education and some had been officials under the imperial regime. Some had degrees from universities in America and Europe, and many had studied in Japanese colleges and military schools. Now mostly of middle age, these leaders had formed student friendships abroad, and variously had conspired to overthrow governments, gathered and dispensed funds for revolution, smuggled arms, spread propaganda among troops, worked with underworld secret societies, participated in parliamentary struggles, established literary and political journals, taught in colleges, organized trade unions, commanded armies, governed provinces, and engaged in business ventures. They came from all regions of China and had their local ties, though most of them were from Kwangtung and the Yangtze valley provinces. They formed a network of relationships with the traditional and the more modern sectors of Chinese society.

The party needed to be galvanized into action. Apparently Dr Sun was too engrossed in financial and military problems to pay much attention to the Kuomintang, though he called upon the Shanghai office from time to time to execute diplomatic missions or propaganda campaigns, and doubtless to forward money. In October 1923 Sun turned his attention to revitalizing the party. Michael Borodin, the chief adviser sent to him by Soviet Russia, arrived in Canton on 6 October, and for the next seven weeks the two men regularly consulted on plans for party reorganization.

Background of Soviet interest in the Kuomintang

In the early 1920s Soviet Russia had national strategic interests in China as well as revolutionary ones. Russia and China shared a long border, and the Soviet government desired to establish diplomatic relations with the Peking government for the many advantages this would bring. An important Russian strategic objective was to acquire control over the Chinese Eastern Railway (formerly a Russian state enterprise), which traversed Manchuria and was a vital link in the Trans-Siberian Railway that joined the Russian maritime provinces with Central Siberia. Russia and China were rivals for dominance in Outer Mongolia, which China considered its own, but which was ruled by a Mongolian regime recently placed there by the Red Army. Russia's unwillingness to permit China to control this buffer area was the stumbling block which prevented three Russian missions from effecting formal inter-governmental relations with Peking. In September 1923 the deputy commissar for foreign affairs, Lev M. Karakhan, arrived in Peking as envoy plenipotentiary to try once more to open negotiations.

China fitted into Russia's world revolutionary strategy as a region which should be liberated from capitalist exploitation. In 1919 Lenin organized the Third, or Communist, International to be the general staff of world revolution with its headquarters in Moscow. At its Second Congress in 1920 he articulated a strategy for undermining the great capitalist states by driving a wedge between them and their colonies. The Comintern, as well as the communist parties in the dominant countries and in their colonies, should concentrate on this liberation struggle as a preliminary stage of the world revolution. Lenin foresaw that the rising bourgeoisie in the colonies must inevitably lead these liberation movements, and he argued that it was the duty of each nascent communist party in a colony to assist the bourgeoisie in the national liberation struggle. This was a united front strategy. However, the communist party must maintain its separate identity, grow in strength by organizing and training the proletariat and poor peasantry, and prepare for the second revolutionary stage – the struggle to overthrow the bourgeoisie and establish a socialist state. The Communist International elaborated this basic strategy and propagated it in such colonial regions as its emissaries could penetrate. China, though not a colony, was fitted into this scheme and the Comintern sent its agents there.

Soviet emissaries had a double task in China: to help create a communist movement, and to find that national revolutionary organization which Soviet Russia and the Comintern would assist in the liberation struggle. Ignorant about China, the Russian revolutionary leaders needed several years of exploration by scouts before they settled upon the Nationalist Party. (The origin and circumstances of the Chinese Communist Party are discussed in *Cambridge History of China*, Vol. 12, ch. 10.) Once it had been organized, Hendricus Sneevliet – a Dutch Comintern agent who used the pseudonym Maring – went beyond the united front strategy by inducing the Communist Party's members, much against their will, to enter the Kuomintang, since Sun Yat-sen would not agree to an alliance between the parties. The Comintern's Executive Committee (ECCI) approved this tactic as a way for the infant party to gain access to the proletariat in South China, but, more importantly, in the hope that communists could radicalize the Kuomintang and steer it into alliance with Russia. The Russian leaders planned to be at the helm of the revolution.

There was a five-year courtship between Sun Yat-sen and Soviet Russia. At various times in his revolutionary career Dr Sun solicited aid from all the leading powers. Shortly after the Bolshevik Revolution he sent out feelers for an alliance between his party and Lenin's. Later he conceived the hope that the new revolutionary state would help him militarily into the presidency at Peking. Lenin and Gregorii Chicherin, the commissar for foreign affairs, cultivated Sun through occasional correspondence. Three Comintern agents – Voitinsky, Sneevliet and Dalin – tried to persuade him of the need to reform his party. After his defeat by Ch'en Chiung-ming in June 1922 Dr Sun was more than ever eager for foreign assistance, and he began to pin great hopes on Soviet Russia. In the latter part of 1922 he corresponded with Adolf Joffe, Russia's diplomatic delegate in Peking. Joffe failed in his efforts to negotiate a treaty with the Chinese government and went to Shanghai where he had extensive discussions with Dr Sun in January 1923, just after troops in Sun's pay had recovered Canton. The inner details of their deliberations have never been disclosed, but soon thereafter the Soviet leadership made a definite decision to assist Dr Sun and the Kuomintang financially, and to send advisers to help the party's revitalization.[3] Borodin was the person selected to direct this work.

Borodin had very good credentials from the Comintern's point of view. Born on 9 July 1884 he had been a revolutionary since his youth in Latvia. Expelled from Russia in 1906 he spent 11 years in the United States. He then returned to his homeland in the summer of 1918 and plunged into revolutionary work once more. He became well known to Lenin and translated one of his major works. After the founding of the Communist International he became one of its emissaries, visiting Spain, Mexico and the United States for organizational work, and then being arrested and imprisoned in England where he had gone to help reorganize the British Communist Party. Soon after his return to Moscow in the spring of 1923 he was chosen for the China assignment. When he arrived in Canton he was 39 years old, and by all accounts a man of intelligence and magnetic personality.

Borodin's instructions have not been published, but probably he had familiarized himself with past Comintern resolutions regarding China. The ECCI had sent a directive to the Chinese Communist Party in May 1923 that spelled out its role in the national revolution and the terms under which it should cooperate with the Kuomintang. The main thrust of the directive was the necessity to broaden the revolution by aggressively preparing for agrarian revolt and the need to reform the Kuomintang to make it the leader of a democratic anti-imperialist and anti-feudal front.

3 Details of the moves of Dr Sun and Soviet leaders towards an alliance may be found in C. Martin Wilbur, *Sun Yat-sen: frustrated patriot*.

The 'basic demand' of the Kuomintang must be its unconditional support of the workers' movement in China. The Kuomintang should draw the broadest possible masses into the struggle against the northern militarists and foreign imperialism. The Communist Party must continuously influence the Kuomintang in favour of agrarian revolution, insisting on confiscation of land in favour of the poorest peasantry; and it must do whatever possible to prevent alliances between Sun Yat-sen and the militarists. It must demand the earliest possible convocation of a Kuomintang convention to focus upon creation of a broad national democratic front, and it must insist on the abrogation of treaties and agreements imposed upon China by the imperialist powers.[4] Borodin's objectives probably were similar; this is clearly evident in his early activities in Canton.

Rejuvenating the Kuomintang

Borodin met frequently with Sun Yat-sen to discuss Kuomintang problems and offer advice on the coming revolution. He also met with local communists to reassure them of his intention in the long run to work for the strengthening of the Communist Party.[5] On 25 October Dr Sun appointed a Provisional Executive Committee to draft a new party programme and constitution and to prepare for a national congress. He appointed Borodin its adviser. Borodin drafted a new constitution for the Kuomintang, modelling its structure on that of the Russian Communist Party/Bolshevik. His draft, which is similar to the one later adopted, described five levels of organization – national, provincial, county, district and sub-district. An annual National Congress of Representatives was to elect a Central Executive Committee (CEC) and a Central Supervisory Committee (CSC). Between congresses the CEC would run the party, appoint its chief officers, manage finances, and direct its organs and all lower executive committees. Kuomintang members were all to be under strict party discipline. Those having membership in other organizations such as labour unions, merchants associations, provincial assemblies or

---

4 Xenia Joukoff Eudin and Robert C. North, *Soviet Russia and the East, 1920–1927: a documentary survey*, 344–6. Jane Degras, *The Communist International, 1919–1943: documents selected and edited by Jane Degras*, 2. 25–6, extracts.

5 Borodin's reports on his early meetings are found in N. Mitarevsky, *World-wide Soviet plots, as disclosed by hitherto unpublished documents seized in the USSR embassy in Peking*, 130–8. This is a hostile source, but the documents prove genuine when tested by other historical evidence. The best scholarly account of Borodin's life and his work in China until Dr Sun's death is Lydia Holubnychy, *Michael Borodin and the Chinese revolution, 1923–1925*. A biography of Borodin covering his entire life is Dan N. Jacobs, *Borodin: Stalin's man in China*.

the national parliament were to organize themselves into 'party fractions' (*tang-t'uan*) and must always present a united position in the other body in order to steer it.

The Provisional Executive Committee met 28 times, drafted a ringing proclamation and a new party programme. It supervised the re-registration of party members; established a journal to publicize the intended reorganization and explain the party's revolutionary ideology; and set up a school to train members of district and sub-district executive committees. It set the agenda for the National Congress and supervised the selection of delegates from the provinces and major cities of China and from branches abroad.[6]

Sun Yat-sen's hold on Canton became precarious in November 1923, as forces under Ch'en Chiung-ming menaced the city. It was feared the generalissimo might be forced to flee. During this crisis Borodin urged a radical programme to mobilize mass support. He urged Sun and a group of Kuomintang leaders to have the party issue decrees promising land to the peasants through confiscation and distribution of landlord holdings, and promising labour an eight-hour day, a minimum wage and other rights. He argued that these promises would rally support for the troops fighting Ch'en Chiung-ming. However, Dr Sun declined to issue the land decree because of strong opposition among some important followers. After considerable bargaining, he agreed – according to Borodin's reminiscent account – to a decree reducing land rent by 25 per cent and to another providing for establishment of peasant unions.[7] Fortunately for the Nationalists, the troops supporting Sun drove the enemy off. The military crisis passed. Sun did not issue the decree reducing land rents.

Another problem, which would haunt both the Nationalists and the Communists, arose shortly after Borodin and Liao Chung-k'ai, one of the staunchest advocates of Dr Sun's Soviet orientation, left for Shanghai at the end of November to explain to leading comrades the need for party

6 Details of the work of the Provisional Executive Committee were published in eight issues of *Kuo-min-tang chou-k'an* (Kuomintang weekly), Canton, 23 Nov. 1923–13 Jan. 1924. See also *Ko-ming wen-hsien* (Documents of the revolution; hereafter *KMWH*), 8. 1077–9; 1079–80 for proclamation; 1080–4 for draft of the party programme (trans. in Shieh, *The Kuomintang*, 73–85). Borodin's draft constitution is in *Kuo-min-tang chou-k'an*, 25 Nov. 1923; reprinted in *Hsiang-tao chou-pao* (Guide weekly; hereafter *HTCP*) no. 50, 29 Dec. 1923 (this was a communist journal).

7 Louis Fischer, *The soviets in world affairs: A history of the relations between the Soviet Union and the rest of the world*, 637–8. Also A. I. Cherepanov, *Zapiski voennogo sovetnika v Kitae; iz istorii pervoi grazdanskoi revolutionnoi coiny, 1924–1927* (Notes of a military adviser in China: from the history of the first revolutionary civil war in China, 1924–1927), 37–43. Draft trans. of vol. 1 by Alexandra O. Smith, 45–9. The military crisis is well covered in the chronological biography of Sun Yat-sen, *Kuo-fu nien-p'u* (hereafter *KFNP*), 2. 1020–33, but Borodin's recommendation and Sun's rejection are not mentioned.

reorganization. Eleven prestigious members of the Kuomintang's Kwang-tung headquarters, party veterans all, sent a petition to Dr Sun, warning him of communist influence in the new system of party organization and in the draft documents. They accused Ch'en Tu-hsiu, head of the Com-munist Party, of being the man behind the scenes, and charged that the policy of cooperation between the two parties was an element in the Communist International's scheme to stir up class struggle in the capi-talist countries to hasten social revolution and, in nascent capitalist countries, to unite labour, peasants and petty bourgeoisie to produce national revolution. Ch'en Tu-hsiu had brought his adherents into the Kuomintang to take it over, they asserted; and they warned Dr Sun that within five years Ch'en might be elected leader of the Kuomintang. This petition was an early evidence of continuing opposition among conser-vative party veterans towards the Soviet orientation and the admission of communists into the senior party.

Sun Yat-sen rejected the criticism. In a written reply, he explained that Borodin was author of the new constitution and that Ch'en Tu-hsiu had nothing to do with it. It was Russia's idea to befriend the Kuomintang and it was Russia which had advised the Chinese communists to work within the Kuomintang. He asserted that Russia must cooperate with the Kuomintang and not with Ch'en Tu-hsiu. 'If Ch'en Tu-hsiu disobeys our party he will be ousted.' Sun cautioned against suspicion of Russia because of suspicion of Ch'en Tu-hsiu.[8] Despite this show of confidence, the new draft constitution was revised to eliminate the election of the party leader; instead, it named Sun Yat-sen as leader, made him chairman of the National Congress of Representatives and the Central Executive Committee, and gave him veto power over the decisions of both.

The Canton customs crisis, which peaked in mid December, sharpened Sun Yat-sen's anti-imperialism, though Borodin's earlier advice – he was not in Canton during the crisis – must have had its effects as well. The generalissimo and his government demanded a share of the revenues col-lected at Canton by the foreign-controlled Maritime Customs Service, for which there was a precedent. When the diplomatic corps in Peking declined to instruct the inspector-general to allocate revenues as Sun's foreign minister requested, Generalissimo Sun announced that he would

8 'Petition to impeach the Communist Party, presented by the Kwangtung Branch of the Chung-kuo Kuomintang and Tsung-li's criticisms and explanations' (in Chinese) in Central Supervisory Committee of the Kuomintang, *T'an-ho Kung-ch'an-tang liang ta yao-an* (Two important cases of impeachment of the Communist Party), 1-11. Reprinted in *KMWH*, 9. 1271-3, but lacking Sun's comment. The comments are translated in Conrad Brandt, Benjamin Schwartz and John K. Fairbank, *A documentary history of Chinese communism*, 72-3.

seize the Canton customs house and appoint his own officials. This threatened the unity of the customs service, an agency of the Peking government, which all the powers recognized; and the action might have started a trend that would undermine the security of two major indemnities and many foreign loans. The interested powers met Sun's challenge by sending gunboats to Canton to prevent the seizure. The Nationalists were much too weak to fight; instead, they turned to mass demonstrations and propaganda in foreign capitals. The crisis passed, but Sun had made great political capital in China by his challenge to foreign domination. The Nationalist Party became more overtly nationalistic: anti-imperialism became its central theme, exactly as the Comintern advocated.[9]

The National Congress of Kuomintang Delegates convened in Canton on 20 January 1924 with 196 delegates appointed or elected and with 165 present on the opening day. Most were party veterans and about 40 represented overseas branches. Some 20 of the delegates were members of the Chinese Communist Party as well as of the Kuomintang. The 10-day congress heard seven speeches by Sun Yat-sen, reports on party activity in various regions of China and abroad; it debated and adopted a proclamation, party programme and constitution; and it elected two central committees. A report on party membership stated that, after intensive recruitment, there were more than 23,360 registered members in China and about 4,600 members abroad. The congress adjourned for three days to mourn the death of Lenin.[10]

In his opening address Sun Yat-sen called for unity and sacrifice among all party members. The proclamation emphasized anti-imperialism, anti-militarism and the function of the masses, especially poor peasants and workers, in the national revolution. Yet Borodin, who played an important role back-stage, was unsuccessful in persuading Sun Yat-sen to include a clear statement of the movement's united front with Soviet Russia. Nor could he get a statement included in the proclamation on expropriation of lands of large and absentee landlords and distribution of such lands to tenants.[11] The party platform was a reformist programme designed to appeal to many sectors of Chinese society; it promised to solve China's problems through legal instruments.

9 The customs crisis and evidence of Sun's growing hostility towards the imperialist powers are presented in Wilbur, *Sun Yat-sen,* 183–90.
10 *Chung-kuo Kuo-min-tang ch'üan-kuo tai-piao ta-hui hui-i-lu* (Minutes of the National Congress of the Kuomintang of China). *KMWH*, 8. 1100–60 for systematic details on the congress, and *KFNP*, 2. 1052–70 for an overview.
11 Cherepanov, *Zapiski,* 1. 67–71; draft trans., 85–92. Cherepanov states that his account is based upon Borodin's notes.

The issue of communists within the Kuomintang arose once more when a group of delegates tried to include an amendment in the constitution forbidding any Kuomintang member to belong to another party. Li Ta-chao presented a defence of communist intentions in joining the Kuomintang: they did so to contribute to the revolutionary work of the senior party, not to use its name to promote communism. Theirs was an open and upright action and not a secret plot, he assured the delegates, and he begged them not to harbour suspicions. After debate the amendment was rejected. Dr Sun clearly indicated his acceptance of communists within his party by naming 10 as regular or alternate members of the Central Executive Committee, about a quarter of the total.[12]

The newly elected Central Executive Committee met after the Congress closed and organized the party's central headquarters, which were now to be in Canton. They decided upon a Secretariat, an Organizational Bureau to manage party affairs, and eight functional bureaus: propaganda, labour, farmers, youth, women, investigation (later dropped), Overseas Chinese and military affairs. Party veterans were appointed to head the bureaus, two of which were placed under communists who had prior affiliations with the Kuomintang, T'an P'ing-shan for organization and Lin Tsu-han for farmers. A three-man Standing Committee was to manage daily business; it consisted of Liao Chung-k'ai, Tai Chi-t'ao and T'an P'ing-shan, a leftist group. Other members of the CEC residing in Canton were to meet at least once a week thereafter, but a majority of the members and alternates returned to cities in the north where they set up regional executive headquarters in Peking, Szechwan, Shanghai, Hankow, and Harbin, to promote the party. Gradually the central bureaus were given small staffs and the regional headquarters began to function. The leadership devoted much effort to creating propaganda on a nationwide scale; enrolling new members throughout China; organizing labourers, poor farmers and students in Kwangtung; and creating a military force loyal to the party. The work was carried on with a small budget, to which it appears that Borodin initially contributed some Ch.$30,000 a month.[13] Thus the Kuomintang started on its way to becoming a mass organiza-

12 Accounts of the debate, based on minutes, are in Chiang Yung-ching, *Hu Han-min hsien-sheng nien-p'u* (Chronological biography of Mr Hu Han-min), 301–3; and Li Yun-han, *Ts'ung jung-Kung tao ch'ing-tang* (From admitting the communists to the purification of the Kuomintang; hereafter *TJK*), 176–82. The earliest version of Li Ta-chao's statement is probably in *Chung-kuo Kuo-min-tang chou-k'an*, 10 (2 March 1924) 5. The text in Li's handwriting is in *KMWH*, 9. 1243–54.

13 *KMWH*, 8. 1160–7. Borodin's early financial contributions are inferred from Tsou Lu, *Chung-kuo Kuo-min-tang shih kao* (A draft history of the Kuomintang of China), 2nd edn, 390 and 399, f.ns. 21 and 22. Although Tsou says that the party leaders decided to replace Borodin's subsidy with other funds, there is considerable evidence that it continued.

tion with a strong leadership structure, a revolutionary ideology, and a plan for the ultimate seizure of political power in China.

Creating a revolutionary military force

Soviet military advisers who arrived with Borodin or joined him in Canton were appalled at the condition of the military forces supporting Sun Yat-sen in the winter of 1923–4. Most of the troops were poorly trained, badly equipped and led by incompetent officers, in the Russians' opinion. Only Sun's bodyguard of 150–200 men were completely loyal to him; the rest were the private armies of their commanders and their fighting value was nil, it seemed to the Russians. This situation had to be remedied if the Nationalists were to launch a campaign to unify the country with any hope of achieving military success. Necessary reforms would be the centralization of revenue collection, arms procurement, and pay of military units; standardized military training, and the indoctrination of officers and men in a common revolutionary ideology; and the creation of a unified and effective command structure. These were difficult measures to carry out, given the government's slender resources and the fact that unification of finances and command ran against the particularistic interests of the senior officers upon whom the government depended for its territorial base. The local arsenal, when it operated, could producd only enough rifles and machine guns in a year to equip one, or at most two, full-strength divisions, but the arsenal was run like a commercial enterprise: it sold its arms to any general who could pay for them. Importation of arms was difficult, though not impossible, because of an international arms embargo which the Maritime Customs Service attempted to enforce.

Dr Sun tried to strengthen his authority and bring his commanders together by appointing them to important positions within the Kuomintang. He chose Generals T'an Yen-k'ai and Yang Hsi-min, the titular commanders of the Hunan and Yunnan forces in Kwangtung, to be members of the Central Executive Committee. As reserve members of the Central Supervisory Committee he nominated General Hsu Ch'ung-chih, in titular command of Kwangtung Army units which supported Sun, and Gernerals Liu Chen-huan and Fan Chung-hsiu, who commanded small Kwangsi and Honan forces. In March the CEC delegated them, together with Generals Chu P'ei-te, who led a separate Yunnan force, and Lu Shih-t'i, a Szechwanese commanding a mixed corps, to organize party cells in their units. Periodically the generalissimo tried to persuade the various commanders to allow his appointees to collect the taxes and pay their troops, but he had little success. In fact, he seemed compelled to appoint or confirm certain commanders to control such lucrative revenue sources as bureaus for licensing gambling or 'suppressing opium'.

The most important step worked out by Borodin and Sun Yat-sen was the establishment of a military academy to train junior officers who would also be thoroughly indoctrinated with loyalty to the Kuomintang and imbued with its increasingly nationalistic ideology. Planning began just after the Party Congress and by May 1924 the Army Officers Academy (Lu-chün chün-kuan hsüeh-hsiao) at Whampoa, on an island south of Canton, was ready to open its gates to the first entering class of some 500 patriotic students drawn from middle schools and colleges all over China. Dr Sun appointed Chiang Kai-shek as commandant, and the principal military instructors were graduates of Japanese military schools or the Paoting and Yunnan military academies. They were aided by a few Russian officers, graduates of the Frunze Military Academy and the Russian civil war. General Chiang, Liao Chung-k'ai, the Kuomintang representative in the management of the Academy, and such veteran revolutionaries as Hu Han-min, Wang Ching-wei, and Tai Chi-t'ao, gave political instruction. The school was supported from the start by Russian funds supplemented by local taxes.

In June Russia sent a skilled commander, General P. A. Pavlov, to be Dr. Sun's military adviser. He recommended the creation of a military council, and this was organized on 11 July, made up of the principal commanders supporting the military government and a few party veterans. The council was a step towards creating a unified command and a political apparatus in the allied armies. Their military schools were to be improved and elite units be formed in each army for retraining. Unfortunately, General Pavlov drowned while on a reconnaissance on the East River front a month after his arrival in Canton. General Vasilii K. Blyukher, his replacement who used the pseudonym 'Galen' in China, did not arrive until October 1924. By that time the Whampoa Academy had its second class of cadets and a training regiment was being formed which later became the First Division of the National Revolutionary Army, the 'Party Army'. The first substantial batch of Russian arms reached Canton also in October 1924 on the *Vorovsky*, a yacht which had sailed from Odessa bringing a third group of Russian military advisers. Later shipments came from Vladivostok.[14]

14 'The National Revolutionary Army: a short history of its origin, development and organization'. This document was found in the Soviet military attaché's office on 6 April 1927. A translation was forwarded by Colonel S. R. V. Steward, the British military attaché in Peking, to the Foreign Office. It may be seen in the Public Record Office, London, FO 371: 12440/9156. A study of militarism as institutionalized in China is Ch'i Hsi-sheng,

Efforts to create a mass movement

Comintern representatives had repeatedly urged Sun Yat-sen to bring the masses into the national revolution, and this was also on the agenda of the Chinese Communist Party, which intended to organize the proletariat and link it to the poor peasantry, also under its direction. In the mass movement the two parties became rivals. The CEC of the Kuomintang set up its bureaus for labour, farmers, youth and women early in 1924, but the first two bureaus soon fell under the influence of vigorous young communists. The Socialist Youth Corps, the Communist Party's adjunct, was gaining a wide influence among educated youth.

Liao Chung-k'ai, as head of the Labour Bureau, tried to bring all unions in Canton into a single federation under his office, but was unsuccessful since many well-established unions were suspicious that communists on his staff would penetrate the unions and control the workers. The Communist Party hoped to bring railway workers, seamen, telegraph and telephone operators, postal employees and electricity workers into a single federation under its control. These were industries vital to a successful revolution. Despite such rivalries, Canton labour did rally in support of Chinese employees in the British and French concessions on the island of Shameen, who struck to protest at a system of passes the foreign authorities tried to impose after a Vietnamese revolutionary attempted on 19 June to assassinate the governor-general of Indo-China, who was visiting the island. Liu Erh-sung, a communist labour leader, is credited with being the main organizer of a complete strike and blockade of Shameen that lasted over a month, with strongly anti-imperialist overtones. Experience gained in the strike was well used a year later in the great Canton-Hong Kong strike and boycott.

The Communist International gave much attention during its Fourth Congress in November-December 1922 to the problem of organizing the peasantry in oriental countries. Its 'General theses on the oriental question' stated that in order to draw the peasant masses into the national liberation struggle the revolutionary parties must force the bourgeois-nationalist parties to adopt a revolutionary agrarian programme of land expropriation and redistribution to the landless. In May 1923 the ECCI instructed the Chinese Communist Party to draw in the peasant masses and press forward in preparation for agrarian revolution.[15] Actually, the Chinese Socialist Youth Corps could claim some credit already for the

Warlord politics in China, 1916–1928. The efforts of Soviet military advisers are treated systematically in Dieter Heinzig, *Sowjetische militärberater bei der Kuomintang 1923–1927.*

15 Eudin and North, *Soviet Russia and the East,* 151 and 233; and 344–6.

work of one of its leaders, P'eng P'ai, who organized tenant farmers in his native Hai-feng hsien east of Canton during 1922 and 1923, with the help of other Youth Corps members. A large-scale rent strike ended in arrests of many members, but P'eng escaped and came to Canton in the spring of 1924 and was soon the leading figure in the Kuomintang's Farmers Bureau.[16]

Planning for work of the Farmers Bureau began slowly, but by June 1924 the Kuomintang announced a simple scheme for farmers' associations (*nung-min hsieh-hui*), which were to be autonomous bodies permitted to organize guards recruited only from their own members. Local units were to be made up of farmers owning less than 100 *mou* (16 acres) of land and must exclude certain undesirable types. The CEC authorized the appointment of 20 special deputies to go into the field to investigate rural conditions, spread propaganda, and organize farmers' associations. In July the Bureau set up a Farmers' Movement Training Institute to prepare such workers, and P'eng P'ai directed the first class; the students received theoretical and practical instruction, including military training. (Other communists directed each of the successive classes up to the sixth, of which Mao Tse-tung was director from May to October 1926.) By October 1924 some 175 students had graduated from the Institute's short courses, and most of them were organizing farmers' associations in their native counties. The plan was to unite such associations on a county-wide, province-wide, and finally into a national organization that would not be under the control of the Kuomintang nor of its government. Why such autonomy was necessary became the topic of much theoretical argument.[17]

The Chinese Communist Party intended to control the peasant movement. A communist writer, probably Lo Ch'i-yuan, who was director of the Institute's second class and influential in the farmers' movement, revealed in a 1926 report that the CCP organized a peasant committee in 1924 'to direct the Kuomintang Farmers Bureau'. He asserted that the committee directed the Provincial Farmers Association when it was

---

16 See his biography in Donald W. Klein and Ann B. Clark, *Biographic dictionary of Chinese communism, 1921-1965*, 2. 720-4; Howard L. Boorman and Richard C. Howard, *Biographical dictionary of Republican China*, 3. 71-3. On his organizing work, see Shinkichi Etō, 'Hai-lu-feng – the first Chinese soviet government', pt I, *The China Quarterly (hereafter CQ)*, 8 (Oct./Dec. 1961) 160-83; and for P'eng's own account, Donald Holoch, trans. *Seeds of peasant revolution: report on the Haifeng peasant movement by P'eng P'ai*. P'eng is treated extensively in Roy Hofheinz, *The broken wave: the Chinese communist peasant movement, 1922-1928*.

17 'First proclamation of the revolutionary government on the farmers' movement', in *Chung-kuo Kuo-min-tang chung-yao hsuan-yen hui-pien* (Collection of Important Proclamations of the Kuomintang of China), 247-51. Lo Ch'i-yuan, 'Short report on the work of this [Farmers] Bureau during the past year,' *Chung-kuo nung-min*, 2 (1 Feb. 1926) 147-207; 158-9 for CEC decision. There is considerable detail on the Training Institute.

organized in May 1925, as well as local farmers' committees and the special deputies. The report also boasts that 99 per cent of the special deputies were 'comrades'.[18] During a confidential discussion among the Russian military advisers on reasons for Kuomintang hostility towards Chinese Communists, 'Nilov' (Sakanovsky) cited the communists' attempt to monopolize the labour and peasant movements, with the result that in setting up a preparatory committee for the National Peasant Conference, which was to meet in May 1926, the communists tried to place a few Kuomintang members on the committee 'for the sake of appearances'. They failed, he said, 'because there are no KMT members working among the peasantry'. In a resolution on the peasant movement dated July 1926 the Communist Party's Central Committee stated that peasant associations must be kept organizationally independent of the Kuomintang and not become its appendages. However, 'our party must devote the utmost effort to gaining the position of leadership in all peasant movements'.[19] The 'soul and spirit of the movement' in Kwangtung were Lo Ch'i-yuan, P'eng P'ai, and Juan Hsiao-hsien;[20] all had been early recruits to the Socialist Youth Corps in Kwangtung, and then became members of both the Communist Party and the Kuomintang.

The organizing of farmers' associations began in the Canton suburbs and nearby counties; by April 1925 there were some 160 associations with a reported membership of 20,390 – a tiny fraction of the rural population in areas under the revolutionary Canton government.[21] Communist organizers had greater success in Kwang-ning county, bordering Kwangsi, where graduates of the Training Institute led by P'eng P'ai organized tenant farmers and succeeded, with military help from Canton, in defeating landlords in a protracted rent reduction struggle. Thereafter they were able to organize many more associations in the county, reportedly 294 with nearly 55,000 members by April 1925.[22] P'eng P'ai was able to return to Hai-feng county on the heels of the Eastern Expedition at the

18 *Kwang-tung nung-min yun-tung pao-kao* (A report on the farmers' movement in Kwangtung), 124 and 53.
19 C. Martin Wilbur and Julie Lien-ying How, eds. *Documents on communism, nationalism, and Soviet advisers in China, 1918–1927*, 258 and 301.
20 T. C. Chang [Chang Tzu-ch'iang], *The farmers' movement in Kwangtung*, 23.
21 Figures from a map discovered after the Canton Commune of December 1927. See J.F. Brenan, 'A report on results of translations of Russian documents seized in the Russian Consulate, December 14, 1927'. Great Britain: Foreign Office, 405/256. Confidential. *Further correspondence respecting China*, 13583 (Jan.–March 1928) 117. We deduce the date.
22 *Idem*. Ts'ai Ho-sen, 'The Kwangtung farmers' movement on May First this year', *HTCP*, 112 (Special Issue for 1 May 1925) 1030–6. *Kwang-tung nung-min yun-tung pao-kao*, 64–83 and 98–100. 'Experiences in the rent reduction movement of Kwang-ning farmers', in *Ti-i-tz'u kuo-nei ko-ming chan-cheng shih-ch'i ti nung-min yun-tung* (The Farmers' movement during the First Revolutionary Civil War period), 139–47. Reprinted from *Kwang-tung nung-min yun-tung ching-kuo kai-k'uang,* Jan. 1927.

end of February 1925 and to revive his shattered movement there. Membership grew rapidly to a reported 70,000, with 12,000 in neighbouring Lu-feng county, but Ch'en Chiung-ming's troops recovered these counties in the summer and again the movement was driven underground.[23]

Rural revolt brought on suppression. Farmers' associations tried to protect their members from oppression, mobilize them against heavy taxation, and pit tenants against landlords in rent reduction movements. Men of property frequently sent hired toughs, bandits, or militia (*min t'uan*) to enforce customary payments. Organizers were murdered and some villages burned. Farmers fought back, sometimes supported by Nationalist troops, as in the two most successful areas.[24] Rural revolution could not be easily constrained; it threatened the alliance between an essentially reformist Kuomintang and the militant Communist Party.

Conflict within the revolutionary camp and in the Kwangtung base

By June 1924, what Kuomintang leaders in Shanghai and Canton had learned about the Communist Party's infiltration tactics and efforts to steer their party generated strong anti-communist sentiments in both cities.[25] Members of the Central Supervisory Committee petitioned Sun Yat-sen about the dangers and confronted Borodin with documentary evidence found in resolutions of the Socialist Youth Corps and the Communist Party's Central Committee that showed how communists intended to use the senior party for their revolutionary purposes. They objected particularly to the system of communist fractions within all levels of the Kuomintang, which contradicted Li Ta-chao's assurances at the Kuomintang Congress that the Communist Party was not 'a party within the Party'. The petitioners feared for the Kuomintang's future. In his debate with Chang Chi and Hsieh Ch'ih, two Kuomintang stalwarts, Borodin made clear that Russian assistance depended upon continued communist participation in the Kuomintang.[26]

23 A letter from P'eng P'ai reporting his triumphal reception and organizing work is quoted in Ts'ai, 'The Kwangtung Farmers' Movement . . .', 1031. For other details, see Shinkichi Etō, 'Hai-lu-feng', 149-81; See 151-2.
24 *Ibid.* 159 for a list of 195 peasant leaders killed up to May 1926, based upon Juan Hsiao-hsien, 'An outline report on the farmers' struggles in Kwangtung province during the past year', in *Chung-kuo nung-min*, 6/7 (July 1926) 611-29. This journal reports many specific cases.
25 Su-ch'ing (pseud.), *Kung-ch'an-tang chih yin-mou ta pao-lu* (The plots of the Communist Party exposed). This gives an extensive account of the discoveries and the mounting controversy.
26 Central Supervisory Committee of the Kuomintang, *T'an-ho Kung-ch'an-tang liang ta yao-an* (Two important cases of impeachment of the Communist Party), reprinted in *KMWH*,

In July the Kuomintang Central Executive Committee discussed the problem and issued a proclamation urging members not to be suspicious of each other. Dr Sun, on the advice of Borodin, created a special organ, the Political Council, to deal with major policy issues: it was made up of a few trusted Kuomintang leaders, and he appointed Borodin its adviser. Borodin was uneasy about the growing tide of opposition in the Kuomintang: he feared that left and right were coming together against the communists, though they dared not take decisive action for fear of their party's total isolation – that is, from external (that is, Russian) support.[27]

Chinese communist leaders were also restive. Ch'en Tu-hsiu, Ts'ai Ho-sen, and Mao Tse-tung of the Central Committee advocated a break with the Kuomintang. The committee even sent a secret circular letter to all district committees of the party and to all cells, directing them to prepare for a break.[28] But Borodin and Voitinsky, now the Comintern's official representative, insisted that the advantageous arrangement continue.

The issue was temporarily set at rest by decisions of the Political Council endorsed by the Second Plenum of the Kuomintang Central Executive Committee in August. The Plenum issued an 'Instruction on questions relating to admission of communists', which credited the Communist Party with special responsibility for the proletariat, recognized its need for secrecy, and exhorted the comrades to cooperate with each other to complete the national revolution.[29] This was a victory for Comintern policy and for those in the Kuomintang who formed the emerging left wing.

Another conflict arose from the heavy taxation imposed by Sun's military government and by the voracious 'guest armies', as well as from the increasing evidences of radicalism and social conflict. To protect themselves, merchant leaders created a militia as a counter force. When the generalissimo discovered in August 1924 that the merchants had imported a large shipment of arms from Europe, he ordered the arms confiscated, which was accomplished by Chiang Kai-shek's Whampoa cadets with

---

9. 1278–86. The impeachment is also given in Tsou Lu, *Chung-kuo Kuo-min-tang shih kao* (A draft history of the Kuomintang of China) Taipei edn, 413–21. 'Records of the questions of Central Supervisory members, Hsieh Ch'ih and Chang Chi, and the answers of Borodin' in *T'an-ho kung-ch'an-tang*, 25–30, and *KMWH*, 9. 1286–91.

27 V. I. Glunin, 'Comintern and the formation of the communist movement in China (1920–1927)', (in Russian), in *Komintern i Vostok; bor'ba za Leninskuiu strategiiu i taktiku v natsional'no-osvoboditel'nom dvizhenii* (Comintern and the Orient; the struggle for the Leninist strategy and tactics in the national liberational movement), 242–99; see p. 271. The article, based upon Russian archives, was abstracted for me by the late Lydia Holubnychy.

28 *Ibid.* 271–3.

29 The instruction is reprinted in *KMWH*, 16. 2773–6. See *TJK*, 324–31, and *KFNP*, 2. 1117–19 for discussions of the debates at the plenum.

the help of a Cantonese naval vessel. After two months of indecisive bargaining and one bloody clash Dr Sun ordered all the forces he could command to suppress the Merchants' Corps. They did so on 15 October, destroying much of Canton's commercial quarter by fire and looting. This action seriously tarnished Dr Sun's reputation in Cantonese commercial communities in China and abroad.[30] However, on 13 November, the ageing leader left for Peking, his hopes for the presidency revived by Feng Yü-hsiang's *coup d'état* against his superior, Wu P'ei-fu, on 23 October 1924.

While Dr Sun was in Peking dying of cancer, units of the Kwangtung Army under General Hsu Ch'ung-chih, together with the two training regiments of the Party Army, commanded by Chiang Kai-shek and staffed by officers and cadets of the Whampoa academy, launched a campaign against Ch'en Chiung-ming and his supporters. This is now known as the First Eastern Expedition. During February, March and April 1925 the combined revolutionary forces, with only diversionary help from the Yunnan and Kwangsi 'guest armies', succeeded in driving clear to the eastern borders of Kwangtung, taking major cities and capturing much equipment, but failing to destroy Ch'en's army. In June the Eastern Expedition turned back, abandoning most of the captured territory, in order to deal with the Yunnan and Kwangsi armies, which had taken firm control of Canton.

Several features of the Eastern Expedition presaged the later Northern Expedition. One was the good discipline and high morale of the lower officers and troops of the Party Army, who were thoroughly indoctrinated and who fought under a harsh 'law of collective responsibility' (*lien-tso fa*), decreed by General Chiang. Another was the propaganda squads that preceded or accompanied the revolutionary army, distributing leaflets and haranguing the populace to obtain support. As a result, farmers brought supplies and acted as spies, message carriers, guides and porters. As in the later Northern Expedition, Russian officers served as military advisers, planning strategy, aiding on transport and commissary, and directing artillery fire. The 19 Russian officers learned a great deal about the realities of Chinese warfare as practised in the south and thereafter worked energetically to prepare the revolutionary forces for more effective combat. Finally, there was the rivalry and disunity on the enemy side, and the friction between the commanders in the revolutionary camp. Even in the lower officer ranks there were the seeds of conflict between communists organized in the League of Military Youth, and other Kuo-

---

30 An extended account of the 'Merchants' Corps incident' is found in C. Martin Wilbur, *Forging the weapons: Sun Yat-sen and the Kuomintang in Canton, 1924,* 89–93, 100–5.

mintang officers who created a rival organization, the Society for the Study of Sun Yat-sen's Doctrines.[31]

The intensified revolutionary atmosphere in 1925

Dr Sun Yat-sen died on 12 March 1925, leaving behind a testament for his followers that was drafted by Wang Ching-wei and signed by the dying leader on 11 March. During the following month there were memorial meetings in all the major cities of China with much emphasis upon Dr Sun's revolutionary goals.[32] Shanghai University, conducted jointly by the Kuomintang and Chinese Communist Party, actively engaged in revolutionary propaganda and encouraged students to become involved in organizing labour. Communist leaders were reviving their labour movement with strongly anti-imperialist overtones and directed primarily towards Japanese-owned textile mills in Shanghai. During the first week of May a conference of some 280 delegates of unions throughout the country met in Canton and organized a National General Labour Union under communist leadership. It was designed to bring all unions into the national revolution under a single militant organization, though many anti-communist unions stayed aloof. The 26 man executive committee was dominated by communists, while all its principal officers were members of the party.[33] Then in Shanghai a strike in a Japanese factory lit the fuse that led to the May Thirtieth Incident.

On 15 May Japanese guards fired on a group of Chinese workers who invaded the temporarily closed mill, demanding work and smashing machinery. One of the leaders, a communist, died from his wounds. Other labour leaders and students of Shanghai University immediately

31 Sources on the First Eastern Expedition are Ch'en Hsun-cheng, *Kuo-min Ko-ming-chün chan-shih ch'u-kao* (A preliminary draft of the National Revolutionary Army's battle history), in *KMWH*, 10 and 11. 1523–677; Mao Ssu-ch'eng, comp. *Min-kuo shih-wu nien i-ch'ien chih Chiang Chieh-shih hsien-sheng* (Mr Chiang Kai-shek up to 1926; hereafter Mao, *CKSHS*) Taipei reprint, 403–63. National Government of the Republic of China, Ministry of Defence, *Pei-fa chan-shih* (A battle history of the northern punitive expedition; hereafter *PFCS*), 1. 137–276; National Government of the Republic of China, Ministry of Defence. *pei-fa chien-shih* (A Brief History of the northern punitive expedition), 13–25; and Cherepanov, *Zapiski*, 138–202, draft trans. 183–263.

32 The death-bed wills and a farewell letter to the leaders of Soviet Russia, and memorial services are discussed in Wilbur, *Sun Yat-sen*, 277–82.

33 Accounts of the congress are [Lo] I-nung, 'Chung-kuo ti-er-tz'u ch'uan-kuo lao-tung ta-hui chih shih-mo', *HTCP*, 115 (17 May 1925) 1063–4; Teng Chung-hsia, *Chung-kuo chih-kung yun-tung chien-shih* (A brief history of the Chinese labour movement). I used Central China, New China Bookstore, 1949, 116–38; Ch'en Ta, *Chung-kuo lao-kung wen-t'i* (Chinese labour problems), 122–8 and 593; Chung-kuo lao-kung yun-tung shih pien-tsuan wei-yuan-hui, comp. *Chung-kuo lao-kung yun-tung shih* (A history of the Chinese labour movement), 2. 356–61; Chang Kuo-t'ao, *The rise of the Chinese Communist Party, 1921–1927*, 414–22; Jean Chesneaux, *The Chinese labor movement, 1919–1927*, 258–61.

began wide-scale agitation directed against imperialist capitalists, making a martyr of the slain communist worker, and then demanding the release of students arrested in the International Settlement for demonstrating. The communist leaders of a recently organized labour union that operated in the safety of the native city strove in every way to persuade workers of the Japanese factory to stay on strike. Demonstrators took up another issue, four new regulations for the International Settlement that were to be voted upon by the foreign rate-payers on 2 June: they objected to foreigners determining rules for Chinese within the Settlement. Chinese wanted to roll back the 'unequal treaties', not to permit extensions.[34]

Probably no one planned a riot nor anticipated a shooting when, on Saturday, 30 May, students from eight colleges in the Shanghai area gathered in the International Settlement to preach against the unequal treaties and the military rulers of China, and to demand that their six arrested colleagues be freed. Police of the Settlement under orders from their commissioner attempted to stop the street demonstrations, arrested students who refused to desist, and soon were in head-bloodying conflict with students and sympathetic Chinese bystanders. When a large and angry crowd pressed on the Lousa Police Station where the arrested students were held and where arms were stored, the officer in charge, Inspector Everson, feared the crowd would rush the station, according to his testimony at the later inquest and trial hearings. To stop it he ordered his Chinese and Sikh constables to fire into the infuriated throng.

34 Important sources on the May 30th Incident and its aftermath include *Kuo-wen chou-pao*, 2. 21 (7 June 1925) and 22 (14 June) and subsequent issues into Sept.; *Tung-fang tsa-chih* (hereafter *TFTC*), special issue in July 1925; *HTCP*, 117 (6 June 1925) to 134 (30 October); U.S. Department of State, *Records relating to internal affairs of China, 1910-1929*, Microcopy no. 329, Roll no. 137, for USDS 893.5045/112, dispatch from Edwin S. Cunningham, American consul-general in Shanghai, 10 June 1925, enclosure 1: 'Extracts from police reports for period May 16 to June 5; enclosure 2: Inquest; enclosure 5: 'Extract from Mixed Court register for Tuesday, 2 June, 1925' (preliminary trial hearing); USDS 893.5045/147: 'Extract from Mixed Court register for Tuesday, 9 June, 1925' (175 pp. of testimony and cross-examination followed by nine exhibits). The trial record is available in *Report of the trial of the Chinese arrested during the riots of May 30, 1925* (I have not seen this); USDS 893.5045/158, dispatch by Ferdinand Mayer, chargé d'affaires, Peking, 3 July 1925: report of the investigation by a delegation sent to Shanghai by the diplomatic corps, with 23 annexes; USDS 893.5045/274: separate findings of a commission of three judges – American, British and Japanese – who conducted an inquiry from 12 Oct. onwards. The covering letter from Justice E. Finley Johnson, chairman of the International Commission of Judges, to Secretary of State Frank B. Kellogg, is dated Shanghai, 14 Nov. 1925. The proceedings of the inquiry were published as: International Commission of Judges, 1925, *A report of the proceedings of the International Commission of Judges* (I have not seen this work). The gist of a vast number of letters, press clippings, translations of Chinese publications, photos of propaganda posters, etc., included in reports of U.S. diplomatic and consular personnel in the above mentioned Microcopy no. 329, Rolls 43-45 and 136-38, may be found in U.S. Department of State, *Papers relating to the foreign relations of the United States*, 1925 (hereafter *FRUS*), 1. 647-721. A good recent account is in Nicholas R. Clifford, *Shanghai, 1925: urban nationalism and the defense of foreign privilege*.

That volley at 3.37 p.m. left four Chinese dead and many wounded on the pavement. Eight later died of their wounds. Five or possibly six of the slain were students. Relations between Chinese and foreigners were never to be the same again.

The May Thirtieth Incident gave a tremendous spur to the national revolution. Local leaders and political activists in Shanghai immediately organized a city-wide protest which developed into a general strike on Monday morning, 1 June. Further rioting, countered by police repression, lasted several days and 10 more Chinese lost their lives. The International Settlement became an armed camp as the Shanghai Volunteer Corps and some 1,300 marines from five powers patrolled the streets. The Chinese press spread detailed accounts and student groups issued innumerable pamphlets and cartoons and dispatched telegrams and letters to other cities calling for support to the strikers and opposition to the imperialists. Demonstrations occurred in at least 28 cities. Anti-foreign riots broke out in the British concession in Chinkiang, in Hankow where more Chinese were killed and wounded, and in Kiukiang where the Japanese and British consulates were destroyed. Funds poured into Shanghai from all over the country, from Chinese overseas, and from Soviet Russia to support the strikers. The Canton tragedy of 23 June, in which scores of parading Chinese were machine-gunned from the Shameen concessions, intensified the hatred of foreign privilege. As a result of the protracted strikes and boycotts, the policies of Great Britain and the other powers changed significantly. Thus the 'May Thirtieth movement' was a nation-wide protest; it also aroused public opinion throughout the world against the archaic treaty system.

The Kuomintang and the Communist Party both grew rapidly. Students flocked to Canton to enter the Military Academy. The Communist Party's vigorous leadership of strikes and boycotts attracted thousands of new members. The party suddenly found the key to rapid unionization of Shanghai's labour force through relief payments to the strikers, and became dominant in the labour movement there. During the Hong Kong-Canton strike and boycott, Canton labour became much more militant. At the same time an anti-communist tide grew within the Kuomintang in Shanghai, and Chinese entrepreneurs in many cities became wary of communist leadership of their workers. In short, while nationalism flamed and social revolution grew more intense, the seeds of counter-revolution were also nourished.

Consolidating the southern revolutionary base

Canton's reaction to the May Thirtieth Incident was delayed due to the precarious situation of the remaining radical leadership there. The city was controlled by the Yunnan and Kwangsi armies under Generals Yang Hsi-min and Liu Chen-huan, because most of the other Nationalist forces were in eastern Kwangtung regrouping after the successful Eastern Expedition. They planned to return to Canton and subdue the forces of Yang and Liu, but until this battle was fought it was scarcely possible to mount anti-foreign demonstrations in Canton against the opposition of the two generals, who were courting foreign support.

The battle for Canton lasted from 6 to 12 June inclusive. The Eastern Expeditionary troops marched back and, on 8 June, captured Shih-lung on the south-eastern approaches to Canton along the railway from Kowloon. Other Nationalist units closed the ring west and north of the city. At dawn on 12 June the main Nationalist force attacked enemy emplacements north of Canton while a mixed force led by Whampoa cadets wearing red scarves crossed the river from Ch'ang-chou Island and landed east of Canton at Tung-shan to plunge into the fray. The battle raged from Tung-shan to White Cloud Mountain, north-west of the city, when at noon Cantonese troops crossed from Honam Island to deal with enemy forces in the city. By 3 p.m. the Nationalists were victorious. General Liu abandoned his troops, fled to the British concession in Shameen, and took steamer for Hong Kong; two days later General Yang followed him there.[35] Russian military advisers led by General Blyukher played important roles both in developing the strategy and overseeing its execution.[36] Chiang Kai-shek, who played a leading part in this campaign, became garrison commander and soon brought disorders in the city under control. It was now possible to create a new government with some grip on the city's finances, and also to join in the nationalistic agitation that was sweeping the country.

As soon as Canton had been secured, the Nationalist leaders set out to

35 Ch'en Hsun-cheng wrote a general account of the campaign, reprinted in *KMWH*, 11. 1704–6. This is the basis for a similar account in *PFCS*, 1. 280–7, with two maps. Also Mao, *CKSHS*, (1–14 June 1925) 484–6; USDS 893.00/6396 and /6458, dispatches of Consul-General Douglas Jenkins, Canton, 12 and 17 June 1925; and *New York Times*, 7–13 June.
36 Cherepanov gives a detailed account of the campaign, in which he participated with the Whampoa cadets, though the account is based in part on the Soviet mission archives, apparently. He portrays General Blyukher as author of the plan of attack and in charge of all operations, and depicts the Russian advisers with the scattered Nationalist units as forming a communications net and enforcing Blyukher's orders exactly. Cherepanov, *Zapiski*, 1. 201–38, draft trans., 291–314. This account is marked by a hostile bias towards Chiang Kai-shek. There were only some 20 Russian advisers with the Nationalist armies at this time.

establish a 'national government' in Canton, replacing the generalissimo's headquarters, which had been Dr Sun's central organ. The Kuomintang Political Council resumed meetings in Canton on 14 June with Borodin advising, and decided on a structure of government with nine ministries united by a Government Council, a reorganization of the armies into the National Revolutionary Army, and reform of military and financial administration to bring the sword and the purse under Kuomintang control. All organs were to be under the party's direction. The Government Council and a parallel Military Council were to take policy direction from the Kuomintang Central Executive Committee, but effectively this meant direction from the extra-statutory Political Council, consisting of Wang Ching-wei, Hu Han-min, Liao Chung-k'ai, Wu Ch'ao-shu (C.C. Wu), and Hsu Ch'ung-chih after early July. Wang, Hu and Liao seemed to be a triumvirate in the Political Council, Government Council, and Military Council, but Wang became chairman of each of these bodies. Generals T'an Yen-k'ai and Hsu Ch'ung-chih were also prominent along with Wu Ch'ao-shu, the mayor of Canton. Chiang Kai-shek had not yet risen to political importance, though he was a member of the Military Council, commandant of the Military Academy, and commander of the Party Army. Wang's rise was apparently at the expense of Hu Han-min, whose position declined from deputy generalissimo after Sun Yat-sen's departure, to minister of foreign affairs in the new government, which had no formal foreign relations.[37] The national government was proclaimed on 1 July 1925.

One week earlier the tragic 'Shakee massacre' of 23 June set off the massive Canton-Hong Kong strike and boycott that lasted for 16 months.[38] With the Yunnan and Kwangsi troops defeated, patriots in Canton began to organize an appropriate protest against the May Thirtieth Incident in Shanghai and subsequent repressions of demonstrations in other foreign concession areas. Labour leaders travelled to Hong Kong to persuade union leaders there to join in a strike and boycott planned to begin on 21 June, with Canton to provide sanctuary for Hong Kong workers who went on strike. While four communist-dominated unions in Hong Kong went out earlier, a general strike began simultaneously on the appointed day in the British concession on Shameen and in Hong Kong. Striking

37 Basic documents in *KMWH*, 20. 3801–20. *TJK*, 373 quotes the resolution from the minutes of the 14th Session of the Central Political Council of 14 June 1925, preserved in the Kuomintang Archives. Mao, *CKSHS*, 494 gives resolutions adopted by the Central Executive Committee the next day. Other details in Chiang Yung-ching, *Hu Han-min hsien-sheng nien-p'u*, 331–2.

38 The paragraphs on the beginnings of the Hong Kong-Canton strike and boycott are condensed from a manuscript based upon research by the author in Chinese, Russian, British and American sources.

workers poured into Canton, where organizers planned a massive demonstration on 23 June. Apprehensive British and French authorities brought up gunboats and marines and prepared the defences of their concession, fearing it would be attacked.

On 23 June after a huge noon-time rally directed against the unequal treaties, an orderly parade of Chinese passed through the crowded Canton streets and approached the bund facing Shameen Island. It was composed of more than a hundred contingents of workers, farmers, merchants, school children, boy scouts, college students, Whampoa cadets, and units from the Party Army and the Hunan and Kwangtung armies. As the parade was passing the heavily-guarded British bridge across the narrow strip of water which separated the two sides, someone started firing. Which side fired first immediately became a matter of dispute.[39] In the subsequent fusillades from both sides, one foreigner was killed and eight or nine wounded on Shameen, but fire from the British and French side killed at least 52 Chinese and wounded 117, including students, civilians of various occupations, cadets and troops.

Cantonese fury at this slaughter is scarcely describable. Many clamoured for war, but the political and military authorities strove to calm the populace to prevent an attack on the concessions. The Canton authorities adopted a policy of economic warfare against their foreign enemies coupled with diplomacy. They supported the strike of Chinese workers in Hong Kong, which was only partially successful in crippling the colony, and stoppage of all trade with Hong Kong and a boycott of British goods. On the diplomatic front they attempted to divide the powers and concentrated vengeance on Great Britain. These measures lasted for many months, and only came to an end in October 1926, after the Northern Expedition was under way and after many efforts to negotiate a settlement.[40] Canton became the driving force of the Chinese nationalist

39 The most extensive source giving the Chinese side of this dispute is Ch'ien I-chang, ed. 'Sha-chi t'ung shih' (The tragic history of Shakee), original in Kuomintang Archives 230/ 1780; partially reprinted in *KMWH*, 18. 3330–58 and intermittently to p. 3419. Also *June Twenty-third: the report of the Commission for the Investigation of the Shakee Massacre June 23, 1925, Canton China*, distributed 'With compliments of the Commission'. For testimony presented by Shameen observers that the firing began from the Chinese side, see Great Britain, Foreign Office, Cmd. 2636, China no. 1 (1926), *Papers respecting the first firing in the Shameen affair of June 23, 1925*. Also US Department of State, 893.00/6464, dispatch, Douglas Jenkins, Canton, 26 June 1925; 893.00/6314, telegram, Shameen, 24 June; and two telegrams from commander-in-chief, Asiatic Fleet to Operation Department of the U.S. Navy, delivered to the State Department in paraphrase, 893.00/6352 and /6359. I find it impossible to determine the fact of the first firing on the basis of evidence available to me.

40 A full account of periodic attempts to negotiate, primarily based on Foreign Office archives but also using Chinese sources, is found in David Clive Wilson, 'Britain and the Kuomintang, 1924–28: a study of the interaction of official policies and perceptions in Britain and China', University of London, School of Oriental and African Studies, Ph.D. dissertation, 1973.

movement. Citizens rallied behind its government. Patriotic students flocked to the city and many enrolled in the Whampoa Military Academy. Canton was filled with unemployed strikers whose support became a drain upon the city's financial resources, though contributions poured in from other parts of China, from overseas Chinese, and from Soviet Russia. The Chinese merchant community suffered serious losses due to the enforced stoppage of their normally extensive trade with Hong Kong. The well-organized strikers, with armed pickets and led by the Chinese Communist Party, became an imperium within the revolutionary movement. Thus, while the strike and boycott helped at first to consolidate the revolutionary base, it also divided the leadership. These results were part of the skein of conflict that led to the crushing of the organized left in Canton in April 1927.

COMPETITION AND DISSENSION WITHIN

Aborted counter-revolution

Counter-revolution showed its hand on 20 August 1925 in the assassination of Liao Chung-k'ai, an ardent supporter of Sun's alliance with Soviet Russia and his efforts to mobilize the masses. Immediately after the tragedy, Borodin proposed the formation of a special committee of three with full powers to deal with the crisis. Hsu Ch'ung-chih, Wang Ching-wei and Chiang Kai-shek made up the triumvirate, with Borodin as adviser. Investigations revealed a plot among a group of conservative Kuomintang leaders and some commanders in the Kwangtung Army to overthrow the radicals in the Canton power establishment. Within a week many suspects were arrested, some executed, while others of the plotters had fled. Chiang and Borodin decided to send Hu Han-min to Russia, and within a month Chiang Kai-shek expelled his rival, Hsu Ch'ung-chih, titular commander of the Kwangtung Army. Two party veterans who obstructed the expansion of Russian influence, Lin Sen and Tsou Lu, were sent north on a 'diplomatic mission'. These men later became leaders of a prestigious faction within the Kuomintang opposing the remaining leadership in Canton.[41]

There were other important consequences of the crisis. Wang Ching-wei and Chiang Kai-shek became key figures in the revolutionary movement and for six months held greatest influence in the Canton regime.

---

41 Sources on this complex series of events: *TJK*, 375–92; Wang Ching-wei, 'Political report' made to the Second Kuomintang Congress, in *KMWH*, 20. 3851–70; Chiang Kai-shek, 'Military Report' in *KMWH*, 11. 1756–63; Chiang's 'Diary' for the period 15 Aug.–23 Sept.; and reports of British and American consuls in Canton.

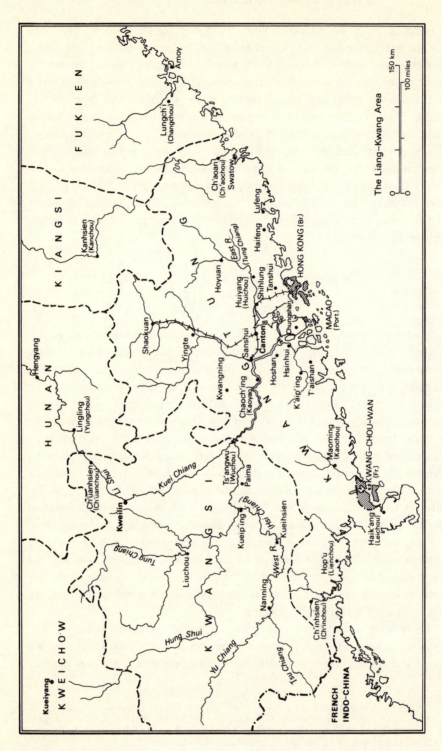

MAP 1. Kwangtung and Kwangsi in the early 1920s

The military forces upholding the regime were reorganized into five corps of the National Revolutionary Army: First Corps from the Party Army, commanded by Chiang Kai-shek; Second Corps of Hunanese, commanded by T'an Yen-k'ai; Third Corps of Yunnanese, Commanded by Chu P'ei-te; Fourth Corps drawn from the Kwangtung Army, placed under the command of Li Chi-shen; and Fifth Corps made up of Li Fu-lin's private army. To consolidate the Kwangtung Army, with its scattered units lodged in local bases, was not easy, but the newly designated Fourth Corps was gradually converted into a unified and effective fighting force. Another effort to unify financial administration was also ultimately successful.[42]

From October 1925 through January 1926 the reorganized National Revolutionary Army fought three campaigns which solidified its hold on Kwangtung. By early October Canton was menaced once more by the revived forces under Ch'en Chiung-ming on the east, a Szechwanese corps under Hsiung K'o-wu in the north-west, and Kwangtung troops under Teng Pen-yin and Wei Pang-p'ing in the south-west. The Second Eastern Expedition, made up principally of divisions of the First and Fourth Corps and a mixed force under Ch'eng Ch'ien, which later became the Sixth Corps, decisively defeated Ch'en Chiung-ming's coalition. The Fourth Regiment of the First Corps captured Ch'en's seemingly impregnable bastion of Hui-chow (Waichow) on 14 October with great courage and much loss of life, according to Cherepanov, who witnessed the battle and describes the courage of communist officers and political commissars.[43] Thereafter in a series of battles, the expeditionary force under Chiang Kai-shek's overall command captured towns *en route* to Swatow, while Ch'eng Ch'ien cut off the enemy's escape into Kiangsi and Fukien.[44] As in the previous eastern expedition political workers mobilized popular support and Russians advised each of the main units.

Also during October units of the Second and Third Corps drove the Szechwanese north across the Kwangtung border. Before the Eastern Expedition was finished parts of the First and Fourth Corps had to be

---

42 Wilbur and How, *Documents*, 186–99, contains a valuable report by 'Kisan'ka' (N.V. Kuibyshev), probably dated early in 1926, detailing important elements in the military reorganization and centralization. I have dealt with military unification in Kwangtung in 'Military separatism and the process of reunification under the Nationalist regime, 1922–1937', in Ping-ti Ho and Tang Tsou, eds. *China in crisis*, 1. 203–63, especially, 227–33.

43 Cherepanov, *Zapiski*, draft trans., 334–54. See *supra*, f.n. 31 for other accounts of the three campaigns.

44 N.I. Konchits, 'In the ranks of the National Revolutionary Army of China', (in Russian), *Sovetskiie dobrovoltsy v pervoi grazhdanskoi revolutsionnoi voine v Kitae; vospominaniia*, (Soviet volunteers in the First Revolutionary Civil War in China; reminiscences), 24–95. Pages 37–62 follow Ch'eng Ch'ien's campaign in a diary account.

sent to the southern front where, with help of units from the Second and Third Corps, they defeated the enemy by late December and went on to take Hainan Island. Thus were most of the elements of the National Revolutionary Army battle-tested and hardened before the Northern Expedition.

After Kwangtung had been brought under Nationalist control, three generals in neighbouring Kwangsi brought their province into alliance with Canton. Huang Shao-hsiung, Li Tsung-jen and Pai Ch'ung-hsi joined the Kuomintang and permitted the party to operate in regions they controlled. Their forces were designated the Seventh Corps, with General Li in command. General T'ang Sheng-chih, who commanded a division in southern Hunan, also negotiated in the spring of 1926 for incorporation of his troops, which were designated the Eighth Corps. These eight corps were the major units of the National Revolutionary Army when the Northern Expedition began. The total force numbered some 150,000, though only about 100,000 could be used outside the two-province base.[45] The NRA was still a rather heterogeneous force, but had been improved in training, equipment, indoctrination and battle experience during two-and-a-half years of reorganization with Russian help.

Polarization of the Kuomintang

In the summer of 1925 Tai Chi-t'ao issued two books, both of which presented a conservative interpretation of Sun Yat-sen's philosophy and arguments against communist participation in the Kuomintang.[46] Tai argued that the Three Principles of the People were the sole doctrine of the Kuomintang, which, he asserted, was the only party working for the national revolution. Communists and any others who did not accept these principles unreservedly should be excluded from the Kuomintang. In effect, Tai called for an end to the system by which communists were permitted to work within the senior party; he accused them of being parasitic, stirring up conflict between leaders, seeking to oust non-communists from Kuomintang posts, and absorbing its members into their party and youth corps. Tai's friend, Shen Ting-i, who had joined the Communist Party, turned against it. On 5 July he called a meeting of the Kuomintang's Chekiang Provincial Committee, which issued a manifesto echoing Tai's ideas and denouncing the concept of class struggle.

---

45 *KMWH*, 12. 1802-5 and *Pei-fa chien-shih*, chart following p. 46.
46 Boorman, *Biographical dictionary*, 3. 202. The late Miss Julie How analysed the main points in *Kuo-min ko-ming yü Chungkuo Kuomintang* in Wilbur and How, *Documents*, 206-7.

The Shanghai Executive Headquarters printed this document and sent it to all Kuomintang offices under its jurisdiction; it also issued an instruction forbidding Kuomintang members to advocate class struggle.[47]

The Communist Party responded to this challenge. Ch'en Tu-hsiu, the party's leader, published an open letter to Tai, dated 30 August, in which he defended communist motives in joining the Kuomintang and warned that Tai's writings were being used by reactionaries as propaganda.[48] The Central Committee held an enlarged plenum in Peking in October which passed a resolution on relations between the Communist Party and the Kuomintang. The resolution attacked Tai and others like him as the principal enemies and re-emphasized the policy of alliance with the left wing of the Kuomintang against the right. The resolution attempted to set standards for classifying members of the two factions but expressed doubts as to the real strength of the left.[49]

A group of Kuomintang veterans met in the Western Hills near Peking in November 1925 in what they called a plenum of the Central Executive Committee of the Kuomintang. Actually the party was so riven by controversy over the radical course being followed in Canton that neither the Peking group nor the leaders in Canton could muster a quorum of the CEC. Nevertheless, the 'Fourth CEC Plenum' decided to expel communists from the Kuomintang and declared that national revolution and class revolution could not go forward together. The group declared Borodin's relationship with the party terminated, dissolved the Political Council, which had no constitutional basis, and suspended Wang Ching-wei from party membership for six months. These measures had no binding effect. In retaliation the leaders in Canton used the CEC name to issue a manifesto denouncing Tsou Lu and Hsieh Ch'ih for their leadership of the Western Hills group, and in an open letter, Chiang Kai-shek defended Wang, Borodin and the Chinese communists. The Western Hills faction set up headquarters in Shanghai, seized the local membership records, took over the *Min-kuo jih-pao* as its mouthpiece, and planned to call the Second National Congress of the Kuomintang.[50]

The leaders in Canton succeeded, however, in assembling their Second National Congress first. It met in Canton from 4 to 19 January 1926, with 253 voting delegates, and heard a variety of reports on party work, includ-

47 *TJK*, 411–12, based on the documents preserved in Kuomintang Archives.
48 Ch'en Tu-hsiu, 'Letter to Tai Chi-t'ao', *HTCP*, 130 (18 September 1925) 1196–7.
49 Wilbur and How, *Documents*, 234–7.
50 'Important documents of the Western Hills Conference expelling communists from the Kuomintang, November 1925', *Kuo-wen chou-pao*, 4. 14 (17 April 1927) 14–16; Tsou Lu, *Hui-ku-lu* (Reminiscences), 1. 180–9; Tai Chi-t'ao, *Tai Chi-t'ao hsien-sheng wen-ts'un* (Collected writings of Mr Tai Chi-t'ao), edited by Ch'en T'ien-hsi, 3. 975–8 and 985; *TJK*, 413–34 (based on Kuomintang Archives); Wilbur and How, *Documents*, 209–12.

ing T'an P'ing-shan's discussion of party membership. This was still under 200,000, though later T'an spoke of half a million in China and overseas – an exaggeration. He gave round-number figures for membership in each of 11 formally organized provinces, five in the process of organization, and three special municipalities, which totalled 183,700; but he had to omit figures for Shanghai and Hankow, which had failed to report, and he left out figures for enrolments in army corps, naval vessels and the Canton police, all of which had special branches.[51]

Some 90 of the Kuomintang delegates, more than one third, were members of the Communist Party as well.[52] They operated as a caucus. The Congress debated the culpability of the dissident conservatives and how they should be punished. Opinion was sharply divided, but in the end Wang Ching-wei's plea for leniency – for not splitting the party further – was passed by a show-of-hands majority. Hsieh Ch'ih and Tsou Lu were to be expelled, 12 others who had attended the Western Hills conference should receive letters of warning, and Tai Chi-t'ao would be exhorted to repent.[53] As a direct response to the Western Hills group's expulsion of Borodin, the Second Congress unanimously passed a resolution to send him a letter of thanks together with a silver vessel inscribed with the words 'united struggle'.[54]

Since one of the principal demands of the Western Hills group was the expulsion of communists from the Kuomintang, that issue could not be avoided. Indeed, the debates showed an undercurrent of criticism of communist secret activities and implied doubts about their ultimate loyalty to the senior party. Several communist spokesmen heatedly defended their party. Then the issue was again set aside with a decision that the Central Executive Committees of the two parties should meet together to work out a solution.[55] No such joint meeting was ever held.

Another triumph for the left was the election of the new central committees of the Kuomintang. None of the dissident Peking group was re-elected. Communists won seven, and possibly eight, of the 36 seats on the CEC, and six among the 24 alternate positions, a slightly higher proportion than they held in the first CEC. Only two won positions on the Central Supervisory Committee, but there had been no communist in the previous CSC. Leftists, whose identification is less certain, won nine

51 *Chung-kuo Kuo-min-tang ti-erh-tz'u ch'üan-kuo tai-piao ta-hui hui-i chi-lu* (Minutes of the Second National Congress of Kuomintang Delegates; hereafter *Minutes*). CEC of the Kuomintang, April 1926, pp. 29 and 31.
52 *TJK*, 463.
53 *Minutes*, 134, and Li Yun-han, *TJK*, 466–9.
54 *Minutes*, 18–19.
55 *Ibid.* 165–9.

seats in the regular CEC and three among the alternates; they won two in the CSC. Chiang Kai-shek became a new member of the CEC, sharing the highest number of votes with Wang Ching-wei, T'an Yen-k'ai and Hu Han-min. Hu clearly was a potential right-wing leader and was still in exile in Russia for his alleged role in the Liao Chung-k'ai assassination plot. His virtually unanimous election must have been carried through by prearrangement.[56]

The clearest evidence of the drift leftward was the election by the new Central Executive Committee of its nine-man standing committee; the actual operating body. This contained three leftists – Wang Ching-wei, Ch'en Kung-po and Kan Nai-kuang; three communists – T'an P'ing-shan, Lin Tsu-han and Yang P'ao-an; and Chiang Kai-shek, T'an Yen-k'ai and Hu Han-min.[57] The leftist and communist leaders in Canton enjoyed their triumph for only two months.

Politicization and communist penetration of the National Revolutionary Army

The National Revolutionary Army of the Kuomintang was deliberately politicized to make it an effective revolutionary instrument. The armed forces were to be under the Kuomintang's civilian control and officers and troops to be indoctrinated with the party's ideology. The main instruments of control were the National Government Military Council, subordinate to the Political Council of the Kuomintang Central Executive Committee, the Political Training Department, which was directly under the Military Council, and party representatives in all major units of the armed forces. The Political Training Department was modelled on the Soviet Central Political Administration (PUR), and party representatives were equivalent to the political commissars in the Red Army. The system of control and indoctrination was worked out gradually, beginning with the establishment of the Whampoa Military Academy in the spring of 1924; by mid March 1926, shortly before the start of the Northern Expedition, a political structure had been created within most larger units of the armed forces. Politicization was a partial substitute for

56 Election scores in *Minutes*, 145–6. The top four each won 248 of the 249 valid votes cast. Naturally, the three highest scorers at the meeting could not vote for themselves on signed ballots. According to Chang Kuo-t'ao, who attended the congress, the absent Hu actually received 249 votes but at Wang Ching-wei's instigation, the secretary-general of the congress, Wu Yü-chang, reduced Hu's vote by one and placed his name third in the rank order, behind those of Wang and Chiang (actually behind Wang and T'an, but ahead of Chiang, according to the published Minutes). Chang, *The rise of the Chinese Communist Party*, 1. 282 and 708, f.n. 14.

57 *TJK*, pp. 473 and 519, f.n. 33, based upon minutes in the Kuomintang Archives, with the scores in the voting.

technical modernization; it also was conceived of as a means to control military officers whose loyalty to the Kuomintang might be questionable.[58]

The Political Training Department was an instrument both for control and indoctrination. It was established in about June 1925 and by October had begun to function. The Military Council appointed the head of the department, with confirmation by the Kuomintang Political Council. Ch'en Kung-po held the position in March 1926, but was to be replaced. A table of organization of that date showed some 29 officers, who operated in three sections: general affairs, propaganda and party affairs. Actual work within the armed forces was carried out through party representatives and political sections, and the department, at least in theory, controlled all party representatives in army corps, independent divisions, the bureaus of the navy and the air force, in the Central Political and Military Academy, and in the General Staff and Administration of Supplies. All party, political and cultural work in the armed forces was supposed to be done under the Political Training Department's instructions, but instructions issued to higher level party representatives had to bear the signature of the chairman of the Military Council as well as that of the head of the department. However, there were elements of friction and conflict between the department and high level party representatives, who were mostly party veterans. Chou En-lai, a communist, was deputy and often acting head of the department.

As of mid March 1926, the Political Training Department had planned a three-month programme of political instruction for officers and for troops; had set up a commission to prepare a textbook in reading and writing for illiterate soldiers; and it issued a daily newspaper, *Political work*, which was distributed in 18,000 copies, mostly to officers and political workers in the armed forces. The editor of *Political work* was a communist and the local committee of the Chinese Communist Party wrote its feature articles as a means of instructing political personnel and,

58 The following discussion is based primarily on a series of unpublished documents seized in the raid on the Soviet military attaché's offices in the Russian embassy in Peking on 6 April 1927. The original documents were in Russian, and the British military attaché in Peking, Colonel J.R.V. Steward, sent an English translation to the British minister, Sir Miles Lampson, who forwarded them to the Foreign Office. They are now in the Public Record Office in London, filed under F.O. 371–12502 (F8322/3241/10). The documents in the series consist of 'Political work in the National Revolutionary Army' and 15 annexes, of which three are missing. They date from around mid March 1926, and the first annex, 'Regulations governing the political directorate of the National Revolutionary Army', dated 15 March 1926, and the undated sixth annex, 'Regulations governing political commissaries [*sic*] in the National Revolutionary Army', are confirmed by almost identical regulations issued by the National Government Military Council on 19 March 1926, and reprinted in *KMWH*, 12. 1814–21. It is planned to publish these Soviet documents in a revised and enlarged edition of Wilbur and How, *Documents*.

through them, the officers and troops. To coordinate publishing efforts of political sections in various army corps and divisions, a committee of representatives from these units planned to issue 16 pamphlets with such titles as 'What and how to teach soldiers', 'What are the "Unequal treaties"?' and 'The history of the Kuomintang'. Five were already in press, and in addition other pamphlets, leaflets, books, journals, wall newspapers and cartoon posters were being published in large numbers by various organs.

Party representatives were the political watch-dogs and official propagandists of the Kuomintang within units of the National Revolutionary Army. By March 1926 the system operated in all army corps and ships of the navy as well as in central military administrative organs. The first article of the 'Regulations for party representatives in the National Revolutionary Army' announced their purpose – 'to inculcate the revolutionary spirit, to increase fighting power, to tighten discipline, and to develop San Min Chu-i (Three Principles of the People) education'.[59] The party representative was responsible for the political and moral condition of his unit, overseeing the execution of Kuomintang instructions, guiding the party nucleus, and carrying out all political and cultural work. He had to be well acquainted with the officers and men of his unit, study their states of mind, and try to remedy all defects. He was an officer with the right to command, and his orders were be obeyed just as those of the unit commander. In battle he was to be an exemplar of bravery, protecting the civilian population from the army during campaigns, and was expected to establish connections with farmers' associations and labour unions in localities where the troops were quartered.

Party representatives were part of a separate chain of command, parallel but not subordinate to the military chain. They were observers of the loyalty of military officers. Higher level party representatives were appointed by the Military Council to headquarters of corps and divisions, to the Navy Bureau, the General Staff, and other high organs, and were to act jointly with their opposite numbers of the military command. Orders issued by the military commander without their signature were invalid. In case of disagreement, the party representative should sign but report the case to his superior; but if the commander committed some illegal act, the party representative should frustrate it and report immediately to his superior and to the chairman of the Military Council. The party representative, or 'commissar', and the military commander 'being one and an indivisible whole, should always and everywhere work toge-

---

59 *KMWH*, 12. 1818, with a different translation in annex 6, cited above.

ther trying to attain one common aim: the unification of China under the banner of the Kuomintang'.

According to the information available to the Russian author of our basic source as of about mid March 1926, there were 876 political workers in the National Revolutionary Army. About 75 per cent of them were communists or members of the Kuomintang left, about 20 per cent were careerists without principles, and the remaining 5 per cent were right wing members of the Kuomintang, who were extremely hostile to both the communists and leftists. One of the annexes numerates 241 communists doing political work in the National Revolutionary Army or more than a quarter of the known political workers. There were 887 communists known to be in the army, more than half of them in the First Corps and the Central Political-Military Academy – still a minute fraction of the 65,000 combat troops at that time. A Russian adviser, V. A. Sakanovsky ('Nilov'), in discussing the reasons for the 20 March coup, stated that communist political workers manned the most important posts in the army, appointed members of their own cliques to various positions, and secretly pursued tasks unknown to the respective commanding officers, which aroused the jealousy and indignation of the military officers of all ranks as well as of non-communist workers. He reported that the chief of the Political Department of the First Corps, four out of five commissars of its divisions, and five of the 16 regimental commissars were communists.[60]

All communists received directives to penetrate Kuomintang organizations and gain influence therein, according to the Russian author of 'Political work in the National Revolutionary Army'. The current slogan was 'A good communist is a good member of the Kuomintang nucleus'. This penetration, and particularly in the key area of political indoctrination of troops, intensely concerned some Kuomintang leaders. Furthermore, the Kwangtung Provincial Committee of the Chinese Communist Party had established a special Military Section at Canton to direct the work of communists in the army. It was a small, secret body whose membership was unknown to the mass of party comrades, and it directed the secret work of communist nuclei in the army. It was also supposed to organize armed detachments of workers and peasants, establish nuclei in secret societies, landowners' detachments and other armed groups, and organize nuclei on trunk railways and waterways to disrupt the enemy's

---

60 Wilbur and How, *Documents*, 259, deductively dated as between 10 and 16 April 1926. A disappointingly vague account of communist penetration of the Political Department is in *Kuo-chün cheng-kung shih-kao* (Draft history of political work in the National Army) 1. 212–221, esp. p. 221, where such penetration is blamed upon Ch'en Kung-po.

rear and put down counter-revolutionary uprisings. Communists who, in the guise of Kuomintang members, penetrated clubs and societies in the army, such as the League of Military Youth and the Society for the Study of Sun Wen-ism, were to follow the directives of the Military Section. They were also to watch the behaviour of officers and report any harmful activity to higher organizations of the Communist Party. In short, it was the communist intention to influence insofar as possible the politicization of the National Revolutionary Army even though they could not entirely direct it.

How well this secret system was kept from knowledge of the Kuomintang leadership is unknown. Nevertheless, communist organizational and propaganda work within the military could not be entirely concealed.

Communist leadership of mass movements before the Northern Expedition

The Chinese Communist Party committed itself to organizing the Chinese masses – labourers, peasants, soldiers and students – and to radicalizing these groups in preparation for that future day when the revolution would move to its second stage, the socialist revolution. The leadership intended both to control mass organizations and to infuse the party's own ranks with proletarians in order to make it a mass party. An enlarged plenum of the Party's Central Committee held in Peking in October 1925 adopted a series of 'Resolutions on the question of organization' which show these intentions. The second resolution exhorted:

... We must on the one hand assemble and organize the proletariat; on the other hand, we must provide it with political training and education. Through study we have come to understand the means of unifying the peasantry and allying it with other democratic elements. Before we can perform this historically significant duty, however, we must first of all expand our party by absorbing into the party the proletariat and the most revolutionary elements of the advanced intelligentsia. ... It is absolutely true that the future destiny of the Chinese revolutionary movement depends entirely upon whether or not the Chinese Communist Party will be able to organize and lead the masses.[61]

The following year was marked by considerable success in enlarging the Communist Party and its Youth Corps and changing the social composition of their memberships. For example, the Communist Youth Corps, as it was renamed in February 1925, grew from less than 2,500 in early 1925 to some 12,500 in November 1926. Prior to 30 May 1925, 90 per cent of its members were students but by September they made up only

---

61 Wilbur and How, *Documents*, 100–1. Other parts of the resolutions instruct party members how to absorb proletarian elements and they criticize past mistakes in mass organization.

49 per cent. In November 1926 students constituted 35 per cent; workers, 40 per cent; and peasants, 5 per cent.[62] The Communist Party also grew rapidly as a result of the revolutionary upsurge in mid 1925. Near the end of 1926 the Party, which had been made up almost entirely of intellectuals, had changed its composition with a reported 66 per cent classified as proletarians, 22 per cent as intellectuals, 5 per cent as peasants, and 2 per cent as soldiers.[63] These proportions may, however, include both the Party and the Youth Corps.

Communists worked diligently to try to expand the National General Labour Union (Ch'üan-kuo tsung-kung hui) which they organized at a conference in Canton in May 1925, and which they controlled.[64] By the time of the next congress in May 1926 the membership in constituent unions was said to have grown from 540,000 to 1,241,000.[65] Because of repression, however, many of the unions had been driven underground. For example, in Shanghai the General Labour Union announced on 28 July 1925 that it had 218,000 members in 117 unions. This rapid growth was a result of the great patriotic June strikes and the fact that many workers received strike pay only through their unions. There was also coercion and intimidation by the unions' pickets. A year later the Shanghai General Labour Union claimed only 43,000 members (another account gives 81,000 for May 1926)[66] after the union's headquarters had been forcibly closed and such militant leaders as Li Li-san and Liu Shao-ch'i

62 See 'Report of the communistic movement of youth of China', *China illustrated review*, Peking, 28 Jan. 1928, 14–16. This is a document seized in the Peking raid; it was brought to my attention by Mrs Carol Andrews. Also, 'Report of the Young Communist International at the Sixth World Congress of the Communist International', *Lieh-ning ch'ing-nien*, 1. 10 (15 Feb. 1929) 69–94, 84. Files are in the Library of Congress.

63 Robert C. North, *Moscow and Chinese communists*, 131, citing *Report on the activity of the Communist International, March-November, 1926*, 118. Another account of membership composition at the time of the Fifth CCP Congress in May 1927 gives the following: Workers, 53.8 per cent; intellectuals, 19.1; peasants, 18.7; military men, 3.1; middle and small merchants, 0.5 per cent. Pavel Mif, *Chin-chi shih-ch'i chung ti Chung-kuo Kung-ch'an-tang* (The Chinese Communist Party in critical days) (trans. from the Russian), 37.

64 See *Supra*, f.n. 33.

65 'Lo-sheng' (pseud.), 'Ti-san-tz'u ch'üan-kuo lao-tung ta-hui chih ching-kuo chi ch'i chieh-kuo' (Experiences and results of the Third National Labour Congress), *HTCP*, 155 (5 May 1926) reprinted in *Ti-i-tz'u kuo-nei ko-ming chan-cheng shih-ch'i ti kung-jen yun-tung* (The workers' movement during the First Revolutionary Civil War period), 219. An important item which I have not seen used is Liu Shao-ch'i's report on the Chinese labour movement in the past year, i.e., up to May 1926, in *Cheng-chih chou-pao*, 14 (Canton, 5 June 1926) which is available in U.S. National Archives Microfilm 329, Reel 56, 893.00/7980.

66 Numbers in Chesneaux, *The Chinese labor movement*, 269 (based upon police daily report for 7 August 1925. I believe the exact figure was 217,804); and Chesneaux, 339. A British labour expert visited Shanghai in 1926 and was told that the Shanghai Federation of Labour Unions – i.e., the General Labour Union – claimed only 81,000 members in 15 unions with 47 branches in May 1926. Col. C. L'Estrange Malone, *New China, report of an investigation. Pt. II. Labour conditions and labour organizations 1926*.

had been driven from Shanghai the previous September. Despite such reverses and the rivalry and opposition of non-communist unions and federations, there were now many experienced labour organizers in the Communist Party after five years of work, and not a few among them were actual proletarians.[67] Moreover, Canton communists dominated the strike committee, which managed the Hong Kong-Canton strike, controlled the armed picket corps, and assumed some aspects of judicial and police authority.

The farmers' movement was greatly expanded in the year between May 1925 and May 1926, when the First and Second Congresses of the Kwangtung Farmers' Associations met in Canton. A fairly reliable figure for April 1925 showed 172,185 members in 557 villages or *hsiang*, in only 22 of Kwangtung's 94 counties.[68] A detailed report for May 1926 showed 626,457 members in 4,216 *hsiang* associations in 66 counties.[69] Still, this was a small proportion of the millions of farm families in the province. The nearly five-fold increase resulted from active organizing by graduates of the Farmers' Movement Training Institute, always headed by a communist member of the Kuomintang, which turned out 478 specialists, many of them farmers, from the five classes held between July 1924 and December 1925.[70] When the associations are plotted by counties on a map of Kwangtung, the greatest concentrations appear in the south-east (Hai-feng, Lu-feng and Wu-hua counties, where P'eng P'ai was the leader), in a few delta counties near Canton (especially Shun-te, Tung-wan and Hsiang-shan), and in Kwang-ning county in the north-west, where the movement had its first great success. In regions not controlled by the National Revolutionary Army, such as the north-east, or only recently conquered, such as the south-west, there were very few farmers' associations and memberships were small. The reason seems clear. Farmers' associations were agents of social revolution as well as instruments for the national revolution. It was difficult to organize and sustain them in areas where nationalist military power did not reach.

Local associations repeatedly engaged in struggles to eliminate socioeconomic grievances, which pitted them against local power-holders such as wealthy landowners and taxing authorities, who often controlled local

---

67 This theme is developed by Chesneaux, *The Chinese labour movement*, 400–2.

68 See *Supra*, f.n. 21. The official figures for May 1925 were 210,000, but I consider them unreliable.

69 Lo Ch'i-yuan, 'Hui-wu tsung pao-kao' (General report of the association's work), *Chung-kuo nung-min*, 6/7 (July 1926) 639–87, 654. This gives exact figures for each county. There are detailed figures for later in 1926, showing 823,338 members in 6,442 associations, in 71 counties. See Chang, *The farmers' movement in Kwangtung*, 15–16.

70 Etō, 'Hai-lu-feng', 1. 182, based upon detailed reports in *Chung-kuo nung-min*. Hofheinz, *The broken wave*, 78–92 discusses the Institute.

militia. Better organized farmers' associations had their trained and armed guards. A good deal of bloodshed and intimidation by both sides marked these struggles. A list of 164 incidents of conflict during the first three-and-a-half months of 1926 categorizes the majority as struggles against oppression by *min t'uan*, 'local bullies and evil gentry'; looting and killing by bandits; and harassment by army units and oppression by officials. Others arose from more strictly economic causes.[71] Statements by the communist leadership emphasized the support given by farmers' associations to the National Revolutionary Army's campaigns in Kwangtung and to the Hong Kong strike and boycott. In short, they supported the revolution as well as engaged in class struggle.

The Russian role by early 1926

Soviet Russia and the Comintern advised and financed the Chinese revolutionary movement, and attempted to steer it to success in the defeat of imperialism and Chinese militarism. (A detailed account is beyond the scope of this book, but a summary as of early 1926 may help to explain developments.)

The extent of Russian financing of Chinese revolutionary activities is still secret; here it is possible only to give scattered examples based upon seemingly reliable evidence. In March 1923 the Russian leadership decided to assist Sun Yat-sen and voted to render financial aid in the amount of Ch.$2 million.[72] Borodin provided part of the initial financing of Whampoa Military Academy, and he later told Louis Fischer that the Soviet government had made a grant of 3 million roubles (about Ch.$2.7 million) for the organization and initial running expenses of the school.[73] Entries in Blyukher's diary show that the monthly subsidy was Ch.$ 100,000 in November 1924.[74] The shipment of arms which came to Canton on the *Vorovsky* in October 1924 was a gift, but later the Canton government was expected to pay for arms and munitions shipped from Vladivostok, as shown by documents seized in the Soviet military attaché's office in Peking in April 1927. Egorov, the attaché, drafted a tele-

71 Lo Ch'i-yuan, 'Hui-wu tsung pao-kao', 667-8; summarized with examples in Chang, *The farmers' movement*, 24-30.

72 R. A. Mirovitskaia, 'Mikhail Borodin (1884-1951)' in *Vidnye Sovietskie kommunisty – uchastniki Kitaiskoi revolutsii* (Outstanding Soviet communists – the participants in the Chinese revolution), 22-40, esp. p. 24, based on Soviet archives.

73 Fischer, *The soviets in world affairs*, 640. 'The National Revolutionary Army', written by members of the Soviet military mission in Canton, ending about 19 April, states that 'This school was organized by us in 1924 and at first was maintained at our expense.'

74 A. I. Kartunova, 'Vasilii Blyukher (1889-1938)', in *Vidne Sovietskie kommunisty – uchastniki Kitaiskoi revolutsii* (The outstanding Soviet communists – participants in the Chinese revolution), 41-65, pp. 62-3.

gram to 'Galen' (Blyukher) on 4 July 1926 informing him that military supplies already provided to Canton as of 1 December [1925] had cost 2.5 million roubles, and must be paid for immediately; in future Canton's orders were to be executed as far as possible only for cash payments.[75] In August 1924, when Dr Sun established a central bank in Canton, Russia promised to underwrite the bank to the extent of Canton $10 million, though apparently only $30,000 was transmitted at that time.[76] Russia also subsidized the Kuomintang, through Borodin, at the rate of about Ch.$35,000 a month in 1924, according to Ma Soo, a confidant of Dr Sun, who visited Canton in October; and Blyukher's diary entry for 1 December indicates that Borodin had been making payments for salaries of Kuomintang officials and providing subsidies for party newspapers and journals.[77]

When Chinese workmen went on strike at the Japanese textile mills in Shanghai in February 1925, *Izvestia* stated on 3 March that Profintern, 'The Red International of Trade Unions,' was sending 30,000 roubles to support the workers; it also published a translation of the strike committee's acknowledgment of assistance.[78] After the explosive May Thirtieth Incident, Russian trade unions quickly sent 148,000 roubles to support the striking Chinese workers in Shanghai, according to the Moscow press.[79] Probably one would need to see Borodin's account books to know how much was provided to support Hong Kong workers who settled in Canton during the protracted strike and boycott of 1925–26, for a document found in the Peking raid, which provides a history of the strike as of March 1926, mentions only that funds were 'partly subscribed throughout China and abroad among the Chinese and the proletariat.'[80] In the north, Soviet advisers trained and equipped the army of General Feng Yü-hsiang. Between April 1925 and March 1926 Russia supplied Feng

75 Reprinted in *The China yearbook 1928*, 802. Alexandr Il'ich Egorov, a hero of the Russian civil war, came to Peking late in 1925 to take over the position of military attaché.

76 C. Martin Wilbur, *Sun Yat-sen: frustrated patriot*, 212 and 352, f.n. 99.

77 USDS 893.00/6393, dispatch, Mayer, Peking, 9 June 1925, enclosing Jenkins' dispatch from Canton, 29 May, reporting an interview with Ma Soo published in the *Hong Kong Telegraph* on 27 May. Kartunova, 'Vasilii Blyukher', 62–3. Both accounts identify Liao Chung-k'ai as the Kuomintang official negotiating with Borodin and, later, with Blyukher for allocation of Russian funds.

78 USDS 893.5045/53, dispatch, Coleman, Riga, 9 March 1925, trans. from Moscow *Izvestia*, No. 51, 3 March.

79 USDS 893.00B/156, telegram, Coleman, Riga, 17 June 1925. In addition Rub. 5,000 contributed in other countries was transmitted through Moscow.

80 GBFO F6462/3241/10 (now filed in FO 371/12501) and printed in FO 405/254. Confidential. *Further correspondence respecting China*, 13315, July–Sept. 1927, no. 27. Teng Chung-hsia, who was a leader of the strike, gives a total of Ch.$5,170,000 as the income of the strike committee to June 1926, with sources specified in round numbers; among these is 'other sources – 200,000'. Teng Chung-hsia, *Chung-kuo chih-kung yun-tung chien-shih*, 184.

with more than 6 million roubles' worth of arms and ammunition, according to his signed receipts.[81] I have seen no verifiable estimate of the extent of the Comintern's financial assistance to the Chinese Communist Party.

Money bought influence, but not absolute authority. The Russians in China suffered frustrations and disappointments. Despite the great growth of membership in the Chinese Communist Party and the Socialist Youth Corps in the latter half of 1925, and the apparent success of the party in organizing striking workers from Hong Kong and Kwangtung farmers, leaders of the Chinese party were restive at the constraints of working within the Kuomintang. Comintern advisers had to curb efforts to withdraw the Communist Party from the internal alliance.[82] On 13 March 1926, the Executive Committee of the Comintern passed a resolution on China which insisted on the 'fighting alliance of the Kuomintang with the communists'; scolded the party for slowness in organizational development because of its 'narrow sectarian views' on admission of workers; and warned against two deviations: 'right-wing deviationism' – a formless merging with the general democratic national movement – and 'left moods' – trying to skip over the revolutionary-democratic stage straight to the proletarian dictatorship and Soviet power, forgetting the peasantry. Once more the ECCI insisted, as it had since 1923, that 'the fundamental problem of the Chinese national liberation movement is the peasant problem'. It called upon the Chinese comrades 'to unite all existing peasant organizations into common revolutionary centres . . . which would be capable of rousing the whole peasantry to an armed struggle against the militarists and the administrators, middlemen and gentry who bolster up the semi-feudal order in the villages'.[83] This was an assignment easy to make in Moscow but not so easy to execute in China where, as late as July 1926, a plenum of the Executive Committee of the Communist Party admitted that there were barely 120 persons responsible for party work, when at least 355 directing personnel were needed.[84]

Russia had made a large investment in North China, attempting to strengthen and win over the Kuominchün, The National People's Army, organized by Feng Yü-hsiang and other generals after the coup against Wu P'ei-fu in October 1924. Beginning in late April 1925 a team of Soviet

81 Wilbur and How, *Documents*, 333 and 521, f.n. 93. The total may have been nearly Rub. 11 million.
82 *Ibid.* 92.
83 'Resolution on the Chinese question of the Sixth ECCI plenum' in *International press correspondence*, 6. 40 (6 May 1926) as quoted in Helmut Gruber, *Soviet Russia masters the Comintern*, 457-61.
84 Wilbur and How, *Documents*, 115.

military advisers began working with General Feng's First Kuominchün and by November there were 42 Russians working in his base at Kalgan. They did not succeed in getting close to Feng – let alone control him in Russia's interest – but they laboured hard to improve the junior officer corps by establishing a variety of technical schools. They had no such success politically as their colleagues seemed to be having in Canton. In June 1925, a team of 43 Russians arrived in Kaifeng, Honan, to work with the Second Kuominchün, commanded by Yueh Wei-chün. They were frustrated on every hand, and only a few of them remained to see the collapse of Yueh's army in early March 1926 under attack from rural 'Red Spears'. Russian advisers tried, but failed, to link up with the Third Kuominchün; it, too, disintegrated in February 1926.

By the end of 1925 Kuo Sung-ling's effort to overthrow Chang Tso-lin, Russia's enemy, had failed. This was partly due to ineffective support from the Kuominchün – though 18 members of the Russian Kalgan mission assisted Feng's offensive – and partly because the Japanese army in Manchuria intervened to protect Chang Tso-lin. General Feng then went into retirement and the commanders of his First Kuominchün were preparing to withdraw beyond the Great Wall to avoid war with the combined forces of Chang Tso-lin and a revived Wu P'ei-fu, who was no more friendly to Russia than was General Chang.[85] During Kuo Sung-ling's rebellion, Chang Tso-lin had sent for reinforcements from Heilungkiang, but the Russian manager of the Chinese Eastern Railway, A. N. Ivanov, refused to allow the troops to be moved on the railway without prepayment of the expense. The troops proceeded south by another route, but after suppression of the rebellion the returning troops commandeered several trains for the return to Harbin. Ivanov retaliated by shutting down the Changchun-Harbin section of the railway, and was in turn arrested by the Chinese troops on 22 January 1926. Karakhan issued an ultimatum, and the problem was settled through negotiations at Mukden. Chang Tso-lin was now fully aware of Russian power in the north of his domain and of Russian assistance to his domestic enemies.[86]

In February, shortly after and during these events, a commission from Moscow, headed by A. S. Bubnov, was in Peking studying the work of

85 Based upon a chapter written by the late Mrs Julie How Hwa for the forthcoming expanded version of Wilbur and How, *Documents*. Her basic sources were documents seized in the Peking raid as clarified by other contemporary evidence. A young Russian woman worked as an interpreter with the advisers in Kalgan and was in Peking during the first month of 1926. Her vivid account of these events is in Vera Vladimirovna Vishnyakova-Akimova, *Dva goda v vosstavshem Kitae, 1925–1927: vospominania,* trans. by Steven I. Levine, *Two years in revolutionary China, 1925–1927,* see 80–122.
86 Sow-theng Leong, *Sino-Soviet diplomatic relations, 1917–1926,* 282–3; and O. Edmund Clubb, *China and Russia: the 'great game',* 217–19.

the Russian advisers in North and South China and looking into general questions of Soviet aid to the Chinese revolution. The commission met with Ambassador Karakhan, the military attaché, Egórov, and some advisers who had worked with Feng Yü-hsiang and in Canton. In spite of apprehensions about General Feng's true dedication to revolution, Bubnov and Karakhan decided he should continue to be courted.[87]

On 18 March a grave incident occurred in Peking which strained relations of the First Kuominchün with the Kuomintang and Communist Party, and may have further discouraged the Russian embassy. The incident was an outgrowth of an ultimatum which eight Boxer Protocol powers handed to Tuan Ch'i-jui's government on 16 March, demanding removal of all obstacles to their communications between Peking and the sea, in conformity with the Boxer Protocol of 1901. Next day representatives of Chinese civic and political organizations in Peking petitioned the government to reject the ultimatum, but were driven off and many petitioners were injured. On the morning of 18 March a mass meeting adopted resolutions demanding abrogation of the Boxer Protocol and all 'unequal treaties'. Leaders of the Kuomintang and the Communist Party jointly organized the protest, which iterated a basic objective of both parties. About two thousand demonstrators, many of them students, marched towards the cabinet offices but were attacked by government guards and 47 demonstrators were killed, almost as many Chinese as had been slain in the Shakee massacre. The government issued a warrant for the arrest of five prominent Kuomintang figures in Peking, one of whom, Li Ta-chao, was a founder of the Communist Party. All went into hiding, Li taking sanctuary in the Russian embassy. Tuan Ch'i-jui's government had survived through Feng Yü-hsiang's support. A Kuominchün general was garrison commander and chief of police in Peking, but seemingly did nothing to prevent the massacre. Hence, the Kuomintang's Peking municipal headquarters laid the blame for the incident upon Kuominchün leaders and stated in a resolution that the Kuomintang would break off friendly relations with the Kuominchün unless Tuan and other high officials were arrested and executed. This did not occur.[88]

In South China, the Russian aid mission probably numbered fifty or more adult workers early in March 1926. Six Russian ships plied regularly between Vladivostok and Canton bringing oil, weapons and disassembled aircraft.[89] The head of the military mission was N. V. Kuybyshev

---

87 See *supra*, f.n. 85.
88 *Idem.*
89 This is an estimate, for the numbers changed as new advisers arrived, some coming from

('Kisan'ka'), who had replaced General Blyukher, but his relations with Chiang Kai-shek, head of the Party Army and commandant of the Military Academy, were strained.

These problems and uncertainties help to explain a remarkably interesting resolution on China and Japan passed by a special commission of the Politburo of the Russian Communist Party on 25 March 1926, and formally approved by the Politburo a week later.[90] The Politburo commission, headed by Leon Trotsky, expressed considerable apprehension concerning the correlation of Chinese internal forces and the danger of consolidation of imperialist forces after the signing of the Locarno treaties of December 1925. The commission feared that Great Britain and Japan might join against the Chinese revolution and Soviet Russia. The Soviet Union needed an extended respite and the Chinese revolutionary movement needed to gain time. To meet these dangers and to protect Russian interests in Manchuria, the commission decided it was necessary to reach an understanding with Japan and Chang Tso-lin that would assure both the Japanese and the Russian positions in Manchuria. It was necessary to be 'reconciled to the fact that southern Manchuria will remain in Japanese hands during the period ahead'. The accommodation policy had to be submitted for approval to the Chinese Communist Party and the Kuomintang, recognizing how difficult it would be for them to accept the line in view of Chinese hatred for Japan. The orientation towards coming to 'a certain understanding with Japan' was to be carefully prepared so that Chinese revolutionary forces would not interpret it incorrectly as 'a sacrifice of Chinese interest, for the purpose of a settlement of Soviet-Japanese political relations'. To orient public opinion properly it would be necessary to strengthen revolutionary and anti-imperialist influences on the Chinese press.

If Manchuria were to become autonomous, which the commission said Japan desired, Russia should get Chang Tso-lin to give up 'meddling in the internal affairs of the rest of China'. The Chinese Eastern Railway should be brought completely under Russian control, though masked by

reduced or abandoned military missions in the north. C.C. Wu told the German consul, probably late in October 1925, that there were 38 Russians in the Canton government's service, GBFO 405/248 No. 251 (F 5914/194/10). Vishnyakova-Akimova, who arrived in Canton 28 February 1926, mentions six newcomers on her ship, and describes many she met in Canton, but does not give a total figure. She names the six Russian vessels. *Dva goda v vosstavshem Kitae*, Levine trans., 141, 149, 176–88.

90 The document is in the Trotsky Archives at Harvard University. 'Problems of our policy with respect to China and Japan' in Leon Trotsky, *Leon Trotsky on China: introduction by Peng Shu-tse*, 102–10. Abstract in Gruber, *Soviet Russia masters the Comintern*, 462–7, under a different title and translation; and commented upon in Leong, *Sino-Soviet diplomatic relations*, 286–9. Other members of the special commission were Chicherin, Dzerzhinsky and Voroshilov.

measures of a cultural nature called Sinification. In negotiations with Chang Tso-lin, Russia should encourage Chang to maintain good and stable relations with Japan. Russia would not encroach on such relations, but should make clear that it was to the Manchurian government's advantage to maintain good relations with Russia also, to guarantee itself a certain independence in relation to Japan. It could be pointed out to Chang Tso-lin that certain Japanese circles were ready to have him replaced by another buffer general, 'but that we see no reason for him to be replaced . . . while normal relations exist.' One of the points of agreement with Chang, and later with Japan, should be to protect revolutionary Mongolia from Chang's encroachment.

Before entering negotiations with Japan, Russia should concentrate on actually improving relations and influencing Japanese public opinion. The commission contemplated a possible tripartite agreement (Soviet Union, Japan, China), but 'the ground should be prepared politically and diplomatically in such a way that it will be impossible for the Chinese to interpret any concessions China may find itself temporarily forced to make to Japan as a division of spheres of influence with our participation'. Left-wing circles should be made aware that Russia was prepared to tolerate only those Chinese concessions to Japanese imperialism that were necessary to defend the revolutionary movement from a united imperialist offensive. The possible joint negotiations should have as their objective, at the cost of some concessions, to drive a wedge between Japan and Britain.

Russia was openly to declare its full sympathy with the struggle of the Chinese masses for a single independent government; however, it would reject the idea of any military intervention by Russia: the Chinese problem must be solved by the Chinese people themselves. Until realization of a unified China, the Soviet government 'attempts to establish and maintain loyal relations with all governments existing in China, central as well as provincial.' Hence, looking southwards, the commission considered that if the people's armies [that is, Kuominchün] had to surrender ground to Wu P'ei-fu for a long period it might be expedient to reach an agreement with Wu in order to weaken his dependence on Britain, 'the main and implacable foe of Chinese independence'. The Canton government was to be encouraged to perceive its area not only as a temporary revolutionary beach-head but also a country needing a stable administration, and to concentrate all its efforts on internal reform and defence. Stalin added to the approved text that in the present period the Canton government should 'emphatically reject any idea of an aggressive military campaign and, in general, any activity that would push the imperialists onto the path of military intervention' – a caution against Chiang Kai-shek's plan for a Northern Expedition. A note directed that the Soviet ambassador in Paris should explore the possibility that the Canton government might work out a *modus vivendi* with France and send a representative there to sound out this possibility.[91]

In short, as one specialist on Sino-Soviet relations during this period summarized the thrust of the document, the Russian tactic 'was to divide the imperialist camp by isolating Britain as the chief target of antiforeignism and buying off Japan at China's expense.'[92] Events transpiring in Canton at this very time make it evident, however, that Russia could not control the direction of the national revolution. Apparently the implications of Chiang Kai-shek's 20th March coup were not yet appreciated by the top leadership in Moscow by the end of March, or at least did not affect their basic strategy, which was concerned with the north.

Readjustment of power relations in Kwangtung

The reasons for the '*Chung-shan* gunboat incident' of 20 March 1926 and Chiang's power-play thereafter are too complex and confused to detail here.[93] Apparently Chiang developed a hostility towards three of the top Russian military advisers in Canton because of their domineering attitudes and control over allocation of Russian arms and funds, their lack of support for a Northern Expedition, and his suspicions that N. V. Kuybyshev was conniving with Wang Ching-wei and others to have him sent off to Russia. He also became hostile to Wang, his main political rival, whom he suspected of working hand-in-glove with the Russians against him.[94]

Suspicious comings and goings of the gunboat *Chung-shan* on 18 and 19 March, which was anchored off Chiang's headquarters at Whampoa with full steam up, may have led Chiang to believe that a plan to abduct him and send him to Russia was underway. On the morning of 20 March he had the vessel seized, arrested Li Chih-lung, the acting chief of the Naval Bureau and a communist, declared martial law in Canton, and had

---

91 The Gruber translation says, to send 'the president of the Canton government', rather than 'a representative' of the government. This is interesting in view of the fact that one outcome of Chiang's 20 March *coup d'état*, was that Wang Ching-wei left for France in May.
92 Leong, *Sino-Soviet diplomatic relations*, 287.
93 Two valuable recent studies are Wu Tien-wei, 'Chiang Kai-shek's March twentieth coup d'etat of 1926', *JAS*, 27 (May 1968) 585–602, and *TJK*, 489–94. A brief account is in Wilbur and How, *Documents*, 218–24.
94 Evidences of Chiang's growing suspicions are found in his 'Diary' (Mao, CKSHS) for the period from 19 Jan. to 15 March 1926. He made a series of charges against Wang early in April in Chiang Kai-shek, 'A letter of reply to Wang Ching-wei', later published in Wen-hua yen-chiu she, comp. *Chung-kuo wu ta wei-jen shou-cha* (Letters of China's five great leaders), 246–53.

his troops disarm the guards protecting the residences of the Russian advisers and the headquarters of the communist-controlled Hong Kong-Canton strike committee.[95] This sudden action, executed without consultation with Wang Ching-wei or forewarning to the Russian advisers, created a political storm which only ended with the Russians' agreement to deport the three advisers to whom Chiang most objected, the withdrawal of communist political workers from the First Corps, and the departure of Wang Ching-wei for France on 9 May.

On 29 April Borodin returned to Canton, together with Hu Han-min, Eugene Chen, and several leftist leaders. Thereafter there was intense bargaining between Chiang and Borodin, in which it seems that Borodin made most of the concessions. Chiang agreed to expel a group of more conservative Kuomintang officials and to continue cooperation with Soviet Russia and the Chinese Communist Party, while Borodin agreed to continue Russian aid and to support the Northern Expedition, which had been opposed by the Russian advisers and the Chinese Communist Party. Communists would restrict very considerably their activities in the Kuomintang.

Chiang called for a plenary meeting of the Kuomintang Central Executive Committee, which was held from 15 to 25 May, and which worked out severe restrictions on Communist Party influences within the Kuomintang. Chiang formulated most of the proposals that were adopted, with verbal modifications. Once more a joint council of high-level Kuomintang and communist representatives was planned to settle obstacles to inter-party cooperation with the help of a representative of the Third International. Members of 'another party' in the Kuomintang were forbidden to criticize the leader and his Three Principles of the People. The other party must turn over to the chairman of the Kuomintang CEC a list of its members who had joined the senior party, and such members might not occupy more than one third of the positions in executive committees of the Kuomintang in central, provincial or metropolitan headquarters, nor serve as heads of bureaus of the central organ. All orders of another party to its members in the Kuomintang must first be submitted to and passed by the joint council, and members of the Kuomintang might not join another party without permission. Violators of these conditions were to be expelled immediately. A new office was created with large powers, that of chairman of the standing committee of the Kuomintang's Central Executive Committee. Chiang Kai-shek's patron, Chang Jen-chieh (Ching-chiang), was elected to the position,

95 Mao, *CKSHS*, entries for 22 and 23 March, and 20 April, reprinted in *KMWH*, 9. 1291–300, give Chiang's account of the incident.

though he was not even a member of the committee. All Kuomintang members were to be re-registered; they were to pledge their allegiance to specified major writings of Sun Yat-sen and to the manifestos and re-solutions of the First and Second Congresses; and those who had joined other political bodies not authorized by 'our party' must withdraw from them.[96] As an earlier part of the settlement, the Communist Party withdrew its members who were Kuomintang party representatives in the Army's First Corps on 10 April.[97] But many others retained their positions.

Such were some results of the negotiations between Chiang and Borodin. Communists within the Kuomintang must restrain their criticisms and curtail their active roles in high levels of the parent party; a mechanism was devised to adjudicate inter-party conflict; and the Kuomintang was somewhat further centralized. Communists relinquished important posts in the Kuomintang's Organization Bureau and the bureaus of propaganda and farmers, and in the Secretariat. Chiang, himself, became head of the Organization Bureau with his close associate, Ch'en Kuo-fu, as his deputy. Rightists also were curbed with the departure of Hu Han-min for Shanghai on 9 May, the imprisonment of Wu T'ieh-ch'eng on the 30th, and the expulsion of C.C. Wu, the foreign minister, who was replaced by the leftist, Eugene Chen. Planning for the Northern Expedition now resumed with full purpose.

THE DRIVE TO UNIFY CHINA – FIRST PHASE

Planning for the Northern Expedition

Planning had long been underway for a military campaign from Kwangtung province northwards to the Yangtze. General Blyukher presented a partial plan in March and June 1925, and drew up a more complete one in September while in Kalgan recuperating from Canton's sultry climate, both thermal and political.[98] The September plan estimated the enemy's potential resistance against an expedition made up of regrouped and better trained Nationalist forces, and predicted no difficulty in the ex-

96 Abstracted from the minutes of the plenum, quoted in *TJK*, 504–9, and Mao, *CKSHS*, 15–25 May.
97 Wilbur and How, *Documents*, 222.
98 A. I. Kartunova, 'Blucher's "grand plan" of 1926', trans. by Jan J. Solecki with notes by C. Martin Wilbur, *CQ*, 35 (July–Sept. 1968) 18–39. In Oct. 1925 the Russian embassy in Peking sent A. Khmelev to Canton to investigate conditions, and he reported on the constant friction between 'Galen' and Borodin, as a consequence of which Blyukher had been compelled to leave Canton. 'Extract (pp. 27–30) from the "Report *Journey to Canton* in October, 1925" by A. Khmeloff', a document from the Peking Raid of 6 April 1927. Trans. now in Hoover Institution on War, Revolution and Peace, Stanford, California, Jay Calvin Huston Collection.

pedition taking the Wuhan cities on the middle Yangtze and then capturing Shanghai. It was a remarkably prescient prediction.

On 16 April 1926 a joint meeting of the Kuomintang Political Council and the Military Council appointed Chiang Kai-shek, Chu P'ei-te and Li Chi-shen as a committee to plan for the Northern Expedition.[99] After Borodin's return and promise of support for the northern campaign, Chinese and Russian staff members did further planning, and when Blyukher returned to Canton late in May he refined the plans and presented them to the Military Council on 23 June.[100] Blyukher emphasized a single thrust through Hunan towards Hankow, with forces deployed to protect Kwangtung from Fukien on the east and other forces to protect the expedition's right flank from attack by Sun Ch'uan-fang in Kiangsi. The expedition was to begin only when all troops were in position, because of the difficulty of coordination, given the primitive facilities for communication between units.

In preparation for the campaign Chiang Kai-shek organized a General Headquarters of the National Revolutionary Army, which eventually replaced the Military Council, a collegial group of leading political and military figures, as the principal command organ. General Li Chi-shen was appointed chief-of-staff, with General Pai Ch'ung-hsi as his deputy. Li was commander of the Fourth Corps and was to remain in Canton with two divisions as garrison commander. General Pai was a graduate of the Paoting Military Academy and was one of the triumvirate of young Kwangsi officers (the others being Li Tsung-jen and Huang Shao-hsiung) who had unified Kwangsi and brought it into alliance with the Nationalist government in Kwangtung. Pai was a noted strategist. As part of the reorganization, the Political Training Department of the Military Council was placed under General Headquarters, and renamed the General Political Department. Teng Yen-ta was appointed its chief, replacing Ch'en Kung-po, and Kuo Mo-jo became deputy chief and head of the Propaganda Department. Teng, an ardent revolutionist, had been a student at Paoting Military Academy, a regimental commander in the Kwangtung First Division that brought Sun Yat-sen back to Canton in 1923, one of the organizers of Whampoa Military Academy and assistant director of its training department. In 1925 Teng went to Germany where he became acquainted with a number of Chinese communists, and returned to China through Soviet Russia. Chiang Kai-shek then appointed him dean of the

99 Minutes of the Kuomintang Political Council, no. 131. Strangely this meeting is not mentioned in Chiang's diary, although he did attend.

100 A. I. Kartunova, 'Vasilii Blyukher (1889-1938)', 62-3. For that date Chiang's 'Diary' does not mention any such meeting, though he chaired a meeting of the Political Department of the commander-in-chief's headquarters on work to be done when battle began.

academy, but he was arrested along with a number of communists during the 20 March coup, and soon sent to Ch'ao-chow to head the branch of the academy there. Teng's appointment as head of the General Political Department put a leftist in charge. Kuo Mo-jo was a noted literary figure, who had been active in the May Thirtieth movement and had helped to transform the Creation Society, a literary group, into an agency promoting the national revolution. A devotee of Marxism-Leninism, Kuo later joined the Chinese Communist Party. Under the General Political Department there were political departments attached to the headquarters of the various corps and divisions making up the National Revolutionary Army.[101]

Three military coalitions stood in the way of the Nationalists' hopes of reunifying China through a military-political campaign in the late spring of 1926. Wu P'ei-fu had been trying since mid 1925 to form a coalition in Hupei, Honan and northern Hunan that could overthrow both the Kuominchün in the north and the Kuomintang in the south. Divisions under his direct command were reputed to be well-disciplined and excellent fighters, but he was also dependent upon many unreliable generals. Nationalist historians portray Wu's coalition as numbering more than 200,000 troops, probably a greatly exaggerated figure. Sun Ch'uan-fang headed an 'Alliance of Five Provinces' in east China – Fukien, Chekiang, Kiangsu, Anhwei and Kiangsi. Based on the wealthy lower Yangtze region, this coalition had great financial resources, but the alliance was one of convenience. It too, was reputed to number more than 200,000 men. Chang Tso-lin headed the most formidable coalition, whose members dominated Manchuria, Shantung and much of Chihli. This relatively well-armed force was believed to number about 350,000 men. Chang Tso-lin and Wu P'ei-fu, though enemies of long standing, jointly supported a government in Peking and were attempting to drive Feng Yü-hsiang's forces out of their base around Nan-k'ou and Kalgan. Russia supported Feng's army, the First Kuominchün, with arms and advisers. In May 1926 Feng went to Moscow to seek more aid, and he sent delegates to Canton to work out an alliance with the Nationalists. Other military groups in West China had to be considered in strategic planning, though they were not strong enough to be menacing. Two naval concentrations on the east coast might play an important strategic role, one at Foochow and the other at Shanghai. The Shanghai ships were particularly dangerous because of the possibility that they might be

---

101 Biographies in Boorman, *Biographical dictionary*. The organizational system of the General Political Department and its subsidiaries is given in *Kuo-chün cheng-kung shih-kao*, 1. 264–72. Pictures of Teng and Kuo, p. 281.

used to disrupt military crossings or transport of troops on the lower Yangtze.[102]

The National Revolutionary Army had been enlarged by the recent addition of Kwangsi forces under the triumvir of Li Tsung-jen, Huang Shao-hsiung and Pai Ch'ung-hsi, designated as the Seventh Corps, and by a South Hunan division under T'ang Sheng-chih which was to become the Eighth Corps. The total force may have reached 150,000 men, but since many would have to guard the base area, the forces available for the campaign probably were less than 65,000 at the beginning.

Provincial origin, past history and recent politics determined the orientation of the corps and divisions making up the National Revolutionary Army. The First Corps was initially built up from training regiments at the Whampoa Military Academy. Many of the troops in these regiments had been recruited in Chekiang, Kiangsu and Anhwei. There were also regiments and divisions formed out of units in the Second Kwangtung Army. Ho Ying-ch'in, the commander, was a native of Kweichow and a graduate of a Japanese military school. He had participated in the Revolution of 1911–12 on the staff of Ch'en Ch'i-mei, a patron of Chiang Kai-shek. Before joining the staff at Whampoa he had been an officer in the Kweichow Army and then dean of studies at the famed Yunnan Military Academy. At Whampoa he was responsible for training the regiments which became the First Division. Most of the officers of the First Corps had been instructors or cadets at the Whampoa Military Academy commanded by Chiang Kai-shek, and the corps was considered his base of power. Members of the conservative Society for the Study of Sun Wen-ism dominated the political apparatus of the First Corps. The corps had five divisions and a total strength of 19 regiments, much more than any other in the National Revolutionary Army.

The Second Corps was made up largely of Hunanese. Its commander was the scholar-politician, T'an Yen-k'ai, who had several times been governor of Hunan after the 1911 Revolution, and also been associated with Sun Yat-sen's separatist governments in the south. He was a leading member of the coalition which ruled Kwangtung after Dr Sun's death. The actual field commander of the corps was Lu Ti-p'ing, a Hunanese general. A French-trained communist, Li Fu-ch'un, headed the political department, and many of the political workers at regimental level were communists. The Second Corps had four divisions and a strength of 12 regiments.

The Third Corps was mainly a Yunnanese force, commanded by Chu P'ei-te. General Chu was a long-time revolutionary who had commanded

102 *KMWH*, 12. 1780–9 *PFCS* 1. 62–8; *Pei-fa chien-shih*, charts, 46ff.

units of the Yunnan Army campaigning in neighbouring provinces, had assisted Sun Yat-sen's return to Canton in 1923, and Dr Sun selected him to head his personal guard. The Third corps had three divisions, made up of eight regiments and two battalions, one being artillery.

The Fourth Corps was a battle-hardened force built up from the old First Division of the Kwangtung Army, loyal to Sun Yat-sen. Li Chi-shen commanded the corps, and most of the officers were men of long revolutionary association. Besides its four divisions there was an independent regiment commanded by Yeh T'ing, a communist who had studied in the Red Army Academy and the University of the Toilers of the East, and he had recruited a number of communist cadets from Whampoa Academy as platoon commanders. The Fourth Corps had a total strength of 13 regiments and two artillery battalions and it rivalled the First Corps.

Li Fu-lin's Fifth Corps was essentially a garrison force south of Canton. Some of its units participated only briefly in southern Kiangsi.

The Sixth Corps was the last to be formed in the revolutionary base. Ch'eng Ch'ien was its commander. General Ch'eng was a Hunan military officer with a long career as a revolutionary and supporter of Sun Yat-sen. The Kuomintang party representative in the Sixth Corps was Lin Po-ch'ü (Lin Tsu-han), a Hunanese revolutionary associate of Ch'eng Ch'ien. Lin was a leader of both the Kuomintang and the Chinese Communist Party. Communist political workers who left the First Corps after the March 20th incident were assigned to the Sixth Corps. This rather mixed force had three divisions with nine regiments and two artillery battalions.

The Kwangsi force, named the Seventh Corps, was organized in brigades rather than divisions, and consisted of 18 regiments and two artillery battalions. Li Tsung-jen commanded the units which participated in the Northern Expedition, about half the force. The head of its political department was Huang Jih-k'uei, a communist who had been active in the student movement and was appointed secretary of the Kuomintang Youth Bureau after the Second Kuomintang Congress. However, Li Tsung-jen left Huang at rear headquarters and appointed Mai Huan-chang, a non-communist trained in France, to be in charge of political work among troops at the front.

The Eighth Corps of T'ang Sheng-chih was only being formed. It soon grew into six divisions in 17 regiments. The Kuomintang party representative was Liu Wen-tao, a man of considerable revolutionary experience, educated in China, Japan and France. He joined the Kuomintang in 1925.

There were also two infantry regiments made up of cadets at the Central

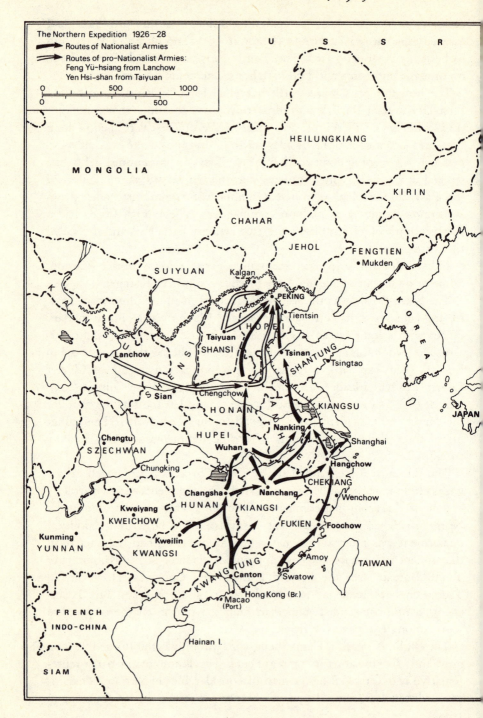

MAP 2. The Northern Expedition 1926–28

Military Political Academy, as the Whampoa Academy had been renamed, and two regiments of students of the fifth class; also a police regiment, and Lai Shih-huang's independent regiment, which was soon to become the Fourteenth Corps.[103]

Two routes from the provinces in the south led into Hunan, the first target of the Northern Expedition. A railway led northwards from Canton about 140 miles to Shao-kuan, from which point there was a toilsome ascent to a pass and a 30-mile portage to a tributary of the Hsiang River, which flows northwards through Hunan towards the Yangtze. The other route led from Kweilin in northern Kwangsi province through an easy connection to the headwaters of the Hsiang River in south-western Hunan. Hengyang, an important town in southern Hunan, was the place where the two routes joined. It was also T'ang Sheng-chih's main base, but in May 1926 General T'ang's hold on it was threatened from the north by another Hunanese general, Yeh K'ai-hsin. The first military movements in what became the Northern Expedition were the dispatches into Hunan of a brigade from Kwangsi and Yeh T'ing's independent regiment from Kwangtung to stiffen T'ang's resistance. On 2 June General T'ang accepted the post of commander of the Eighth Corps of the National Revolutionary Army, and on 5 June the Nationalist Government appointed Chiang Kai-shek as commander-in-chief of the army.

The Northern Expedition begins

By early July two divisions of the Fourth Corps, the 10th under Ch'en Ming-shu and the 12th under Chang Fa-k'uei, had joined Yeh T'ing's independent regiment in south-eastern Hunan, and more brigades of the Seventh Corps had entered South-west Hunan. Two rivers join the Hsiang about 50 kilometres south of Changsha, the Lien from the west and the Lu on the east. Advance Commander T'ang Sheng-chih ordered an offensive by the units of the three corps now in place on the west and east of the Hsiang River. Units of the Eighth Corps crossed the Lien, while on 10 July the Fourth Corps captured Li-ling on the P'ing-hsiang–Chu-chow railway line in the east. This breach of the Lien–Lo line left Changsha exposed; General Yeh K'ai-hsin retreated through the provincial capital into northern Hunan, and General T'ang entered Changsha

103 The careers of commanders and chief political workers are outlined in Boorman, *Biographical dictionary*. Tables of organization showing commanders of corps, divisions, regiments and battalions are given in *KMWH*, 12. 1802–3 (which I have followed), and in *PFCS* 2. 322ff., and *Pei-fa chien-shih*, 46ff.

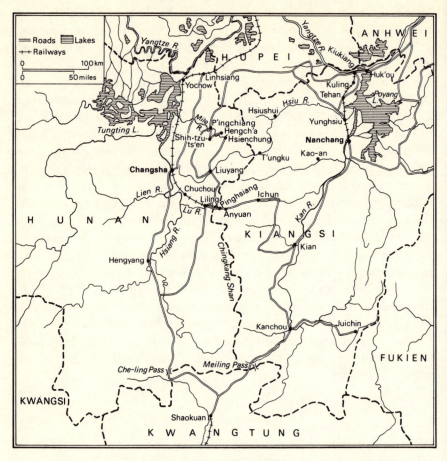

MAP 3.   Hunan and Kiangsi during the Northern Expedition

on 11 July. While this campaign was underway Chiang Kai-shek formally
accepted the post of commander-in-chief of the National Revolutionary
Army during a ceremony which officially launched the Northern Expedition on 9 July. Thus, with little fighting the revolutionary forces had
captured most of the Hsiang River valley.

Major battles lay ahead as Wu P'ei-fu began to send divisions southwards
and as the Second Division of the First Corps and the Sixth Corps were
brought into Hunan as general reserves, and the Second and Third Corps
were brought up to guard the right flank against an attack by Sun Ch'uan-
fang from Kiangsi in the east. However, the Nationalists in Canton had
been negotiating with Sun Ch'uan-fang to try to keep him neutral as
long as possible. They also were negotiating with Yuan Tsu-ming, the
military governor of Kweichow on the west, and on 11 July Chiang Kai-

shek telegraphed T'ang Sheng-chih to say that Yuan and a subordinate general had joined the revolutionary side. On 20 July the Military Council of the national government appointed his two subordinates, P'eng Han-chang as commander of the Ninth Corps and Wang T'ien-p'ei as commander of the Tenth Corps. (This system of co-opting potential enemies or enrolling turncoat forces went on during most of the Northern Expedition, resulting in a tremendously bloated National Revolutionary Army, greatly diluted in quality.)[104]

Chiang Kai-shek left Canton for the front on 27 July accompanied by members of his staff and General Blyukher and a group of Russian advisers. Arriving at Changsha on 11 August he called a military conference to decide on next moves. The conference was attended by Pai Ch'ung-hsi, Teng Yen-ta, Ch'en Kung-po as head of the War Area Political Affairs Committee, Ch'en K'o-yü, deputy commander of the Fourth Corps, Li Tsung-jen, T'ang Sheng-chih, and various division commanders, Blyukher, and other advisers. The group finally decided to drive straight for Wuchang, the capital of Hupei province, and postpone the attack on Nanchang, the capital of Kiangsi, which apparently was Chiang Kai-shek's first objective. The Fourth Corps was to lead an attack on P'ing-chiang, a strongly held fortress on the Milo River and then race for Ting-ssu bridge on the railway leading to Wuchang. The Seventh Corps was to proceed north-east towards Wuchang, and the Eighth Corps to proceed on the west along the railway itself.

The Fourth Corps, with much dash and bravery, took P'ing-chiang on 19 August, with Huang Ch'i-hsiang's 36th Regiment of the 12th Division the first to enter the city. The victory at Ting-ssu bridge, defended by a strong force brought down by Wu P'ei-fu, and considered impossible to take from the south, was accomplished on the night of August 26/27, when local farmers guided the 36th Regiment through shallow waters for an attack on the bridge from behind. This was one of the crucial battles of the first phase of the campaign. General Wu P'ei-fu personally supervised the defences of Ho-sheng bridge, the next objective. Again the 12th Division led the fight, supported by the 10th Division and elements of the Seventh Corps. Despite Wu's desperate efforts to prevent his troops from retreating, they were defeated at many points on 30 August and fled.

104 An interesting report on Canton's negotiations is found in a document dated 3 June, 1926 and based upon reports from Borodin. Wilbur and How, *Documents*, p. 269. Donald A. Jordan, *The Northern Expedition: China's national revolution of 1926–1928*, 276–86, treats defections systematically. See also C. Martin Wilbur, 'Military separatism and the process of reunification', 244–5. A valuable account of the Northern Expedition as remembered by one of its top commanders is in Te-kong Tong and Li Tsung-jen, *The memoirs of Li Tsung-jen*.

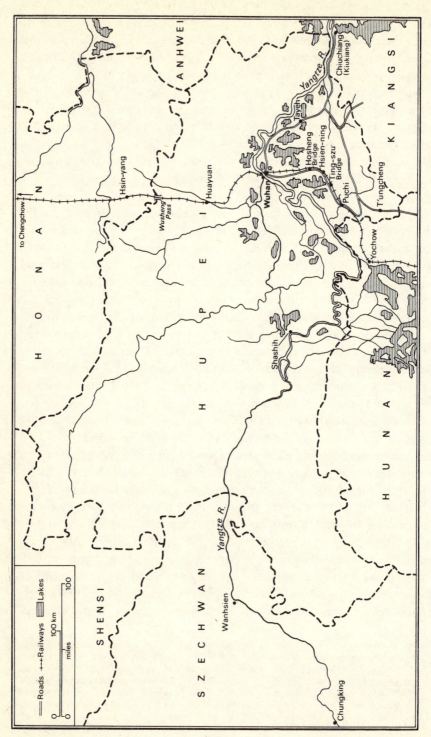

MAP 4. Hupei

General Wu narrowly escaped by train to Wuchang and crossed the Yangtze to Hankow. The Fourth Corps suffered heavy casualties in these battles and, together with the Seventh and Eighth Corps, captured thousands of enemy troops and mountains of equipment.[105] The road to Wuchang was now open.

Pursuing revolutionary forces arrived in the suburbs of Wuchang on 31 August, too late to prevent the enemy from withdrawing behind the city's massive walls. After three costly night-time attempts by 'dare-to-die' troops to scale the walls, in which Yeh T'ing's independent regiment lost heavily, the Fourth and Seventh Corps and the Second Division of the First Corps settled down to what became a seige of forty days. On 6 and 7 September the Eighth Corps, which had crossed the Yangtze, took Hanyang and Hankow after General Liu Tso-lung, the garrison commander, defected; later, Liu was given the title of commander of the Fifteenth Corps. Wu P'ei-fu retreated north along the Peking-Hankow Railway with his remaining troops to Wu-sheng Pass on the northern border of Hupei, but the pursuing Eighth Corps took the pass on 15 September, and Wu retreated into Honan. Finally, on 10 October, the Wuchang garrison surrendered and Hupei had been brought under the authority of the national government.

The assault on Kiangsi proved much more difficult. The most important topographical feature of that province is the Kan River, which starts near the northern border of Kwangtung and flows northeastwards into the great Po-yang Lake, which joins the Yangtze. Nanchang, the capital, lies in the northern part of the province on the east bank of the Kan in a rich plain which extends to the lake. The city was connected with Kiukiang on the Yangtze by a 79-mile railway. While Chiang Kai-shek and Sun Ch'uan-fang negotiated through representatives, both sides sent troops into the province. The general plan of the National Revolutionary Army was to send forces, which had so far done little fighting, eastwards from Hunan to capture Nanchang, while other units from Hupei would capture the railway and take Kiukiang. The southern part of Kiangsi was left to the Fourteenth Corps of Lai Shih-huang, who had defected to the Nationalist side. These movements took place during the first two weeks of September.

Then on 19 September Ch'eng Ch'ien's Sixth Corps by rapid march

---

105 These battles are described in *KMWH*, 12. 1904–31, and *PFCS*, 2. 355–431, both with lists of casualties, enemy prisoners, and booty; *Pei-fa chien-shih*, 55–9; Jordan, *The Northern Expedition*, 75–9; and in A. I. Cherepanov, *Severnyi pokhod Natsional'-no-Revoliutsionnoi Armii Kitaia (zapiski voennogo sovetnika 1926–1927)* (The Northern Expedition of the National Revolutionary Army of China – Notes of a military adviser 1926–1927), 158–64, from a Russian viewpoint.

succeeded in capturing Nanchang with help from the local garrison and students and workers within the city, and with support from the First Division of the First Corps. But an enemy counter-attack drove these forces from the city and the railway with very heavy losses, while the Third Corps allegedly stood by without giving support. Chiang Kai-shek personally directed a second attempt to take Nanchang with the Second Division of First Corps and two divisions of the Second. By 13 October this attack had failed, as well as efforts by elements from the Third, Sixth and Seventh Corps to capture towns on the railway, which they proved unable to hold. The double failure brought on a general retreat and reorganization while General Blyukher and his Russian staff directed careful preparations for a coordinated general attack with all units in proper communication and working on a single timetable. Four regiments of the Fourth Corps were called in from Wuchang as well as the Second Independent Division of Ho Yao-tsu, a Hunanese commander who had recently joined the Nationalists. Chiang Kai-shek was still ne-gotiating with a representative of Sun Ch'uan-fang as late as 28 October, but by then negotiations were obviously a screen. More importantly several enemy regiments and brigades were negotiating to turn over.

The general offensive began at the end of October with the Seventh Corps, the Second Independent Division, and the 12th Division of the Fourth Corps attacking the centre and northern sector of the railway to take Kiukiang; the Third and Sixth Corps attacking stations near Nan-chang; and the Second and Fourteenth Corps moving on Nanchang from the south. This well-planned and hard-fought campaign lasting a week succeeded in clearing the railway, capturing Kiukiang on 5 November and Nanchang on the 8th. Aside from some 7,000 of the enemy who defected, the Nationalists disarmed more than 40,000 of Sun Ch'uan-fang's troops. The National Revolutionary Army lost nearly 15,000 killed and wounded in the two months' campaign in Kiangsi.[106]

---

106 An account dated 5 Dec. 1926 and based upon information in Blyukher's headquarters was written by A. Khmelev, who was in Nanchang 24–30 Nov. Preserved in Russian archives, his report quotes a 15 Nov. telegram from 'Galen' which gives these casualty figures, and adds another 10,000 for the previous campaigns. Apparently Blyukher was counting losses only of the corps which had been organized in Kwangtung, the original NRA. He deprecated the actual fighting of the Seventh Corps and Ho Yao-tsu's Independent Second Division in the Kiangsi campaign, though these forces captured most of the enemy's arms. Blyukher's mid Nov. figures for forces campaigning outside Kwangtung are as follows:

Corps from Kwangtung	Outside Corps
First: more than 3,000	Seventh: about 7,000
In Fukien 8,000	Eighth: 25–30,000 (15,000 as
Second: 6,000 of inferior battle-fitness	battle-fit)
Third: around 3,000	Ninth and Tenth: unclear

While the campaign in Kiangsi was being fought, General Ho Ying-ch'in was directing another campaign in the coastal province of Fukien. Two divisions of the First Corps, the Third and 14th, guarded the eastern border of Kwangtung against a possible attack from the Fukien military governor, Chou Yin-jen, an ally of Sun Ch'uan-fang. General Ho negotiated with an enemy corps commander, Li Feng-hsiang, and his division commanders, Ts'ao Wan-hsun and Tu Ch'i-yun, to defect to the Nationalist side, and with leaders of the navy stationed at Foochow. Kuomintang members in Fukien negotiated with various 'people's armies' to assist in ousting Chou Yin-jen, a northerner. Chiang Kai-shek instructed General Ho to negotiate for peace on condition that Chou not send troops into Kwangtung or Kwangsi. These preliminaries occurred in August and September.[107]

The enemy in Fukien reportedly outnumbered the Nationalist forces in men and equipment by the order of five to one. Chou Yin-jen on 27 September sent forces to invade Kwangtung with the purpose of capturing the major East River cities, but General Ho received inside information on these plans and ordered an offensive against Chou's base at Yungting across the border. On 10 October the First Corps' Third Division captured the city and then returned to Kwangtung to deal with the invaders at Sung-k'o. In these initial battles the Nationalists captured thousands of prisoners with their rifles, machine guns and cannon. On 14 October the enemy's Third Fukien Division defected, as planned, and was reorganized as the Seventeenth Corps of the National Revolutionary Army. These initial battles were so successful that on 16 October Chiang Kai-shek appointed General Ho as commander of the Eastern Route Army made up of the First, Seventeenth and Forteenth Corps (Lai Shih-huang's force, which was to enter Fukien from Kiangsi), and ordered him to proceed to conquer the province.

Fourth: 3,500 original and 2,500   Fourteenth: about 500
      newcomers   Fifteenth: 5–6,000 inferior
Sixth: more than 3,000   Seventeenth: 8,000

'Iz istorii severnogo pokhoda Natsional'no-Revolutsionnoi Armii' (From the history of the Northern Expedition of the National Revolutionary Army), in *Istoricheskii arkhiv* (The historical archives), 4 (1959) 113–26, Doc. 3, 116. Other accounts of the Kiangsi campaign are *KMWH*, 13. 2047–179 (with many telegrams); *PFCS*, 2. 499–564; *Pei-fa chien-shih*, 69–90; Cherepanov, *Severnyi*, 189–201 (with a hostile bias towards Chiang Kai-shek); Jordan, *The Northern Expedition*, 83–92.

107 I have used Ch'en Hsun-cheng's account of the Fukien campaign as the basic source. *KMWH*, 14. 2187–212, and 2212–20 for documents. A. I. Cherepanov was Ho Ying-ch'in's military adviser, but his account of the campaign is brief and not always accurate because he lacked documents. *Severnyi*, 172–8. Other accounts in *PFCS*, 2. 575–96; *Pei-fa chien-shih*, 91–8; Jordan, *The Northern Expedition*, 93–6. The Kuomintang Archives contain *Kuo-min ko-ming-chün tung-lu-chün chan-shih chi-lüeh* (A brief record of the battle history of the Eastern Route Army of the National Revolutionary Army), 465/30, which gives voluminous details.

Pacification of Fukien proceeded methodically, with the main forces following the coastal route and taking major centres such as Chang-chou (8 November) and Ch'üan-chou (21 November). As the forces approached the Min River, the navy switched sides, trapping retreating troops who were disarmed by the thousands. On 3 December the navy occupied Foochow, the provincial capital, and on 18 December Ho Ying-ch'in occupied the city with two divisions of the First Corps. In the more mountainous central part of the province 'people's armies' assisted the Seventeeth Corps' advance. Chou Yin-jen retreated with his remnants to the Chekiang border, hoping to link up with Sun Ch'uan-fang, but was blocked by General Ch'en I, who was negotiating to join the Nationalist side.

Thus, by the end of December 1926 the Nationalists had taken the capitals and major cities of Hunan, Hupei, Kiangsi and Fukien, adding them to the original base of Kwangtung and the adjacent province of Kwangsi, which had joined through negotiations. The military governor of Kweichow had also brought his province nominally under the Nationalist government. These seven provinces had a population of approximately 170 million, and the four conquered provinces of 110 million.[108]

Many factors account for this success in only six months. Of prime importance was two years of training and equipping the original National Revolutionary Army with Russian help, and the battle-hardening of campaigns in Kwangtung during 1925. Another was the political indoctrination of troops and officers, giving them the cause for which to fight – essentially an ardent spirit of nationalism. Important, too, was the fiscal reform carried out in Kwangtung, which brought most of the province's tax revenues into the Nationalists' treasury, created trust in the currency and made it possible to borrow by selling treasury notes. Negotiations with enemy forces and the use of silver bullets to induce defections were also useful. The decisive factor, however, was the valour of the National Revolutionary Army in the long-awaited Northern Expedition, particularly the sacrificial spirit of the First and Fourth Corps, though some other units also fought well when committed to battle.

Russian advisers played an important role in the campaigns. General Blyukher developed the general strategy and he and his staff executed detailed, professional plans for particular campaigns. Each of the engaged corps had its Russian advisers, as did some of the divisions. These men tried to assure that plans were executed exactly by their units, and they provided Blyukher an intelligence network during the battles and valuable

108 George Babcock Cressey, *China's geographic foundations: a survey of the land and its people*, 55, based upon the Chinese Post Office estimate of 1926.

summations thereafter. Some actually led attacks. They also provided political assessments of the Chinese generals whom they advised. A few daring Russian aviators scouted enemy dispositions, dropped leaflets into beseiged cities, terrorized enemy troops, and lofted bombs onto strategic targets. Several Russians became seriously ill, one with cholera, others with dysentery. After the Kiangsi campaign, 'a considerable per cent of our workers' were admitted to the Nanchang American hospital.[109]

Mobilizing the masses

Another important reason for the quick military success was political work. Special political officers accompanying the armies, as well as Kuomintang and Communist Party members behind enemy lines, supported the campaign by winning over local populations and attempting to suborn enemy units. Troops of the National Revolutionary Army, coached to treat the populace well, were forbidden to loot or to press-gang labourers. There are many reports of their enthusiastic welcome, of farmers selling food to the troops, acting as spies, guides and porters, and serving as litter bearers for the wounded. In some cases crudely armed units of farmers attacked the enemy rear. Railway workers sabotaged enemy communications. Some 400 miners from An-yuan joined Yeh T'ing's independent regiment. Within besieged Wuchang, revolutionaries secretly posted placards and distributed subversive leaflets to undermine enemy morale. Students and police in Nanchang helped with the first brief capture of that city and many paid with their lives when it was lost.[110]

As soon as major cities were taken by the National Revolutionary Army, labour organizers began to form or to revive labour unions. Most of the organizers were communists, some with much experience in the labour movement through work in Shanghai after the May Thirtieth Incident and in Canton directing the great strike and boycott against Hong Kong.

109 Khmelev's report in 'Iz istorii', 125. Cherepanov, *Severnyi*, 124–69, and Vishnyakova-Akimova, *Two Years*, 242–3 and 247. Three reports from the front by Russian advisers are translated and published in Wilbur and How, *Documents*, nos. 43, 44 and 49. Other reports are briefed in the forthcoming revision of that work. Ch'en Hsun-cheng's accounts of the capture of Wuchang and Nanchang praise the work of 'our airforce', without mentioning that the aviators were Russians. *KMWH*, 13. 1991–2, 2163–4.

110 Two early accounts of specific forms of assistance to the advancing army are reprinted in *Ti-itz'u . . . nung-min*, 293–7 (14 Sept. 1926) and 298–301 (4 Nov 1926). An early account by an Australian observer is H. Owen Chapman, *The Chinese revolution 1926–27: a record of the period under communist control as seen from the Nationalist capital, Hankow*, 21–7. Jordan, *The Northern Expedition*, 75–9, 241–6, for examples and an appraisal. Angus McDonald, 'The Hunan peasant movement: its urban origins', *Modern China*, 1.2 (April 1975) 188–9, and in his book, *The urban origins of rural revolution*, 264–70, deprecates the role of farmers in assisting the troops, crediting urban workers as more important.

In Hunan the labour movement was quickly revived under the direction of Kuo Liang, a Hunanese communist, who had been active in organizing railway workers in 1922, only to see the union crushed in the repression of 1923. He joined the Kuomintang and was a member of the party's underground nucleus in Changsha in 1924. At the Third Congress of the All China General Labour Union held in Canton in May 1926, he was elected to the Central Committee, and then returned to Changsha. Soon after the city was taken by the Eighth Corps, scores of unions had been formed and there followed a wave of agitation and strikes for higher wages and better working conditions. Political officers supported the unionization movement, and armed picket corps enforced the strikes. In September a provincial federation of Hunan unions was established and a December congress passed a series of resolutions which sought to regularize union structure and governance, to impose discipline in the labour movement, and prevent unauthorized strikes. Twenty-seven-year-old Kuo Liang became chairman of the Hunan General Labour Union. By spring of 1927 the provincial federation claimed over 400,000 members, of whom 90,000 were industrial workers.[111]

Revolutionary fervour mounted steadily in Hankow and Hanyang after their capture early in September. The cities were soon plastered with posters denouncing imperialism and warlords, and calling for support of the national revolution. The political department organized daily meetings and parades, and the Kuomintang began recruiting among students, lower level officials, women, labourers and others groups. By the end of December it had taken in some 31,000 new members. The Central Committee of the Communist Party sent Chang Kuo-t'ao from Shanghai to direct work in Wuhan; he arrived on 11 September and was followed by several comrades with rich experience in labour organizing, Li Li-san, Liu Shao-ch'i, Hsiang Ying, and Hsu Pai-hao. The labour movement had been repressed but not destroyed in the years after the brutal suppression of the Peking-Hankow Railway strike in February 1923. Now it quickly revived. On 14 September a preliminary meeting of union delegates planned the formation of a Hupei General Labour Union, which was officially inaugurated on 10 October. A list of unions published towards the end of November named 73 in the Wuhan cities with a reported membership of 82,000, and six unions in the iron mining centre of Ta-yeh with 11,000 members. Sometime in November the communist-dominated All China General Labour Union set up a management office in Hankow to direct the unionization process.[112]

111 *Ti-i-tz'u . . . kung-jen,* 316–74 for documents on unionization in Hunan. Chesneaux, *The Chinese labor movement,* 322.
112 *Ibid.* 321–2; Chang, *The rise of the Chinese Communist Party,* 1. 532–50; *Chung-kuo lao-kung yun-tung shih,* 2. 597–601.

In November a wave of strikes hit the Wuhan cities, directed against both native business and foreign concerns. Printers, postal workers, clerks in silk shops, coolie labourers, servants and employees in Japanese homes and businesses walked out, and the British cigarette company was closed down. Unions used armed picket corps to enforce strikes, which they did with brutality in some cases. Most strikes were quickly settled by wage increases, but unions tried to impose their authority on management, which stiffened resistance. The strikes had a depressing effect on business. Eleven Chinese banks failed on settlement day, 19 November, including two of the largest. Chinese business leaders began to organize to protect themselves and even threatened a commercial stoppage if the government did not respond to two demands: that pay increases be negotiated directly between employers and employees without interference of unions, and that coercion by picket corps be forbidden. The government responded by establishing a mediation commission with two representatives each from the Nationalist government, the Kuomintang, the Chamber of Commerce and the General Labour Union. The commission was to investigate the rising cost of living and the ability of business to pay increased wages. A number of government leaders arrived on 11 December from Canton, via Nanchang, and quickly sought to establish more orderly government. However, disruptive economic forces had already been set in train that ultimately contributed to the demise of the Wuhan government.[113]

The most dramatic and portentous involvement of the masses in the revolution was the rapid expansion of the farmers' movement in the newly liberated provinces. Before the Northern Expedition began, the Canton headquarters of the movement knew of only 161 local associations in Hunan, Hupei, and Kiangsi, with a total of 43,423 members. Six months later, at the end of 1926, communist leaders of the movement were claiming more than one-and-a-half-million farmers organized in associations spread through 91 counties of Hunan and Hupei alone. Such figures cannot be accurate, but they point to a frenzy of organizing by the few hundred cadres able to devote themselves to this phase of the revolution.[114]

Local communists who had worked surreptitiously before the Nationalist troops arrived, could now organize farmers openly with the help

113 *Ibid.* 612–22 on strikes, business reaction and the mediation commission. USDS 893.504/ 40 Consul-general Lockhart, Hankow, to secretary of state, 28 Dec. 1926, p. 15 on strikes and bank failures. *China year book 1928*, p. 984 on picket brutality. Wang Chien-min, *Chung-kuo Kung-ch'an-tang shih kao* (A draft history of the Chinese Communist Party), 1. 400–4, for a general treatment of communist labour organizing in Hupei.

114 Enrolment figures from *Ti-i-tz'u . . . nung-min*, 17–18 for 3 June 1926; 257–62 for Hunan in November; 395 for Hupei at end December. Li Jui asserts that more than 40,000 farmers had been organized in Hunan before the expedition began, but does not substantiate it. *Ibid.* 267.

and protection of political officers. Among the organizers of the rural mass movement were graduates of the Farmers Movement Training Institute in Canton, 65 of whom were natives of Hunan, Hupei and Kiangsi. Another 85 graduated early in October from the class which Mao Tse-tung directed. Local organizers knew the poor farmers' grievances, and they had a repertoire of propaganda slogans and organizing techniques. In Hunan, they first concentrated on enlisting farmers to help the revolutionary troops, then turned to drawing them into associations and defence corps. At first they played down rural class struggle and emphasized benefits to the poorer farmers by opening granaries and calling for reduction of rent and interest rates, renegotiation of land contracts, and reducing food prices by prohibiting export of grain from one district to another. Such policies could only arouse fierce opposition from the powerful, and rural Hunan was soon embroiled in conflict. 'Local bullies and evil gentry' became the targets for attack and humiliation, along with large landlords and 'corrupt officials'. Their property should be confiscated, and when possible it was. However, it was not only communists and Kuomintang leftists who were organizing farmers' associations. More conservative provincial Kuomintang members as well as local notables organized associations or gave an official name to existing agricultural societies. A Left Society based in Changsha attempted to steer the farmers' movement into reformist channels. Thus there was inter-organizational conflict as well as class conflict within the agrarian movement.[115]

As violence spread there were reports of local tyrants being executed and, on the other side, of villages attacked and burned, and of farmer leaders slain. In some regions poor farmers, or their spokesmen, were demanding 'solution of the land problem' – that is, expropriation and division of landlords' land, or other forms of 'land equalization'. The farmers' movement spread geographically but was strongest in the Hsiang River valley and along the borders of Hupei, areas conquered by the National Revolutionary Army. By November there were reported to be 6,867 local farmers' associations in Hunan with a total membership of more than 1,267,000. Local groups were linked in a structure of 462 district associations and 29 formally organized county associations, with more being formed. An analysis of the class composition of the associations showed that over 60 per cent were hired agricultural workers or tenants, with 'semi-independent peasants' making up 18 per cent. 'Independent

---

115 Etō, 'Hai-lu-feng', 1. 182 for graduates of the FMTI. On early developments see accounts in *Ti-i-tz'u . . . nung-min*, 270–5, 281–4, 293–301, 322–5; Hofheinz, *The broken wave*, 130–4. McDonald 'The Hunan peasant movement', 190–5 argues the variety of associations in rivalry.

peasants' and handicraftsmen made up most of the remaining 20 per cent. The movement as organized by the leftist leadership seems clearly to have attracted the rural poor.[116]

The Hunan provincial farmers' association was organized at a congress at Changsha which lasted most of December. One-hundred-and-seventy delegates reportedly represented the more than 1.3 million organized farmers. The opening meetings were held jointly with a congress of labour delegates who were said to represent more than 326,000 unionized workers in Hunan. Many days were spent in discussing and then adopting resolutions that had been prepared by the organizers in advance. A proclamation adopted on 2 October by a conference of the Hunan provincial Communist Party branch had set forth the minimal political and economic demands of the farmers, and this provided the outlines for the resolutions adopted by the congress in December. The resolutions called for local self-government in which farmers' associations must participate, self-defence organizations controlled by farmers themselves, the smashing of domination by 'local bullies and evil gentry', support for the revolutionary policies of the Kuomintang and Chinese Communist Party, reduction of rent and of interest on loans, abolition of exorbitant taxes and likin, storage of grain against famine and other relief measures, and confiscation of property of reactionaries – that is, warlords and their subordinates, corrupt officials, 'local bullies and evil gentry'. One of the architects of the provincial association, who became its secretary-general, was Liu Chih-hsun, a Hunanese communist, aged 19, a graduate of Ya-li (Yale-in-China at Changsha), and friend of Mao Tse-tung. Mao, who had recently become head of the Communist Party's peasant committee, attended the latter part of the congress and delivered two speeches in which he insisted that the peasant problem was the central issue of the national revolution; unless it were solved, imperialism and warlordism could not be overthrown nor industrial progress be achieved. He excoriated those who would restrain the peasantry and called for unremitting struggle.[117] After the congress Mao travelled in five counties near

116 On executions, see reports in GBFO 405/252. Confidential. *Further correspondence respecting China*, 13313, Jan.–March 1927, nos. 44, 74, and 91; *North China Herald* (hereafter *NCH*), 15 Jan. 1927, p. 62; Mitarevsky, *World-wide Soviet plots*, 139–40, trans. of a report by a Kuomintang official. Communist writers emphasized how few executions of tyrants there were. See *Ti-i-tz'u . . . nung-min*, 281, 312, 381; and 282–3, 329 on killing of rural leaders. Hofheinz, *The broken wave*, 49–50, leans towards this interpretation. Apparently killings increased after the turn of the year. On November membership and class composition, *Ti-i-tz'u . . . nung-min*, 257–62, and Suguru Yokoyama, 'The Peasant movement in Hunan', *Modern China*, 1. 2. 204–38, chart on p. 217, but possibly based upon a different source.

117 *Ti-i-tz'u . . . nung-min*, 275–8 for Li Jui's account of the congress and Mao's speeches; 322–5 for the Communist Party proclamation (trans. in Yokoyama, cited, 220–2); and 326–80 for the proclamation and resolutions adopted by the congress.

Changsha to investigate the agrarian revolution; he then wrote a stirring – and later famous – report.

In Hupei the agrarian movement followed a similar course. From a
small base of 38 associations with a membership of a little more than four
thousand as reported on 3 June, the membership rose by December to a
reported 287,000 in 34 counties. In Kiangsi, which was conquered only
with great difficulty, development was not so rapid. In June there were
only 36 associations with about 1,100 members; in October a reported
6,276 members (probably mostly in the south); and in November, after
the capture of Nanchang, when a preparatory conference for a provincial
association was held, the figure of 50,000 was being used. However,
Kiangsi was Chiang Kai-shek's special sphere: the agrarian movement
apparently was held in check.[118]

The anti-imperialist movement

At the heart of the Nationalist movement was opposition to the political
and economic privileges of foreigners in China, privileges which derived
from 'unequal treaties' imposed by the powers during the previous 80
years. The Nationalist leaders systematically sought to arouse the populace
with barrages of propaganda in support of their pledge to win back
China's lost rights. Although nationals of many countries enjoyed special
treaty rights, the Nationalists' strategy (and behind it, Russian advice)
was to focus hostility upon Great Britain in order to avoid a simultaneous
confrontation with Japan, the United States and France. Great Britain
held the predominant position in China and hence was a natural target.
Anti-imperialism was, of course, a fundamental tenet of the world communist movement, and Bolshevik Russia, which supported and advised
the Nationalists, regarded Great Britain as its major foe. Russia was
particularly fearful of being drawn into conflict with Japan. The strategy
of focusing Chinese hostility upon Great Britain became clear after the
May Thirtieth and June Twenty-third Incidents of 1925, for Japan was
an initial target in the first incident and France had been as guilty as
Great Britan in the second, but in efforts at retaliation their roles were
played down. The anti-imperialist movement brought great benefits in
popular support for the Nationalists and the Communists – both parties
grew rapidly from mid 1925 on – but it involved risks also. It seemed
likely that Great Britain, if pushed too far, might retaliate militarily against

118 *Ti-i-tz'u . . . nung-min*, 17–18 for June figures; 395 for Hupei; 420 for Kiangsi. As late as
    May 1927 Kiangsi reported only 82,617 members. Hofheinz, *The broken wave*, 104, presents
    figures claimed by organizers from 1924 to 1927 for four provinces, but not Kiangsi.

Canton, or that the powers might adopt a policy of outright support for the Nationalists' enemies, the northern 'warlords'.

The strike against Hong Kong and the boycott against trade with Great Britain had gone on for a full year in Kwangtung when the Northern Expedition began. There had been several circuitous attempts to negotiate a settlement, for both sides wanted the conflict ended. The strike no longer inconvenienced Hong Kong but the boycott seriously harmed British trade and shipping in South China. Support for the strikers was a heavy drain on the resources of the Canton government, and the independent power in Canton which the strike committee had developed was an embarrassment. Armed and unruly pickets created many problems for the Canton leadership. The strike committee itself was the prime obstacle to a termination of the boycott because it insisted upon a large financial settlement to pay off the strikers for their year of unemployment, but the Canton government could not find the money and the Hong Kong government refused absolutely to pay what it regarded as blackmail. There was also the serious problem for the Canton authorities of employment for thousands of former Hong Kong workers when their financial relief ended. Eager to end the conflict, the Nationalist government consented to negotiate directly with the Hong Kong government, instead of continuing the pretence that it played only a mediating role. Formal negotiations from 15 to 23 July foundered again on the issue of payment. Then, on 4 September a brief action by ships of the British navy in Canton harbour and the unrelated Wan-hsien incident on the upper Yangtze the next day, apparently convinced the Canton authorities that Great Britain intended to try to force an end to the boycott by military action, though this was not the case. A telegram to Chiang Kai-shek at the front warned of this imagined danger and he ordered the strike and boycott ended. On 18 September Eugene Chen, acting foreign minister, told the acting British consul-general in Canton that the boycott would end on or before 10 October, and that his government would levy extra taxes in order to pay off the strikers. Thus, on 10 October the strike and boycott ended by unilateral decision on the Chinese side, and the Canton government imposed surtaxes on imports and exports that accorded with the 2.5 per cent surtaxes promised at the Washington Conference, though never officially brought into effect. To this imposition of new tariffs the British government turned a blind eye. The Foreign Office was happy to see the troublesome boycott ended and was trying to formulate a new policy more friendly towards the Nationalists.[119]

119 Wilson, 'Britain and the Kuomintang', 335–401, gives a judicious account of the settlement based upon British Foreign Office Archives and Chinese published sources. The minutes

Foreign missionary activity had long been a target of hostility for ardent Chinese nationalists, many of whom scorned religion and objected particularly to a foreign religion which, they argued, enslaved the minds of its converts. Missionary schools were a particular target because of foreign control over the education of Chinese youth. The nationwide propaganda campaign against missionary education that began in 1922 was not particularly associated with the Kuomintang, but soon that party and the Communist Party supported a vituperative anti-Christian movement. During 1925 Kwangtung saw many evidences: explicitly anti-Christian parades, street lectures and inflammatory handbills, and invasion and destruction of some mission properties, on two occasions by Nationalist troops. Disruptive activities occurred in a number of mission colleges and middle schools in central China where communist and Kuomintang influences were strong among students. For example, in both 1924 and 1925 provocateurs stirred up 'student storms' in Ya-li (Yale-in-China) in Changsha. The Second National Congress of the Kuomintang held in Canton in January 1926 endorsed a strong resolution supporting the anti-Christian movement, and charging schools, journals and churches run by missionaries as being 'the tongues and claws of imperialism'. In Kwangsi, after it had been brought into alliance with the Nationalist government, there were several anti-Christian riots with some looting of mission properties during the first half of 1926. The anti-Christian movement was, in short, a part of the broader anti-imperialist movement, but foreign missionaries and their institutions were immediate and very vulnerable targets.[120]

There was, however, an ambivalence. Some leaders of the Kuomintang were Christians, as Sun Yat-sen had been, and some were themselves graduates of missionary institutions. Violent attacks on Christian institutions damaged the reputation of the Kuomintang abroad as well as among Chinese Christians. The Nationalist military campaign seemed, at the beginning, to face dangerous odds; there was good reason to try to avoid arousing foreign opposition. In a resolution adopted by a plenary

of the Kuomintang Political Council for the first half of 1926, contain many cases of action by the strike committee or the pickets, which the Political Council found unruly and attempted to curb. Teng Chung-hsia and Su Chao-cheng of the strike committee often attended these meetings when such issues were on the agenda. Teng Chung-hsia, *Chung-kuo chih-kung yun-tung chien-shih*, 188-94; *Chung-kuo lao-kung yun-tung shih*, 2. 544-6, 551-6, 583-90 for varying Chinese accounts of ending the strike and boycott.

120 Much information on anti-Christian activities is in Leon Wieger, *Chine moderne*, 5, 6 and 7, covering the years 1924 through 1927; and in volumes of *Foreign relations of the United States* dealing with China for those years. Also Jessie G. Lutz, 'Chinese nationalism and the anti-Christian campaigns of the 1920s', *Modern Asian Studies*, 10. 3 (1976), 394-416; and Ka-che Yip, 'The anti-Christian movement in China, 1922-1927', Columbia University, Ph.D. dissertation, 1970, published as *Religion, nationalism and Chinese students*, 1980.

session of the Chinese Communist Party's Central Committee, which met in Shanghai from 12 to 18 July 1926 just as the Northern Expedition was getting under way, the following attitude towards the Christian church was laid down:

In our verbal propaganda, we should do our utmost to depict the [Christian] Church as the vanguard of imperialism. . . . The Church wishes to deceive all oppressed peoples and lead them to forget their own actual sufferings in order to ensure a strong and lasting foundation for imperialist oppression.

We must not at this time create any opportunity of actual conflict with the Church. This condition is imposed by our present situation (the Church is allied with militarists everywhere under the pretext of treaty protection) . . .

On 20 August after he reached Changsha, the commander-in-chief, Chiang Kai-shek, issued a proclamation to the world in which he explained the patriotic purposes of the Northern Expedition to liberate China from the warlords and win its rightful place of equality among the nations, with friendship for all. He promised protection of life and property for all foreigners in China who did not obstruct the operation of the revolutionary forces or assist the warlords. Two days later, Hsiang-ya, the Yale-in-China hospital and medical college in Changsha, received an order to send doctors to attend General Chiang. The American missionary surgeon who extracted an impacted tooth was favourably impressed by Chiang Kai-shek's apparent friendliness. The Hsiang-ya faculty had feared their hospital would be expropriated, but instead Chiang's headquarters set up a well equipped military hospital across the street, and for a time the two hospitals cooperated. General Chiang permitted no attacks on foreigners by troops under his control.[121]

After fighting had moved beyond Hunan, conditions changed markedly. An anti-British boycott was started in the province. Demonstrations in Changsha and other towns took on a fiercely anti-foreign character. In October many mission stations were under harassment, their buildings plastered with hostile posters and their Chinese employees or the students in their schools organized into unions that made demands that clearly had a common orchestration. Missionaries were driven from their stations in Li-ling and Nan-hsien. In Changsha all mission schools were under attack. As concern mounted, an American journalist submitted

---

121 Communist resolution, Wilbur and How, *Documents*, 299–300. Chiang's proclamation in Mao, *CKSHS* for 20 Aug. 1926; trans. in Wieger, *Chine moderne*, 7. 113–15 (dated 19 Aug.). The next item in *Chine moderne* is an anti-Christian statement issued by the Political Department of the Fourth Corps, dated 25 August. On the tooth episode, Ruth Altman Greene, *Hsiang-Ya journal*, 45–7. Reuben Holden, *Yale in China: the mainland, 1901–1951*, 157, states that at this time Chiang 'maintained excellent discipline among his troops and permitted no offenses against foreigners.'

questions to Chiang Kai-shek in Nanchang. He replied on 19 November 'I have no quarrel with Christianity and missionaries will always be welcome as heretofore. The elimination of missions from China is not part of our programme, and they may function in this country without interference as always.' Yet in Hunan threats of violence and other forms of pressure grew so intense that by the year's end most mission schools were closed and missionaries of several nationalities had fled to the Hankow sanctuary or were preparing to do so. No one had been killed, but many churches and mission properties had been seized by unions or military units. American businesses in Changsha had not been molested, and Japanese and Germans were generally left undisturbed.[122]

The British Foreign Office began work during November on a policy statement that might open the way to fuller accommodation to Chinese nationalism and improved relations with the Nationalist regime. Austen Chamberlain, the foreign secretary, personally directed the attempt to formulate a fresh and forward-looking policy, and his memorandum was approved by the cabinet on 1 December 1926. The text was cabled to the new British minister to China, Miles Lampson, who was then in Shanghai on his way to Peking. The statement (later known as the Christmas Memorandum because of its publication on 26 December) was actually directed to the other powers. It urged each to declare its willingness to negotiate on treaty revision and all other outstanding questions as soon as an authoritative Chinese government should emerge; but that pending such time, they should deal with local authorities and consider sympathetically any reasonable proposals, even if contrary to strict interpretation of treaty rights, in return for fair treatment of foreign interests by them. Protests should be reserved for attempted wholesale repudiation of treaty obligations or attacks upon the legitimate and vital interests of foreigners in China; and such protests should be made effective by united action of the powers. The memorandum stated the British government's view that some of the Commission on Extra-territoriality's recommendations for revision should be carried out at once, and that the powers should immediately and unconditionally authorize the Washington surtaxes without specifying how the proceeds were to be handled or used.[123] The memorandum, while showing a desire to accommodate to the aspirations of Chinese

122 Chiang Kai-shek's statement in NCH, 12 Feb. 1927, p. 230; but a very different summary in Wieger, Chine moderne, 7. 51. Catherine M. McGuire, 'The union movement in Hunan in 1926-1927 and its effect on the American community', Columbia University, M.A. essay in history, 1977, citing U.S. Consular archives from Changsha and correspondence from Hunan mission stations.
123 Wilson, 'Britain and the Kuomintang', 434-41; Dorothy Borg, American policy and the Chinese revolution, 1925-1928, 228-30.

patriots, was much too restrictive to satisfy the demands of the Nationalist movement.

Recognizing that the Nationalists seemed well established on the Yangtze, the British Foreign Office was considering the possibility of diplomatic recognition as soon as the Kuomintang government was sufficiently established to assume full responsibilities for all treaties and other obligations of the government it would succeed. Until that time Great Britain would endeavour to deal in a friendly spirit with any Kuomintang administration exercising *de facto* authority in any part of China. The Foreign Office authorized Lampson to visit Hankow even before taking up his post in Peking. Thus it was that the British minister to China held his first diplomatic discussions with Eugene Chen, the Nationalist foreign minister, from 9 to 17 December. The central issue in their exploratory discussion was the conditions for possible British recognition, and the main difficulty was Lampson's insistence that the Nationalists accept the existing treaties as binding until new treaties had been negotiated. The talks allowed each side to appraise the limits to which the other side would go in accommodation. Eugene Chen tried imaginatively to find a formula to bridge conflicting positions, for he seemed eager to win the advantage that recognition would bring his government. He insisted that Minister Lampson's departure be arranged to appear as only a temporary suspension of talks, and Lampson obliged him in this.[124]

Seizure of the British concession in Hankow

There were, however, others among the Wuhan leaders who opposed an attempt to come to an agreement with Great Britain. Anti-British agitation, which had mounted in November, causing alarm in the Hankow British concession, was held in check during Lampson's visit. After his departure on 18 December the public was again systematically subjected to propaganda against British imperialism. Evidently Borodin was eager to keep the anti-British fever burning, as evidenced by his advice in meetings of the Provisional Joint Council of Party and Government leaders (the top policy making body in Wuhan) and corresponding resolutions adopted by a Committee of Wuhan Citizens to Oppose British Imperialism which held a giant rally on 26 December. Li Li-san, a veteran communist labour leader who had won his spurs directing the anti-

---

124 Wilson, 'Britain and the Kuomintang', 464–7, based upon Lampson's cables, which the writer also has read in the Public Record Office. Eugene Chen's account as presented to the Kuomintang Third CEC Plenum on 13 March 1927 is in Chiang Yung-ching, *Bo-lo-t'ing yü Wu-han cheng-ch'üan* (Borodin and the Wuhan regime; hereafter, *Borodin*), 89–90. Professor Chiang bases his study on original documents in the Kuomintang Archives.

British strike in Shanghai during the summer of 1925, presided and gave a speech, as did other communist leaders. The Christmas Memorandum was published in China on the same date, and Borodin proposed the propaganda line to use in denouncing British policy, and this was adopted by the Kuomintang Central Propaganda Department. An issue which troubled relations was the arrest of 17 Kuomintang members in the British and French concessions in Tientsin on 23 November. After trial they were handed over to Chinese authorities and the Kuomintang office was sealed. The Nationalist government, still in Canton, had protested and announced that it held Great Britain responsible for what might happen to the Kuomintang members in enemy hands. Towards the end of December the Nationalist leadership, now in Hankow, revived the issue when seven of their Tientsin fellows were executed. This incident became part of the propaganda argument for the recovery of foreign concessionary areas. Yet direct conflict with Great Britain, the main enemy, had to be avoided.[125]

With the revival of anti-British demonstrations, the authorities of the Hankow British concession placed barricades at the entrances and manned them with police, small detachments of marines, and members of the Hankow Volunteers. Individual Chinese were permitted to pass through but not crowds or armed soldiers. The first two days of January saw celebrations and parades in the Wuhan cities to welcome – that is, to hasten – the Nationalist government's establishment there. The third saw a giant anti-British rally. That afternoon a large crowd of Chinese gathered outside one of the barricades listening to the anti-imperialist harangues of members of a propaganda squad. The crowd was being aroused to a passion of hatred for British imperialism when suddenly someone began flinging stones at the men on the barricades. This led to a clash between marines, using their bayonets, and the angry crowd. Five Chinese and three marines were injured, though no shots were fired. First reports said one or many Chinese had been killed. The Provisional Joint Council was just in meeting when this dangerous situation was reported. It decided immediately to try to forestall a worse conflict by persuading the crowd to disperse and by demanding that the British authorities withdraw the marines and leave the Chinese police, backed by troops,

---

125 Chiang Yung-ching, *Borodin*, 93-8. Borodin summarized his thoughts on the Christmas memorandum thus, 'Our present policy is to bring Britain and Japan, and Japan and Fengtien into increasing conflict.' In a speech on 20 December before several thousand delegates – possibly of the Committee to Oppose British Imperialism – Borodin stated that Lampson 'has been here with sweet words but his heart is sour. The British are working behind our backs to destroy us. The only way to combat this is first a boycott of everything British.' *NCH*, 24 Dec. 1926, as quoted in Wilson, 'Britain and the Kuomintang,' 468. An account of the 26 December anti-British rally is in *Ti-i-tz'u . . . kung-jen*, 383-4.

to maintain order. The crowd did disperse upon the urging of Hsu Ch'ien and Chiang Tso-pin, who promised that the government would solve the problem in 24 hours. The British consul-general, Herbert Goffe, in consultation with Rear-Admiral Cameron, prudently accepted Eugene Chen's proposal – delivered virtually as an ultimatum – in order to avoid a repetition of the May Thirtieth and June Twenty-third Incidents. The Volunteers withdrew and the marines went back to their ships. Chinese police replaced them on the 4th.

But in fact, the barricades were now open. Urged on by agitators, crowds rushed into the concession and the consul-general had to ask for Chinese troops to maintain order. Next day the Chinese and Sikh members of the concession police quit and the situation became tense when a mob began to stone the police station. The municipal council decided to hand the station over to the Nationalist authorities, making them responsible. British and American women and children were put on board ships and sent to Shanghai, while the men were concentrated in a building near the shore from which they could be evacuated quickly in case of necessity. The Nationalists set up a commission to administer the concession. Thus was the British concession wrested from British control, not by design but in response to a dangerously escalating development. On 6 January the small British enclave in Kiukiang was also taken over by crowd action, without British resistance, but with considerable looting and destruction. These victories for Chinese nationalism added enormously to the Kuomintang's prestige. They also had unforeseen consequences.[126]

One consequence was an increasing number of missionary refugees from interior stations ordered by their consuls to leave for places of safety. Another was concern for the security of the International Settlement in Shanghai, which had the greatest concentration of foreign residents and was a hub of British economic interests in China. Shanghai was clearly the next objective of the Nationalist military campaign. On the basis of predictions and estimates of the British naval commander-in-chief for the Far East and H.M. consul-general in Shanghai, the Cabinet in London debated sending a greatly augmented military force to protect the Settlement from enforced take-over. On 21 January the Cabinet

126 Accounts from the Chinese side are in Chiang Yung-ching, *Borodin*, 99–104, based upon minutes of the Provisional Joint Council; *Kuo-wen chou-pao*, 4.2 and 3, 9 Jan. (with pictures of Hsu Ch'ien and Chiang Tso-pin) and 16 Jan. 1927; *Ti-i-tz'u . . . kung-jen*, 384–93, reprinting Canton *Min-kuo jih-pao* accounts; and Chang, *The rise of the Chinese Communist Party*, 1. 562–6, for a reminiscent account. Wilson, 'Britain and the Kuomintang', 484–97, using British archives and Kuomintang documents, concludes convincingly that the seizure of the concession was not planned by the Nationalist leadership. A British eye-witness account is by E.S. Wilkinson in *NCH*, 15 Jan. 1927, pp. 46–7; also the *Hankow Herald* for January.

made the final decision to send a cruiser squadron and an entire British division instead of the single Indian battalion then on stand-by basis in Hong Kong. News of this decision, which reached China very quickly, created for the Nationalists the spectre that Great Britain might attempt to retake the concessions in Hankow and Kiukiang, or that the British force would assist Sun Ch'uan-fang against the planned capture of the Shanghai area. In fact, the British government had quickly set aside the idea of retaking either concession by force, and Miles Lampson, now in Peking, sent two members of his legation staff to Hankow to negotiate for their retrocession.

Owen O'Malley, the counsellor, and Eric Teichman, the Chinese secretary of the British legation, arrived in Hankow on 11 January and negotiations between Eugene Chen and O'Malley over the Hankow concession lasted until 12 February. For the Nationalist side the negotiations conveyed the appearance of British recognition, and a successful conclusion would add to the Nationalist government's prestige. For the British, the negotiations were seen as a test of the utility of conducting relations with the Nationalists: what the British government wanted was a restoration of face in China and assurance that the Nationalists would make no new attempt to abrogate treaty terms by force. In order to set a favourable stage, the Nationalist foreign ministry proclaimed on 10 January that during the negotiations the anti-British and anti-Christian campaigns were to cease. To reciprocate for the lull which did occur O'Malley persuaded the Hankow British community to resume business on 24 January. The shut-down had begun on 5 January because of the perceived danger, but it had continued as a form of economic pressure on a city already struggling with a depression of trade and unemployment. Some 30 out of 140 Chinese banks failed at Chinese New Year (26 January). Eugene Chen also issued a statement to the effect that the Nationalist government preferred to have all questions outstanding between itself and the foreign powers settled by negotiations and agreement. On the retrocession issue the two sides worked out a face-saving formula by which the Chinese commission would continue to administer the concession while the British Municipal Council wound up financial affairs; then a ratepayers' meeting would formally approve the passing of authority to a joint Chinese-British committee having a Chinese chairman and a Chinese majority – an arrangement based on the precedent of the retrocession of the German concession in Hankow some years earlier. The agreement was to be signed on 30 January, but a new issue arose with the arrival in Shanghai of the Indian battalion on 27 January and knowledge that many more British contingents were on the way. Eugene Chen now demanded assurances that the British force in Shanghai was intended only for defensive purposes; and he threatened not to sign the agreement unless the forces *en route* were stopped short of Shanghai. The compromise was a formal statement by Minister Chen that it was not the policy of his government to use force to effect changes in the status of concessions and international settlements, and British foreign secretary Chamberlain's statement in Parliament that if the Hankow agreement were signed, and no further emergency arose, the remaining British forces would be held in Hong Kong. After these gestures, the Chen-O'Malley agreement was signed on 19 February and a similar agreement on Kiukiang on 2 March. The Chinese side emerged from the negotiations with enhanced prestige while Great Britain had tested its new policy of accommodation towards the Nationalists. Furthermore, the Wuhan leftists had scored a triumph that strengthened their position relative to their rivals in Nanchang.[127]

CONFLICT OVER REVOLUTIONARY GOALS

Dissension within the revolutionary camp

Disunion was inherent in the composition of the Kuomintang leadership, a group riven by factionalism, and also in the situation of the Communist Party, with its distinct philosophy and separate goals, participating with the Kuomintang in guiding the national revolution. There was no consensus as to what forms of activity 'national revolution' embraced. By early in 1927 the Nationalist leadership was divided over a number of issues. What should be the next move in the military campaign – towards Shanghai or towards Peking? Where should the organs of authority be located – in Wuhan or in Nanchang? Behind this issue was a more important one – which leaders within the Kuomintang should make the major decisions? And behind the issue of authority lay a more divisive problem – how much social revolution should be encouraged and how rapidly should it be allowed to proceed? A similar problem, with strategic implications, was whether to stimulate or to restrain the anti-imperialist movement. Conflict over such issues during the first three months of the year resulted in disruption among the Kuomintang leaders, a realign-

---

127 This account is based primarily on Wilson, 'Britain and the Kuomintang', 498–530, which examines evolving British and Chinese response to the Hankow Incident on the basis of documents and accounts from both sides. Nationalist documents on the case are in *KMWH*, 14. 2343–78. See also, Iriye, *After imperialism*, 101–3; Chiang Yung-ching, *Borodin*, 104–09. Mr Chiang believes Borodin engineered the delay in signing of the agreement.

ment in April, and a purge of communists within much of the revolutionary domain.

When the remaining leadership in Canton proceeded northwards to set up the Nationalist government in Wuhan, they went in two separate parties, going overland to Nanchang, where Chiang Kai-shek had established the headquarters of the National Revolutionary Army. After a week of conferences, the first contingent went to Hankow, arriving 10 December. On Borodin's advice this group on 13 December formed the Provisional Joint Council, composed of a few members of the Kuomintang Central Executive Committee and of the National Government Council. They elected Hsu Ch'ien their chairman and Borodin their adviser. This small, extra-constitutional body soon became the chief policy-making group in Wuhan, in effect usurping the authority of the Kuomintang Political Council. Leftists predominated and the Joint Council became an important instrument of Borodin's influence.[128] The authority it began to assert was soon contested by another prestigious group in Nanchang that included not only Chiang Kai-shek, but Chang Ching-chiang (Chang Jen-chieh), acting chairman of the CEC Standing Committee, and T'an Yen-k'ai, acting chairman of the Nationalist Government Council, who arrived in the second travelling party from Canton on 31 December, together with central party headquarters and some government ministers.

In the first days of January, Chiang Kai-shek held a military conference at his headquarters in Nanchang to discuss the financing and reorganization of the swollen armies and to plan the next phase of the campaign. Chiang's intention was a drive on Shanghai by two routes, one down the Yangtze and the other northeastwards through Chekiang. General Blyukher opposed this strategy, as did T'ang Sheng-chih and Teng Yen-ta, the powerful head of the Political Department. The reasons on both sides were strategic and political. For Chiang and his followers, success would mean dominance of the wealthy and relatively industrialized lower Yangtze region and a potential capital at Nanking. For the Hankow group, a campaign northwards could mean a juncture with the Russian-assisted army of Feng Yü-hsiang and then the possibility of the big

128 Initial members were Soong Ch'ing-ling (Mme Sun Yat-sen), Hsu Ch'ien, Teng Yen-ta, Wu Yü-chang, Wang Fa-ch'in, T'ang Sheng-chih, Chan Ta-pei, Tung Yung-wei (Tung Pi-wu), Yü Shu-te, Chiang Tso-pin, Sun Fo, Eugene Chen, and T.V. Soong. All were either regular or reserve members of the Second CEC except T'ang Sheng-chih, commander of the strongest military force in the area and emerging as a rival to Chiang Kai-shek, and Chiang Tso-pin, an important Hupei leader in revolutionary activities and long-time associate of Sun Yat-sen. Wu Yü-chang, Tung Pi-wu and Yü Shu-te were also leading members of the Communist Party. The list is from Chiang Yung-ching, *Borodin*, 33, based on minutes of the Joint Council.

political prize, Peking. The strategy adopted by the conference conformed to Chiang Kai-shek's wishes, though it did include the concentration of T'ang Sheng-chih's troops on the southern section of the Peking-Hankow Railway in a defensive position.[129]

The Nanchang groups set up a Provisional Central Political Council, and most of the Central Committee members there advocated that party headquarters and the Nationalist government should be temporarily located at Nanchang, where the military headquarters were. Hsu Ch'ien and his associates demanded, on the contrary, an immediate move to Wuhan. Both factions, one claiming authority of the Joint Council and the other using the name of the Political Council, resolved to call a plenary session of the Central Executive Committee – each at its own locale! – to readjust party affairs. Chiang Kai-shek travelled to Wuhan on 11 January to try to win over his comrades there, but he left a week later, unsuccessful and apparently embittered. He had been publicly denounced by Borodin and had excoriated him in return the next day. From henceforth the two factions operated more and more independently and antagonistically, though emissaries went back and forth trying to patch up differences. However, the breach between Chiang Kai-shek and Borodin on the personal as well as policy level grew steadily worse. In fact, there is reason to believe that Borodin personally instigated a campaign against Chiang in hopes of weakening his position.[130]

The Chinese Communist leadership supported the Wuhan leftists in these controversies. In a political report dated 8 January 1927, the communist party Central Committee stressed that the next military campaign should drive northwards along the Peking–Hankow Railway and that all military forces should be concentrated there. It favoured a movement then emerging for an autonomous Shanghai that would create a buffer zone between Nationalist forces and the Mukden-Shantung troops. (If effective, this might at least delay Chiang Kai-shek's seizure of the Shanghai prize.) The report also approved the Joint Council, though it deplored the emerging conflict among the Nationalist leadership and urged a reconciliation between Chiang and Wang Ching-wei, who had already been invited by the Kuomintang to return and resume his leadership roles. However, in February, communists in Wuhan began a propaganda

---

129 *PFCS* 2. 606–14. This lists all corps and some divisions that would participate.
130 Chiang Yung-ching, *Borodin*, 33–43; *TJK*, 530–41; Chang, *The Rise of the Chinese Communist Party*, 556–62, 567–8. (All these writers discuss the rift and see Borodin as the instigator.) On Borodin's insulting speech, see also 'The letter from Shanghai', in Leon Trotsky, *Problems of the Chinese revolution*, 407. Chiang Kai-shek's account of the confrontation is translated in Wieger, *Chine moderne*, 7. 140–2. On the broadening rift, see also Wilbur and How, *Documents*, 381–8; and from a Soviet Russian point of view, Cherepanov, *Severnyi*, 205–10.

campaign against 'military dictators' and 'new warlords', and began specifically to denounce Chiang Kai-shek's strong supporter, Chang Ching-chiang. Chiang Kai-shek retaliated with a speech on 21 February, denouncing the Wuhan Joint Council as the usurper of party authority and Hsu Ch'ien as the autocrat, defending his own position and his determination to support the loyal old associates of Sun Yat-sen, and threatening to curb the aggressive Communist Party. On 25 February the Nanchang group received word from Ch'en Kung-po of what the Wuhan group planned to achieve through the Third CEC Plenum – essentially a reversion to the organizational system before Chiang Kai-shek acquired the concentration of powers in his own person through decisions of the Second Plenum the previous May, and by his appointment as commander-in-chief. They detected Borodin's machinations and on the next day the Nanchang Political Council resolved to telegraph the Comintern asking it to recall Borodin. When there was no reply, the Council is said to have telegraphed Borodin directly, urging him to leave, but he simply disregarded it. The breach was now very wide.[131]

The revolutionary leadership divided over other issues. Should the anti-imperialist movement be restrained for fear the powers would come to the support of Sun Ch'uan-fang and Chang Tso-lin? More difficult to grapple with was the question whether to rein in the mass movement for fear a powerful counter-revolutionary tide would so strengthen the enemy as to prevent victory in the campaign to unify the country under Nationalist control. Already the violence of the agrarian movement and the ebullience of the labour movement were creating a tide of opposition within Nationalist territory. Some leaders in Wuhan believed labour must be restrained because successive strikes were disrupting commerce, reducing government revenues, and creating a problem of relief for the unemployed. In the countryside, aroused farmers were executing local enemies, and larger landlords and merchants were fleeing to the cities where they spread word of a rural terror. Their flight disrupted rural commerce, particularly in rice, tea and other farm products, which led to depression in trade in Changsha, Wuhan and other cities in the Nationalist domain. The Communist Central Committee in its political report of 8 January expressed concern:

131 Wilbur and How, *Documents*, no. 47, 427-30; and 388-93 on the communist offensive. *KMWH*, 16. 2782-9 for Chiang's speech, and abstract in *NCH*, 12 March, p. 402 and 19 March, p. 439. Chiang Yung-ching, *Borodin*, 42, gives Ch'en's telegraphic report and Nanchang's reaction. *TJK*, 540, mentions the telegram to Borodin but without a substantiating source. 'The letter from Shanghai', dated 17 March 1927 states that Voitinsky, the Comintern representative, visited Chiang Kai-shek and then requested Moscow to recall Borodin because 'otherwise Chiang Kai-shek would not make any serious concessions.' Trotsky, *Problems*, 406.

In the provinces of Hunan, Hupei, and Kiangsi now occupied by the Northern Expeditionary Forces, the mass movement has entered the revolutionary path and revolutionary work has penetrated deeply into the villages. . . . Assassinations of local bullies and bad gentry continue to occur without end. . . . A violent reaction would ensue should there be a military setback.[132]

Just at this time Mao Tse-tung was making a field study of farmers' revolt in the counties around Changsha. In his report, which later became a classic revolutionary declaration, Mao gloried in the violence and the peasants' seizure of local power. He urged his comrades to support this absolutely necessary period of violence if the poor were to overthrow their centuries-old oppressors. As Mao presented it, peasant violence was entirely spontaneous.[133]

But the communist leaders became extremely apprehensive. A Central Committee Political report of 26 January surveyed emerging attitudes among the powers and the trend of political opinion in China towards the communists' role in the developing revolution. The following are key passages:

The right wing of the Kuomintang is daily becoming more powerful. . . . There is currently an extremely strong tendency within the Kuomintang to oppose Soviet Russia, the Communist Party, and the labour and peasant movements.

The tendency towards the right is due first to the belief of Chiang Kai-shek and Chang Ching-chiang that only one party should exist in the country, that all classes should cooperate, that class struggle should be prohibited, and that there is no need of a Communist Party. . . .

The second reason is their idea that the national revolution will soon succeed, that there will soon be a movement for class revolution, and that the greatest enemy at present is not imperialism or militarism but the Communist Party. . . . For these reasons, a great anti-Communist tide has developed within the Kuomintang. . .

The most important problem which requires our urgent consideration at the moment is the alliance of foreign imperialism and the Kuomintang right wing with the so-called moderate elements of the Kuomintang, resulting in internal and external opposition to Soviet Russia, communism, and the labour and peasant movements. This would be an extremely dangerous thing and is, furthermore, entirely within the realm of possibility . . .

How did the communist leadership propose to combat this danger? First, the party should quiet the Kuomintang's fears, based on the belief that the Communist Party, close to the masses, opposed the national

132 Wilbur and How, *Documents*, 428.
133 *Selected works of Mao Tse-tung*, 1. 21–59 ('corrected' in spots). Partial translations in Brandt, Schwartz and Fairbank, *A documentary history*, 80–9, and Stuart R. Schram, *The political thought of Mao Tse-tung*, rev. edn, 250–9. Hofheinz, *The broken wave*, 310–11, for a bibliographic note on various versions of Mao's report. It has been commented on by all Mao's biographers.

government, and that there would soon be a communist revolution. To do so, the party should urge the masses to give financial and military support to the government, and, through propaganda, explain that victory for the national revolution was still distant, discredit the bourgeoisie and its ideology, and warn the Kuomintang not to join the bourgeoisie against 'the real revolutionaries', the workers and peasants. In foreign policy, the party should concentrate on the anti-British movement and delay extending the anti-imperialist movement to Japan, France and the United States, in order to isolate Great Britain. 'These policies', the report concluded with a show of confidence, would, if properly executed, 'lead to complete success. They will prevent united attack on us by the foreign powers and eliminate the Kuomintang's fear of the Chinese Communist Party.'[134]

Still, the tide of events – events such as myriads of actions and reactions in the Chinese countryside and cities (strikes, business failures, land seizures, murders), propaganda, developing sentiments among Chinese of local and regional influence, and decisions in major power centres in China, and in Moscow, London, Tokyo, Paris and Washington – this tide was leading inexorably to head-on conflicts within the revolutionary movement.

The growing split among the revolutionaries

In February and early March the rift between the Wuhan group and Chiang Kai-shek and his supporters became clearly evident. They took separate roads, the radical left establishing itself more firmly in Wuhan and attempting to curb Chiang's power, and the commander-in-chief suppressing communists in his domain, sending forces off to conquer the lower Yangtze, and searching for new support, Chinese and foreign.

Leaders of the Kuomintang left, Hupei communist leaders, and some Russian advisers had worked for several months to create a military alliance around T'ang Sheng-chih against Chiang Kai-shek. On 5 March a secret Russian report, apparently written in Hankow, reported a line-up of armies opposed to Chiang, naming the Third Corps (Chu P'ei-te), the Fourth (Chang Fa-k'uei, now deputy commander), the Seventh (Li Tsung-jen), the Eighth (T'ang Sheng-chih), the Eleventh (reformed from the 10th Division of the Fourth Corps, Ch'en Ming-shu), and other less effective units. The document warned, however, that the internal struggle

---

134 Wilbur and How, *Documents*, no. 48, 431–4.

to destroy Chiang had not been entirely successful.[135] The Russian author misjudged the sentiments of Ch'en Ming-shu, the garrison commander at Wuchang, who had been sent to Nanchang to persuade CEC members to come to Wuhan to attend the controversial plenum there. He returned from Nanchang on 6 March and that very evening was forced to give up his command of the Eleventh Corps and depart.[136] The corps was turned over to Chang Fa-k'uei, a leftist.

In Nanchang, meanwhile, General Blyukher and members of his Russian staff at Chiang's headquarters worked on plans for a campaign to take the lower Yangtze area, although they opposed an immediate breakthrough to the east. Blyukher favoured an advance on Honan against the Mukdenese, a juncture with Feng Yü-hsiang's army, and then a move east along the Lunghai Railway. Borodin favoured a move directly against Chiang Kai-shek, according to Cherepanov, whose work is based in part on Russian archives. As planned by Blyukher, the lower Yangtze campaign should be preceded by a thrust north along the Peking–Hankow railway towards Chengchow and Loyang for the juncture with Feng, whose forces were now concentrated on the Shensi-Honan border.[137] Both sides were negotiating with Feng Yü-hsiang's representatives. In fact, both sides negotiated in the first months of 1927 with various commanders to ease the path of victory – among them Generals Chin Yun-ao and Wei I-san in Honan, Ch'en T'iao-yuan and Wang P'u in Anhwei, Meng Chao-yueh in Kiangsu, and Admiral Yang Shu-chuang and General Pi Shu-ch'eng in Shanghai.

Chiang Kai-shek negotiated indirectly with Chang Tso-lin, the most powerful of the 'warlords'. He did so on the basis of a decision reached at a conference with Borodin and a group of Kuomintang leaders on 7 December to eliminate Sun Ch'uan-fang and ally with Chang Tso-lin.[138] If Sun were to be eliminated it was important to persuade Chang Tso-lin

135 Wilbur and How, *Documents*, 435–6 and discussion of the anti-Chiang alliance, 393–96. Cherepanov, *Severnyi*, 299–300, quotes Blyukher's opinion in January 1927 that the Second, Fourth, Sixth and Eighth Corps would support the leftists and communists against a conspiracy of the rightists, but that the Third and Seventh Corps would constitute a serious obstacle.

136 *TJK*, 541–2 and Chiang Yung-ching, *Borodin*, 43–4; Wilbur and How, *Documents*, 531. Basing themselves on Kuomintang Archives, Professors Li and Chiang attribute Ch'en's enforced departure to T'ang Sheng-chih, Teng Yen-ta and Borodin.

137 Cherepanov, *Severnyi*, 300, and 225 for planning. R. A. Mirovitskaia, 'Pervoe destiatiletie' (The first decade), in *Leninskaia politika SSSR v otnoshenii Kitaia* (The Leninist policy of the USSR with regard to China). Moscow, 'Nauka', 1968, 20–67, p. 44 for quotation from a 'Memorandum on the liquidation of the enemy in the area of the Lower Yangtze', dated 6 Jan 1927 and now in the archives of the Ministry of Defence of the USSR. Marc Kasanin, *China in the twenties*, trans. from the Russian by Hilda Kasanina, 194–201, provides a colourful account of his work on Blyukher's staff in Nanchang.

138 Mao, *CKSHS*, for 7 Dec.

not to support him. Sun, however, had already effected an alliance with Chang and his subordinate, Chang Tsung-ch'ang; the latter then sent his Shantung army southwards to support – or displace – Sun. Chiang Kai-shek's negotiations went on through intermediaries well into March, and were intended to postpone war with the powerful Fengtien Army; but possibly Chiang was looking for additional strength against his rivals in Wuhan. Chang Tso-lin's terms for neutrality and divided spheres apparently included the condition that Chiang break with the Chinese Communist Party and suppress it.

In February and March communist writers protested against Chiang Kai-shek's 'crimes' in negotiating with Chang Tso-lin and with Japan.[139] There is ample evidence that Chiang was seeking an understanding with Japan, both to aid his negotations with Chang Tso-lin and in anticipation of the drive on Shanghai. Through various means he tried to assure Japan, as well as the other powers, that they need not fear the consequences of the capture of Shanghai by his forces.[140] The Japanese government, well briefed on the developing rift in the Nationalist camp, moved towards the opinion that accommodation might be reached with Chiang.[141]

As always, Chiang needed money for the campaign to take Shanghai; one of his complaints against the Wuhan government was that it did not provide the funds. Being a native of the Ningpo area and having long been a resident of Shanghai with its large Ningpo community, powerful both in business and the underworld, Chiang had useful connections in the metropolis. Late in 1926 the chairman of the Shanghai Chinese Chamber of Commerce, Yü Hsia-ch'ing (better known as Yu Ya-ching) visited Chiang at Nanchang and allegedly offered handsome support

139 Letter from the CC of the CCP to the Northern Regional Committee dated 13 Feb. 1927, in Mitarevsky, *World wide Soviet plots*, 119-20; 'A warning', signed in the name of the Chinese Communist Party and a number of communist-dominated organizations and dated Canton, 27 Feb., in Robert C. North and Xenia J. Eudin, *M. N. Roy's mission to China: the Communist-Kuomintang Split of 1927*, 150-5. Ch'en Tu-hsiu in *HTCP*, 190 and 191 (6 and 12 March) 2045-6, 2056-7.

140 In an interview with a Japanese visiting Nanchang and published in *Jiji press* on 9 Feb., Chiang is reported to have said he did not think of taking the Shanghai concessions by force, and that if any country were to assist the Nationalists out of sympathy 'we would not refuse such assistance; rather we would shake hands with that country. . . . We would be glad to shake hands with Japan.' Dispatch, Sir John Tilley, Tokyo, to Sir Austen Chamberlain, 14 Feb. 1927, in GBFO 405/252. Confidential. *Further correspondence respecting China*, no. 13313 (Jan.–March 1927), no. 172 enclosure. Chiang sent Tai Chi-t'ao to Japan as an emissary. In a press interview in Tokyo on 27 February Tai explained that his mission was to secure Japan's proper understanding of the Nationalist position and future policy, and stated the conviction that the foreign concessions would be recovered by peaceful means. *NCH*, 5 March p. 352. Huang Fu was another important intermediary, according both to contemporary press reports and the autobiography of his widow, Shen I-yün, *I-yun hui-i* (Reminiscences of Shen I-yun), 247-90.

141 Much presumptive evidence of both sets of negotiations is presented in Wilbur and How, *Documents*, 389-91. See also, Iriye, *After imperialism*, 110, 119-21.

from the Chinese business leadership to help him take the city. Huang Chin-jung, leading underworld figure and also chief of Chinese detectives in the French concession, is said to have been another caller. Huang Fu, Chiang's sworn brother, served as an intermediary in Shanghai fund raising. He carried Chiang's confidential message to Chang Chia-ao, deputy governor of the Bank of China, requesting additional financial aid from the bank, and Chang complied with several hundred thousand Chinese dollars in January 1927. Chiang also sent his quartermaster-general, Yü Fei-p'eng, to Shanghai to arrange loans; Yü succeeded in extracting a million more from the Bank of China and presumably, by using similar tactics, a good deal more elsewhere. George Sokolsky may have helped in persuading the British–American Tobacco Company to advance two million dollars against future tax stamps, the money being deposited in the Bank of China to finance Ho Ying-ch'in's First Corps.[142]

Actions and counter-actions

Chiang Kai-shek's plans to capture Shanghai moved a step forward when Hsueh Yueh's First Division of the First Corps captured Hangchow on 18 February 1927. His drive on the capital of Chekiang from eastern Kiangsi was aided by the Second Division and by the Twenty-sixth Corps under General Chou Feng-ch'i, who had defected to the Nationalists in December. General Ho Ying-ch'in was in overall command of the Eastern Route Army but General Pai Ch'ung-hsi commanded the troops at the front.[143] After the capture of Hangchow, 130 miles by rail from Shanghai, the Nationalist forces pushed cautiously forward to Kashing, a vital point about 47 miles away, and both sides prepared for the inevitable battle for Shanghai. Marshal Sun Ch'uan-fang conferred with his new ally, Marshal Chang Tsung-ch'ang in Nanking and ceded the defence of Shanghai to the Shantungese. During a transitional period Sun's subordinate, General Li Pao-chang, retained his position as Shanghai-Woosung defence commander. During this transition the city's communist leaders, with as much cooperation as they could get from

142 Yen-p'ing Hao, *The Comprador in nineteenth century China: bridge between East and West*, 290, f.n. 83, cites a late source to the effect that Yü Hsia-ch'ing promised Chiang a loan of $60 million from the Chekiang financial clique. Harold Isaacs, *The tragedy of the Chinese revolution*, rev. edn, 143, tells of Huang's visit to Chiang, 'on behalf of the Shanghai bankers and merchants'. Chang Chia-ao in an unpublished autobiography on file in Columbia University reports Chiang's efforts to have the Bank of China support his campaign. Mr Sokolsky recounted his role in an interview with the writer in 1962, now on deposit in Special Collections Library of Columbia University.
143 Jordan, *The Northern Expedition*, 102–5; *PFCS*, 2. 619–29; *Pei-fa chien-shih*, 104–8. Cherepanov, *Severnyi*, 227–36. Cherepanov was adviser to Ho Ying-ch'in.

other groups, brought about the second 'Shanghai uprising' against Marshal Sun, which lasted from 19 to 24 February, effectively disrupting the city.[144]

The uprising apparently had two purposes: to disrupt Sun Ch'uan-fang's rear and thus to assist the Nationalist's advance; and to seize as much control of the Chinese cities as possible for instruments of the Communist Party and the left Kuomintang before the National Revolutionary Army arrived. The uprising was enforced by intimidation squads of the General Labour Union and by several assassinations of Chinese labour foremen and others opposing the strike.[145] Li Pao-chang suppressed the uprising ruthlessly, sending broadswordsmen into the streets of the Chinese city to behead agitators, many of them students. Nevertheless, the uprising brought some hundreds of thousands of workers (reported numbers differ widely) out on a political strike, and demonstrated the power of the Shanghai communists. It also hardened the resolve of leaders in the Chinese business community and rightists within the Kuomintang to oppose them. It strengthened the British government's determination to prevent another 'Hankow incident', and France, Japan and the United States advanced their preparations to protect their nationals. Thus the uprising probably assisted Chiang Kai-shek in his search for allies and sharpened the danger foreseen in the 26 January political report of the Communist Central Committee – 'an alliance of foreign imperialism and the Kuomintang right wing with the so-called moderate elements of the Kuomintang' against Soviet Russia, communism, and the labour and peasant movements.

On 10 March the long-awaited and much debated Third Plenum of the

144 There are many sources on this brief uprising. Primary ones are Chao Shih-yen ('Shih-ying'), 'Records of the Shanghai general strike' in HTCP, no. 189, 28 Feb. 1927, with documents: reprinted in Ti-i-tz'u . . . kung-jen, 450-72; 'Three Shanghai uprisings', Problemi Kitaii, 2. 10-11. 'Letter from Shanghai', 409-12; NCH, 26 Feb. 1927, pp. 317-21, and 19 March p. 472, for Municipal Gazette Police Reports for February; China Yearbook 1928, 820-3, reprinting 'Minutes of the military section', a communist document found in the 6 April raid on the Soviet embassy in Peking. USDS 893.00/8822, Dispatch, Gauss, Shanghai, 9 April 1927, 'Labour, student and agitator movements in Shanghai during February, 1927'. 34 pp. containing much factual detail.
   Secondary accounts are Chung-kuo lao-kung yun-tung shih, 2. 637-40; Wang, Chung-kuo Kung-ch'an-tang, 1. 276-9; Jordan, The Northern Expedition, 209-11 (all with a hostile bias). Harold Isaacs, The tragedy of the Chinese Revolution, 132-6; Chesneaux, The Chinese labor movement, 354-5 (both favourable).

145 Evidence for this statement comes from NCH, 19 March p. 472, Municipal Gazette News: police reports for February; and 'Minutes of the military section', 823 in a report by comrade Chow (probably Chou En-lai), dating before 10 March, which states 'The campaign of red terror has been successfully carried out at Shanghai. More than 10 strike-breakers, provokers and people opposed to the workers at the factories have been killed. This campaign had a sobering effect on the above mentioned people. . .'. (The figure may have included some executions after 24 Feb.)

Kuomintang Central Executive Committee opened in Hankow with 33 delegates, but without Chiang Kai-shek, who remained in Nanchang preparing for the campaign down the Yangtze. All but three of the participants were identifiable as Kuomintang leftists (at that time) or as communist members of the party.[146] Meeting for a week, the plenum passed a series of resolutions designed 'to restore power to the party'. These restructured all top party and government committees and councils, elevating Chiang's rival, Wang Ching-wei, who was still en route from Moscow, to the first position in all of them. They placed Chiang as one among equals in several committees, but left him out of the praesidium of the Political Council, the party's main policy-making body. The plenum re-established the Military Council, which had been abolished in favour of the commander-in-chief's headquarters when the Northern Expedition was about to begin. Chiang was chosen to be a member of its seven-man praesidium but Wang Ching-wei's name headed the list and three of the other members were Chiang's opponents, T'ang Sheng-chih, Teng Yen-ta and Hsu Ch'ien. Wang Ching-wei was elected head of the Party's important Organization Department, replacing Chiang, and Wu Yü-chang, a communist member of the Kuomintang, was to head the office until Wang arrived.

Another affront to Chiang Kai-shek and his faction was a resolution to invalidate the elections to the Kwangtung and Kiangsi Provincial Party Headquarters and the Canton Party Headquarters, which had been reorganized under the direction of Chang Ching-chiang and Ch'en Kuo-fu. A resolution on unifying foreign relations forbade any party members or government officials – including specifically military officers – not in responsible foreign office positions to have any 'direct or indirect dealings with imperialism', unless directed to do so, on pain of expulsion from the Kuomintang. This pointed to Chiang Kai-shek, whose forces would inevitably soon come in contact with foreign powers in Shanghai.[147] Other resolutions called for greater cooperation between the Kuomintang and the Communist Party; determined to cease criticism of the other party in Kuomintang journals; revived the idea of a joint commission with participation of representatives of the Comintern to settle inter-party conflicts; called on the Communist Party to appoint members to

---

146 *TJK*, 545. Li gives a detailed account of the plenum based upon documents in the Kuomintang Archives, some of which are published in *KMWH*, 16. 2689–95. See also Chiang Yung-ching, *Borodin*, 46–51; Wilbur and How, *Documents*, 397–400, based largely on translations of resolutions published in *Min-kuo jih-pao*, official organ of the Kuomintang, 8–18 March 1927, in USDS 893.00/8910, a dispatch from American Consul-General F. P. Lockhart, Hankow, 6 April 1927.

147 Li, *TJK*, 547.

join the Nationalist government and provincial governments; urged joint direction of mass movements, particularly of farmers and labourers; and decided to send a three man delegation to the Comintern to negotiate on problems of the Chinese revolution and its relation to world revolution.[148]

While these decisions were being taken in Hankow to reduce Chiang's power, his faction took action against communists and leftists in Kiangsi. On 11 March one of Chiang Kai-shek's subordinates executed Ch'en Tsan-hsien, the communist leader of the General Labour Union in Kanchow, a major town in the southern part of the province, and broke up the union. On 16 March, as he was about to launch the campaign down the Yangtze, Chiang Kai-shek ordered the dissolution of the Nanchang Municipal Headquarters of the Kuomintang, which supported the Wuhan faction, and ordered his subordinates to reorganize it. A few days later, after he reached Kiukiang, his subordinates violently suppressed the communist-led General Labour Union and the Kuomintang Municipal Headquarters there. On 19 March Chiang arrived in Anking, the capital of Anhwei, which had come over to the Nationalist side through the defection of Generals Ch'en T'iao-yuan and Wang P'u. On the 23rd a struggle between five hastily organized anti-communist provincial associations (one of them taking the name of General Labour Union) and communist partisans culminated in the dispersal of the latter.[149] These were portents.

The capture of Shanghai and Nanking

Chiang Kai-shek organized the drive to capture the important lower Yangtze cities along two routes. One was to drive down both banks of the great river, with the right bank army under Ch'eng Ch'ien aimed at Nanking and the left or north bank army under Li Tsung-jen directed towards cutting the Tientsin–Pukow Railway, the enemy's north–south lifeline. The other route was directed against Shanghai, which stands at the east end of a triangle with Hangchow at the south-west and Nanking at the north-west corners, and with the Grand Canal and Lake Tai forming a baseline on the west. By mid March, the forces that had taken Hangchow

148 *Ibid.* 548; Chiang Yung-ching, *Borodin*, 50.
149 *TJK*, 565-8, 594-8, and 660-2; Chang, *The rise of the Chinese Communist Party*, 578; Liu Li-k'ai and Wang Chen, *I-chiu i-chiu chih i-chiu er-ch'i nien ti Chung-kuo kung-jen yun-tung*, 55. Chesneaux, *The Chinese labor movement*, 352, summarizes these actions. Tom Mann, British labour leader and member of the International Workers' Delegation to China in 1927, passed through Kanchow on 19 March where he learned details of the execution of Ch'en Tsan-hsien. When he arrived in Nanchang on 25 March 'revolutionaries were in the ascendency but other forces had been dominant.' Tom Mann, *What I saw in China.*

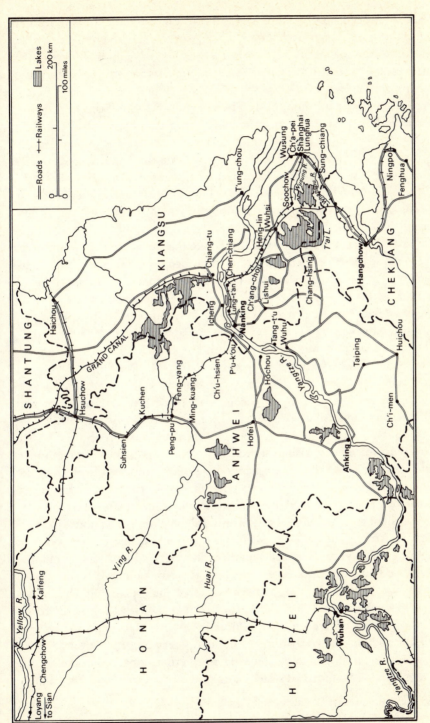

Map 5. The Lower Yangtze region

were positioned only a few miles from Shanghai under front commander Pai Ch'ung-hsi, while Ho Ying-ch'in's army was ready to press northward on both sides of Lake Tai to cut the Shanghai–Nanking Railway, the main escape route for Sun Ch'uan-fang's remnants and the fresh Shantung troops under General Pi Shu-ch'eng. The commander of the Chinese fleet at Shanghai, Admiral Yang Shu-chuang, had long been negotiating with the Kuomintang through its chief representative in Shanghai, Niu Yung-chien. On 14 March Admiral Yang declared his flotilla for the Nationalists; he had already sent three vessels up the Yangtze to Kiukiang for Chiang Kai-shek's use. Preliminary battles in the third week of March, and strikes and sabotage on his railway lines, made it imperative for Chang Tsung-ch'ang to withdraw his troops towards Nanking or face entrapment.

On 18 March a Nationalist attack broke the Sungkiang front and northern troops retreated into Shanghai, but not into the foreign settlements which were protected by a multi-national army manning barricades at all entrances. Pi Shu-ch'eng negotiated his own surrender, gave the battle plans to Niu Yung-chien,[150] then escaped by Japanese ship to Tsingtao and made his way to Tsinan, where he was apprehended and executed.

On 21 March, a Monday, as Pai Ch'ung-hsi's forces approached the city's southern outskirts, the General Labour Union began the 'third uprising'. By now the Workers' Inspections Corps numbered some 3,000, trained by Whampoa cadets, and some armed with rifles and pistols. Some guerrilla groups had also infiltrated the city, and intimidation squads – called 'black gowned gunmen' in Western reports – were active again. The uprising started at noon with pickets and gunmen attacking police on the streets, capturing police stations in sections of the Chinese cities, and seizing arms. Simultaneously thousands of workers came out on a general strike, enforced where necessary, although the atmosphere was one of celebration and welcome for the National Revolutionary Army. The city was filled with Nationalist flags. After a day of fighting in a very confused situation, it appeared that a communist-organized underground force with support from the masses had liberated the Chinese cities, although the amount of joint planning with Kuomintang agents is unclear. Some four to five thousand northern troops still were concentrated in Chapei near the North Station on the railway leading to Nanking. According to contemporary reports there was much looting, arson and killing, some by northern troops and some by the irregular forces which had seized parts of the city. Probably some of these

---

150 Ch'en Hsun-cheng, 'The capture of Chekiang and Shanghai' in KMWH, 14. 2231–309, p. 2288 on Pi's defection.

irregulars were not affiliated with either the Nationalist or the Communist parties. The uprising, nevertheless, had the appearance of an effort by some of the Communist Party leadership to seize control of the Chinese sections of Shanghai in preparation for a provisional government that they already had formed. Chou En-lai, Chao Shih-yen, Lo I-nung, and Wang Shou-hua were among the guiding hands.

General Pai Ch'ung-hsi arrived on 22 March with 20,000 troops and set up his headquarters at the Arsenal on the southern edge of the city. His subordinate, General Hsueh Yueh, commanding the powerful First Division, subdued the remaining northern troops, most of whom were thereupon interned behind the foreign defence lines. General Pai proclaimed his authority for maintaining order, demanded that all irregulars be incorporated into his army or surrender their arms, and promised the foreign authorities that he would not permit an effort to take over the foreign settlements by force. He ordered an end to the general strike, and his order was carried out on 24 March. Between the 23rd and the 26th General Pai's troops in a variety of attacks against guerrilla centres rounded up 20 self-styled generals, including a communist leader, and many 'black gunmen'; most of the leaders reportedly were executed. Several large units of the Labour Inspection Corps, well armed, remained in three centres, and the Corps extended its control into Pootung, across the Whangpoo River.[151]

Northern troops retreated from Nanking on 23 March, followed during the night by entering troops of the Nationalists' Right Bank Army, commanded by General Ch'eng Ch'ien. On the morning of the 24th groups of Nationalist soldiers systematically looted the British, American and Japanese consulates, wounded the British consul, attacked and robbed foreign nationals throughout the city, killed two Englishmen, an American, a French and an Italian priest, and a Japanese marine. At 3 : 30 pm. two American destroyers and a British cruiser laid a curtain of shells around the residences of the Standard Oil Company to assist the escape of some fifty foreigners, mostly American and British. The bombardment of this sparsely populated area killed, according to separate Chinese inves-

151 Some contemporary accounts of Shanghai's capture are in *Kuo-wen chou-pao*, 27 March 1927. An article by Chao Shih-yen, using the pseudonym 'Shih-ying', and several GLU proclamations in *HTCP*, no. 193, 6 April 1927, and reprinted in *Ti-yi-tz'u . . . kung-jen*, 473–90. *NCH*, 26 March, pp. 481–8, and 515; 2 April p. 16. USDS 893.00/8406, 8410, 8414, 8415, 8421, 8422, telegrams from Consul-General Gauss, Shanghai, 19–24 March, some published in *FRUS*, 1927, 2. 89–91; and 893.000/8906, Gauss' long dispatch dated 21 April 1927, 'Political conditions in the Shanghai Consular District', covering the period 21 March to 20 April. 'Report on the situation in Shanghai', by British Vice-Consul Blackburn, dated 15 April, in GBFO 405/253. Confidential. *Further correspondence respecting China*, 13304, April–June 1927, no. 156, enclosure 2. Secondary accounts, as in the note on the 'Second Uprising'.

tigations, four, six or 15 Chinese civilians and 24 troops.[152] Early published Chinese and Russian reports asserted that thousands of Chinese had been killed. The bombardment quickly discouraged further attacks on foreigners. General Ch'eng, who entered the city in the afternoon, restored order among his troops and, on the 25th all foreigners who wished to leave were evacuated without harm, although foreign properties were looted and burned for several more days.[153]

Who the persons directly responsible for the Nanking Incident were, aside from the soldiers in Nationalist uniform actually engaged, seems not to have been judicially established. On March 25 Ch'eng Ch'ien issued a public statement asserting that 'reactionary elements in Nanking . . . incited enemy forces and local ruffians to loot foreign property, burn houses and there were even incidents of wounding and slaying.' On the same day Yang Chieh, commander of the 17th Division, Sixth Corps, told the Japanese consul, Morioka Shōhei, that the soldiers had been instigated by communists in Nanking. The consul reported to his government that the acts of violence had been planned by party commissars and communist officers of lower grade within the Second, Sixth and Fortieth Armies, and by members of the Communist Party's Nanking branch. Reports to Wuhan by Nationalist officers continued to attribute the attacks to northern troops and rascals dressed in Nationalist uniforms, but Western diplomats in China, and their home offices, very soon accepted the Japanese consul's version – communist instigation.[154] This explanation was also later adopted by the Chiang Kai-shek faction of the Kuomintang.

The Nanking Incident was a unique event during the Northern Expedition: previously there had been no such extensive attacks on resident foreigners resulting in killings and wide-scale property losses. The event

---

152 NCH, 16 April 1927, p. 108, for the 'diligent inquiry' of a Chinese man, who reported four Chinese killed; KMWH, 14. 2381–2 for telegraphic report of General Chang Hui-tsan of the Nationalist Fourth Division, dated 5 April, who reported five or six killed; and telegraphic report of Li Shih-chang, head of the Political Bureau of the commander-in-chief of the Right Bank Army, dated 5 April, reporting an officer and 23 soldiers killed and 15 civilians.

153 Foreign eye-witness accounts in FRUS, 1927, 2. 146–63; GBFO, China no. 4 (1927), Papers relating to the Nanking Incident of March 24 and 25, 1927. vol. 36, comd. 2953; China yearbook, 1928, pp. 723–36 'The Nanking outrages'; Alice Tisdale Hobart, Within the walls of Nanking, 157–243. Chinese documents and studies, KMWH, 14. 2378–92; Chiang Yung-ching, Borodin, 117–24; TJK, 584–8. Other accounts in Borg, American policy and the Chinese revolution, 1925–1928, 290–317. Iriye, After imperialism, 126–33.

154 KMWH, 14. 2379 for Ch'eng Ch'ien's report as published in TFTC, 24. 7 (10 April) 128–9; and 2378–83 for other reports. Iriye, After imperialism, 128–9, for Morioka's report. Iriye suggests that Yang Chieh's statement may have been a fabrication. The American consul, John K. Davis, came to believe that troops of the Fourth Division (Second Corps), commanded by Chang Hui-tsan, were responsible for the attacks. FRUS, 1927, 2. 158.

created an atmosphere of crisis in the foreign settlements in Shanghai. In Peking the British, American, Japanese, French and Italian ministers consulted among themselves and with their governments concerning reprisals. They reached agreement on a set of demands for retribution but their governments could not agree on sanctions if apologies from the Nationalist government and punishments of those guilty were not forthcoming. The Japanese government under the influence of Foreign Minister Shidehara Kijūrō, attempted to restrain Great Britain and the other powers from too bellicose a posture, while at the same time hoping to persuade Chiang Kai-shek and the other moderate leaders of the Kuomintang 'to solve the present issue and eventually stabilize conditions throughout the south.' In short, Chiang was to be encouraged to act against the radicals in his party. The Japanese consul-general in Shanghai, Yada Shichitarō, passed this advice to Chiang Kai-shek through his close associate, Huang Fu. The British government's policy towards the Nationalists hardened. Great Britain now had the power in place to execute a variety of punishments, but the American government would not consent to participate in sanctions. In the end, after protracted international debate, the powers did not take direct sanctions: developments in the power struggle within the Kuomintang superseded such ideas.[155]

The Wuhan government was at first poorly informed on the Nanking Incident. The foreign minister, Eugene Chen, learned the details of what had happened to the foreign community in Nanking from Eric Teichman, the British representative in Hankow, with confirmation from the American and Japanese consuls. Not until 1 April did the Political Council, now fully informed about the Incident and with some inkling as to reaction in foreign capitals, consider seriously how to deal with the situation. Great Britain and America, it appeared, were preparing to intervene, while Japan's policy was still unclear. Borodin put the matter bluntly – 'if the imperialists should actually help the counter-revolutionaries, it could bring about the destruction of the Revolutionary Army.' His proposals were rather familiar: divide Great Britain and Japan. This could be done by allaying Japanese fears of the revolution and by ensuring that Japanese in China were protected, particularly in Hankow where, according to Eugene Chen, Japanese residents were fearful their concession would be seized. Propaganda laying the blame for the Nanking Incident upon imperialism, and with moral appeals, should be addressed

155 Iriye, *After imperialism*, 130–3, describes Shidehara's policy and instructions to his officials in China, based on Japanese Foreign Office documents. Wilson, 'Great Britain and the Kuomintang', 575–91 describes the British reaction based on British Foreign Office and Cabinet documents. American policy is covered in *FRUS*, 1927, 2. 164–236; and in Borg, *American policy and the Chinese revolution*, 296–317.

daily to foreign countries, and particularly to the Japanese and British people to arouse them against intervention. At the same time the policy of the Political Council that foreigners in China should be protected must be clearly explained to all Chinese mass organizations and 'especially to our armed comrades.' To this prescription, the Political Council assented.[156]

Events soon overran the Political Council's determination to reassure Japan about the safety of its concession in Hankow. On 3 April, after a fight between a Japanese sailor and a rickshaw coolie in which the coolie was killed, an angry crowd killed two Japanese (or, according to a Chinese account, seized 10). In this inflamed situation Japanese marines were landed and opened fire with machine guns, killing nine Chinese and wounding eight. Japanese authorities evacuated most of the Japanese women and children, closed and manned the concession boundaries, and brought up more warships. In keeping with its policy, the Wuhan government tried both to minimize the gravity of the incident and to cool Chinese passions. It gave strict orders against retaliation.[157] Its order was one of many efforts by the Wuhan leadership to gain control over fast-moving revolutionary developments.

The struggle for control of Shanghai

Chiang Kai-shek arrived in Shanghai on the afternoon of Saturday, 26 March, and there immediately began an alignment of forces in a complicated struggle for control of the Chinese city, although this was but one aspect of the larger contest for authority over the national revolution. Communists and Kuomintang leftists had on their side the General Labour Union with its armed picket corps; several 'mass organizations' of students, women, journalists and street merchants; and the local Communist Party members. To this side Soviet Russia lent advice and some material support. On the other side were ranged the commanders of the Nationalist armies in and around the city, except perhaps for Hsueh Yueh; members of the Kuomintang 'old right wing', who had long made Shanghai their stronghold and who had good connections

---

156 From the minutes of the Political Council, 1 April 1927, in the Kuomintang Archives. Chiang Yung-ching, *Borodin*, 124-26, quotes Borodin's recommendations to the Council in full. The Wuhan reaction to the Nanking Incident is well analysed in Wilson, 'Great Britain and the Kuomintang', 562-75.

157 H. Owen Chapman, *The Chinese revolution 1926-27*, 72. Chapman was an Australian missionary doctor, in Hankow at the time. Chiang Yung-ching, *Borodin*, 138-9. USDS 893.00/8555, /8608, /8609 Telegrams, Lockhart, Hankow, 3, 4 and 6 April and 8952 dispatch, 14 April 1927; *NCH*, 9 April, pp. 53 and 55; and 16 April, p. 112, based on a letter from Hankow.

with Chinese financial, commercial and industrial leaders, persons who had their own reasons to oppose the militant labour movement; and, ultimately, leaders of Shanghai's underworld gangs, whose control of the city's workers the General Labour Union challenged. Benevolently inclined towards this side – the side of law and order and the continuation of privilege – were the foreign administrations and the police of the International Settlement and the French Concession; behind these most of the foreign consuls; and behind them the power of some 40 warships and 16,000 foreign troops. It seemed an unequal contest, but it took more than three weeks to work itself through.

The leftists tried to arouse the support of the Shanghai masses. On Sunday the General Labour Union opened new offices in the Huchow Guild in Chapei and Wang Shou-hua presided over a meeting at which representatives of many organizations passed resolutions demanding retrocession of the concessions, pledging support for the National government and the Shanghai citizens' government, and urging General Hsueh Yueh to remain in Shanghai, it being rumoured that his division was to be sent away. In Pootung a number of Chinese workers charged with being counter-revolutionaries were reportedly executed by order of the General Labour Union. In the afternoon a huge rally at the West Gate near the French Concession heard fiery speeches demanding the immediate occupation of the concessions on pain of a general strike. Nationalist troops prevented the parade which followed from bursting into the French Concession. The American consul-general reported the situation extremely tense and he doubted that Chiang Kai-shek had either the will or the power to control it.[158]

General Chiang tried to quiet the tense situation and possibly to lull his opponents. That same evening, 27 March, he met with several American reporters and expressed friendliness for their country. He deprecated the foreign preparations to defend the concessions as signs of 'panic'. He denied any split in the Kuomintang and said he recognized the communists as participants in the revolutionary movement regardless of their political creed. He also blamed the Nanking Incident on northern troops in southern uniform. In another interview on 31 March he protested at the foreign bombardment of Nanking, which had aroused enormous anti-foreign feeling, and pleaded that the Incident itself not be exaggerated. He requested the foreign authorities at Shanghai to take measures to lessen the tension between the Chinese populace and the foreign community, and stated that he had already issued instructions

158 *NCH*, 2 April, pp. 6, 16, 19, 37 and 3; USDS 893.00/8506, telegram, Gauss, Shanghai, 27 March, 6 p.m.

against mob violence or any acts harmful to foreign lives and property. He asked the foreign authorities to end martial law, withdraw their troops and warships, and leave protection of the foreign settlements to the Nationalists. The General Labour Union, too, had issued a proclamation the previous day denouncing rumours of a breach between the Nationalist Army and the labouring class; and it declared it false that the foreign settlements would be stormed by pickets under its guidance.[159]

Chiang Kai-shek was urged from several directions to suppress the militant labour movement in Shanghai and to curb the communists, but preparations took time. Leaders of the Chinese business community headed by Yü Hsia-ch'ing, Wang I-t'ing, compradore of a large Japanese shipping firm, and C.C. Wu, formed a federation of commercial and industrial bodies and sent a delegation to see Chiang on 29 March. They emphasized the importance of restoring peace and order in the city immediately, and offered financial support.[160] The Japanese consul-general, Yada, saw Chiang's sworn brother, Huang Fu, several times shortly after Chiang's arrival to urge the general to suppress disorderly elements as well as make amends for the Nanking Incident. An editorial of *North China Daily News*, Shanghai's leading British paper, commented that if General Chiang were 'to save his fellow countrymen from the Reds he must act swiftly and ruthlessly'.[161]

A prestigious group of Kuomintang veterans led by Wu Chih-hui pressed Chiang to purge their party of its communist members. The group was part of the Central Supervisory Committee, elected in January 1926 at the 'leftist' Second National Congress in Canton. On 28 March five of the 12 regular members met informally and passed a resolution proposed by Wu Chih-hui to expel communists from the Kuomintang. The effort would be called 'The movement to protect the party and rescue the country.' Others at the meeting were Ts'ai Yuan-p'ei, 'dean' of Chinese intellectuals, Chang Ching-chiang, the wealthy patron of both Sun Yat-sen and Chiang Kai-shek, Ku Ying-fen, veteran of the 1911 Revolution and Sun Yat-sen's financial commissioner, and Li Shih-tseng, a leader among the French returned students. On 2 April the group met again, with Ch'en Kuo-fu, Chiang's protégé and deputy head of the party's

159 *NCH*, 2 April, pp. 2, 9 and 18.
160 *NCH*, 2 April, pp. 7 and 20; *CWR*, 9 April. The amounts actually advanced to Chiang are uncertain, but three, seven and 15 million dollars are mentioned in Western reports, according to Isaacs, *The tragedy of the Chinese Revolution*, 151-2 and 350, f.n. 27. On 8 April Consul-General Gauss learned that local bankers had advanced Chiang three million dollars, but were insisting they would not support him further unless the communists were ejected from the Kuomintang. USDS 893,00B/276.
161 Iriye, *After imperialism*, 130-1 and footnotes. *NCH*, 2 April, p. 13, editorial dated 28 March.

Organization Department, and two alternate members of the Central Supervisory Committee, Generals Li Tsung-jen and Huang Shao-hsiung, attending. Li and Huang were leaders of the Kwangsi group, and Huang had come to Shanghai in response to a telegraphic request from Chiang Kai-shek. This meeting produced a list of 197 communists or near-communists holding important positions in the Kuomintang and resolved to send the list to the Central Executive Committee with the request that the persons thereon be placed under surveillance.[162]

Chiang Kai-shek conferred with the principal generals of the National Revolutionary Army who would accept his request to come to Shanghai. They included Ch'eng Ch'ien, Ho Yao-tsu, and Ho Ying-ch'in from Nanking; Li Tsung-jen from the Left Bank Army, Huang Shao-hsiung from Kwangsi and Li Chi-shen from Kwangtung; and Pai Ch'ung-hsi, already at Shanghai. Others were Ch'en Ming-shu, who had been driven from Wuhan; Po Wen-wei and Wang P'u of Anhwei, and Chou Feng-ch'i of Chekiang. All of them were anti-communist.

Wang Ching-wei arrived in Shanghai on 1 April, having returned from his 'vacation' in Paris, via Moscow, where he received a handsome welcome. Probably he was the only leader with enough prestige to bridge the widening split in his party. During the next few days he was in a swirl of discussions with T.V. Soong, who had been sent from Wuhan; with Wu Chih-hui, Ts'ai Yuan-p'ei and Li Shih-tseng of the Supervisory Committee faction; with his old colleague, Hu Han-min; with his rival, Chiang Kai-shek; and with Ch'en Tu-hsiu, the general-secretary of the Chinese Communist Party. On 3 April Chiang issued a telegram to all commanders of the National Revolutionary Army announcing Wang's return in most flattering terms and stating that now the administration of all military, civil, financial and foreign matters should be centralized under Chairman Wang's direction; Chiang only had general direction of the several armies and would obey the chairman, as should all other commanders. Thus would authority in the party truly be centralized in order to complete the national revolution and hasten fulfilment of the Three Principles of the People. Privately, Chiang urged on Wang the necessity of expelling Borodin and purifying the party of its communist members. He warned Wang against going to Wuhan where he could not escape becoming a communist pawn. Others begged Wang to join the party purge, but he advocated a plenary meeting of the Central Executive Committee to decide so serious a matter, and urged his comrades not to act independently.[163]

162 KMWH, 17. 3086–93 (list on 3091–92); TJK, 611–14; Chiang Yung-ching, Borodin, 158–60.
163 TJK, 615–17. Chiang's telegram in KMWH, 16. 2797–8; it was abstracted in NCH, 9 April, p. 52.

The outcome of discussions between Wang and Ch'en Tu-hsiu was their joint statement published in the Shanghai papers on the morning of 5 April. The statement first emphasized the continuing need for unity within the revolutionary camp and denied that the Communist Party, 'no matter what its faults', had ever advocated overthrowing its friendly party, the Kuomintang. China was unlikely to have a proletarian dicta- torship even in the future; what was needed now was a democratic dictatorship of all oppressed classes to deal with counter-revolution. The statement called for a spirit of cooperation between members of the two parties and reminded Kuomintang members of Leader Sun's policy of allying with the communists. It tried to set at rest two 'rumours' current in Shanghai – that the Communist Party intended to organize a workers' government, invade the foreign concessions, subvert the nor- thern expeditionary army, and overthrow the Kuomintang; and that the Kuomintang leaders planned to expel the Communist Party and suppress the labour unions and their inspection corps. Neither party had any such intentions. The statement ended by exhorting all comrades to rid themselves of suspicions, end rumours, and consult with mutual respect and good will 'for the good of the revolution and the good of the two parties.'[164]

That same morning Wang attended a stormy meeting with an enlarged group of party veterans and Nationalist generals determined to expel the communists, and then in the evening he secretly boarded a steamer for Hankow. In letters to Chang Jen-chieh (Chang Ching-chiang) and Chiang Kai-shek, he explained that he was going to Wuhan to arrange for a plenary meeting of the Central Executive Committee to be held in Nan- king on 15 April to settle the disputes within the Kuomintang.[165] The Wuhan centre was reasonably well informed of the Shanghai meetings, both through the Chinese press, and from Ch'eng Ch'ien's personal report about April 6. General Ch'eng had left his army at Nanking to come

164 *KMWH*, 16. 2798–800; trans in Warren Kuo, *Analytical history of the Chinese Communist Party*, 1. 424–6; abstract in *NCH*, 9 April, p. 74. According to Wang Ching-wei's later account, Ch'en Tu-hsiu wrote the statement to refute the charges against the Communist Party that Wu, Ts'ai and Li had made to Wang. See his speech of 5 November 1927 in *Wang Ching-wei hsien-sheng tsui-chin yen-shuo chi* (Mr Wang Ching-wei's most recent speeches collected), 126. Ch'en, himself, later called it a 'shameful' statement, and blamed its position on Comintern policy of that time. Ch'en Tu-hsui, 'A letter to all comrades of the party', 10 Dec. 1929, trans. in *Chinese Studies in History*, 3. 3 (Spring 1970) 231.
165 *TJK*, 617–19, with a list of those attending. New names included Generals Li Chi-shen and Pai Ch'ung-hsi; and Po Wen-wei, T.V. Soong and Kan Nai-kuang of the Central Executive Committee. Kan was a member of the Standing Committee and had been con- sidered a leftist. Wang's reminiscent account is in his speech of 5 Nov., cited above, 123–5. Wu Chih-hui wrote a very critical account of Wang's position, 'Shu Wang Ching-wei hsien-sheng hsien tien hou' (Written after Mr Wang Ching-wei's telegram of the 16th [i.e. of April]), *Chih-hui wen-ts'un*, first collection, 1–14.

to Wuhan after conferring with Chiang Kai-shek in Shanghai, and also
meeting with Wu Chih-hui and Li Shih-tseng.[166] There was nothing
effective the Wuhan centre could do to restrain Chiang Kai-shek and his
fellow plotters, and besides, Wuhan was absorbed with its own problems.

Mounting violence among the revolutionaries

Radical and counter-radical actions broke out in widely scattered cities
during the two weeks prior to 12 April, manifestations of the now intense
conflict within the revolutionary camp itself. These actions were not
merely struggles for power; behind the conflicts were issues of great
revolutionary import. Was the goal of the national revolution, at least
in its current phase, simply the reunification of China by eliminating the
warlords and ending imperialist privileges, or was it also to be a class
revolution to emancipate the impoverished masses from their bondage?
In the countryside, were mobilized tenant farmers to seize the land or be
content with rent reduction? In the cities, was the proletariat to force
upon the capitalists not only better wages and working conditions but
also, through the unions, some control over their enterprises? Was mass
violence, including murders, an acceptable way to achieve lower class
emancipation from the bonds of feudalism and capitalism? In short, what
degree of social revolution should accompany the national revolution?
Nationalism unites; social revolution divides.

Leaders at all levels held passionate beliefs about these issues, but
they differed across a broad spectrum from radical to conservative.
Struggles for control over local Kuomintang headquarters and governing councils, and competition in the indoctrination of junior officers
and troops, arose from these differences in commitment. Among the revolutionaries – for all considered themselves as such – there were rival
organizations of youth, labour, farmers, merchants and shopkeepers.
Some were strongly influenced or dominated by the Communist Party;
others were anti-communist. In the labour movement, rivalry between
non-communist labour union organizers and the communist activists
who had been determined to dominate the union movement as the preserve of the Communist Party dated from the previous six years.

There was a pattern to the conflicts that erupted in the cities. The
radicals tried to win support by propaganda and street lecturing, and by

166 *TJK*, 623, citing minutes of an emergency meeting of the Wuhan Political Council, 7 April.
   Ch'eng's written report dated 5 May tells of his meetings in Shanghai, and of a military
   conference which he refused to attend. The conferees were anti-communist. Report is in
   the Kuomintang Archives, no. 1–5/804.

mobilizing the masses in patriotic rallies and parades, with handbills and slogans, some among which denounced conservative Kuomintang leaders. Armed workmen of the General Labour Union – the so-called 'inspection corps' – which were characteristically controlled by communists, protected the radicals' establishments and enforced strikes. Counter-radical action also followed a pattern which points to central direction: for example, the same slogans – 'Uphold Commander-in-Chief Chiang', 'Expel Borodin' – were used in widely scattered places. As conflict intensified in some locality, military commanders might order the arrest of suspected communists and closure of the organizations they dominated. In several cases Whampoa cadets loyal to Chiang were involved. Assisted by troops, a rival labour organization would attack the local offices of the General Labour Union and disarm its inspection corps. The crushing of the Shanghai Inspection Corps on 12 April could not have been a surprise.

In Hangchow, the capital of Chekiang, conflict developed after its capture on 18 February between leftist Kuomintang party headquarters, the General Labour Union, and the Students' Association on the one side, and an anti-communist Labour Federation, the Whampoa Cadets Association, and the rear-guard of the Eastern Route Army on the other. Hsüan Chung-hua, a communist very influential in the provincial Kuomintang headquarters, attempted to have the leaders of the Labour Federation arrested and the Federation broken up, but he was opposed by the head of the Public Security Bureau and the commander of the rear guard. After a bloody conflict on 30 March between parading clerks and workers of the Federation and the armed inspection corps of the General Labour Union, the rear-guard commander forbade the Union to hold a rally and parade the next day on pain of suppression by arms. When students and workers led by the inspection corps paraded anyway, troops fired on the marchers, surrounded and fired on the leftist Kuomintang headquarters, and disarmed the inspection corps. Rioters wrecked the headquarters of the General Labour Union.[167]

On the same day, 31 March, but far in the west, Chungking in Szechwan witnessed the crushing of the General Labour Union and other leftist organs, and the execution of many suspected communists. Conflict in

---

167 *TJK*, 645-60. Li reports Hsüan Chung-hua and another influential communist, An T'i-ch'eng, executed early in May. *Chung-kuo lao-kung yun-tung shih*, 2. 669-70. According to this source, the Chekiang Political Council called together representatives of the GLU and the army and worked out a settlement, which permitted the GLU to continue, but restricted the inspection corps to the union's headquarters. Later, under a reregistration procedure both the federation and the union were dissolved. *NCH*, 9 April, p. 67, report dated 5 April.

Chungking between left and right factions of the Kuomintang went back to 1925. One of the chief rightist leaders was Shih Ch'ing-yang, a party veteran and a member of the anti-communist Western Hills Conference of late 1925. During most of 1926 there were two provincial party headquarters, two general labour unions, and other competing organizations. Rival propaganda squads brawled in the streets. Two communists among the leftist leaders were the veteran revolutionary, Wu Yü-chang, and the later famous Liu Po-ch'eng. In November 1926 Liu Hsiang, the Szechwanese general controlling Chungking, suddenly turned towards the left and ordered the dispersal of right-wing organizations.[168] This was during the flush of the first phase of the Northern Expedition when the leftists in the Kuomintang seemed ascendant. Probably early in 1927 Chiang Kai-shek and the Nanchang Political Council ordered two anti-communists, Hsiang Fu-i and Lü Ch'ao, back to Szechwan to urge Liu Hsiang and Wang Ling-chi, the Chungking garrison commander, to take action against the communists. In February Lü brought a contingent of Whampoa cadets to work in Liu Hsiang's army. Other anti-communist groups were also organizing, and apparently most of the military commanders developed hostile sentiments towards the radicals. To strengthen their side, the Kuomintang leftists planned a great rally for 31 March, ostensibly to oppose British and American imperialism in response to the bombardment of Nanking a week before, but also to arouse sentiment against Chiang Kai-shek. Garrison Commander Wang, with General Liu Hsiang's concurrence, sent soldiers to surround the meeting place and arrest suspected communists; he also sent troops to search two schools that had been managed by Wu Yü-chang, and to seal up the provincial, county and municipal headquarters of the Kuomintang, the offices of the provincial farmers' association, the city General Labour Union, and the *Szechwan daily*, all controlled by communists, according to our source.[169] When the workers inspection corps resisted the troops in their arresting, much blood was shed. Six important local communists were beaten to death, and according to a report by another communist to the Wuhan centre, over 400 persons were killed and the inspection corps was completely smashed. Thereafter the purge spread throughout Szechwan.[170]

Leftists had their turn to overthrow their rivals on 2 April in Nanchang. Kiangsi was an arena of competition between the two Kuomintang fac-

---

168 *Chung-kuo lao-kung yun-tung shih*, 2. 566–9.
169 Li, *TJK*, 666.
170 *Ibid*. 666–8. *Chung-kuo lao-kung yun-tung shih*, 2. 649, estimates the killed at more than 70 and the wounded at more than 100. *NCH*, 9 April, carried a brief Reuters dispatch from Peking dated 1 April (presumably deriving from the British consulate in Chungking) on the clash.

tions. After the province was taken by the Northern Expeditionary troops, many communists were active there, though their influence was checked during the period when Chiang Kai-shek made Nanchang his headquarters. The Kuomintang provincial executive committee and the government council were made up predominently of 'pure' Kuomintang members. A prestigious old revolutionary, Li Lieh-chün, served as provincial governor. The Kuomintang's Nanchang city headquarters, however, was controlled by leftists. When Chiang Kai-shek left Nanchang in mid March 1927 he ordered the dissolution of the municipal party headquarters; but with his departure, the Wuhan centre increased its influence in Kiangsi. On 26 March the Central Executive Committee in Wuhan appointed a committee of eight to reorganize the provincial executive committee and the provincial government; six of the eight were dual party members. On 30 March the CEC appointed Chu P'ei-te, commander of the Third Corps, as governor, in a bid for his support. In order to carry out Wuhan's decisions, leftists mobilized their supporters among students and labourers, and staged a riotous coup on 2 April. In this case, Nanchang's garrison commander, Wang Chün, a subordinate of Chu P'ei-te, apparently cooperated or remained neutral. The later famous communist general, Chu Te, who then was in command of an officers training regiment and a military academy in Nanchang, supported the coup. A number of Kuomintang members holding positions in the provincial government were arrested and some twenty people were killed. Li Lieh-chün departed and Chu P'ei-te assumed the coveted governorship and restored order. After receiving a stern telegram from Chiang Kai-shek, he protected the Kuomintang officials who had been arrested, though some had been tried by a people's court and condemned to execution.[171]

In Foochow the balance of forces seems to have been more even, and developments took a somewhat different course. Two communist members of the Kuomintang, Ma Shih-ts'ai and Li P'ei-t'ung, came to dominate the provincial party headquarters, sent deputies to organize Kuomintang branches in various counties, and established a political training institute in which a number of the teachers were communists. Through party headquarters they set up the usual organizations of youth,

171 TJK, 594–8, Chiang Yung-ching, Borodin, 128, naming persons executed. Kao, Chronology, 252, mentions more than 20 persons killed by the General Labour Union and some 800 arrested. Mr Ch'eng T'ien-fang, who, as provincial educational commissioner, was one of those arrested, described his harrowing experiences in an interview with the writer in Taipei in 1962. His book, A history of Sino-Soviet relations, 138–9, gives a brief account. Chu Te's American biographer, Agnes Smedley, describes his work at Nanchang but passes over the incident of 2 April. Smedley, The great road: the life and times of Chu Teh.

women, farmers and workers. On the other side, 'pure' Kuomintang activists created anti-communist organizations of youth, women workers, and even a general labour union and a provincial farmers' association. Furthermore, General Ho Ying-ch'in while still in Foochow did not permit the communist-controlled labour union to form an inspection corps nor allow creation of farmers' guards. During March both sides tried to rally their forces in demonstrations of power and there were street conflicts between them, which the garrison commander suppressed. On 19 March a Foochow branch of the Whampoa Cadets Association was established, adding to the strength of the anti-communist side. On 4 April the conservative forces rallied in a meeting 'To uphold Commander-in-Chief Chiang and to protect the party.' They passed resolutions to support the commander-in-chief as leader of the revolutionary army, to expel Borodin, and to punish Hsu Ch'ien, Teng Yen-ta and T'an P'ing-shan. The inspiration for such resolutions could only have come from Shanghai. The meeting also resolved to punish those local communists and leftists who had 'destroyed party work'. including Ma and Li. The American consul in Foochow reported 'what virtually amounts to anti-communist *coup d'état* involving complete change in provincial administration . . . said to have been directly under orders of Chiang Kai-shek.' On 7 April, a group of more conservative party leaders formally established a new provincial headquarters. On the same day, Ma Shih-ts'ai and a few others fled from Foochow, but some ten of the defeated faction 'sooner or later fell into the net and were executed.'[172]

On 6 April the foreign diplomatic corps gave permission for the Peking metropolitan police to conduct a raid on certain buildings in the Soviet embassy compound. The grounds for the search warrant was the suspicion that Chinese communists were using the offices of the Chinese Eastern Railway and the Dalbank in planning an insurrection in Peking. During the raid the police arrested 22 Russians and 36 Kuomintang members in hiding there, including Li Ta-chao, one of the founders and principal theoreticians of the Chinese Communist Party. Six of the nine members of the Executive Committee of the Kuomintang Municipal Headquarters were taken. The police discovered documents of the Chinese Communist Party, as well as Kuomintang and communist banners and seals, and some arms and ammunition. Furthermore, when they saw that Russians in the Soviet military attaché's office were burning their papers,

---

172 *TJK*, 650–5, based upon archival materials including a report from Ma Shih-i. What happened to Li P'ei-t'ung is not stated. USDS 893.00/8615, telegram, MacMurray, Peking, 7 April.

they put out the fire and removed seven truckloads of documents.[173] The immediate effects of the raid were to disrupt Kuomintang and communist operations in the north and, probably, to disrupt the communications of the Russian military advisers with the military attaché's office in Peking. On the next day the authorities of the French Concession in Tientsin searched Soviet establishments there, and in Shanghai the Municipal Council ordered police to surround the Soviet consulate and prevent access. Thus did the Western powers attempt to cripple Soviet assistance to the revolutionaries. After trial by a Chinese court in Peking, Li Ta-chao and 19 other Chinese seized in the raid were executed on 25 April. Ten others received prison sentences. Among those executed were several Kuomintang members regarded with suspicion by the Peking communist organization.

In Shanghai many actions presaged the final break of Chiang Kai-shek and his supporters with the Wuhan centre and the Chinese Communist Party. Two of Chiang's intimates, Yang Hu and Ch'en Ch'ün, reportedly were his intermediaries with Tu Yueh-sheng, one of the top leaders of the Ch'ing-pang, the most powerful underworld society in the lower Yangtze region. They persuaded Tu to lead an anti-communist action. Tu created a 'Society for Common Progress' to carry this through. By 3 April the International Settlement police department had learned that leaders of the Ch'ing-pang had recruited several hundred armed gangsters for the society and that they were lodged in the French Concession where, incidentally, Tu had his lavishly appointed home. Allegedly, Chiang had paid the leaders Ch.$600,000. By 7 April the International Settlement police learned that the gangsters' purpose was to attack the headquarters of the General Labour Union.[174] Tu and Wang Shou-hua, the communist head of the Shanghai General Labour Union, were acquainted. More exactly, they were rivals for control over some sectors of the Shanghai labour force.

During the first three days in April, General Liu Chih, commander of

173 An account of the raid and of the authenticity of the documents discovered is given in Wilbur and How, *Documents*, 8-37. In the months following the raid many of the documents were published, revealing details of Russian espionage and aid to the Kuomintang and Feng Yü-hsiang, as well as much historical information about the revolutionary movement as it involved both parties.

174 Yang and Ch'en had been part of Ch'en Ch'i-mei's organization during the 1911 Revolution and after, as had Chiang. Rather shadowy figures, they were appointed by Chiang to important posts in the Shanghai garrison command. Tu Yueh-sheng was one of the most obscure but influential Chinese in Shanghai. See Y.C. Wang, 'Tu Yueh-sheng (1888–1951): a tentative political biography', *JAS*, 26. 3 (May 1967) 433–55. On the 'Society for Common Progress', see Chesneaux, *The Chinese labor movement*, 393–4, citing Police Daily Reports of 3 and 7 April. *Ti-i-tz'u . . . kung-jen*, 492–3, from a report of the GLU dated 15 April, which says that several days before 12 April the union received repeated reports that the gangsters would attack the union and the inspection corps.

the Second Division of the First Corps, on orders from Chiang Kai-shek and Pai Ch'ung-hsi, sent troops to attack concentrations of armed guerrillas, including one detachment of the inspection corps, killing some dozens and arresting others, who were sent to Lung-hua for trial. His adjutant told a reporter for the *North China Daily News* on 4 April that 'approximately a division' of irregulars had been disarmed but that, since the labour corps under the General Labour Union did not interfere with military affairs, 'the members would not be disarmed yet.' If, however, the corps caused any breaches of the peace, 'they would also be suppressed and disarmed.' On 5 April Chiang Kai-shek instituted martial law and ordered the disarming of all bearers of arms not properly enrolled in the Nationalist Army. Next day, Pai Ch'ung-hsi sealed the office of the Central Political Bureau established by order of the Wuhan centre, and ordered censorship of all telegrams and letters from Hankow. On the 8th he conducted a raid on a union headquarters in Nanshih, the formerly walled city adjacent to the French Concession. Nineteen suspected communists were arrested.[175] About the same time, General Chiang transferred the First and Second Divisions to Nanking,[176] where he had business to perform.

Chiang's purpose in going to Nanking was to gain control of the site of the government he and his allies intended to establish. To do this it was necessary to defend the city from the northern forces and to eliminate potentially subversive elements within. Chiang ordered the Second and Sixth Corps to cross the Yangtze to face the enemy and sent two divisions of the First Corps to the city as reinforcement. Most of the officers of the two divisions were former Whampoa instructors or graduates, and Chiang could count on them to obey his orders.[177]

Within Nanking a complex struggle was under way. The political departments of the Second and Sixth Corps were headed by dual party members, Li Fu-ch'un, a young returned student from France on the radical wing, and Lin Tsu-han, a veteran of the 1911 Revolution and an

---

175 *NCH*, 9 April, pp. 50, 51, 55, 77; Chesneaux, *The Chinese labor movement*, 346, from police daily report of 8 April.

176 Kao, *Chronology*, 9 April, implying the divisions had arrived. Leon Trotsky in *Problems of the Chinese revolution*, 276, quotes from a report by Chitarov, who had returned from China, that Hsueh Yueh offered to the Central Committee of the Chinese Communist Party that he not submit to Chiang's order to move his division, but instead stay in Shanghai and fight together with the workers. The responsible communist leaders turned him down because they did not want a 'premature conflict' with Chiang Kai-shek.

177 *TJK*, 623, states that Chiang ordered the crossing to be completed by 6 April. General Ch'eng, who was then in Wuhan, telegraphed his commanders not to go, but the telegram was discovered by Chiang's headquarters so 'Ch'eng's plot was foiled'. On 5 May Ch'eng Ch'ien wrote a bitter letter to the CEC in Wuhan describing these events and the destruction of his army. Kuomintang Archives 1–5/804.

important Kuomintang leader and member of its Central Executive Committee. After Nanking was occupied on 24 March the usual pattern of setting up a general labour union and other mass associations began under the leadership of the two political departments. Lin Tsu-han had not been with the Sixth Corps when it captured Nanking, but travelled there at the end of March and stayed a few days to develop support for the Wuhan side. On 1 April the Kiangsu Provincial Party Headquarters moved from Shanghai to Nanking; it was a leftist group in which two alleged communists, Chang Shu-shih and Hou Shao-ch'iu, were prominent. Chang had represented the Kiangsu Provincial Party Headquarters at the Third CEC Plenum, and came down from Hankow to Nanking on 3 April. His later report to Wuhan central is a first-hand if biased source of information on the developing conflict in Nanking. He learned that two 'counter-revolutionary gangsters' had organized a rival Kuomintang municipal headquarters, but the political department of the Sixth Corps shut this down and arrested some of its partisans. He also learned the ominous news that Chiang Kai-shek had appointed 'the wrecker of the Anhwei Provincial Party Headquarters, the gangster Yang Hu' to be in charge of the Nanking special area, and another 'counter-revolutionary gangster' to carry out the wrecking. These men organized a Labour Association 'especially to hire gangsters'. The political department was unable to shut this down because it was protected by the chief of the Public Security Bureau. The leftists planned a rally to close down the Labour Association by mass action, but the Public Security Bureau forbade this meeting on pain of forcible suppression. Provincial Party Headquarters then decided to hold an assembly to celebrate the union of soldiers and the people on 8 April, and on the next day to hold a rally to celebrate Wang Ching-wei's return. The first meeting was a disappointment because the Second and Sixth Corps had already crossed the Yangtze, and only the political department of the Sixth Corps and a few armed comrades attended. None came from the First Corps.[178] This signalled the shift in military power. Meanwhile in Hankow, Borodin called an emergency meeting of the Political Council on 7 April after hearing reports from Ch'eng Ch'ien and Li Fu-ch'un on Chiang's plans. The meeting

---

178 Chang Shu-shih, 'Kiangsu sheng tang-pu tai-piao pao-kao' (Report of the representative of the Kiangsu provincial party headquarters), Kuomintang Archives, Kiangsu collection, 2/99; date about 27 April. Quoted in Chiang Yung-ching, Borodin, 133-5. According to Pai Ch'ung-hsi, lower and middle ranking communist officers in Hsueh's division and the 21st Division of Yen Chung had either been dismissed or arrested. Pai Ch'ung-hsi, Shih-liu nien ch'ing-tang yun-tung ti hui-i (Recollections of the party purification movement of 1927), Propaganda Department of the Kuomintang Kwangsi Party Reconstruction Committee, 1932, p. 10.

resolved that central party headquarters and the National government should move to Nanking.[179] But it was already too late.

Chiang Kai-shek and Ho Ying-ch'in arrived in Nanking on the morning of 9 April, leaving Pai Ch'ung-hsi and Chou Feng-ch'i to hold Shanghai. Nanking was put under strict martial law. Those who had planned the great rally to welcome Wang Ching-wei found it advisable to add some posters and banners welcoming Chiang! But apparently that rally was never held. A gang of armed ruffians – hired for four Chinese dollars a day – attacked and smashed the Kuomintang provincial and city headquarters, bound up staff members, including the heads of the provincial farmers department and merchants department, the secretaries of the propaganda department and women's department, and officials of the secretariat, and dragged them off to the public security office. Several were alleged communists. Chang Shu-shih hid during this raid, but later was captured and held overnight. It was thus he learned that Commander-in-chief Chiang was behind these acts. To counter this attack, the leftists sent labourers to the commander-in-chief's headquarters to petition him to protect the provincial and city headquarters of the Kuomintang and the General Labour Union, but to no avail. Next day the leftists succeeded in holding a rally, after which 'the masses' went again to the commander-in-chief to beg for protection. This time they came into conflict with troops and police, and many persons were wounded. There were two days of terror on 10 and 11 April: armed gangsters attacked the General Labour Union, and military police searched hotels and other places where Chang Shu-shih's comrades lived, arresting a number. Hou Shao-ch'iu was among those killed. Chang, himself, escaped through the water gate in a small boat and finally made his way to Hankow.[180] Nanking no longer was safe for Wuhan supporters.

Similar conflicts in Amoy and Ningpo on 9 and 10 April resulted in victories for the conservative side. In Canton the American consul reported on 9 April that the situation was becoming very tense and a clash between moderates and communists was expected at any time. The Chinese press had published telegrams from Li Chi-shen stating that, since the Hankow administration was controlled by communists, its mandates need not be obeyed.[181] This was only a hint of the terrible purge that was to begin on 15 April.

In spite of all these acts and portents, there was little the communist

---

179 Li, *TJK*, 623.
180 This paragraph is a synthesis of Chang's first-hand account and that of Li Yun-han, based on archival material. It is unclear how many of those arrested were executed. *Chung-kuo lao-kung yun-tung shih*, 2. 646–7 stresses the other side of the story.
181 *Ibid.* 670–1; *NCH*, 16 April, p. 100. USDS 893.00/8642, MacMurray, Peking, 11 April.

leadership in Shanghai could do to ward off an attack. Since no inner party documents are available for the first two weeks of April, it is difficult to learn what preparations the Central Committee and the leaders of the General Labour Union made. Ch'en Tu-hsiu later revealed that the Comintern instructed the Communist Party to hide or bury all the workers' weapons to avoid a military conflict with Chiang Kai-shek. The telegram was sent on 31 March, according to A. Mandalian. Apparently the order to hide the arms was not carried out.[182] Rather, the leadership tried to assert strict discipline over the unions and the inspection corps, to win public support, and prepare for a general strike in case the enemy tried to disarm the workers. After a secret meeting aboard a strike-bound ship in the river, the Shanghai General Labour Union held a more open meeting on 4 April under the chairmanship of its dynamic leader, Wang Shou-hua, where it was resolved – that is, announced – that the pickets must obey explicitly the General Labour Union regulations on the use of their fire-arms, and workers must not declare strikes without orders from the union. The public should be informed why it was necessary to maintain armed pickets. The joint statement by Wang Ching-wei and Ch'en Tu-hsiu the next day aimed at easing tension and gaining public support. But the Executive Committee of the General Labour Union resolved to order a general strike if anyone tried to disarm the workers. In Chapei the workers inspection corps held a parade, arms in hand, in a show of power: and on the 7th an assembly of labour union delegates resolved that, should anyone harm the picket corps or take armed action against it, all Shanghai workers must rise in support and use the power of the masses to stop it. Resolutions passed at a leftist meeting the same day indicate the radicals' concerns: the right wing of the Kuomintang in Rue Vallon should be suppressed and its members arrested and punished; the Kuomintang in Shanghai should come under the control and direction of the CEC in Hankow; General Liu Chih should be dismissed and punished, and General Hsueh Yueh be urged to stay in Shanghai and control military affairs; all counter-revolutionaries should be suppressed and all workers be armed.[183]

The spreading anti-communist purge

Pai Ch'ung-hsi, Yang Hu, Tu Yueh-sheng and their associates planned carefully for the disarming of the powerful workers inspection corps in

---

182 Ch'en Tu-hsiu, 'A letter to all comrades of the party', 231; North and Eudin, *M.N. Roy's mission to China*, 54, quoting an article in *Pravda*, 159 (16 July 1927) 2–3; and Chang, *The rise of the Chinese Communist Party*, 1. 587.
183 *NCH*, 9 April, p. 80; *TJK*, 570–1; *NCH*, 9 April, p. 50, resolutions 8–12 and 18.

Shanghai. Tu's gangster recruits were armed with pistols, formed into squads with specific targets of attack, and dressed in workmen's outfits with armbands carrying the word 'worker.' Several hundred troops from Pai's force were similarly disguised. On the night of 11 April Wang Shou-hua came by invitation to dinner at Tu Yueh-sheng's house. As he was leaving he was abducted, killed and the corpse dumped at Lung-hua. Chou Feng-ch'i's troops were positioned during the night near concentration points of the inspection corps and the headquarters of the General Labour Union. Authorities of the International Settlement and the French Concession were informed in advance. After midnight they were told of the impending attack; they ordered the barricades around the two settlements closed, preventing escape into the foreign sanctuaries. Yet Tu's 'workers' were permitted to move out from the French Concession and Pai's disguised troops to pass through the International Settlement just before dawn on 12 April.[184]

Between 4 and 5 a.m. the attacking parties, numbering about 1,000 in all, began firing upon concentrations of the inspection corps in Chapei, adjacent to the International Settlement, in the old south city next to the French Concession, in Pootung across the river, and in Woosung where the Whangpoo enters the Yangtze. In some places the defenders resisted fiercely but in others they were tricked into submission. In some places uniformed troops of Chou Feng-ch'i's Twenty-Sixth Corps joined the attack, in others they pretended to restore order between feuding labour organizations. According to early reports, some 25 to 30 of the resisters died in the fighting. Captured leaders on the leftist side were sent to General Pai's headquarters where, according to a news report, 145 were executed. Chou En-lai and Ku Shun-chang, a communist leader of the inspection corps, were among those arrested, though both escaped. General Chou Feng-ch'i made a great haul of workers' arms, some 3,000 rifles, 20 machine guns, 600 pistols, much ammunition, and quantities of axes and pikes. After disarming the inspection corps, troops and gangster-workers searched and sealed up the offices of various leftist organizations.[185]

---

184 On Wang's death, *Chuan-chi wen-hsueh*, 11. 1 (July 1967) 97; Taipei *Hua pao*, 4 and 5 Oct. 1961, an article on Tu Yueh-sheng by a former secretary, Hu Shu-wu. Both say Tu's sub-ordinates did the killing, and imply Yang Hu and Ch'en Ch'ün were involved. A written reply to questions asked of Pai Ch'ung-hsi in 1962, stated, 'I arrested Wang Shou-hua ... and the chief communist representative Hou Shao-ch'iu and others ... the leaders were punished according to law ...'. USDS 893.00/8906, dispatch, Gauss, Shanghai, 21 April 1927, 'Political conditions in the Shanghai consular district', states that Wang was arrested 11 April and executed at Pai Ch'ung-hsi's headquarters. For Pai Ch'ung-hsi's reminiscent account of the preparations, see Pai Ch'ung-hsi, *Shih-liu nien*, 11.

185 *Ti-i-tz'u ... kung-jen*, 494–500, for an early account from the communist side; and *NCH*, 16 April, pp. 102–4, and USDS 893.00/8906, just cited, for outsiders' reports. Secondary accounts in Isaacs, *The tragedy of the Chinese revolution*, 175–7; Chesneaux, *The Chinese labor*

The defeated tried to rally their supporters. The leaders of the General Labour Union called a general strike and, despite General Pai's order forbidding it, more than 100,000 workers, many under picket intimidation, stayed away next day. But the strike could not be sustained for long. After a rally in Chapei on the 13th, demonstrators marched on Chou Feng-ch'i's headquarters to petition for the release of those arrested and the return of the workers' arms. Among the marchers were both armed men, and women and children. When guards at the headquarters fired on the procession, scores of innocents were slain. Among the 90 or so captured, more than 40 were former soldiers of the Shantung Army, hired as corps members. That evening a newly organized Committee on the Unification of Trade Unions took over the headquarters of the General Labour Union; it was to be Chiang's instrument to bring the labour movement under conservative control. The fearful repression of 12–14 April shattered the left-directed mass movement in Shanghai. Hundreds had been killed and thousands fled in terror. The leaders of the General Labour Union could do nothing but call off the strike on 15 April, and send to the Wuhan government a report bitterly denouncing Chiang Kai-shek and begging for help.[186]

Canton, the nursery of the revolution, underwent an equally brutal suppression of communist-led organizations, and many noted radicals were slain. General Li Chi-shen, who had been 'dismissed' by the Wuhan centre, returned to Canton on 14 April, fresh from the conservative conferences in Shanghai. He called a secret emergency meeting that night. The conferees set up a special committee, headed by General Li, to plan and execute 'party purification'. General Ch'ien Ta-chün, Canton garrison commander, proclaimed martial law beginning 15 April, and the head of the Canton Police Bureau issued a similar proclamation saying he had received orders from the commander-in-chief of the National Revolutionary Army to arrest without delay all Communist Party elements in Canton and to disarm the pickets of various labour unions. In the pre-dawn hours of 15 April the purge began.

Battalions of troops and 2,000 armed police surrounded the headquar-

movement, 369–70; and Tien-wei Wu, 'Chiang Kai-shek's April 12 coup of 1927', in F. Gilbert Chan and Thomas H. Etzold, eds. *China in the 1920's: nationalism and revolution*, 146–59, 155–7. General Pai Ch'ung-hsi told the writer there is no truth whatsoever in André Malraux's account, in *Man's fate*, of arrested radicals being executed by pitching them into the flames of a locomotive fire-box.

186 *TJK*, 628–9. *Ti-i-tz'u . . . kung-jen*, 516–18; GLU report on pp. 530–3. The original handwritten report dated 15 April, with a covering letter on the stationery of the GLU and with its seal, are in the Kuomintang Archives, Shanghai file, 1.8/423. They were to be brought to Wuhan by Wang Ssu-tseng, and were transmitted to the CEC on 27 April. The version in *Ti-i-tz'u . . . kung-jen* is the same. The original is quoted in part in Chiang Yung-ching, *Borodin*, 161–2.

ters of the Hong Kong strike committee, the Canton Congress of Workers' Delegates, and scores of radical unions, where they disarmed the guards and arrested the leaders. At Wongsha station, the terminus of the railway leading towards Hankow, a pitched battle broke out between the railwaymen's union and their old rivals, the conservative mechanics union. Supported by troops, the mechanics prevailed. There were raids also on Chung-shan University and two middle schools where radical influences were strong, and upon the offices of two Nationalist newspapers, which were then reorganized under conservative direction. Posters appeared on the streets on 16 April in support of Chiang Kai-shek and removal of the government to Nanking, which he was about to effect. Because communist influence was thought to be strong among cadets at Whampoa, they were all disarmed, but the majority supported the commander-in-chief. On 18 April some 200 cadets suspected of being communists were arrested while some others fled. A few unions were able to mount a protest strike which lasted from 23 to 25 April, but as a result some twenty or thirty more labour leaders were arrested. Seven persons caught distributing anti-government propaganda were executed, including two girl students. Forty-three unions were forced to reorganize. Raids continued until 27 April. By then some 2,000 suspected communists had been captured. Among the scores executed were Liu Erh-sung, Li Sen (Li Ch'i-han) and Hsiao Ch'u-nü, all well-known leftist militants, who had joined the Communist Party.[187]

Li Chi-shen and the special committee also reorganized the provincial government. Ku Ying-fen, an old associate of Sun Yat-sen and a conservative nationalist, became the leading civil official in Canton, while General Li remained, in effect, the military governor. The new government declared its independence from the Wuhan centre, and this had two serious consequences for the leadership there. The Central Bank at Canton, with eight million Chinese dollars in silver reserves, no longer supported Wuhan, thus weakening its already suspect currency. Further, the three provinces adhering to Wuhan were now cut off from the sea on the south; they were already only tenuously connected on the east via the Yangtze.

187 GBFO 405/253. Confidential. *Further correspondence respecting China*, 13304, April-June 1927, no. 127, a dispatch from British Consul-General J.F. Brenan, Canton, 21 April 1927, which includes translations of proclamations of the 15th and of other documents concerning the purge. Also GBFO 228, F3609/8135. USDS 893.00B/286, 290, 292 and 296, telegrams from American consul-general. Canton, 15, 16, 22 and 25 April. *Ti-i-tz'u . . . kung-jen*, 534–9, an article published in 1931. *TJK*, 655–9, and Chiang Yung-ching, *Borodin*, 164–5, both based partly on a report by Han Lin-fu to the Wuhan leaders on 15 May. (Han, a communist, escaped from Canton and made his way to Hankow.) *Chung-kuo lao-kung yun-tung shih*, 2. 673–7. Liu Li-k'ai and Wang Chen, *I-chiu i-chiu*, 57.

Similar repressions took place in several cities in Kwangsi province on orders from General Huang Shao-hsiung, one of the Shanghai conferees, and also in the port cities of Swatow, Amoy and Ningpo. Yang Hu supervised the reorganization in Ningpo. Kuomintang branches and labour unions in several lesser cities in Kwangtung, Chekiang and Kiangsu were also purged of leftist leaders. These actions in the southern and eastern coastal provinces did not spell the end of the labour union movement, which had grown rapidly since 1920, but communist influences were sharply reduced. Party members had either to go underground or flee to the sanctuary of Wuhan – a temporary sanctuary only, as it proved to be.

The radical labour leaders in Wuhan may have felt a sense of revenge for the killing of their comrades in Shanghai with the execution on 14 April of eight veteran union organizers who had opposed the Communist Party's domination of the unions in Hupei. They were arrested by Teng Yen-ta's political department and denounced as 'labour thieves'. On 10 April communist labour leaders in Wuhan called a meeting of delegates of the Hupei General Labour Union and the meeting resolved that the eight be turned over to 'the masses' for execution. A few days later, Kuo P'in-po, Lu Shih-ying, Yuan Tzu-ying, and five others were condemned by a court and executed by firing squad on the streets of Hankow.[188] In Changsha, a focus of radicalism, an estimated 30 to 40 Chinese who had foreign business connections were reported to have been executed.[189] Among them was the noted scholar and conservative, Yeh Te-hui.

Establishing a government at Nanking

The conservative Kuomintang leaders in Shanghai widened their breach with Wuhan by setting up a rival central apparatus and a separate Nationalist government in Nanking. They had gathered there ostensibly to await the Wuhan members of the Central Executive Committee for the plenum that Wang Ching-wei was supposed to arrange. When Wang and the others did not come, nine members of a self-styled Central Political Council coopted nine others, and this group resolved on 17 April to establish the central government in Nanking the next day. Of those who made this decision, only five were members of the Central Executive Committee, which numbered 36 with 24 alternates. Eight were members of the Central Supervisory Committee, which had 12 members and eight

188 *TJK*, 568–9; Chiang Yung-ching, *Borodin*, 129; *Chung-kuo lao-kung yun-tung shih*, 601–2; Chesneaux, *The Chinese labor movement*, 326.
189 USDS 893.00/8802, telegram, Lockhart, 17 April, 'wantonly killed by the Communists', was the way Lockhart reported the information.

alternates. The remaining five were generals.[190] The Wuhan group had more legitimacy if measured by the number of Central Committee members active there, yet the Nanking group had several very prestigious persons, notably Hu Han-min, Wu Chih-hui, Ts'ai Yuan-p'ei, Li Shih-tseng, Chang Ching-chiang and Teng Tse-ju. After the formal inauguration of the government, which Hu Han-min now chaired, there was a manifesto both revolutionary and anti-communist in tone, for it was important to legitimize the 'party purification movement' already underway. After the Political Council had discussed the 2 April resolution of the Central Supervisory Committee, which urged expulsion of communists from the Kuomintang, the new government issued an appropriate order to the commander-in-chief and other officers and officials, naming Borodin, Ch'en Tu-hsiu, Hsu Ch'ien, Teng Yen-ta, Wu Yü-chang and Lin Tsu-han as particularly evil, but warning against communist leaders everywhere and appending a list of 197 persons to be arrested. Not all were members of the Communist Party so far as is known; probably the Central Supervisory Committee in drawing up the list had mainly to rely on its suspicions.[191] The next few weeks were occupied in setting up a central and various local purge committees to supervise the cleansing of the Kuomintang in those places where the influence of the Shanghai-Nanking group could reach. The government, itself, had little substance and its locale was quite insecure.

On 17 April the Central Executive Committee in Wuhan expelled Chiang Kai-shek from the Kuomintang and relieved him from all his posts. The Nationalist government at Wuhan issued a mandate elaborating his 12 great crimes, and the Chinese Communist Party issued a declaration on 20 April in support. This explained the class basis of the new reactionary tide and stated that the proletariat now no longer need be restrained from direct struggle against feudal-bourgeois elements.[192] Such verbal onslaughts scarcely touched the real power structure.

MOUNTING PROBLEMS FOR THE WUHAN REGIME

Wuhan's struggle to survive

The leadership in Wuhan now faced enormous difficulties. To the north were the powerful military forces of Chang Tso-lin; elements of the National Revolutionary Army on the east and south seemingly supported

190 *TJK*, 632; minutes of the meetings on the 17th in *KMWH*, 22. 4211–16.
191 An imperfect list in *KMWH*, 16. 2826–7; corrected lists in *KMWH*, 17. 3091–2 and *TJK*, 635–7.
192 *Chinese correspondence: weekly organ of the Central Executive Committee of the Kuomintang*, 2. 6 (1 May 1927); and *China yearbook, 1928*, 1367–70.

Chiang Kai-shek; and on the west were Szechwanese commanders apparently in league with him. The only bright patch on the military horizon as seen from Wuhan was in the north-west where Feng Yü-hsiang's revived army stood poised to descend down the Lung-Hai Railway into Honan; it was being re-equipped with Russian arms and had a cadre of experienced southern political officers working among the troops. Imperialism appeared menacing. The Arcos raid in London and raids on Soviet establishments in China, which had required international sanction, raised fears of concerted action against Russian support for revolutionary movements. The Nanking Incident, with the threat of foreign retaliation, had still to be settled, and foreign forces in Shanghai now had the power to retaliate. The river that divided the Wuhan cities was filled with foreign gunboats. Relations with Japan were strained because of the April Third Incident in the Japanese concession in Hankow.

However menacing the external scene may have seemed, it was internal economic problems that threatened the regime's survival. The confluence of rivers and two railway lines made the Wuhan cities the gathering place for agricultural and mineral products from a vast hinterland and the distribution point for manufactured goods from down river and abroad. Yet by April this trade was stagnating as a result of class warfare in Hunan and Hupei, and strikes and business failures in the main cities. There was even fear of a rice shortage in the revolutionary capital because revolutionaries in Hunan were holding back rice on the theory that if it were not shipped out from a community, prices there would remain low and the poor could afford to eat. In Wuhan there was massive unemployment: more than 100,000 workers idle, a potential danger and costly charge on the government. Foreign business activity was much curtailed, partly due to the exodus of foreigners from Hankow (on 12 April the foreign population was down from a normal 4,500 to 1,300), and partly due to strikes and lockouts. Mills and wharves in the Japanese concession were deserted. A strike of the Chinese staffs of foreign banks, which had begun on 21 March, contributed to the stagnation since the banks could not perform the financial functions essential to trade. Shipping on the middle Yangtze was much reduced, partly because China Merchants' Steam Navigation Company ships had been withdrawn to avoid commandeering, and partly because pilfering of cargoes and labour disorders on Hankow wharves discouraged foreign shipping. Business stagnation reduced the government's tax revenues while its currency was under inflationary pressures. To protect dwindling reserves of specie, the government on 18 April forbade Chinese banks to redeem their own notes in silver and imposed an embargo on its export. As the British legation's Chinese secretary, Eric Teichman, noted after three months in Hankow, 'The revolution has dislocated the whole economic life of Central China.' He wondered whether 'the puny figures of the Nationalist government, riding like froth' on the revolutionary wave, could control 'the storm and turmoil they have created'.[193]

At this very time the Wuhan centre planned to resume the Northern Expedition to link up with Feng Yü-hsiang. In view of the critical situation, Borodin recommended a 'tactical retreat.' On 20 April he proposed to the Central Political Council five ameliorative measures which amounted to a sharp change of course. (1) The government and the unions should set up a commission to enforce 'revolutionary discipline' on the workers, and the unions should form a tribunal to try and punish recalcitrant workers. (2) The government should reach agreement with foreign banks and other enterprises so they could conduct business freely in the areas under Wuhan's jurisdiction; and the government and unions should form a committee to enforce the agreement, using, if necessary, the inspection corps and armed forces. (3) Workers in foreign banks and other enterprises should not be allowed to strike without permission of this committee. (4) The government should do all in its power to fix maximum prices of commodities in terms of copper currency. (5) The government should set up a relief bureau and mess halls to take care of the unemployed, and the Finance Ministry should allocate $30,000 in copper coins to the General Labour Union to be used to exchange the workers' notes for cash. These measures, Borodin assured the councillors, would eliminate the excuse for foreign intervention, while restoration of foreign economic activity would benefit the workers themselves. After only brief discussion to clarify the powers of the proposed new organizations, the Council resolved to adopt Borodin's proposals and to appoint the head of the Kuomintang's Labour Bureau, the head of the Government's Labour Department, the foreign minister and the finance minister to implement the new course.[194]

The Wuhan leaders then acted decisively. Eugene Chen met with foreign business men on 23 April and promised them an improved climate

193 GBFO 405/253. Confidential. *Further correspondence respecting China,* 13304, April–June 1927, no. 112, enclosure, a dispatch by Eric Teichman from Hankow on 7 April. The economic situation in Wuhan was well reported by the American consul-general, Frank P. Lockhart, in telegrams and dispatches, including his monthly 'Review of commerce and industries'. Figures on exodus of foreigners, by nationality, in *China Yearbook, 1928,* 755.

194 Chiang Yung-ching, *Borodin,* 175–9, and *TJK,* 680–2, both based on minutes of the Political Council for 20 April in the Kuomintang Archives. The four persons appointed were Ch'en Kung-po, Su Chao-cheng, Eugene Chen, and Chang Chao-yuan, to replace the absent T.V. Soong. Ch'en was chairman.

for their enterprises; thereafter he attempted to solve their particular problems. The new policy was announced in the *People's Tribune* the same day, along with the new restraints imposed upon workers. Wang Ching-wei called a discussion meeting of leaders of the Nationalist and Communist Parties, and on 25 April a joint session of the Central Committee of the Communist Party and communist leaders of the Hupei General Labour Union issued a declaration which repeated the substance and much of the wording of the resolution passed by the Kuomintang's Political Council five days earlier, though altering the sequence to emphasize the relief measures for unemployed workers. Point five stated, 'Not a single strike can take place in foreign enterprises or firms without consent of the commission' that was to implement an agreement with foreign enterprises and banks. The resolution concluded, 'The basic requirement of the present moment is revolutionary discipline, self-sacrifice and the unity of the revolutionary forces.'[195] On 30 April at a meeting of all major political and military figures, army political bureau workers, and delegates of various local mass organizations, presided over by Sun Fo, Borodin made a long report on foreign policy, differentiating as always between Great Britain, America and Japan, but emphasizing the present need for conciliation. The finance minister sought to reassure the gathering that the government's financial situation was sound, and that even though economic conditions were serious, the city would be supplied with grain from Hunan through the cooperation of the people there; coal would begin to arrive soon; river boats could now freely sell salt; the government had bought a large supply of copper and intended soon to mint copper coins; remittances for trade with Shanghai would be facilitated by a deposit of more than a million dollars sent to banks in that city; and the government's paper currency was to be made stable by limiting the amount that might be printed and backing it with silver. So, 'all may rest easy'.[196]

The Wuhan leaders also forbade provincial leaders from deciding foreign policy questions, such as the Hunan decision to confiscate the American Standard Oil Company stocks and to form a committee to sell them. They sent Lin Tsu-han to Changsha and Ch'en Ch'i-yuan to Nan-chang to explain the new foreign policy, and both emissaries on their return reported unanimous endorsement by the leadership meetings

195 Quoted in North and Eudin, *M.N. Roy's mission to China*, 186–7; Lockhart's telegrams in *FRUS*, 1927, 2. 112–13 and 115–16; *People's tribune* for 23 and 24 April. Isaacs writes disapprovingly of the measures followed by the Wuhan regime to curb labour and restore amicable foreign relations. *The tragedy of the Chinese revolution*, 204–6.
196 Minutes of the meeting of 30 April 1927 in the Kuomintang Archives.

they assembled. Tax revenues had declined alarmingly in the provinces due to the business recession. Yet it was not possible to cool down the revolutionary fever quickly. Both passion and power were involved. In some parts of Hupei mission properties, churches and schools were returned to their Chinese custodians, while near Wuhan several foreign-owned properties that had been occupied by Chinese troops were restored to their owners. Settling strikes on terms acceptable both to the unions and the owners proved difficult and protracted (some negotiations extended into June), and foreign managers in Hankow complained to Eugene Chen in May that union inspection corps still interfered with resumption of business. Yet discipline was quickly restored on the wharves and shipping took a turn for the better. Larger Chinese enterprises and their workers had similar difficulties in getting operations resumed. Relief for the unemployed was only beginning to be implemented by mid May. The result of a variety of remedial measures in Wuhan was a slight revival of commerce and industry there in May and June, but economic disruptions had been so widespread and severe that a real revival would take much longer to accomplish.[197]

Trying to manage rural revolution

The Wuhan government held only tenuous authority over three provinces – Hunan, Hupei and Kiangsi – with a combined population of some 80 millions and a territory larger than France. In parts of this huge area a rural revolution (arising from poverty, inequity and land hunger) spurred on by radicals among the farmers' movement activists, was gathering momentum, with executions of local despots and land seizures by tenants, all without sanction of the central authorities. These local actions disrupted the rural economy and brought on fierce retaliation just when a tide of reaction was endangering the regime at Wuhan. The leadership of both the Nationalist and the Communist Parties became deeply concerned. What could be done to restore order in the affected areas?

Participants at the Third Plenum of the Kuomintang's Central Executive Committee had passed resolutions and issued a 'Manifesto to the Farmers' on 16 March, which stressed the party's determination to help them. All local armed groups must be controlled by new self-governing village bodies. Self-defence units were authorized to press the struggle

197 Chiang Yung-ching, *Borodin*, 186–94 and 228–9; Chapman, *The Chinese revolution*, 134–6. On settlement of strikes and relief measures, the Kuomintang Archives has minutes of the Committee on Relations between Labour and Foreign Capital for May and June. Consul-General Lockhart, Hankow, to secretary of state, 6 June 1927, 'Review of commerce and industries for the month of May' in US National Archives, Record Group 59.

against 'local bullies and evil gentry', and lawless landlords. The CEC affirmed the Kuomintang's support for farmers in their struggle to possess the land, and suggested confiscation of the lands of counter-revolutionaries which, together with public and temple lands, should be turned over to local land commissions under the jurisdiction of district and village self-governing organs for distribution among the people. Most of these proposals had appeared as resolutions of the December congress of the Hunan Farmers' Association, and were Comintern policy. The plenum also authorized establishment of a Central Land Commission to work out details of the new, more militant, social policy.[198]

On the basis of this lead, local organizers, particularly in Hunan, began a campaign in March to extend self-government under the direction of farmers' associations to all villages. In mid April the Hunan Provincial Farmers' Association, on the authority of the Third Plenum resolutions, sent a directive to all county associations to set up farmers' self-defence forces; and the provincial Kuomintang Propaganda Office issued a propaganda outline that emphasized the need for struggle against feudalism: the time had come, it said, to support the peasants' demand for land. At the end of the month the Provincial Farmers' Association held a propaganda week, presenting what became the radicals' standard argument for the need to 'solve' the land problem now: the peasantry must be mobilized behind the Nationalist government to save it, but the government, to mobilize them, must solve their need for land. Solution of the land problem, it was argued, would also solve the government's financial problem, for the new owner-farmers could pay more taxes since they would no longer pay rent to landlords. Solving the land problem would provide the basis for a flourishing economy in the future; but nothing could be accomplished unless the existing feudal system in the villages was eradicated: landlords must be overthrown and the tillers be given land and political power.[199] By April leaders of the Provincial Farmers' Association were estimating between five and six million members in

---

198 The CEC Plenum's resolution of 10 March is quoted in full in Tien-wei Wu, 'A review of the Wuhan debacle: the Kuomintang-Communist split of 1927,' *JAS*, 29 (November 1969) 129–30. Also, Carol Corder Andrews, 'The policy of the Chinese Communist Party towards the peasant movement, 1921–1927: the impact of national on social revolution', Columbia University, Ph.D. dissertation, 1978, ch. VII, 61–2, based upon a collection of documents issued by the Kuomintang Central Farmers Bureau on 30 June 1927. Kuomintang Archives, 436/138. Chiang Yung-ching, *Borodin*, 268–71, quoting some passages from the resolutions. The Manifesto is also in *Chung-kuo Kuo-min-tang chung-yao hsuan-yen hui-pien*, 359–65. December resolutions in *Ti-i-tz'u . . . nung-min*, 332–40; 373–4. 'Thesis on the situation in China', of the Seventh Plenum of the ECCI, 22 Nov–16 Dec. 1926, in North and Eudin, *M.N. Roy's mission to China*, 139.

199 Andrews, *The policy of the Chinese Communist Party*, ch. 7, based upon contemporary documents in the Kuomintang Archives.

Hunan, though six months earlier they had been under 1.4 million.[200] Whatever the actual figures may have been, a rapid expansion of farmers' associations probably gave the organizers a sense of new power to force the pace of rural revolution.

There were many scores to be settled. During the latter part of 1926 land-owning gentry in many parts of the province had tried to quell the rising farmers movement that threatened their prestige, power and property. They had banded together in property protection societies, used local corps to suppress incipient farmers' associations and searched out activists for arrest and execution.[201] Most of the repression probably came from the landlord side at first, but the tide apparently began to turn in some areas of Hunan, Hupei and Kiangsi late in 1926, to judge from Mao Tse-tung's report of his investigation in counties around Changsha in January, and the alarm expressed by a resolution of the Communist Party's Central Committee on 8 January, which said 'Assassinations of local bullies and the bad gentry continue to occur without end. . . . A violent reaction would ensue should there be a military setback.'[202]

In the countryside theories were being translated into action. Struggle against local despots meant arrests and killings; struggle for the land led to flight of landlords and dividing their property. A report by the finance commissioner of Hunan about executions by farmers' associations in his province – he was concerned about losses of tax revenues as a result of the terror – brought on a debate in the Wuhan Joint Council at the end of January. How should such actions be managed? Tung Pi-wu reported executions in several hsien in Hupei; he thought the government should adopt a tolerant attitude towards the demands of the masses. Borodin advised that the people should not be permitted to act on their own but should submit requests for executions to local party and government offices, which should have authority to decide such cases. The Joint

200 Chiang Yung-ching, *Borodin*, 269, report of Ling Ping on 19 April: over five million organized farmers in Hunan representing some 20 million. Mann, *What I saw in China*, 27, was told in Changsha about 20 April that no less than 5,130,000 peasants were organized in unions in Hunan, in 53 of the 75 counties. Lin Tsu-han, 'Report on an investigation of the Hunan land question, financial question, and party conditions', 2 May (1927), Kuomintang Archives, Hunan 5/53: Now (ca. 30 April) there are farmers' associations in 65 hsien with more than six million members. Lin named six 'most advanced' hsien with a combined membership of 1.6 million, but all his figures were given in the hundred thousand. November 1926 figure in *Ti-i-tz'u . . . nung-min*, 258–62.

201 Li Jui, *The early revolutionary activities of Comrade Mao Tse-tung*, 302–6, for quotations from contemporary leftist Changsha journals concerning actions against the farmers' movement and brutal killings. Li insists that far more peasants were killed than local bullies and evil gentry.

202 'Report of an investigation into the peasant movement in Hunan', in *Selected works of Mao Tse-tung*, 1. 21–59, particularly the final section, 'Fourteen great deeds'. Wilbur and How, *Documents*, 428.

Council then resolved that the revolutionary government forbid executions carried out by the people or their organizations; they must make their accusations to local party and government offices, which would decide on appropriate punishments. The resolution also provided for a revolutionary court at the provincial level with final authority to grant executions. Apparently the central authorities wished to bring rural retributive violence under some system of control. In March Hsia Hsi, a prominent young communist member of the Hunan provincial Kuomintang headquarters, reported approvingly that by then party headquarters in eight hsien, which he named, were able to represent the masses in beating down 'local bullies and evil gentry' through executions and imprisonments. Debate continued at the Third CEC Plenum, with Mao Tse-tung favouring direct action by the masses, and Tung Pi-wu introducing regulations proposed by the Hupei provincial Kuomintang headquarters for punishing local despots, including execution or a lifetime prison sentence, in accordance with the gravity of their offences. The county courts issuing sentences were to be revolutionary commissions of persons elected by specified mass organizations, meeting under the chairmanship of the county magistrate, with majority vote prevailing. A similarly elected provincial court of appeals would hold final authority. The special provincial court in Changsha was established on 5 April and, according to a hostile source, it granted numerous group executions, as did the special courts at the county level. Changsha was filled with people who fled there from their rural homes. Ling Ping, another Hunan communist leader, reported on 19 April to the Central Land Commission that the provincial Kuomintang headquarters had executed several tens of 'local bullies and evil gentry', but this was not enough. What really was needed to suppress the counter-revolutionaries, he argued, was the power of the farmers' own guards.[203]

In the heat of revolution there were many anomalies and irregularities, of which the following are merely examples. The father of the prominent communist labour leader, Li Li-san, was executed by the farmers' association of his home village in Li-ling county, in spite of a letter from the son guaranteeing that his father would not oppose the association. The magistrate of Hsin-hua county, also in Hunan, reported to Central (Kuomintang Central Headquarters) the case of a group that dominated

203 Chiang Yung-ching, *Borodin,* 257-64, 269. Hofheinz, *The broken wave,* 49-51, infers that executions of despots were not numerous, but without substantiating evidence. Li Jui, *The early revolutionary activities,* 306, says that no more than several dozen persons were directly executed by the peasants. Angus W. McDonald, Jr. tabulated the reported executions of bad gentry and local bullies in Hunan up to early May and found 'perhaps 119 province-wide'. McDonald, *The urban origins of rural revolution,* 312. (However, some cases probably never were reported in media still available.)

the local revolutionary organs, using their authority to wreak private vengeance on opponents and to execute local despots without trial so as to divide the property among themselves under the guise of official confiscation. During 'red week', according to the accusation, they executed more than 10 people, and no one dared to interfere. They even shot the head of the likin bureau without trial; he was under arrest and should have been sent to the magistrate for trial. The well-known authoress, Hsieh Ping-ying, in an autobiographical account, described a mass trial of three persons over whom, as a girl soldier, she had stood night guard. The judge who passed the sentence was a mere lieutenant of the company passing through. The three were summarily shot.[204]

There was great disagreement among the leaders of the Comintern in Moscow and of the Chinese Communist Party at Wuhan, as well as between Borodin and a newly arrived Comintern figure, the Indian, M.N. Roy, whether the agrarian revolution should be pressed forward or restrained at this time, that is April 1927.[205] Verbally, all could agree that an agrarian revolution was essential, but if this meant large-scale confiscation and redistribution of farm lands, such action would imperil, and probably destroy, the united revolutionary front between the communists and the Kuomintang, which was sacrosanct Comintern policy. A renewed northern campaign was just then being mobilized. Borodin believed the agrarian revolution should be restrained while that operation to 'widen' the revolutionary base was underway. Roy opposed the campaign northward and argued for 'deepening' the revolution in the present base, that is, to encourage rural revolt in Hunan and Hupei. By April, however, farmers in some regions were already seizing and dividing the lands of the wealthy and of those they saw as enemies. Reports of these actions implied they were spontaneous with the poor farmers themselves.[206]

204 Chang, *The rise of the Chinese Communist Party*, 1. 606. Mr Chang uses the case of Li's father to illustrate how seriously the peasant movement had got out of hand. Telegram of Magistrate Li Hsien-p'ei and others, dated 6 June, 1927 in Kuomintang Archives, Hankow Archive: Hunan dispute, 1–5/704. Most of the members of the ring were killed in a conflict with the magistrate's force but the leaders escaped. The telegram urges their capture 'to rid the people of this scourge for good'. Hsieh Ping-ying, *Autobiography of a Chinese girl*, 120–5. The event apparently occurred in Hupei during the resumed northern expedition in the spring of 1927, but the book in translation is not without errors.
205 North and Eudin, *M.N. Roy's mission to China*, 32–83, trace the controversy from Dec. 1926 to May 1927, with quotations from various parties to the dispute.
206 Mann, *What I saw in China*, 27, recalling what he was told in Changsha, about 20–25 April and Lin Tsu-han, 'Report on a investigation of the Hunan land question', on what he learned at the end of April. The 'Resolution on the agrarian question' adopted at the Fifth Congress of the CCP on 9 May states 'Furthermore, in Hupei and Hunan the peasants are starting to resolve the land problem by confiscating and distributing lands belonging to the gentry and the bandits.' In a speech on 13 May Stalin said the peasants of Hunan, Hupei, and other provinces were already 'seizing the land from below'. North and Eudin, *M.N. Roy's mission to China*, 86 and 260.

During this time of rising turbulence and mounting hostility towards the militant farmers' movement, the Central Land Commission met in Hankow between 2 April and 9 May to draw up a land policy for adoption by the Kuomintang leadership. Teng Yen-ta was the commission's chairman; he had recently been made head of the Kuomintang Farmers Bureau, but his main position was chief of the National Revolutionary Army Political Department. Other members were the eminent jurist, Hsu Ch'ien, and Ku Meng-yü, a former professor of economics at Peking University, both of whom were at the pinnacle of the left-wing Kuomintang leadership alignment. Two communist members were T'an P'ing-shan, fresh back from the Seventh ECCI Plenum in Moscow, and Mao Tse-tung, head of the Communist Party Peasant Department. The commissioners met five times but found the problem so complex that they decided to gather more information and opinion by holding enlarged conferences. Five of these were held between 19 April and 6 May, participated in by provincial level Kuomintang leaders, functionaries involved with the farmers' movement in various provinces, military commanders and political officers, and some persons familiar with conditions in northern provinces which the Wuhan leaders hoped to bring under their control through the renewed military campaign. Some Russian advisers attended to recount experiences in 'solving the land question' in the Soviet Union, and to provide what information they had gathered about agrarian conditions in China. Borodin appeared once and cautioned against too hasty and too drastic a programme in actuality.[207]

The result of many hours of discussion and clash of opinion was a report signed by the commissioners on 9 May, and drafts of seven resolutions. All conferees were agreed, the commission reported, that the land problem required urgent solution, but there was much discussion whether all land should be confiscated and nationalized, or whether there should be only partial confiscation now. They had agreed that, in view of the objective situation, it was only possible at present to carry out partial, that is, political confiscation. The land of small landlords and of Nationalist military men should be protected, for it was believed that most officers came from landlord families, and there seemed to be a growing animosity among the troops towards the farmers' movement. The central authority should only establish general principles, leaving details of implementation to provincial authorities in the light of local conditions.

207 Chiang Yung-ching, *Borodin*, 276–308, provides texts of the resulting draft resolutions and an account of the debates. A lively and rather different account of positions taken by various protagonists, is in Hofheinz, *The broken wave*, 36–45, based partly on notes taken by the present writer from minutes of the meetings now in the Kuomintang Archives. The following account is based on these notes.

The draft 'Resolution on solving the land question' indicated that land of large landlords and officials, public land and wasteland should be distributed to farmers with no land or insufficient land to sustain themselves. To assure that the land problem was indeed solved, it was necessary for the farmers to have political power; hence, the Nationalist government should assist them in their struggle against big landlords and other feudal elements. A draft for a 'Law on disposition of rebel property' defined 'rebels' as all who were enemies of the national revolution, instruments of imperialism, those who fleece and oppress the people, currency manipulators, militarists, bureaucrats, corrupt officials, 'local bullies', gentry, and other counter-revolutionaries. All their property should be confiscated. Yet the draft also carefully specified which governmental organs should do the confiscating on the basis of what kinds of evidence, all in accordance with law. Furthermore, the proceeds of enemy property distributed during the war were to be used for expenses of the army and the government. In the case of confiscated village land, 30 per cent was to be used for village improvement (such as farmers' banks), and the remainder held for distribution to revolutionary soldiers returning from the war. Distributed property might not be sold or transferred by the recipient and was subject to governmental redistribution after his death. The more detailed draft 'Decision on the land question' showed that the writers considered the land given out was to be on tenure, for the recipients were to pay rent, the proceeds to go to the government.

The commission clearly intended to regularize confiscation instead of having lands and other property seized spontaneously by the masses. Yet no one could answer the 'prior question' asked by Professor Ku Meng-yü: could the comrades 'in the peasant movement in Hunan and Hupei' say whether or not the villagers would obey the regulations drawn up so carefully in the commission's chambers?

The commission also wrestled with the complex problems of farm tenancy. Its draft resolution on this subject stipulated that no tenant should have to pay more than 40 per cent of the crop and should not pay anything else. It even went into details about rental contracts, perpetual lease, times of payment, reduction of rent in times of hardship, and other complexities of Chinese tenancy systems. Clearly, the commission hoped the Kuomintang would actually start on its unfulfilled promise to protect and benefit tenant farmers.

Leaders of the Chinese Communist Party were also struggling to develop a policy towards the agrarian revolution, with some of the top leadership urging restraint while some who worked at the provincial level wanted to press the pace. On the same day that the Kuomintang

Land Commission submitted its report, 9 May, the Fifth Congress of the CCP adopted a somewhat more radical 'Resolution on the agrarian question'.[208] All communal, ancestral, temple and school lands, and lands belonging to the Christian church, and company-owned property, should be confiscated and transferred to the tenants who tilled them. Land committees should decide whether such lands would be cultivated communally or be divided among the peasants. Landlord estates should be transferred through land committees to those who had tilled them, but land belonging to small owners and to officers of the revolutionary army should not be confiscated. Soldiers who had no land were to be granted some after the revolutionary war was over. Confiscated land should be exempt from all duties except the progressive land tax payable to the state, and rent rates should be lowered to a level corresponding to that tax. Tenants cultivating unconfiscated land should enjoy permanent tenure, pay a fixed rent, and be exempt from all other dues. Landlords and gentry were to be deprived of all political rights, and their military forces disarmed and replaced by peasant militia. Accumulated debts were to be annulled and interest rates lowered and limited by law. This slightly more radical disposition of the agrarian question, and the underlying analysis in the preamble of the resolution, put the Communist Party on record in support of social revolution – 'revolution from below' – during the national revolution, but social revolution must still be guided by regulations.

When the Land Commission's recommendation for solving the land question came to the Kuomintang Political Council for decision on 12 May, several leaders expressed fears that if it were passed and publicized it would adversely effect the national revolution's chances for victory. In the end, the three who voted to adopt the resolution, even though it would be kept secret – Lin Tsu-han, Wu Yü-chang (both dual party members) and Teng Yen-ta – were outvoted by their eight colleagues. The proposed law was set aside 'temporarily'. Some of the other resolutions were adopted, though not all were to be publicized. In the end it made very little difference because events on the battlefield, and those soon to occur within the revolutionary base, would nullify these efforts of the leaders in Wuhan to legislate revolution.

Soldiers decide

During May both wings of the Nationalist Party resumed their northward campaigns along the railways, the Wuhan wing into Honan and the

Nanking group into northern Anhwei and northern Kiangsu. Feng Yü-hsiang drove eastwards out of Shensi along the Lunghai Railway in coordination with Wuhan's campaign. Each wing also stationed defensive forces to guard against attack by the other. The Wuhan drive under the overall command of T'ang Sheng-chih, was opposed first by the remnants of Wu P'ei-fu's armies and then by the powerful Fengtien Army. Nanking faced the remnants of Sun Ch'uan-fang's forces and the stronger Shantung Army of Chang Tsung-ch'ang. By 1 June Feng Yü-hsiang's Kuominchün and T'ang Sheng-chih's armies met at Chengchow, where the Peking–Hankow Railway crosses the Lunghai, and the Fengtien Army had retreated north of the Yellow River. Two days later, the Nanking forces took Hsuchow, where the Lunghai crosses the Tientsin–Pukou Railway, and Sun and Chang retreated into Shantung to regroup their forces.[209] Somewhat concerned by the campaign towards Shantung, where there were many Japanese residents, the Japanese government dispatched troops to Tsingtao, and later to Tsinan, the provincial capital, arousing a storm of protest among nationalistic Chinese.

The Wuhan drive began first with the Fourth Front Army under Chang Fa-k'uei and the Thirty-Fifth and Thirty-Sixth Corps under T'ang Sheng-chih, some sixty to seventy thousand strong, moving up the railway towards the border of Honan, the remaining preserve of Wu P'ei-fu and his generals. Wu's subordinates were divided into two factions, one wishing to join Chang Tso-lin in opposition to Wuhan and the communists, and the other opting for Feng Yü-hsiang. Several of the second group were receiving subsidies from the Wuhan Military Council and they opened the way into Honan. Wu P'ei-fu attempted a stand at Chu-ma-tien, and was decisively beaten on 14 May. This ended his long and illustrious military career. Wu fled to eastern Szechwan under the protection of Yang Sen.[210] His defeat opened the way for major battles against heavily-armed Fengtien forces under the command of Chang Hsueh-liang, the son of Chang Tso-lin. Chang Fa-k'uei's 'Ironsides' defeated the Fengtien forces in northern Honan in bloody battles on 17 and 28 May, while Feng Yü-hsiang rushed eastwards against little

209 Accounts of these campaigns are in PFCS, 3. 677–755, with maps; KMWH, 15. 2412–92, with documents; Jordan, The Northern Expedition, 129–32; James E. Sheridan, Chinese warlord: The career of Feng Yü-hsiang, 220–4, with maps.
210 Odoric Y. K. Wou, Militarism in modern China: the career of Wu P'ei-fu, 1916–1939, 143, for the factionalism among Wu's subordinates and his defeat. Kuomintang Archives, 441/22, a military budget and accounting for April 1927, shows Chin Yün-ao receiving $320,000, Wei I-san receiving $100,000, and Fan Chung-hsiu, $44,000 that month. Feng Yü-hsiang, who the Wuhan group hoped to hold as an ally, was given $730,000, and his representative at Wuhan, Liu Chi, was paid $37,360. Feng's stipend was more than any other commander received except Chang Fa-k'uei, who got a little over $900,000 for his two corps.

opposition to seize the lion's share of the spoils. The Wuhan armies suffered some 14,000 casualities, while Feng lost a mere 400. Hospitals in Hankow were soon filled with wounded.[211] Nanking's effort, spearheaded by Ho Ying-ch'in, Li Tsung-jen and Pai Ch'ung-hsi, was much less costly.

In sending its best troops northwards and leaving only light garrison forces to protect the rail lines and major cities in Hunan and Hupei, the Wuhan regime created a golden opportunity for its enemies. General Yang Sen, one of those who came over to the Nationalist side during the early phase of the Northern Expedition and was rewarded by being appointed commander of the Twentieth Corps – his own Szechwanese troops – seized the opportunity to move eastwards from his base at Wan-hien to attack Ichang in western Hupei. Hsia Tou-yin, commander of the 14th Independent Division, who guarded Ichang and was subsidized by the Wuhan Military Council, withdrew in order to launch an attack on the Wuhan cities. Hsia claimed to be opposing communism, and sought support from generals garrisoning the revolutionary base. Both moves seem to have been inspired by Chiang Kai-shek.[212]

Wuhan's crisis came in mid May, when a regiment of Hsia's division, estimated by aerial reconnaissance to number five or six hundred, came within striking distance of Wuchang from the south, with the rest of the division only 50 miles away. Apparently most of the garrison forces in the tri-city areas were secretly in sympathy, if not in league, with Hsia.[213]

The Wuchang garrison commander, General Yeh T'ing, and his recently organized and only partially equipped 24th Division of the Eleventh Corps, stiffened by a few hundred cadets of the Wuhan Military Academy led by Yün Tai-ying, determined to drive Hsia away. Both men were members of the Communist Party, and another communist, Chang Kuo-t'ao, directed emergency security in Wuchang city. He was particularly concerned that collaborators might try to topple the leftist regime from within. M.N. Roy prepared a declaration for the Communist Party in which the party of the proletariat sought to reassure its partners, the 'petty bourgeoisie', that it had no intention of overthrowing them, and

211 Sheridan, *Chinese warlord*, 346, f.n. 45, citing a report by Wang Ching-wei in the Kuomintang Archives, and a dispatch from Consul-General Lockhart of 30 June 1927.
212 USDS 893.00/8929, telegram, Lockhart, Hankow, 18 May, reporting Hsia only 40 miles from Hankow and 'Believed to have allied self with Chiang Kai-shek'. On 1 June M. N. Roy implied the same in an article prepared for *International press correspondence*, calling Yang, Hsia and Hsu K'e-hsiang, who by then also had revolted, 'marionettes who are brought into motion by strings which are pulled from Shanghai by way of Nanking.' Sun Fo also made the charge against Chiang in a report dated 20 June, now in the Kuomintang Archives, 484/283. Chiang Yung-ching, *Borodin*, 311, 313; and *TJK*, 693-4, for the same assertion and a document of 20 May showing Chiang's close knowledge of the developments.
213 *TJK*, 696, citing a report to Nanking of an anti-communist organization in Wuhan.

also disclaiming responsibility for the 'excesses' of the peasant movement. He also prepared a propaganda appeal to the troops of Hsia Tou-yin, begging them not to be deceived by their commander's profession of anti-communism; he was really against their 'brother-peasants in Hunan' because they were taking the land from landlords and gentry. On the morning of 19 May Yeh T'ing's force routed the invading troops.[214]

The fighting south of Wuchang cut all communications with Changsha, the most revolutionary city in China at that time, where mass organizations led by communists were growing ever more militant and where there had been many executions of their opponents in April. A bitter anti-communist sentiment was gaining adherents, and there were plots to suppress the radicals. The city was full of rumours: that Wuhan had fallen, Wang Ching-wei had fled and Borodin been executed. Because the Wuhan regime had sent its most effective forces northwards, Changsha was sparsely garrisoned. General Ho Chien, commander of the Thirty-fifth Corps of T'ang Sheng-chih's Hunan Army, left one regiment under Hsu K'o-hsiang as his rearguard in Changsha, and there were other Hunanese units in the city and scattered throughout the province. In some of these outlying places troops clashed with farmers' associations, killing some of the leaders, while in Changsha there was mounting friction between garrison forces and armed pickets of the General Labour Union. Apparently both sides were preparing for a showdown.[215] There were rumours that farmers' guards and labour union pickets planned to disarm the troops. Merchants closed their shops. To lessen the tension some communists organized a joint meeting of mass organizations and troop units on 18 May, with pledges of revolutionary discipline and support for the Nationalist government.[216] But the situation was fast growing beyond anyone's control. The next day, according to a later report from the acting provin-

214 Chiang Yung-ching, *Borodin*, 311–25, and *TJK*, 693–9, give hostile accounts of communist activity in respect of Hsia's threat, but also quote a valuable account of the battle by Kao Yü-han. For the communist side, Chang, *The rise of the Chinese Communist Party*, 1. 627–32 and North and Eudin, *M. N. Roy's mission to China*, doc. 21 and 22, pp. 286–92. Sun Fo, in his report of 20 June, cited, did not mention Yeh T'ing's role, saying, 'But fortunately the Sixth and Second Corps returned and drove off Hsia Tou-yin, then defeated Yang Sen.' (In 1930, Hsia became garrison commander of the Wuhan cities, and in 1932, chairman of the Hupei Provincial government.)

215 Ho Chien in *KMWH*, 25. 5284–5, names four persons who planned a coup. Self-justifying telegrams, signed by Acting Provincial Chairman Chang I-p'eng, and by many officers, accused the radicals of planning an attack upon the garrison forces. Kuomintang Archives, Hankow Archive, Hunan dispute, 1–5/692, 695, and 700, dated 1, 4 and 7 June 1927. A reminiscent communist account says that communist leaders knew an attack was coming, and tried to prepare. *Ti-i-tz'u . . . nung-min*, 383.

216 Chiang Yung-ching, *Borodin*, 328–30, quoting from reports to the Wuhan government by various persons in Changsha in early June. Professor Chiang interprets the joint meeting as a communist defensive strategy.

cial governor, banners carried in a parade were inscribed, 'Overthrow the Thirty-fifth Corps; confiscate their arms'. On the same day, some troops in the city clashed with the General Labour Union, and the union's inspection corps reportedly invaded Ho Chien's residence and arrested and beat up his father.[217]

Two days later, on the night of 21 May, Hsu K'o-hsiang, with the support of many other commanders, took violent repressive measures against the headquarters of the provincial labour union and farmers' association, killing those who resisted and arresting a large number of suspected communists, closing down many radical organs and, in effect, dissolving the provincial government. A grain purchasing mission which had been sent from Hankow to persuade the Provincial Farmers' Association to release grain for the capital, got caught in the conflict and some of its members were killed.[218] For several days thereafter, the provincial capital witnessed a bloodbath, and the counter-revolution spread to many other counties.[219] In Hupei, Hsia Tou-yin's defeated troops went on a rampage of smashing farmers' associations and the terror spread to other districts in South and West Hupei.[220] Those slain in the two provinces probably numbered in the thousands.

The Changsha coup threw the Communist Party into confusion and presented the Kuomintang leaders with terrible dilemmas. While part of their army was in combat, troops in the rear had apparently taken counter-revolutionary action with no authorization from the centre. Whether Hsu K'o-hsiang and the other Hunanese commanders could be disciplined would depend upon the attitude of Generals T'ang Sheng-chih and Ho Chien, who were at the Honan front. Unsure of what had

---

217 Kao, *Chronology*, 258, and Boorman and Howard, *Biographical dictionary of Republican China*, 2. 61. Li Jui, *The early revolutionary activities*, 314, states that, 'Ho Chien had his father-in-law beaten only once'. He lists a series of murderous actions against peasants' associations in places other than Changsha from mid May to 21 May. I have not seen contemporary documentary evidence of the invasion of Ho Chien's home.

218 Kuomintang Archives, Hankow Archive, Hunan dispute, 1–5/709, 14 June 1927, gives an accounting of the purchase money given to the commission, most of which was lost, and an eye-witness account of the attack on the Provincial Farmers' Association head-quarters.

219 Many accounts of the 'Horse Day incident' (21 May) are listed in Wu, 'A review of the Wuhan debacle', 133, f.n. 30. Isaacs, *The Tragedy of the Chinese revolution*, 235–6 gives a vivid but essentially unsourced description of the executions. *TJK*, 699 and 702, says 3,000 persone were arrested and 70 organs closed. In his *TJK* Li Yun-han names three communist leaders executed and several others who fled in disguise.

220 A report submitted by the Hupei Farmers' Association dated 15 June 1927, in the Kuomintang Archives, cited in detail 19 specific places and estimated that four to five thousand persons were killed and many villages devastated. The association begged the Nationalist government to suppress these attacks and punish the perpetrators. Also *TJK*, 699. Isaacs, *The Tragedy of the Chinese revolution*, 227, quotes a pitiful report on the massacre of farmers in Hupei.

actually happened in Changsha, the Political Council, on the advice of Borodin, decided to send a special commission to investigate and, if possible, to restore order. It appointed T'an P'ing-shan, a communist who had just been made head of the government's Famers Department, Ch'en Kung-po, P'eng Tse-hsiang and two others nominated by General T'ang, together with Borodin. The commission started on 25 May but got no further than the Hunan border, where it was stopped and threatened with death in a telegram from Hsu K'o-hsiang. The commission returned hastily to the revolutionary capital. In Changsha, Hsu and other anti-communists set up a party purification commission to reregister all Kuomintang members and reorganize party affairs in the province.[221] A group of communist leaders in Hunan planned a counter-attack for 31 May, and started to mobilize farmers' guards in counties near Changsha.

Both in Wuhan and in Moscow, men trying to steer the revolution debated how to meet the crisis. On 24 May M.N. Roy, possibly still unaware of the gravity of the situation, drafted a resolution for the communist Politburo on relations with the Kuomintang, which proposed a declaration that 'At the present stage of the revolution, collaboration of the Communist Party with the Kuomintang is still necessary'. He then attempted to define the conditions for such collaboration: development of the democratic forces; persevering with the struggle against reactionary elements in the Kuomintang with the aim of isolating and then forcing them out of the party; seizure of leadership by the left wing closely linked with the masses; and defence of the interests of the proletariat and the peasantry.[222] This resolution, with its many details for moderation within the framework of collaboration, was shelved. The communist Politburo, caught in the vice of the Comintern's dominant policy of continuing membership in the other party and cooperation with its left wing, resolved on 26 May that the land problem first had to pass through a propaganda stage; for the time being soldiers were to be exposed to propaganda, and self-governing bodies were to be organized in the villages and counties.[223] This temporizing resolution merely reaffirmed the party's stand. More concretely, on the same day a telegram was sent in the name of the All-China General Labour Union and the National Peasants' Association (which had not yet been formally established) to the Hunan Provincial Farmers' Association and labour unions informing them that the government had appointed a commission, which was on

221 Chiang Yung-ching, *Borodin*, 332–3 and 337.
222 North and Eudin, *M. N. Roy's mission to China*, doc. 23, 302.
223 Brandt, Schwartz and Fairbank, *A documentary history*, 112, quoting the 7 Aug. 1927 'Circular letter of the CC to all party members'.

its way to settle the Changsha incident; it instructed them 'to be patient . . . in order to avoid further friction'.[224]

In far-off Moscow, the Executive Committee of the Communist International was holding its Eighth Plenum (18–30 May) during which Trotsky and the opposition bitterly attacked Stalin and Bukharin for their policy on the Chinese revolution, in particular for continuing to support the Wuhan faction of the Kuomintang, restraining the Chinese peasantry, and for rejecting the immediate creation of soviets.[225] The Chinese Commission was debating whether the time for land revolution in China had come or not. On 27 May Stalin joined the discussion, producing telegrams from Borodin showing that the Kuomintang was resolved to fight against the agrarian revolution even at the price of a break with the Comintern. Should the Communist Party fight or manoeuvre? Stalin asked, according to the later report of Albert Treint, who opposed him in the meeting. Stalin insisted that to fight meant certain defeat; to manoeuvre meant to win time, to become stronger, and to fight later in conditions where victory would be possible. He proposed to send instructions to Borodin directing him to oppose the confiscation and dividing of land belonging to members of the Kuomintang or to officers of the national army.[226] The final ECCI resolution called for the creation of a truly revolutionary army, 'but the Communist Party of China must exert all its efforts directly in alliance with the left Kuomintang.'[227]

The Hunan Provincial Committee of the Chinese Communist Party had mobilized a strong force of farmers' guards in counties near Changsha for a general attack on the city and nearby towns. Just before the appointed day, 31 May, Li Wei-han ordered a halt, probably in response to instructions from Hankow.[228] The order failed to reach the contingent at Liu-yang, which had already begun its march on Changsha. Their

---

224 North and Eudin, *M. N. Roy's mission to China*, 103, quoting *The people's tribune* of 28 May.
225 *Leon Trotsky on China*, 220–48, for Trotsky's speeches and writings during the session.
226 'Documents on the Comintern and the Chinese revolution', with an introduction by Harold Isaacs, *CQ*, 45 (January–March 1971) 100–15, with English and French versions of Albert Treint's retrospective account, written in 1935, but based on a version published in Nov. 1927. The English translation is reprinted in Gruber, *Soviet Russia masters the Comintern*, 490–4. (Stalin's proposed instruction to Borodin would merely reinforce the established policy of the Chinese Communist Party at that time.)
227 North and Eudin, *M. N. Roy's mission to China*, 92–3. They give an extended discussion of the debates on China raging in Moscow in May.
228 Both Ts'ai Ho-sen and P'eng Shu-chih charge Li with the order to halt. North and Eudin, *M. N. Roy's mission to China*, 106, and Brandt, Schwartz and Fairbank, *A documentary history*, 487, f.n. 8. Schram asserts that Mao Tse-tung gave the order on the instruction of Stalin. Li Jui, *The early revolutionary activities*, 315, note. Klein and Clark, *Biographic dictionary*, accept Li's responsibility for the order.

attack was crushed on the afternoon of 31 May, and another force attempting to seize Hsiang-t'an was destroyed to a man.[229]

The day after this disaster Stalin's famous telegram instructing his subordinates arrived in the revolutionary capital.[230] Stalin called for seizure of land by the masses 'from below', and also for combating 'excesses', not with the help of troops but through peasant unions. Vacillating and compromising leaders of the Kuomintang Central Committee were to be replaced by peasant and working-class leaders. Dependence upon unreliable generals had to cease, and several new army corps were to be created by mobilizing 20,000 communists and about 50,000 revolutionary workers and peasants from Hunan and Hupei. A revolutionary tribunal headed by a prominent non-communist Kuomintang leader had to be organized to punish officers who maintained contact with Chiang Kai-shek or who set soldiers on the people. 'Persuasion is not enough', Stalin exhorted. 'It is time to act. The scoundrels must be punished.'

Under the circumstances in China at that moment, with the mass movement suffering cruel oppression and the Communist Party in disarray, such orders were 'like taking a bath in a toilet', as Ch'en Tu-hsiu later characterized them. All Central Committee members realized the orders could not be executed. Everyone present knew not 'whether to laugh or cry', as Chang Kuo-t'ao recalled. Therefore, the party's Politburo telegraphed accepting the instructions in principle, but made it clear they could not be realized immediately.[231] (Roy's indiscretion in showing Stalin's telegram to Wang Ching-wei is discussed below.)

229 *Ti-i-tz'u . . . nung-min*, 338, from the reminiscences of Liu Chih-hsün, published a year later. This has been translated in part in Li Jui, *The early revolutionary activities*, 315–16. On 1 June the Kuomintang CEC sent a letter to the Hunan Special Committee, containing copies of telegrams received from Hsiang-t'an party headquarters and from the farmers' association describing attacks by units of the Eighth, 35th and 36th Corps on labour and farmer groups, making one believe the aggression came from the military before 31 May. Kuomintang Archives, Hankow Archive, Hunan dispute, 1–5/693. The acting governor, Chang I-p'eng, telegraphed Hankow on 30 May describing mass rallies in a number of counties and attacks on various places; then an attack on Changsha 'today at 10 a.m.' by 'hundreds of men with guns and thousands of men with wooden staves'. After a two-hour battle 'the peasants were totally routed'. He quotes prisoner interrogations to the effect that the provincial farmers' union had given the order on the 20th to break into the city and plunder. 'Therefore we came to slaughter.' Kuomintang Archives, Hankow Archive, Hunan dispute, 1–5/692. (The dates are puzzling.)

230 The text is given in North and Eudin, *M. N. Roy's Mission to China*, 106–7, translated from two articles by Stalin, dated 1935. Also in Eudin and North, *Soviet Russia and the East*, 303–4. In 1929 Ch'en Tu-hsiu gave the gist of the Stalin's instructions, which he said came from the Comintern, in 'A letter to all comrades of the party', 333–4, and this was used by Isaacs in *The Tragedy of the Chinese Revolution*, 245–6. It is unclear whether the telegram was addressed to Borodin, Roy or the Central Committee of the CCP.

231 Ch'en Tu-hsiu, 'A letter to all comrades of the party,' 234–5; Chang, *The rise of the Chinese Communist Party*, 1. 637. Roy provided the text of a telegram to the Comintern, dated 15 June, which he said was sent by Ch'en Tu-hsiu at the instruction of the Politburo. North and Eudin, *M. N. Roy's mission to China*, Doc. 29, pp. 338–40. The telegram describes the

Apparently the best that the communist leaders could do was to organize mass demonstrations in Wuhan on 4 and 5 June, with petitions addressed to the national government begging it to halt the slaughter in the provinces and to punish Hsu K'o-hsiang and his allies. The petitioners admitted that the agrarian movement had been marred by puerile actions, but contended that these were inevitable in the early stages of a revolution. They were nothing compared with the atrocities committed by Hsu and his fellow conspirators in league with Chiang Kai-shek; their actions disrupted the rear of the northern campaign and threatened the entire revolutionary movement.[232] The ever loquacious Roy prepared an open letter to the Central Committee of the Kuomintang from the Central Committee of the Communist Party, which called for a punitive expedition to suppress the Changsha counter-revolutionaries, the dissolution of its various committees, and a decree by the national government guaranteeing complete freedom to worker and peasant organizations and the Communist Party in Hunan. It requested an order to return the arms confiscated from workers' and peasants' detachments, and the arming of the peasants as a guarantee against future counter-revolutionary flare-ups. Roy also wrote an 'Appeal to the peasants' in which the Chinese Communist Party called on the Hunan peasants to continue the struggle against large landlords, the gentry, and counter-revolutionary militarists by seizing their land. But the lands of small landlords and of officers fighting at the front should be inviolate. The peasants should not regard soldiers as enemies but should establish close ties with them, drawing the mass of soldiers into peasant unions. Roy's words exhorted the Hunan peasants to demand the surrender of the counter-revolutionary gang in Changsha and to organize an armed uprising to overthrow it. 'Help the national government to restore [its] power in Hunan! Support the Kuomintang against the counter-revolutionary militarists!'[233]

The issue was not to be settled by words but by soldiers. Hsu K'o-hsiang was in telegraphic communication with Generals Ho Chien and T'ang Sheng-chih from the beginning, and he may have been their agent. After the commission of investigation was turned back, T'ang Sheng-chih appointed General Chou Lan, deputy commander of the Thirty-sixth Corps, as his commissioner to go to Changsha, and the Kuomintang

critical situation and the Communist Party's inability at present to carry out the Comintern's instructions.

232 Kuomintang Archives, Hankow Archive, Hunan dispute, 1–5/696 and 697, dated 4 and 5 June, one from the Provisional Assembly of Representatives of Various Circles in Wuhan, the other from the Wuhan Assembly to Celebrate the Capture of Chengchow and Kaifeng. (There are clear evidences of common drafting.)

233 North and Eudin, *M. N. Roy's mission to China*, docs. 26 and 27, pp. 314–20, dated 3 and 4 June.

Central Committee made him its special deputy. General Chou was instructed to take command of all troops in Hunan and enforce discipline. Both sides should cease their conflict. The provincial party apparatus, the provincial government, and farmers' and workers' organizations were to be reconstituted under Central's orders. After Chou Lan arrived in Changsha, Central received a telegram dated 7 June and signed in the names of Chang I-p'eng, four educational officials, and 41 commanders and political officers, including Hsu K'o-hsiang, expressing gratitude for the instructions transmitted by Deputy Commander Chou, justifying their own actions on 21 May, and pledging to carry out absolutely all orders of the central government.[234]

Though the tone was submissive the formidable list of officers who purportedly signed could only have been meant to convey their solidarity. Chou Lan was warmly welcomed by a citizens' gathering on 9 June, where he was urged to join the party purification movement. In fact, he found such a strong anti-communist sentiment in Changsha that he felt unable to carry out his even-handed instructions. He telegraphed Central reporting that farmers' associations opposed the government and asked for troops to exterminate them.[235]

The agrarian movement in Hunan was too widespread, and its communist leaders too few and divided for the disorders to be brought under control quickly. Several more reports came to Central describing conflicts that were blamed on the farmers' movement, including the seizure of the P'ing-hsiang–Chu-chou Railway and the surrounding of the P'ing-hsiang collieries, preventing coal from being shipped or food going to the miners.[236] In a discussion of the Hunan problem in the Political Council on 13 June Wang Ching-wei reported that in an immediately prior meeting of the Military Council Mao Tse-tung had admitted that farmers' associations had damaged the homes of soldiers, but he threw the blame on members of the Ko-lao hui, a powerful secret society in Hunan who he said, had infiltrated the associations. 'They knew neither the Kuomintang nor the Communist Party, but only the business of killing and setting fires', Wang quoted Mao as saying. With respect to the May Twenty-first Incident in Changsha, Mao maintained that it was the troops who had attacked the association, which had only tried to defend itself and was not trying to seize soldiers' rifles. With the concurrence of Mao and Wu Yü-chang, the Political Council then decided to send T'ang Sheng-chih,

234 Kuomintang Archives, Hankow Archive, Hunan dispute, 1–5/700.
235 Chiang Yung-ching, *Borodin*, 338, citing discussion in the Kuomintang Political Council, 13 June.
236 *Ibid.* 343–4, citing documents. The railway seizure was reported in the Political Council on 15 June.

recently back from the Honan battles, to restore order in Hunan, but he should do so without using military force.[237]

After arriving at his base and having been appraised of the situation, T'ang telegraphed on 26 June, recommending that two persons who had been leaders in Hsu K'o-hsiang's party purification movement should be expelled from the Kuomintang, and that Hsu, himself, should be given a demerit. Hsu, however, was not to be humbled by T'ang. He led his troops to South Hunan, where he received a commission from Chiang Kai-shek to join in the party purification struggle.[238]

Another soldier took action against the Communist Party in Kiangsi. Chu P'ei-te and his Third Corps guarded the province against a possible attack from the Nanking faction. Influenced by anti-communist sentiments in his army and by the May Twenty-first Incident in Changsha, he decided to dismiss the political officers in his army, many of whom were communists. On 29 May he sent 142 of them off to Wuhan where they arrived on 1 June. He also freed Ch'eng T'ien-feng and other Kuomintang leaders who had been imprisoned since 2 April and feared execution. On 5 June he ordered 22 leading communists to leave the province, though he treated them with great courtesy and provided them with travel money. Furthermore. he ordered the provincial General Labour Union and Farmers' Association to supend activities, and his gendarmes confiscated 800 rifles and other equipment from the Nanchang farmers' guards. Apparently, General Chu, who was also governor of Kiangsi, was trying to prevent the sort of conflicts that had erupted in neighbouring Hunan. He announced that sending away the political workers had no other purpose than to calm the environment. The Kuomintang organizations were to continue and mass organizations to maintain their structures, though suspending activities until orders came from Wuhan Central. He proclaimed his support for the National government in Wuhan and his opposition to the Nanking government. Still, he sent his resignation as head of the Kuomintang's special commission to manage party affairs, and asked for a new group of commissioners. Presumably he was testing Wuhan's reaction. Out in the province, Chu P'ei-te's order for suspension of activity by the farmers' and workers' movements was interpreted as an opportunity to suppress them. A report sent to Wuhan

237 *Ibid.* 348, and *TJK*, p. 707, both quoting the minutes of the Political Council. Also quoted in Kuo, *Analytical history*, 1. 243. According to Ts'ai Ho-sen, Borodin, too, used the explanation that misdeeds of the Hunan Farmers' Association had been 'led by local villains and the Ko Lao Hui, not by us.' Chiang Yung-ching, *Borodin*, 336, though not exactly dated.

238 A translation of General T'ang's telegram of 26 June is reprinted from *The people's tribune* of 29 June in North and Eudin, *M. N. Roy's Mission to China*, 120–1. The Chinese version in *TJK*, 708; also Chiang Yung-ching, *Borodin*, 350–1.

by the Provincial Farmers' Association stated that some 200 leaders of the movement were slain and that 'local bullies and evil gentry' in a number of named counties had gone on a rampage of smashing local associations and were cruelly killing farmers.

How could this development be dealt with? In Wuhan the communist leadership was in great disagreement. Some, including Roy, demanded that Chu be punished, and planned a general strike to back up their proposal. Borodin was furious at this idea. Others feared that an unsuccessful attempt to topple General Chu would have terrible consequences. When Wang Ching-wei returned from his conference with Feng Yü-hsiang at Chengchow, Hsiang Chung-fa demanded that he order Chu to restore the leaders of the mass movements to their positions. Then, when the Kuomintang Political Council considered Chu P'ei-te's resignation, Wang Ching-wei stated the problem plainly: if Chu were not excused for his actions he might immediately turn over to Nanking, greatly strengthening that overriding source of evil. Therefore the Political Council resolved not even to consider Chu's resignation. Searching for a compromise, the Council decided to send Ch'en Kung-po and Ch'en Ch'i-yuan, together with a few communist cadres, to Kiangsi to confer with Chu P'ei-te, while T'an P'ing-shan, in compliance with a request from Chu, offered to send 40 recent graduates of the Farmers' Movement Training Institute for low-level work in Kiangsi. On 20 June the two Ch'ens and the communist cadres arrived in Kiukiang where they conferred with General Chu. All agreed to a rather vague formula: concentration of power in the Kuomintang; all who did not maintain discipline would immediately be restrained. Thus was the issue compromised, though communist influence in the province, never as strong as in Hunan, had markedly declined.[239]

Separating communists from the left-wing Kuomintang

M.N. Roy revealed the contents of Stalin's telegram to Wang Ching-wei on 5 June, the day before Wuhan notables were to depart for a conference with General Feng Yü-hsiang. At Wang's request, Roy later gave him a translation of the text. Wang was appalled, but it took him and his closest associates some weeks to decide how to meet this menacing turn in Russian policy towards their party.[240]

239 This brief account is synthesized from Li, *TJK*, 709–15, and Chiang Yung-ching, *Borodin*, 354–68, both based on contemporary documents.
240 Wang reported the date and circumstances on 15 July to an enlarged meeting of the CEC Standing Committee, as quoted from the minutes in *TJK*, 736 and Chiang Yung-ching, *Borodin*, 403–4. The first public revelation of the major points in the telegram came in

On 6 June the praesidium of the Kuomintang Political Council travelled to Chengchow to confer with Feng Yü-hsiang.[241] Feng held the whip-hand, for Wuhan's armies had suffered heavy casualties and their rear was in great disorder. The conferees agreed to give Feng control of Honan province and confirmed his appointees in Shensi and Kansu, who were now to be officials of the Nationalist government. Feng's army and a variety of Honan units were to be reorganized into seven front armies under his command. Wuhan's forces were to return to defend their bases. Feng would not agree to join in a campaign against the Nanking faction, although he spoke privately to Wang about Chiang Kai-shek's perfidy. Some of the conferees also discussed Stalin's telegram and laid plans to curb the activities of the Communist Party.[242] The Wuhan contingent then hurriedly left for Hankow on 12 June, leaving Hsu Ch'ien with General Feng – they were old associates – and bringing Yü Yu-jen with them. Ku Meng-yü also stayed behind. Borodin quickly realized that from his point of view the conference had been a failure.[243]

The Wuhan regime faced a precarious strategic situation. At great sacrifice of manpower in Chang Fa-k'uei's Fourth and Eleventh Corps, Honan had been somewhat cleared of opposing armies, but Feng Yü-hsiang, an uncertain ally, now dominated the province. Kwangtung, the original revolutionary base, was controlled by Li Chi-shen, who opposed

August 1927 as a report of the Presidium of the Kuomintang Political Council dated 19 July, and published by the Kuomintang Central Propaganda Office. This is in the Kuomintang Archives. See *TJK*, 745, f.n. 94. On 5 Nov. 1927 Wang recounted the circumstances in a speech in Canton but gave 1 June as the date of Roy's revelation. Wang's speech was published in *Min-kuo jih-pao*, 9 Nov., and is reprinted in *KMWH*, 16. 2851-65, the pertinent section being 2861-2.

241 Wang's report at the 28th meeting of the Political Council on 13 June names T'an Yen-k'ai, Ku Meng-yü, Sun Fo, Hsü Ch'ien and himself as members of the presidium. Other participants mentioned by Wang were Yü Shu-te (the only communist), Wang Fa-ch'in, Teng Yen-ta, and T'ang Sheng-chih from the Wuhan group, and Feng Yü-hsiang, Lu Chung-lin, and Yü Yu-jen. Kuomintang Archives, 005/3. Chiang Yung-ching, *Borodin*, 380, adds Chang Fa-k'uei. Anna Louise Strong and Rayna Prohme accompanied the party, and Miss Strong in a colourful account, says that General Galen (Blyukher) also went, but Borodin could not go as he was sick with fever and had a broken arm. Anna Louise Strong, *China's millions*, 46-8.

242 Chang Fa-k'uei, in an interview with Julie Lien-ying How, remembered that Wang reported the contents of the Comintern resolution – i.e., Stalin's telegram? – and that T'ang Sheng-chih reported on peasant disturbances in Hunan. The decision was made to 'separate the communists', General Chang recalled. Sheridan, *Chinese warlord: the career of Feng Yü-hsiang*, 225-7, for an account of the Chengchow conference based on a variety of sources. See p. 346, f.n. 50, for later reports that the communist problem was discussed. Presumably Yü Shu-te and Blyukher were not included in those talks.

243 USDS 893.00/9106, telegram, Hankow, Lockhart to secretary of state, 15 June 1927, reporting Borodin's depression and his belief that had he been able to attend, the outcome of the conference would have been more favourable. Lockhart added, 'There appears to be a growing [belief] that there will be a gradual elimination of the Russians and the Chinese radicals from Kuomintang councils here.'

the radicalism of the workers and peasants, and was a quasi-ally of Chiang Kai-shek. He blocked Wuhan's access to the sea. To the east, the armies affiliated with the Nanking faction might launch an attack on Wuhan, now that they had driven the forces of Sun Ch'uan-fang and Chang Tsung-ch'ang into Shantung, and there were suspicions that Chiang Kai-shek was still negotiating for a truce with Chang Tso-lin. Within the three-province base – Hunan, Hupei and Kiangsi – the loyalty of T'ang Sheng-chih and his subordinates was uncertain due to their opposition to the militant peasant movement. Chu P'ei-te had just expelled leading communists from Kiangsi and ordered a halt to the activities of the peasant and worker movements, and he seemed to be attempting to play a mediating role between the two Nationalist factions. Complicating these difficulties was the problem of Stalin's order to Borodin and the Chinese Communist Party to encourage land seizures, create an independent military force, punish unreliable generals, and reform the left Kuomintang from below.

Should the left Kuomintang break with the communists in order to placate the generals whose support was essential, but thereby lose Soviet Russia's support? If the break were to be made, when and how should it be carried out? Was there a military solution: a continued drive on Peking, a campaign against Nanking, or a drive southwards to retake Kwangtung? These were the problems that gripped the Nationalist leaders when they returned from Chengchow. A successful drive on Peking would depend on the active participation of Yen Hsi-shan in Shansi, whose army might drive eastward to cut the P'ing-Han railway at Shih-chia-chuang. An attempt was underway to persuade Yen to join with Feng in a northward campaign but his agreement was unlikely. (In fact, he soon declared himself in favour of Nanking.) An eastward campaign against Nanking might succeed if the Kwangsi clique headed by Li Tsung-jen, Pai Ch'ung-hsi, and Huang Shao-hsiung could be induced to turn against Chiang Kai-shek, but for such a campaign Chu P'ei-te's support was essential. A southern campaign was urged by Roy and a few communist leaders and might be attractive to Chang Fa-k'uei, the most loyal military supporter of the left, but his armies had still to recover from casualties in Honan. The Hanyang Arsenal was working night and day, but there were shortages in essential supplies: could it provide arms enough for a second campaign?

By 15 June the Kuomintang Political Council had decided to prepare for an Eastern campaign. According to Ts'ai Ho-sen, this was Borodin's recommendation, and Wang Ching-wei and T'ang Sheng-chih accepted it in the expectation of Russian funds to finance it. In preparation for the campaign, the Military Council proposed new army designations. T'ang Sheng-chih should command the Fourth Group Army made up of two front armies: the First, under T'ang's direct command, made up of the Eighth, Thirty-fifth, and Thirty-sixth Corps; and the Second, commanded by Chang Fa-k'uei, made up of the Fourth, Eleventh, and the newly enrolled Twentieth Corps, commanded by Ho Lung. Before the campaign began, however, they must suppress Yang Sen and Hsia Tou-yin, who were still rampaging in Hupei, send T'ang Sheng-chih to settle matters in Hunan, and send Ch'en Kung-po to negotiate with Chu P'ei-te in Kiangsi (related above).[244]

The communist leaders faced a dilemma. They knew it was impossible to carry out Stalin's orders. Should Communist Party members try to stay within the Kuomintang and continue working for the national revolution under its banner? That policy had brought great benefits in a large membership and influence among students, urban workers and poorer farmers. But many signs pointed to growing hostility among important Kuomintang leaders, and a tide of reaction among the generals against the mass movements and the Communist Party itself. Only by curbing social revolution could the policy of working within the Kuomintang be continued, but many communists saw social revolution as the essence of national revolution. The mass organizations were the Communist Party's real base of support. After heated debate, the communist leadership, on Borodin's advice, seems to have decided about the middle of June to temporize: party members should stay within the Kuomintang and attempt to restrain social revolution. The party would support a campaign against Chiang Kai-shek in the hope, after victory, of rebuilding the shattered ranks and the mass organizations.[245] Their calculations, however, failed to give due weight to Feng Yü-hsiang.

After the Chengchow conference, General Feng sent his representative,

244 Chiang Yung-ching, *Borodin*, 393–4. Kuo, *Analytical history*, 1. 255, for excerpts from Ts'ai Ho-sen, 'History of opportunism'.
245 The fervour of the debate may be sensed from Roy's documents of 9 and 15 June, in North and Eudin, *M.N. Roy's mission to China*, nos. 28, 31 and 32, and the critique of the Central Committee's policy in the 7 Aug. 1927 'Circular letter of the CC to all party members', abstracted in Brandt, Schwartz and Fairbank, *A documentary history*, 102–18. Also Ts'ai Ho-sen's account of debates in the weeks following, in the 'History of opportunism', written a few months later, excerpted in Kuo, *Analytical history*, 1. 255–61, and Chiang Yung-ching, *Borodin*, 393–4. Chang Kuo-t'ao gives a retrospective account in *The rise of the Chinese Communist Party*, 1. 647–9. The Comintern's Executive Committee resolution on the Chinese Question adopted by the Eighth Plenum towards the end of May had forecast a campaign against Chiang Kai-shek in the instruction, 'and conduct intensive demoralization work in the rear and within the armies of Chiang Kai-shek with the aim of liquidating them, which does not exclude, of course, conducting military operations against them at the appropriate moment.' Eudin and North, *Soviet Russia and the East*, 275. Presumably such instructions had been sent by radio to Borodin.

Mao I-heng, to Hsuchow where he met with Pai Ch'ung-hsi and Li Tsung-jen, and it was agreed that Feng and Chiang Kai-shek should meet. An imposing group of Nanking and Shanghai notables then hastened to Hsuchow, where they conferred with General Feng on 20 and 21 June.[246] One important result of the conference was the apparent recruitment of Feng to the Nanking side in consideration of a promised subsidy, reportedly Ch.$2,000,000 a month,[247] which was far more than Wuhan had been paying him. Feng also agreed to use his influence to compel Wuhan to send Borodin back to Russia – something that Chiang had been trying to effect since February – to expel communists, and to persuade loyal Kuomintang members there to come to Nanking to reunite the party and form a single government.[248] On 21 June General Feng sent an ultimatum-like telegram to Wang Ching-wei and T'an Yen-k'ai. After recalling that at Chengchow they had talked about the radicals who had wormed their way into the party and oppressed merchants, factory owners, gentry, landowners, and soldiers, and who refused to obey orders, Feng laid down his terms: Michael Borodin should return to his country immediately; those members of the Central Executive Committee who wished to go abroad for a rest should be allowed to do so; and the rest might join the Nationalist government at Nanking if they so desired. 'It is my desire that you accept the above solution and reach a conclusion immediately.' The next day he told reporters of his 'sincere desire to cooperate with the Nationalists and to extirpate militarism and communism.' He gave them a copy of the telegram.[249]

Within the communist leadership debate raged over strategy. In hopes of overcoming 'the present, dangerous crisis of the revolution', the secretariat of the Chinese Communist Party proposed a desperate scheme on 23 June: the underground Shanghai committee must create within one

246 Mao I-heng, O Meng hui-i-lu (Recollections of Russia and Mongolia), 244–5. The participants from Nanking and Shanghai, besides Chiang, were Hu Han-min, Ts'ai Yuan-p'ei, Chang Jen-chieh (Ching-chiang), Li Shih-tseng, Huang Fu, Niu Yung-chien, Li Lieh-chün, Li Tsung-jen, Huang Shao-hsiung, Pai Ch'ung-hsi, and Wu Chih-hui, who presided. On Feng's side were Li Ming-chung and Ho Chi-kung. TJK, 718, based on Wu Chih-hui's report reprinted in KMWH, 15. 2566. Isaacs, The Tragedy of the Chinese revolution, 256, says that Hsu Ch'ien and Ku Meng-yü accompanied Feng to Hsuchow.

247 Mao I-heng, O Meng hui-i-lu, 245. The British consul-general in Shanghai, Sir Sidney Barton, reported on 30 June that there had been a great drive in the last two weeks in June to collect funds in Shanghai, which he speculated were needed to carry out Chiang's agreement at Hsuchow to finance Feng in return for Feng's support against Hankow and Peking. GBFO 405/254. Confidential. Further correspondence respecting China, no. 13315, July–Sept. 1927, no. 43, enclosure.

248 Chiang Kai-shek's report of 6 July, quoted by Li Yun-han in TJK, 718–19.

249 Isaacs, The Tragedy of the Chinese Revolution, 256, who quotes part of the telegram as published in CWR, 2 July 1927. The Chinese text was published in Kuo-wen chou-pao on 3 July, and is given in TJK, 719–20 and Chiang Yung-ching, Borodin, 382–3.

month a militant anti-imperialist movement more powerful than the May Thirtieth movement of two years before, with students, merchants and workers declaring a general strike and demonstrating within the foreign settlements – even, if necessary, demanding confiscation of imperialist property and taking back of the foreign concessions. If a powerful anti-foreign sentiment were fostered among all sectors of the population – particularly against Japan, which had sent troops into Shantung – and if this were especially virulent among the ranks of Chiang Kai-shek's armies, it would force the imperialists to occupy Nanking and Shanghai – so the secretariat reasoned. This would lead to a nationwide protest which would destroy the roots of Chiang's power and smash the danger from the right in the Wuhan government. 'This movement must burst like an explosion just at the moment when either Chiang Kai-shek attacks Wuhan, or Wuhan attacks Chiang Kai-shek.' The Communist Party could then carry on the social revolution under the banner of a new anti-imperialist war.[250] The Politburo[251] countermanded this scheme with its suicidal potentialities for the remnants of the shattered mass movement in the east. An increasingly hostile situation in the Wuhan cities forced new decisions upon the party leaders.

The Fourth Congress of the National General Labour Union had begun its meetings in Hankow on 19 June with more than 400 delegates, some from the shattered unions of Shanghai and Canton.[252] Also attending were a fraternal delegation from the Profintern (the Red Trade Union International), headed by its president, Aleksandr Lazovskii, representatives from the Kuomintang, the Chinese Communist Party and the Communist Youth League. Both the National General Labour Union and the Congress were controlled by the Communist Party, yet Feng Yü-hsiang now clearly demanded that the Wuhan regime separate itself from that party, and there were rumours that some of Wuhan's generals planned to arrest communists and suppress the labour movement. Who was safe? While the congress proceeded under the chairmanship of Su Chao-cheng, even being favoured by an address by Wang Ching-wei, the communist

250 North and Eudin, M. N. Roy's mission to China, Doc. 35, pp. 361-5. According to Roy, the secretariat sent the letter bearing these instructions to Shanghai, but the Politburo after lengthy debate replaced it by a resolution on the anti-imperialist struggle. Roy does not cite this but quotes his own speech, presumably to the Politburo, opposing this fool-hardy order to the Shanghai comrades. Ibid. 366-9.

251 After the Fifth CCP Congress, the Politburo consisted of Ch'en Tu-hsiu, Chang Kuo-t'ao, Chou En-lai, Ch'ü Ch'iu-pai, Li Li-san, Li Wei-han (pseudonym Lo Mai), T'an P'ing-shan, and Ts'ai Ho-sen, according to Bernadette Yu-ning Li, 'A biography of Ch'ü Ch'iu-pai: from youth to party leadership (1899-1928)', Columbia University, Ph.D. dissertation, 1967, 197.

252 An account of the meetings and some resolutions are reprinted in Ti-i-tz'u . . . kung-jen, 545-2; a description is in Strong, China's millions, 74-88.

Politburo debated what to do about the armed and uniformed pickets – the 'inspection corps' – of the General Labour Union and of the Hupei Provincial Union headed by Li Li-san. The pickets were a source of great animosity in the business community – both Chinese and foreign – which the Wuhan regime was encouraging in every way in order to revive the depressed economy, and provide work for scores of thousands of unemployed. Should the pickets give up their arms as a concession to the Kuomintang? Should they cross the river to Wuchang and enrol in Chang Fa-k'uei's forces? Apparently on 28 June, which was the last day of the congress, the Politburo met in Borodin's home and decided on a further retreat: the pickets would be disarmed voluntarily. That night – either by coincidence or after an understanding – police and troops of the Hankow garrison seized the headquarters of the National Labour Union and the Hupei Provincial Union, and pickets turned in their rifles and removed their insignia and uniforms. Yet the next day the offices were returned to the unions with face-saving apologies, and pickets reappeared, in smaller numbers and without arms. That evening the delegates to the congress were hosts at a festival for soldiers. Wang Ching-wei ordered that no harm should befall the unions.[253]

Pressures for a break between the two parties continued to mount. T'ang Sheng-chih's telegram of 26 June from Changsha, placing the blame for disorders in Hunan upon those who led the peasant movement, was published on 29 June. On the same day General Ho Chien, commander of the Thirty-fifth Corps, issued a proclamation demanding that the Kuomintang expel its communist members. He threatened to arrest any communists his troops could capture. In the face of this threat, the communist leadership decided to move the party's headquarters across the river to Wuchang, and there to hold an enlarged plenum of the Central Committee to fix a policy line. A meeting was first held on 30 June in Borodin's home, attended by Politburo members and two newly arrived Comintern delegates. After acrimonious debate, the participants accepted a series of resolutions that were then adopted on 1 July by the Central Committee. They marked the ultimate retreat of the Communist Party in order to retain working relations with the left Kuomintang. The party of the proletariat resolved that the worker and peasant movements should

253 *TJK*, 731 for Ts'ai Ho-sen's later account of the emergency Politburo meeting; also, Chang, *The rise of the Chinese Communist Party*, 649. Chiang, Yung-ching, *Borodin* 397, for Wang Ching-wei's description of the raids, and USDS 893.00/9159, telegram, Hankow, Lockhart to secretary of state, 29 June, describing the seizures. Miss Strong observed the return of the National Union's headquarters to Su Chao-cheng and describes the festival sardonically. Her account was written in Moscow. See *China's millions*, 87–8. General Li P'in-hsien, garrison commander in Hankow, apparently ordered the raids.

take their orders from, and be supervised by, Kuomintang offices, though the Kuomintang and the government must protect their organizations; armed units of workers and peasants should submit to the government's supervision and training, while those inspection corps in Wuhan that were still armed should be reduced in number or be enrolled in the army; workers and their inspection corps should not exercise judicial authority such as arresting and trying, nor patrol streets and markets without permission from Kuomintang headquarters or the government. Very soon the communist leadership severely reproached itself for these accommodations to the demand for law and order. Another resolution dealt with communists working in the national or local government organs. They should do so as Kuomintang members, not as communists, and to avoid conflict they might ask for leave of absence.[254]

The last days of June saw the beginning of an exodus of Russian military advisers and members of Borodin's staff, persons who had employed much talent and spent great energy in assisting the Nationalist Revolution, for now the end of Russian aid was approaching. Correspondents who called on Borodin early in July found him sick and weary, but determined to stay on as long as hope remained. His wife was in a Peking prison, having been seized on 28 February when the Soviet vessel *Pamiat Lenina*, on which she was travelling to Hankow, was captured by Shantung troops. Mme Borodin's release had to be arranged before he could leave, and apparently Japan was willing to be the intermediary. In the early morning of 12 July a Chinese judge dismissed the charges against her and other Russians who had been seized on the *Pamiat Lenina*. The judge then disappeared, only to show up later in Japan, and the Russian erstwhile prisoners were spirited out of Peking, except for Mme Borodin who was secreted in the city. Her presence was concealed by a series of false news accounts of her arrival in Vladivostok, an interview on the Trans-Siberian, and her arrival statement in Moscow. Towards the end of August she successfully left Peking disguised as a nun.[255]

254 Ho Chien's proclamation is in *Kuo-wen chou-pao*, 4. 29 (21 July 1927), which reprints eight important Wuhan documents concerning the inter-party split. The documents continue in succeeding issues. Chiang Yung-ching, *Borodin*, 399, quotes four of the 11 resolutions as given in the 'Letter to the comrades' from the 7 Aug. [1927] Central Committee Conference, so called. Kuo, *Analytical history*, 259-60, gives seven from the same source.

255 USDS 893.00/9128 telegram, Peking, MacMurray to secretary of state, 23 June, transmitting Hankow telegram of June 22, reporting early departure of Russian aviators. Vishnyakova-Akimova, *Two years in revolutionary China*, 326, tells of her departure soon after 20 June, on Borodin's orders, together with several military advisers. Others followed in contingents during July, and General Blyukher left on 11 Aug, according to Kasanin, *China in the twenties*, 291-2. Interviews with Borodin in Henry Francis Misselwitz, *The dragon stirs: an intimate sketchbook of China's Kuomintang revolution, 1927-1929*, 125; and Vincent Sheean, *Personal history*, 240-1. Sheean details Mme Borodin's escape, in which he nearly played a part (pp. 255-8), and his account is supplemented by Kasanin, cited, 295-6.

The breaking point between the two parties came in the middle of July. Feng Yü-hsiang and Chiang Kai-shek exerted pressure by repeated telegrams from Hsu Ch'ien urging his Wuhan colleagues to dismiss Borodin, and by Chiang bringing his crack First Corps back to Nanking and ordering the Seventh and two other corps to proceed towards Kiangsi. T. V. Soong, Wuhan's finance minister, who had stayed in Shanghai during the previous several months, suddenly returned to Hankow on 12 July, doubtless bearing messages from the Nanking faction. Private meetings in Wang Ching-wei's home were dominated by the more conservative Wuhan leaders, who hoped to find a peaceful settlement with their Nanking rivals. This would require separating from the communists and asking Borodin to leave. (Borodin had already made preparations for departure by an overland route through Mongolia.)[256]

On 14 July the praesidium of the Political Council accepted two proposals by Wang Ching-wei: to send a high-level representative to Moscow to explain Sun Yat-sen's policy of allying with Russia and the Communist Party under the Three Principles of the People, so as to clarify future relationships; and to find a method to manage communists within the Kuomintang so as to avoid intra-party ideological and policy conflicts, and expecially to end the system of two separate and conflicting policy organs. Next day an expanded meeting of the Kuomintang CEC Standing Committee heard Wang's account of Stalin's 1 June telegram, which had so exercised the Political Bureau, and learned that M. N. Roy had left and that Borodin wished to depart. The meeting resolved to call a plenum of the Central Executive Committee within one month to consider the recommendations of the Political Council praesidium – clearly implying separation of communists from the Kuomintang – and before that date entrusting Party headquarters to deal with recalcitrant members. The conferees also agreed that the Political Council should select the delegate to go to Moscow, and it passed resolutions ordering the protection of workers and farmers, as well as the personal freedom of Communist Party members. The decisions were to be kept secret from the rank and file.[257] Thus it appears that at this point the party's civilian leaders planned to postpone the separation and then to take the step peacefully. One element at stake was the hoped for continuation of Russian aid. But on that very day, General Ho Chien's troops were searching the streets for communists,

256 USDS 893.00/9165/9194/9213, telegrams from Peking to secretary of state transmitting information from Hankow and Nanking of 5, 11 and 13 July; and George Sokolsky on the Kuomintang, in *The China Yearbook, 1928*, 1371, for an account of the private meetings, for which T.V. Soong probably was the source.

257 Chiang Yung-ching, *Borodin*, 401–2, and *TJK*, 736–40, citing minutes.

including two Kuomintang Central Committee members, Wu Yü-chang and T'an P'ing-shan, both of whom had disappeared.

They may have gone into hiding along with many other prominent Chinese communists in the Wuhan cities as a result of decisions taken at a meeting on 13 July in response to urgent instructions from the Comintern. Besides blaming the Chinese Communist Party for its opportunistic mistakes, and ordering Borodin back to Russia, the Comintern demanded a proclamation demonstratively announcing the withdrawal of communists from the government. It forbade them, however, to withdraw from the Kuomintang. Even if they were expelled, they should secretly work with the Kuomintang's lower level masses to create resistance to decisions of the leadership and demands for changes in that party's leading organs. On this foundation, communists should then prepare to call a Kuomintang congress.[258] This duplicity was too much for Ch'en Tu-hsiu, the founder of the Chinese Communist Party and its secretary-general, who had often advocated withdrawal from the Kuomintang but always had been over-ruled. Now he resigned his position. The Communist Party's declaration of 13 July denounced the Nationalist government for failing to protect the workers and peasants but actually encouraging reaction, and it announced that T'an P'ing-shan and Su Chao-cheng had resigned their positions. Yet it also stated that communists were neither withdrawing from the Kuomintang nor abandoning the policy of cooperation with it. Borodin then left for a recuperative rest at a mountain resort near Kiukiang. It was just after his wife had been freed from the Peking prison. Accompanying him was the Russian speaking Ch'ü Ch'iu-pai, who was soon to become the party's new secretary-general, at the age of 28.[259]

Separation of the two parties now became a reality. On 16 July, the day the Kuomintang Central Committee published its resolutions restricting communists but ordering their personal protection and no harm to the workers' and farmers' movements, the Communist Party statement of 13 July appeared on posters and in the press. This stimulated the praesidium of the Political Council to publish its account of Stalin's menacing

258 Quoted by *TJK*, 735-6, from Hua Kang's *History of the Chinese Communist Party during the great revolution of 1925-1927*. Isaacs, *The tragedy of the Chinese revolution*, 266-7, quotes 'Resolution of the E.C.C.I. on the present situation of the Chinese revolution,' from *Imprecor*, 28 July, which carries the instructions, but he gives 14 July as its date.
259 The proclamation was reprinted in *Kuo-wen chou-pao*, 4. no. 29 (21 July 1927), and is partially translated in T.C. Woo, *The Kuomintang and the future of the Chinese revolution*, 182. Ch'en Tu-hsiu's position is stated in his 'A letter to all comrades of the Party', 323-33. Vishnyakova-Akimova gives a guarded account of the meeting, presumably based on Russian archives. *Two Years*, 331. Li, *A Biography of Ch'ü Ch'iu-pai*, 221-2. The 13 July 'Manifesto of the Central Committee of the CCP' is translated in Hyobom Pak, *Documents of the Chinese Communist Party, 1927-1930*, 21-9.

telegram, together with a denunciation of communists for withdrawing from the government while planning to stay within the Kuomintang. This amounted to destroying the Kuomintang's policy of admitting communists, the praesidium charged. It ordered all dual party members to resign from one party or the other. Each side issued more excoriating documents. But some leftist Kuomintang leaders deplored the split. Teng Yen-ta issued a condemnation and resigned his positions as head of the National Revolutionary Army's Political Department and of the Kuomintang Farmers Bureau. He had already disappeared and soon was on his way to Russia. Mme Sun Yat-sen issued a statement condemning the anti-revolutionary course on which her colleagues had embarked, and left for Kuling, and later for Shanghai and Russia. Both statements emphasized what was now the underlying and central issue – social revolution. They charged that Wuhan's compromising leaders had turned against it.[260] Eugene Chen also was preparing to leave.

Counter-revolution now moved into the leftist capital. The Wuhan cities went under martial law, troops seized labour union headquarters again, as well as other suspected communist strongholds, and executed many hapless militants. For the communist leaders there seemed to be only two options: flight or revolt. The well-known communists in the Wuhan area went underground or fled to northern Kiangsi, to which province Chang Fa-k'uei's armies were being transferred. There were many communist officers among his forces. By the last week in July, with the inter-party collaboration policy wrecked upon the rocks of class struggle, the Communist Party's core leadership was already planning revolts, now with Comintern encouragement.

Michael Borodin's departure from Hankow symbolized the end of Russia's effort to foster revolution in China through the Nationalist Party – as the first stage. On the afternoon of 27 July, still suffering from fever, Borodin left for Chengchow with a small party of Russian advisers and bodyguards, the two sons of Eugene Chen and an American journalist, Anna Louise Strong, on a train loaded with trucks and heavy-duty touring cars, a great quantity of petrol, and baggage, for a long and uncertain journey homeward. The most important remaining officials in Wuhan saw him off with great courtesy, and Wang Ching-wei presented

---

260 A variety of the documents are in *Kuo-wen chou-pao*, as cited above, and a few are in *KMWH*, 16. 2828–40. Teng Yen-ta's statement is briefed in USDS 893.00/9216, transmitting Lockhart's telegram of 15 July. Chiang Yung-ching, *Borodin*, 409, gives evidence that Teng was in Chengchow by 18 July. Mme Sun's statement is reprinted in T. C. Woo, *The Kuomintang*, 270–3. General accounts of the split, based on KMT documents, are in Chiang, *Borodin*, 401–12, and *TJK*, 741–3. Isaacs, *The tragedy of the Chinese revolution*, devotes a chapter to 'Wuhan: the debacle'.

him with a testamentary letter addressed to the 'Comrades of the Central Politburo of the Communist Party of Soviet Russia.' This expressed the undying gratitude of the Chinese comrades for Borodin's brilliant achievements as adviser to the Kuomintang. The letter also announced that the Kuomintang hoped in the nearest future to send important comrades to Russia to discuss ways of uniting the two countries. Methods of cooperation between the Kuomintang and the Chinese Communist Party still awaited instruction, but Wang professed confidence that Borodin could give a thorough account of the complexities of this matter. The letter closed 'With Revolutionary Greetings', and was subscribed as from the praesidium of the Kuomintang Political Council.[261]

In Chengchow, Borodin received courteous attention from Feng Yü-hsiang, who ordered that he be protected *en route*, and then he travelled westward by rail, taking with him some of General Feng's Russian advisers who knew the route. At the end of the Lunghai Railway, the party loaded its five trucks and five touring cars for the precarious trip west and north through Shensi and Kansu to Ninghsia city, and thence across the Gobi desert to Ulan-Bator, where they arrived in mid September. After a long rest Borodin flew to Verkhne-Udinsk, where he boarded the express train for Moscow. He arrived there on 6 October, at the age of 43.[262]

The two nationalistic parties with their conflicting social philosophies now followed separate ways – the Communists into revolt and the Nationalists into uneasy reconciliation among the various factions. It was not easy for politicians, labour leaders, propagandists and military commanders, who had called each other 'comrade' and worked together for years to rescue China from imperialism and militarism, to disengage. Some simply withdrew, but most of the activists went in one direction or the other. The breach set the main course of Chinese political life for decades thereafter.

---

261 Wang's draft, dated 25 July 1927, is in the Kuomintang Archives, 445/35.
262 An account of the trip is in Strong, *China's millions*. Arrival date from *Pravda*, 7 Oct. 1927. Borodin was born 9 July 1884. In Moscow he held such posts as deputy people's commissar for labour, deputy to the head of Tass, manager of the paper industry and, beginning in 1932, editor of the English language *Moscow news*. Louis Fischer interviewed him 10 times between 26 Feb. and 29 June 1929, according to his *Men and politics: an autobiography*, 138. Fischer recounts, indirectly, what Borodin told him about the Chinese revolution in one chapter of *The Soviets in world affairs*, 2. 632–79. Borodin was arrested in 1949, along with many other Jewish intellectuals, and sent to a prison camp, where he died in 1951 at about the age of 67. *New York Times*, 3 Sept. 1953 and 1 July 1964. More recently, Borodin's reputation has been rehabilitated in the USSR and there are scholarly publications concerning his contributions to the Chinese revolution.

THE COMMUNISTS TURN TO REBELLION

Beginnings of communist revolt

During the latter half of July the Chinese Communist leadership debated plans for a general uprising in four provinces, with encouragement from a newly arrived Comintern delegate, Besso Lominadze, and advice from General Bluykher and some of his staff. An important element of the plan was to seize control of elements in Chang Fa-k'uei's Second Front Army that had moved into northern Kiangsi and in which there were a number of communist commanders and many communist political workers. Details for the revolt were worked out by a group of communists in Nanchang and Kiukiang, and discussed on 26 July in Hankow at a meeting of available members of the party's Central Standing Committee – Ch'ü Ch'iu-pai, who had returned with the plan, Li Wei-han, Chang T'ai-lei and Chang Kuo-t'ao. Lominadze and Bluykher attended together with several other Russians. The plotters hoped that Chang Fa-k'uei could be persuaded to join and lead his troops back to Kwangtung, but if not, then communists would stage a revolt and take over his troops anyway. Moscow had been informed, but at this meeting the Comintern representative reported telegraphic instructions that no Russians were to participate in the uprising, and he also said that no funds were available. Bluykher, who had held a discussion with General Chang only the day before, predicted that should he join the insurrection, there might be 30,000 troops, which would be plenty to fight through to eastern Kwangtung, at which time the communists could cut Chang out; but if the communists split his forces at Nanchang, the uprising would only gain from 5,000 to 8,000 troops. A Moscow telegram cautioned against the uprising unless victory was assured. Therefore Lominadze sent Chang Kuo-t'ao that very night to Nanchang to inform the plotters of Comintern's ambiguous instructions.[263]

263 This description of the Nanchang Uprising is based primarily on accounts by planners and participants in the revolt, Chang T'ai-lei, Li Li-san, Chou I-ch'ün, and Chang Kuo-t'ao, written between early Oct. and early Nov. 1927, shortly after the defeat, and published in the Chinese Communist Party's new journal, *Chung-yang t'ung-hsun* (Central newsletter), 30 Oct. and 30 Nov. They are translated in C. Martin Wilbur, 'The ashes of defeat', *CQ*, 18 (April–June 1964) 3–54. The same documents and some Kuomintang sources are the basis for Wang Chien-min's excellent account in *Chung-kuo kung-ch'antang shih-kao*, 1. 534–52. He gives useful order of battle tables. Another valuable reconstruction based on these primary sources and on the memoirs of Chang Kuo-t'ao and Kung Ch'u, is Hsiao Tso-liang, 'From Nanchang to Swatow' in his *Chinese communism in 1927: city vs. countryside*, 81–104. Chang Kuo-t'ao gives an emotional reminiscent account in *The rise of the Chinese Communist Party*, 1. 672–7, and 2. 3–55, based in part on his own contemporary reports. See also, Harrison, *The long march to power*, 120–3, and Jacques Guillermaz, *A history of the Chinese Communist Party, 1921–1949*, 150–6.

The main architects of the Nanchang uprising were T'an P'ing-shan, Teng Chung-hsia, Yun Tai-ying, Li Li-san, P'eng P'ai, Yeh T'ing, and later Chou En-lai, who was sent by the Centre to supervise. The Chinese Communist Party celebrates 1 August, when the uprising broke out, as the founding date of the Red Army. Several of the commanders who participated went on to illustrious careers in that army – Yeh T'ing, Ho Lung, Liu Po-ch'eng, Chu Te, Nieh Jung-chen, Lo Jui-ch'ing, Ch'en Yi, Hsiao K'o and Lin Piao.[264] Planning had gone so far when Chang Kuo-t'ao arrived and tried to stop the action that 'the arrow was on the bowstring and had to be shot'. General Yeh T'ing, commanding the 24th Division, was prepared to take over the Eleventh Corps, while General Ho Lung, commander of the Twentieth Corps and not yet a member of the Communist Party, was eager to take action in the expectation of re-placing Chang Fa-k'uei, who was just then in conference with Wang Ching-wei, T'ang Sheng-chih, Chu P'ei-te, Sun Fo, and other generals and notables in the mountain resort of Lu-shan.[265]

The uprising was a quick success militarily. Troops under Generals Yeh and Ho disarmed opposing units in the city before daybreak, and Chu Te brought in the remnants of his training regiment to form the cadre of a new division. The conspirators got quantities of arms and ammunition, and a great deal of cash and banknotes from the city's banks and the provincial treasury. Political preparations had not been well worked out, however. Still pretending to be acting under the Kuomintang banner, the leadership announced a 31 member Central Revolutionary Committee of the Kuomintang, naming such absent leaders as Teng Yen-ta, Mme Sun Yat-sen and Mme Liao Chung-k'ai (Ho Hsiang-ning), Eugene Chen, Chang Fa-k'uei and two of his displaced corps commanders, and 17 communists. The only present members of the 'praesidium' were T'an P'ing-shan, Ho Lung, Kuo Mo-jo, and Yun Tai-ying, and all the various named committees were headed by communists, except for Ho Lung and Kuo Mo-jo, who reportedly joined the party *en route*.[266] In setting up a Kuomintang Revolutionary Committee, the leaders claimed legitimacy, but, by their own later admission, they had no firm policies

264 Klein and Clark, *Biographic dictionary*, 1066, lists 40 known participants in the planning or action. Chu Te gave a reminiscent account to Agnes Smedley, published in *The great road*, 200-9.
265 An interesting account of how the news of the Uprising was reported to this conference, of Chang Fa-k'uei's unsuccessful effort to get to Nanchang, and of Wang Ching-wei's outrage at the event, is given in Wang's report on 5 August to the Wuhan Kuomintang Central Standing Committee meeting, reprinted from the minutes held in the Kuomin-tang Archives, in *Kung-fei huo-kuo shih-liao hui-pien* (A compilation of documents on the communist bandits' destruction of the nation) 1. 485-8.
266 Wilbur, 'The ashes of defeat', 31.

on such issues as land revolution, attitudes towards local power-holders, and methods of financing, and they even disputed whether to head for Canton or the East River district of Kwangtung, and about the route of march.

The armies started marching south on the fourth in blistering heat, but lost much equipment along the way. Troop strength dwindled through desertion, dysentery and battle casualties. General Ts'ai T'ing-k'ai escaped with his 10th Division to Chekiang, leaving only the 24th and 25th Divisions of the Eleventh Corps. After suffering serious casualties in battles near Jui-chin and Hui-ch'ang, the marchers were able to leave their seriously wounded in the care of a British missionary hospital at Ting-chou in western Fukien.[267] The army found no support along the way, for the farmers' movement scarcely existed in mountainous eastern Kiangsi and Fukien. Arriving along the Fukien-Kwangtung border after more than a month of marching, the expedition briefly held Chao-chou and Swatow (24–30 September), but found no mass support where only a year before the Hong Kong strike and boycott movement had been very active. By the end of September the scattered units had been completely defeated. Some of the remnants of the 24th Division and of the Twentieth Corps made their way to Lu-feng, on the coast, where the peasant movement organized by P'eng P'ai still had strength; but there Ho Lung's divisional commanders turned over to the enemy side. Many of the communist leaders then escaped in small boats to Hong Kong, and some took ship for Shanghai. The remnants of the 25th Division, commanded by Chou Shih-ti, and the troops under Chu Te, which had served as a rearguard, fled to the mountains. Later Chou and Chu led their force across southern Kiangsi and then split up, Chu Te leading his 600 or so poorly armed men to a junction with Mao Tse-tung in southern Hunan in the spring of 1928.[268]

An immediate result of the Nanchang uprising was the wide-scale arrest of suspected communists in Kiukiang and the Wuhan area and many executions. However, most of the leading communists who were not campaigning southwards were already in hiding and escaped this purge. They were secretly planning to stage a series of rural revolts during the autumn harvest season – normally a time of great tension in the villages when rents had to be paid.

---

267 Smedley, *The great road*, 205. In recalling this in 1937, Chu Te seemed still impressed that 'Dr Nelson Fu and the British doctors in that foreign hospital took charge of our wounded men!'
268 Klein and Clark, *Biographic dictionary*, 247.

Autumn harvest revolts

On orders from the Comintern, Besso Lominadze called a conference of available members of the party's Central Committee on 7 August to reorganize the leadership structure, repudiate past errors – they were to be blamed upon Chinese rather than Comintern strategists – and to ratify a new policy line. Some 22 Chinese communists met for one day in Wuhan under the 'guidance' of Lominadze; 15 of these were members or alternates of the Central Committee, less than half the total number. They elected a new provisional politburo, headed by Ch'ü Ch'iu-pai, to manage party affairs until a new congress convened. The party was now to be rigidly centralized and secret.[269] The August 7th conferees also issued four documents. One, which reportedly was dictated by Lominadze, censured the past Chinese leadership for opportunism, naming particularly, T'an P'ing-shan, but also the party patriarch, Ch'en Tu-hsiu. The other documents laid down an insurrectionist line: the Communist Party would seek to overthrow both the Wuhan and the Nanking regimes, and would organize revolts in the provinces wherever objective situations permitted, looking towards the future establishment of soviets. The revolts were to be conducted under the banner of the 'revolutionary left Kuomintang'.[270]

While the original plan called for rural revolts in Hupei, Hunan, Kiangsi and Kwangtung during the autumn harvest season, the exodus of most of the Kiangsi leaders on the march south after the Nanchang Uprising made another revolt in that province impossible. The new Politburo dispatched Chang T'ai-lei to be in command in Kwangtung as

269 These interpretations are based on the careful study by Bernadette Li, 'A biography of Ch'ü Ch'iu-pai', 232–48. Dr Li identified 14 participants and named the following as the new Politburo: Ch'ü, Hsiang Chung-fa, Li Wei-han, Lo I-nung, P'eng P'ai (in absentia), Su Chao-cheng, and Ts'ai Ho-sen; with four alternates, Chang Kuo-t'ao (in absentia), Chang T'ai-lei, Mao Tse-tung, and P'eng Kung-ta. Hsiao Tso-liang gives a different list based on the memoirs of Chang Kuo-t'ao, who did not attend, and locates the meeting in Kiukiang. Hsiao, *Chinese communism in 1927*, 39–46. Wang Chien-min, *Chung-kuo Kung-ch'an-tang*, 1. 503, and Harrison, *The long march to power*, 123, conclude that Hankow was the meeting site.

270 Documents from the August 7th Conference were published in *Chung-yang t'ung-hsun*, no. 2, 23 Aug. 1927. Some have been reprinted or abstracted in Wang, *Chung-kuo Kung-ch'an-tang*, 1. 504–28 and in *Kung-fei huo-kuo shih-liao hui-pien*, 1. 445–84 (both sanitized to remove references to Chiang Kai-shek). The 'Resolution on the political tasks and tactics of the Chinese Communist Party' is translated in Pak, *Documents*, 45–57, while the 'Circular letter from the conference to all party members' and the resolutions are abstracted in Brandt, Schwartz, and Fairbank, *A documentary history*, 102–23.

Ch'ü Ch'iu-pai, who became head of the Politburo as a result of this conference, made a long report in Moscow about a year later concerning the problems of the Chinese Communist Party in the period leading up to the conference and during his time of leadership. The second half of his report is translated by Man Kwok–chuen and published in *Chinese studies in history*, 5. 1 (Fall 1971) 4–72.

secretary of the Communist Party Southern Bureau and the Provincial Committee. They divided Hupei into seven districts and Hunan into three, hoping to mount extensive peasant revolts in those provinces, but because of a shortage of guiding personnel the theatre was narrowed to the part of Hupei south of Wuhan and the Hunan region east of Changsha. The plotters put Mao Tse-tung in charge of the Hunan operation, to work together with the provincial secretary, P'eng Kung-ta. The provincial secretary for Hupei, Lo I-nung, was involved in the planning, but not the execution of the South Hupei operation, which was directed by a hastily organized special committee. The date set for the two-province insurrection to burst out was 10 September.[271]

Peasant uprisings were to carry through a land revolution, overthrow the Wuhan government and T'ang Sheng-chih's regime, and lead to a people's government. The insurrection must be carefully prepared in its organizational, technical and political aspects, and once launched must never flinch or retreat. Peasants must constitute the main force, though existing troop units and bandit gangs, if converted to the revolutionary cause, could be used as auxiliaries. 'Land to the tillers!', 'Resistance to taxes and rent!', 'Confiscate the land of large and middle landlords!', and 'Exterminate local bullies, evil gentry, and all counter-revolutionaries!' – such were the slogans that should arouse the rural masses. Slaughter of class enemies and local officials would commit the peasantry to a broad rural revolt and to the capture of county seats. Then would follow insurrection in Wuhan and Changsha. So theorized the fugitive Politburo members. Implementation was more difficult.

In southern Hupei the revolt started prematurely with a train robbery on the night of 8 September in which the special committee captured a shipment of money and a few arms. But when it came to attacking two walled and well-defended county seats, as called for in the plan, the local communist leaders backed off, for they lacked the military capability to do

---

271 Basic information on the uprisings is in *Chung-yang t'ung-hsun*, nos. 4–7 and 11, dated 30 Aug. 12, 20 and 30 Sept., 30 Oct., and probably late Nov. 1927. Selected documents from this source are translated in Pak, *Documents*, no. 9 (pp. 59–66) 'Resolution on the plan for insurrection in Hunan and Hupei'; nos. 12–18 (pp. 87–113) on Hunan; nos. 30–32 (pp. 201–15) on Hupei; and no. 23 (pp. 133–45), a post-mortem. Abstracts of the 'Resolution on the plan' and some other items are in Wang Chien-min *Chung-kuo Kung-ch'an-tang*, 1. 533–60; and that resolution and the 'Resolution on political discipline', of 14 Nov. 1927, in which blame for failure was passed out, are translated in Kuo, *Analytical history*, 1. 462–7. The extensive 'Report on the Autumn Harvest Revolt in Hupei', in *Chung-yang t'ung-hsun*, no. 11, was found in corrupt form in Japan, and is translated into Japanese by Taicho Mikami, Tadao Ishikawa and Minoru Shabata, and published by Kansai University Institute of Oriental and Occidental Studies, Osaka, 1961.

Scholarly reconstructions are Roy Hofheinz, Jr. 'The Autumn Harvest Uprising', *CQ*, 32 (Oct.–Dec. 1967) 37–87 with maps; Hsiao, *Chinese communism in 1927*, 39–80, with maps; and Li, 'A biography of Ch'ü Ch'iu-pai', 249–60.

so with their poorly armed and untrained peasant force. Central had forbidden the special committee to contact military units still having some communist officers. This was to be a peasant movement. Thus, the committee was reduced to setting up a revolutionary government in a small town in the mountains on 12 September. Only shortly afterwards they began a move to a market town, Hsin-tien, expecting to get support from a local self-defence force, a group of ex-bandits with 38 rifles, for a joint attack on another county seat. If this proved impossible, then a move towards Yo-chow, across the provincial border, might link them with the uprising in eastern Hunan. Unfortunately for the committee, the leader of the self-defence force, with whom they had been negotiating and who had participated in the train robbery, betrayed them. He disarmed their small force, though allowing the committee members to escape. Thus collapsed the insurrection in south Hupei, after less than 10 days of scattered rioting and killings.[272]

The revolt in Hunan, which Mao Tse-tung was charged with directing, was initially more successful, but also ended in failure. During the organizing stage Mao was in conflict with the Politburo members in Wuhan over several issues. He sensed that without organized military units a revolt could not be sustained, whether or not the troops were called auxiliaries. He also insisted that the available leadership should not be spread too thinly and, in defiance of Central, he restricted his efforts to the Hsiang River counties near Changsha. He also wished the uprising to be fought under the communist banner, not that of the Kuomintang, and he favoured complete land confiscation and the immediate establishment of soviets. Central criticized Mao severely and sent a Russian adviser to Changsha to assist in the directing; it is from reports of this Comrade Ma K'e-fu that some useful information on the uprising and on Mao's 'mistakes' is available.[273]

By the first week in September there were four military units that Mao could throw into the battle. The first was an under-strength regiment made up of fugitives from Chang Fa-k'uei's guards, which had missed the Nanchang Uprising and become depleted through desertions. Its commander and assistant commander were communists, and it was lodged at Hsiu-shui in Kiangsi near the Hunan border. The second was a 'rag-tag' unit made up of deserters from Hsia Tou-yin's force. It was headed by a

272 Hofheinz, 'The Autumn Harvest Uprising', 51-7; Hsiao, *Chinese communism in 1927*, 62-7.
273 An authoritative discussion of Mao's conflict with the Politburo is in Stuart R. Schram, 'On the nature of Mao Tse-tung's "deviation" in 1927', *CQ*, 18 (April-June 1964) 55-66, based on contemporary Russian and Chinese communist documents. The disagreements are also discussed in Hofheinz, 'The Autumn Harvest Uprising', 61-6, and Hsiao, *Chinese communism in 1927*, 46-53.

former bandit and had been in conflict with the so-called first regiment, which had driven it out of Hsiu-shui. The third unit, called the P'ing-chiang–Liu-yang Self-Defence Force, was made up partly of peasants, who had attempted to storm Changsha at the end of May, and partly of local corps and bandits. A graduate of the Wuhan branch of the National-ist Military Academy commanded this unit, which was based in the mountains east of Changsha. The backbone of the fourth regiment, the P'ing-hsiang–Li-ling Self-Defence Force, consisted of unemployed miners from An-yuan, a very militant group under communist leadership. The Hunan Provincial Committee designated these four 'regiments' – scattered in three localities across 150 kilometres, and two of them hostile to each other – as the First Division of the First Army of the Chinese Workers' and Peasants' Revolutionary Army, and gave them communist flags.[274]

The final battle plan called for the first two regiments to attack P'ing-chiang, to the north-east of Changsha, and for the other two to attack Liu-yang, directly east of the provincial capital. Preliminary riots on or before 11 September in the countryside around Changsha were to distract attention from these attacks on walled towns, and guerrilla forces were supposed to harass troops going out to oppose the attackers. The railways leading to Changsha should be cut north and south. After P'ing-chiang and Liu-yang had been captured, all forces would descend on Changsha on the 15th, and the city would respond with a mass uprising from within. However, the Communist Party members who would carry through this plan had been much reduced from the days before the May Twenty-First Incident – from about 20,000 to 5,000 for the province, with only about 1,000 of these in Changsha. Furthermore, the attacking units had relatively few arms.

The An-yuan fourth regiment began its march on schedule on 10 September. Unable to capture P'ing-hsiang, it went on to take Li-ling, a county seat on the railway leading to Changsha, on the 12th. It held the city for a little more than a day, setting up a revolutionary committee and announcing a land confiscation programme. A communist-led peasant unit with only 60 rifles was able to capture Chu-chow, only 50 kilometres from Changsha, throwing the provincial capital into panic on the 13th. According to Comrade Ma, in this area thousands of peasants armed with hand weapons entered the fray and many rifles were captured. Farther

274 This account is based upon Hofheinz and Hsiao, cited, and an interesting reconstruction of Mao's role in Stuart R. Schram, *Political leaders of the twentieth century: Mao Tse-tung*, 120–5. All are based primarily on the *Chung-yang t'ung-hsun* documents, but differ con-siderably in detail.

north, however, the two regiments that were supposed to take P'ing-chiang actually fought each other, and the remnants of the first regiment retreated to the mountains of Kiangsi on the 15th. In the face of this disaster, the Hunan Provincial Committee called off the uprising scheduled for Changsha that day. The third regiment having lost its right flank through the betrayal to its north, gave up its attack on Liu-yang just before the fourth regiment managed to capture the city on the night of the 16th. The next day this best of the communists' regiments was surrounded and almost totally destroyed, and the largely peasant force, the third regiment, met the same fate. 'Comrade Ma' denounced the leadership for cowardice and demanded the attacks be renewed, but to no avail.

Mao Tse-tung had a narrow escape while moving between units in Liu-yang county. He was captured by *min t'uan* and probably would have been shot had he not successfully fled and hid. The exact day on which this happened, and how long Mao was a captive, are not clear, but after his escape he made his way on foot to a mountain town where remnants of the third regiment had gathered and where he ordered the rest of the first regiment to assemble. Overcoming opposition, Mao persuaded the battered force of soldiers, miners, peasants and bandits to retreat to a mountain fastness on the Hunan-Kiangsi border, the famous bandit bastion, Ching-kang-shan.[275] There he took the first step on his long march to power. He did not learn until much later of his dismissal from the Politburo and the punishment meted out to other local communist leaders, whom the Politburo blamed for the Hunan failure.

In Kwangtung, the third area where autumn harvest revolts were ordered, there existed ill-equipped peasant forces in the south-eastern coastal counties of Hai-feng and Lu-feng, where P'eng P'ai had once been able to create a strong movement. In reaction to Li Chi-shen's anti-communist coup of mid April, a communist-led band had succeeded in capturing Hai-feng city on 1 May, executing most of the officials and other counter-revolutionaries who had not escaped. This force was driven out after 10 days, but insurgent units in the hinterland conducted sporadic raids and peasants defied their landlords where possible. On 22 August, heartened by the news that the forces of Yeh T'ing and Ho Lung were approaching, the Communist Party's Kwangtung Committee planned an insurrection timed for their arrival. Communist-led peasant corps were able to capture Lu-feng city on 8 September and Hai-feng on the 17th. Again they evacuated the cities after a period of looting and killing, and regrouped in a prepared mountain base. As the Yeh-Ho

275 In 1936, Mao gave Edgar Snow a vivid account of his escape, immortalized in *Red star over China*.

armies approached Swatow, peasants briefly captured two other county seats, Ch'ao-yang and Chieh-yang, but there was very little coordination between the local forces and the oncoming troops. With the help of a battalion of Yeh T'ing's troops, peasants fought a battle for P'u-ning city, but the battalion commander, a communist, would not permit the peasant force into the city for fear of excessive slaying. With the defeat at Swatow at the end of September, communist hopes of establishing a worker and peasant government in eastern Kwangtung faded temporarily.[276]

In the face of all these defeats, and under increasing danger of being discovered in Wuhan, Ch'ü Ch'iu-pai and some other members of the Politburo made their way in disguise to Shanghai where they re-established the secret headquarters of the Chinese Communist Party about the first of October 1927.

Attempts to unify the Kuomintang leadership

Conciliatory negotiations between the three main factions of the Kuomintang began as soon as the communist leaders had been expelled from Wuhan. The Shanghai faction was made up of a group of prestigious revolutionary veterans united in their opposition to the results of Sun Yat-sen's Russian orientation and admission of communists into the Kuomintang. Some, but not all of this group, had met in the Western Hills outside Peking in November 1925, where they strongly denounced the Communist Party's penetration of the Kuomintang, demanded the dismissal of Borodin, and censured Wang Ching-wei. This dissident group maintained the old Kuomintang headquarters in Shanghai as the party's true centre, and had even held a separate Second Kuomintang Congress in March 1926. A number of the Shanghai leaders cooperated with Chiang Kai-shek and his followers from Nanchang in the anti-communist action in the spring of 1927 and helped in the formation of the Nanking government in April but the group still retained their central party headquarters in Shanghai. A number of them nursed the grievance of having been 'expelled' from the Kuomintang by the Canton leadership, some of whom were now heading the Nanking faction. By late July the Wuhan group had made its break with the Chinese Communist Party and also had lost its most outspokenly radical – and idealistic – members. Reconciliation was not to be easy, because the Wuhan group at its Third

276 Hofheinz, *The broken wave*, 239–48; Eto, 'Hai-lu-feng – the first Chinese soviet government,' II, *CQ*, 9 (Jan.–March 1962) 165–70; and Wilbur, 'The ashes of defeat', 21, 36 and 43.

CEC Plenum in March 1927 had attempted to reduce Chiang Kai-shek's stature and authority, while after Wang Ching-wei's return to China, the Wuhan and Nanking factions had indulged in mutual public denunciations. Each claimed to be the true centre of party authority.

By August, military reverses suffered by the Nanking group and communist-led insurrections in territories claimed by the Wuhan group spurred on the negotiations. Nanking had weakened its northern front to send troops against Wuhan and this led to a recovery by the northern military coalition. Chang Tsung-ch'ang recaptured Hsu-chow on 25 July, and Sun Ch'uan-fang launched a drive towards his old base in the Yangtze delta. In mid to late July Feng Yü-hsiang telegraphed both Nanking and Wuhan urging reconciliation but neither side trusted him, and they were exchanging telegrams and emissaries of their own in early August.[277]

Within the Nanking group there was conflict between the Kwangsi clique, headed by Li Tsung-jen and Pai Ch'ung-hsi, and Chiang's Whampoa adherents. Even Ho Ying-ch'in's support for Chiang was uncertain. It seems the commander-in-chief had many political enemies because of his domineering ways, and that he was an obstacle to reconciliation. Now Chiang's reverses on the northern front, and the Nanking government's financial difficulties in spite of extortionate fund-raising in Shanghai, weakened his prestige. At a meeting of the Military Council at Nanking on 12 August, Chiang stated his intention to resign as commander-in-chief and to leave the defence of the capital to the other generals. When they raised no objection, an intolerable insult, he departed for Shanghai, and was soon followed by Chang Ching-chiang, Hu Han-min, Ts'ai Yuan-p'ei, Wu Chih-hui, and Li Shih-tseng, to try to dissuade him. Chiang's retirement statement published on 13 August, emphasized his sole desire to serve the party; if his retirement would promote unity, he was happy to retire. He reviewed the party's history, Sun Yat-sen's decision to ally with Russia and admit the communists, and justified his own role in expelling the communists for their intrigues within the Kuomintang. He urged his comrades to come together at Nanking and then to complete the Northern Expedition.[278]

After Chiang's departure, emissaries from the two sides met at Lu-

---

277 The complicated process of unification is explored by Professor Li Yun-han on the basis of Kuomintang archival material in his *TJK*, 756-812. *KMWH*, 17. 3104-09, for telegrams exchanged by Nanking and Hankow from 8 Aug. to 20 Sept.

278 There are differing interpretations of Chiang's retirement at this critical moment. His retirement statement is in *KMWH*, 15. 2567-73, and *The China Yearbook 1928*, 1380-5. On extortionate fund-raising by Chiang's agents, see the well-documented study by Parks M. Coble, Jr., 'The Kuomintang regime and the Shanghai capitalists, 1927-29', *CQ*, 77 (March 1979) 1-24, esp. pp. 7-12. See also Dr Coble's book on the same subject.

shan to discuss terms of reconciliation and decided that on 15 September the Central Executive and Central Supervisory Committees should meet in Nanking to settle differences. But before this could happen, Nanking itself was in danger of being captured by the revived forces of Sun Ch'uan-fang, which succeeded in crossing the Yangtze just 15 miles east of the city and had cut the railway leading to Shanghai. This was on 26 August, at a time when elements of Li Tsung-jen's old Seventh Corps and of Ho Ying-ch'in's old First Corps were holding the city, though the two commanders were at odds. Furthermore, T'ang Sheng-chih had sent two corps under Ho Chien and Liu Hsing towards Nanking in coordination with Sun's drive. In this critical situation, Generals Li and Ho set aside their differences and sent their forces into battle, assisted by Pai Ch'ung-hsi and all other available troops. The Nationalists finally defeated the northern invaders in a six-day, seesaw battle which ended on 31 August. Some 30,000 of Sun's troops, their retreat cut off by the Nationalist navy, were taken prisoner, along with a mountain of arms. The Lung-t'an battle was one of the key engagements of the entire campaign. It saved Nanking and the rich delta region, and made possible the reconstitution of the Nationalist government.[279] The First Army then drove Sun's shattered remnants back up the Tientsin–Pukow Railway towards Hsu-chow.

T'an Yen-k'ai and Sun Fo, representing the Wuhan faction, had gone to Nanking for preliminary discussions of party unification, and in early September, with Nanking saved, Wang Ching-wei and most of the other Wuhan leaders followed them to negotiate with their recent rivals. T'ang Sheng-chih, though already in Anking supervising Wuhan's 'Eastern Expedition', declined to come. During talks in Nanking and Shanghai between 5 and 12 September the three factions worked out an ingenious compromise which gave 'face' to all. They would create a Special Central Committee to manage party affairs, to reconstruct the national government and the Military Council, and to prepare for and call the Third Party Congress in January 1928. The congress would then start the party on a new course. Even the method for holding election of delegates to the congress was specified. Thus the Special Central Committee would replace the Central Executive Committees that had been elected at the two rival Second Congresses. In constituting the committee, each faction nominated six representatives and three alternates, and this group was then to elect 14 most prestigious political and military persons – Wang Ching-wei, Hu Han-min, Chang Chi, Wu Chih-hui, Tai Chi-t'ao, Chang

279 *PFCS*, 3. 851–916; *Kuo-min Ko-ming Chün Tung-lu-chün chan-shih chi-lueh*, 94–105; Jordan, *The Northern Expedition*, 138–41. In interviews, Generals Li and Pai remembered the Lung-t'an battle as crucial to the success of the Northern Expedition.

Ching-chiang, Chiang Kai-shek, T'ang Sheng-chih, Feng Yü-hsiang, Yen Hsi-shan, Yang Shu-chuang, Li Chi-shen, Ho Ying-ch'in and Pai Ch'ung-hsi. Thus the Special Central Committee would have 32 members and nine alternates and would include, at least nominally, the most important military leaders. No communists were listed, of course, but the names of Soong Ch'ing-ling, Eugene Chen and even T. V. Soong, were omitted as well.[280]

On 13 September, however, Wang Ching-wei resigned and departed for Kiukiang with some of his close followers. He was dissatisfied that his proposal to call a Fourth Plenum of the Central Executive Committee had been rejected by those who refused to accept the validity of the Third Plenum that had met in Hankow the previous March. Wang professed to consider the Special Central Committee illegal. He followed Chinese practice by issuing a formalistic resignation statement of repentence for his past errors.[281] The other leaders went right ahead to set up the Special Central Committee in Nanking on 15 September by the agreed-upon process. They also issued a telegram rejecting Wang's resignation and requesting Hu Han-min, Wu Chih-hui and Chiang Kai-shek to resume their duties. The Special Central Committee then elected a new Government Council, with Wang Ching-wei, Hu Han-min, Li Lieh-chün, Ts'ai Yuan-p'ei, and T'an Yen-k'ai as its Standing Committee, and appointed four ministers to carry out governmental operations.[282] Neither Wang nor Hu would serve.

The compromise settlement faced obstacles from the beginning. The new committee was vulnerable to the objection of being extra-constitutional, several former Nanking and Shanghai leaders had not been mollified, Chiang Kai-shek still absented himself, and Wang Ching-wei openly opposed it. Early in October the new Nanking group sent a delegation to try to persuade Wang and by the 10th it appeared that a new compromise had been reached. Next day, T'an Yen-k'ai, Li Tsung-jen, Ho Ying-ch'in, and Ch'eng Ch'ien in Nanking issued a circular telegram proposing that the Fourth Plenum of the Central Executive Committee convene in Nanking on 1 November. Even this concession apparently was not enough for Wang and his military prop, T'ang Sheng-chih, who demanded to be appointed commander-in-chief in place of Chiang Kai-shek. On the 21st the Wuhan Political Council, a mere shadow of its former self, issued a manifesto claiming exclusive authority over party, military and political affairs in its territory pending restoration of the

280 Names and details are in *TJK*, 766-69. Also, Kao Yin-tsu, *Chronology*, 268-9.
281 Wang's resignation telegrams are in *KMWH*, 17. 3105-6, and *China Yearbook, 1928*, 1391.
282 *The China Yearbook, 1928*, 1390-7 for lists of names.

Central Executive Committee, and T'ang Sheng-chih denounced Nanking in a circular telegram and announced plans to overthrow the usurpers there. Wang Ching-wei secretly departed for Canton via Shanghai, arriving in the old revolutionary base on 29 October.[283]

T'ang Sheng-chih's challenge probably was a response to the Nanking Government's order of 20 October for a punitive campaign against him. His alleged intrigues with Sun Ch'uan-fang and Chang Tso-lin reportedly had been discovered after the Lung-t'an battle. The campaign against him was to be commanded by Ch'eng Ch'ien, an old Hunanese rival, but the force he led included the armies of Li Tsung-jen and Chu P'ei-te, a naval flotilla, and some aircraft. T'ang, it appears, had many enemies, for Feng Yü-hsiang threatened him from the north, Li Chi-shen from the south, while T'an Yen-k'ai's field commander, Lu Ti-p'ing, sent his forces down the Yangtze from the west. Li Tsung-jen's army methodically pushed Ho Chien's forces on the north side of the Yangtze back towards Hupei, while Ch'eng Ch'ien's army on the south bank drove Liu Hsing's troops towards Kiangsi, where they faced the army of Chu P'ei-te. By early November Nanking's naval units had captured the gateway to the Wuhan cities and Lu Ti-p'ing was pressing on Yo-chow, endangering T'ang Sheng-chih's escape route to Hunan. T'ang's subordinate generals, Ho Chien, Liu Hsing, Yeh Ch'i, Chou Lan, and Li P'in-hsien, decided to retreat to their old bases in Hunan where each would fend for himself. On 12 November, T'ang announced his retirement and secretly fled on a Japanese vessel for safety in Japan.[284] The Northern Expedition military coalition was beginning to fall apart.

Wang Ching-wei returned to Canton to set up a party headquarters in opposition to the Special Central Committee in Nanking. A few leftist Central Committee members such as Ch'en Kung-po, Ku Meng-yü, Kan Nai-kuang, and Ho Hsiang-ning (Mme Liao Chung-k'ai) joined him, while his principal military supporter continued to be Chang Fa-k'uei. After the Nanchang Uprising, General Chang sent his remaining troops – three infantry divisions, an artillery regiment, and a training regiment – on a march to Shao-kuan, near the northern border of Kwangtung at the end of the rail line to Canton, while Chang returned to Canton by sea on the invitation of Li Chi-shen, arriving about 27 September. When his troops reached Shao-kuan he ordered them to Canton, where they probably were a more powerful force than Li Chi-shen commanded, for

283 *TJK*, 775–7 and *FRUS*, 1927, 2. 31–2. Kao Yin-tsu, *Chronology*, 273.
284 *TJK*, 780–2, based in part on Ch'en Hsün-cheng's account of the anti-T'ang campaign and documents in *KMWH*, 17. 2996–3064. Jordan, *The Northern Expedition*, 145. *FRUS*, 1927, 2. 36–7.

Li's troops were spread through the delta towns and he had sent a number of regiments to the Swatow area to suppress the Ho Lung–Yeh T'ing incursion. After that successful operation, General Li began bringing back his troops so that when Wang Ching-wei arrived on 29 October, the military balance between the two generals seemed approximately equal. Li Chi-shen's support for Wang was only nominal, for he had close connections with Huang Shao-hsiung of the Kwangsi clique that supported the Nanking Special Committee and its government. However, the campaign against T'ang Sheng-chih had weakened the Kwangsi clique's hold on Nanking, and the Special Committee itself was in trouble.[285]

Upon arrival, Wang Ching-wei issued a call for the Fourth Plenum of the Central Executive Committee to meet in Canton, inviting the members in Nanking and Shanghai to attend. Li Chi-shen declined to join in this call. More telegraphic negotiations with the Nanking leaders ensued, since they had previously agreed to begin the plenum on 1 November, but in Nanking. It did not meet, but on that day Wang opened central Kuomintang headquarters in Canton. The city's leftist labour movement, which had been severely repressed under Li Chi-shen's anti-communist regime, showed signs of life after Chang Fa-k'uei and Wang Ching-wei returned. Several thousand workers carrying red flags marched on Wang's home, begging him to free labour leaders who had been imprisoned, but the police dispersed them. An effort to revive the anti-British boycott may have indicated a communist initiative, for communists had dominated the old strike committee. Wang's branch political council and the provincial government arranged to disband the remaining strikers from Hong Kong with a monetary gift for each.[286] Apparently Wang's faction was not eager for labour disturbances. As it turned out, Wang's stay in Canton was only fleeting, for early in November Chiang Kai-shek reentered the political arena with a proposal for a Chiang–Wang alliance against Nanking.

General Chiang had departed for Japan on 28 September where, among other activities, he won agreement from Mme Soong that he might marry her youngest daughter, Mei-ling. This would relate him by marriage with Sun Yat-sen's widow, with T. V. Soong, and with the wife of H. H. Kung.[287] He also met privately with the Japanese prime minister, Tanaka Giichi, on 5 November. Baron Tanaka commended Chiang on his timely retirement but told him that only he could save the Chinese revolution.

285 Kao Yin-tsu, *Chronology*, 269–73. *TJK*, 777, has Wang arrive in Canton on 28 Oct.
286 Kao Yin-tsu, *Chronology*, 14 Oct., 1 and 8 Nov. Also S. Bernard Thomas, '*Proletarian hegemony' in the Chinese revolution and the Canton Commune of 1927*, 21.
287 Hollington K. Tong, *Chiang Kai-shek*, 100–1. The marriage was on 1 December, in both civil and Christian ceremonies. Later Chiang Kai-shek adopted Christianity.

He advised Chiang to consolidate the Nationalist position south of the Yangtze and not to become entangled in warlord politics of the north. Japan, the prime minister said, would assist Chiang in his anti-communist efforts so long as international considerations permitted and Japan's own interests were not sacrificed. Chiang responded that a northward drive was imperative and appealed for Japanese assistance so as to wipe out the impression that Japan was aiding Chang Tso-lin. Only thus, he said, could Japan ensure the safety of its nationals in China.[288] Each man had issued an appeal and a warning.

Chiang Kai-shek arranged for T. V. Soong to go to Canton to effect a reconciliation with Wang Ching-wei. Soong arrived on 2 November and Chiang returned to Shanghai on the 10th, when he telegraphed inviting Wang to join him for discussions, agreeing with Wang's fundamental point that the Central Executive Committee should convene to settle all problems in the party. There should be preparatory discussions in Shanghai. T'an Yen-k'ai on behalf of the Nanking Special Committee also telegraphed Wang proposing Shanghai as the site for discussions preparatory to calling the Fourth CEC Plenum.[289]

As Wang Ching-wei and Li Chi-shen prepared to depart for the meeting in Shanghai, General Li asked his associate, Huang Shao-hsiung, to come to Canton to take over control of Li's troops and Wang seconded the invitation. Chang Fa-k'uei agreed to take a trip abroad if Li would support Wang; the trip was financed by a grant of Hong Kong $50,000 from the provincial treasury – that is, by courtesy of General Li, who was happy to see Chang Fa-k'uei gone. General Chang placed his troops under command of his trusted associate, General Huang Ch'i-hsiang, and left for Hong Kong on the 14th, whence he was to sail for Shanghai with Wang and Li.

It was all a ruse, a classic double-cross. Chang Fa-k'uei 'missed' the boat when Wang and Li departed Hong Kong on the 16th. In the pre-dawn hours of the 17th Huang Ch'i-hsiang staged a coup in Canton, supported by Generals Hsueh Yueh and Li Fu-lin. Their troops surrounded the various headquarters and barracks of the Li-Huang forces in Canton and disarmed them. They meant to arrest Huang Shao-hsiung, who, being forewarned, narrowly escaped. Chang Fa-k'uei returned to Canton on the 17th when the coup was over and, together with Ch'en Kung-po and others of Wang Ching-wei's supporters, set up a new

288 Iriye, *After imperialism*, 157-8, based upon Japanese Foreign Office records.
289 Kao Yin-tsu, *Chronology*, 274. GBFO 405/255. Confidential. *Further correspondence respecting China*, no. 13448, Oct.-Dec. 1927, no. 116, enclosure, Consul-General J. F. Brenan, Canton, to Miles Lampson in Peking, 22 Nov. 1927, describing Canton politics of the past few weeks, including T.V. Soong's visit.

provincial government. The coup went by the name of 'Protecting the party'. On board ship between Hong Kong and Shanghai, Li Chi-shen could do nothing, and Wang Ching-wei could profess ignorance of the whole affair.[290]

Very few in Shanghai believed Wang. His political position there was weakened by the coup, though it had strengthened his supporters' hold on wealthy Kwangtung. Party veterans in Shanghai – Hu Han-min, Wu Chih-hui, Ts'ai Yuan-p'ei, Li Shih-tseng and Chang Ching-chiang – scorned Wang for his treachery and some of them refused to see him. Li Chi-shen denounced the coup as a communist plot, recounting a number of incidents before the coup and reports he received shortly after, to back his charge, which Wang, of course, denied. According to Wang the coup was directed entirely against the illegal Special Central Committee. Nevertheless, the charge – not necessarily the facts – proved very damaging to Wang within a few weeks. Li Tsung-jen and Pai Ch'ung-hsi of the Kwangsi clique, who had just won Wuhan from T'ang Sheng-chih, were furious. They even discussed a military campaign to restore Li Chi-shen in Canton. Thus the preliminary discussions in Shanghai towards convening the Central Executive Committee Plenum started off in discord. The discord was particularly intense between those who upheld the Special Central Committee and those, like Wang, who opposed it. An old feud between Hu Han-min and Wang Ching-wei continued unabated. Chiang Kai-shek, having had nothing publicly to do with Kuomintang politics during the past three months, was in a favoured position to mediate. Preliminary 'chats' began in his house in Shanghai's French Concession on 24 November.[291]

A more formal 'preparatory conference' to plan the CEC Plenum met in Chiang's place between 3 and 10 December, with some 35 of the 80 members and alternates of the Central Executive and Central Supervisory Committees attending, but controversy between various factions was as intense as ever. Conflict was fanned by the Nanking government's order on 2 December – the day before the conference was to open – for a military expedition to punish Chang Fa-k'uei and Huang Ch'i-hsiang for their coup 'in league with the Communist Party', since the Nanking government was the creation of the questionable Special Central Com-

---

290 Li Yun-han provides a vivid account, quoting from Huang Shao-hsiung, and from Li Chi-shen's bitter accusation against Chang Fa-k'uei: *TJK*, 790–4. Kao Yin-tsu, *Chronology*, 275; *FRUS*, 1927, 2. 35–6. Consul-General Brenan, in the account cited above, speculated that Li Chi-shen was not tricked but, knowing his position in Canton was undermined, went to Shanghai leaving Huang Shao-hsiung to 'hold the baby'. On the evidence available, this seems unlikely.

291 *TJK*, 792–4; Kao Yin-tsu, *Chronology*, 275–6. *KMWH*, 17. 3113–22 for related documents.

mittee. Charges and threats of impeachment flew back and forth, and only four meetings could be held as one group or another absented itself to caucus. Finally, on 10 December, after Chiang Kai-shek had issued a plea for compromise and unity, Wang Ching-wei offered a resolution requesting Chiang to resume his duties as commander-in-chief. He also intimated his own intention to retire in the interest of party unity. Wang's motion passed unanimously. Indeed, there had been a campaign of circular telegrams from Feng Yü-hsiang, Yen Hsi-shan, Ho Ying-ch'in and other generals demanding that Chiang resume command – a campaign quite probably engineered by Chiang himself. Though General Chiang did not immediately indicate his decision, the preparatory conference also voted to request him to take charge of calling the Fourth CEC Plenum, which should be held between 1 and 15 January. All contentious problems should be settled by that plenum. In short, the Kuomintang leadership was so torn by dissension that the preparatory conference could resolve only routine matters. Chiang's position in the party had been considerably enhanced, and now he might influence strongly, if not determine, which CEC members and alternates might attend the forthcoming plenum that was supposed to reunite the party.[292]

No sooner had the preparatory committee adjourned than Shanghai learned the devastating news of a communist-led uprising in Canton, which began before dawn on 11 December. At first apparently successful in gaining control of parts of the city, the uprising was marked by looting, burning and many executions. Most of Chang Fa-k'uei's troops were off on a campaign against Huang Shao-hsiung, or in the East River district, but he ordered them back. Enough had returned by the third day that General Chang with the help of Li Fu-lin, could suppress the revolt – ferociously. The devastation of Canton had been severe. Wang Ching-wei's political position was irreparably compromised. He first went into a hospital for safety and then sailed for France on a second exile on 17 December. Other leading members of his faction were simply excluded from further participation in high-level Kuomintang work for several years.[293]

292 Kao Yin-tsu, *Chronology*, 276–8; *The China Yearbook, 1928*, 1400; GBFO 405/256. Confidential. *Further correspondence respecting China*, 13583, Jan.–March 1928, No. 154, enclosure, Consul-General Sidney Barton, Shanghai, to Miles Lampson, Peking, 11 Dec. 1927, a well-informed report on the Preparatory Conference. Sir Sidney listed 35 who attended. Hu Han-min was the most conspicuous for his absence. Sir Sidney listed the following as the 'Nanking die-hards', who opposed Wang Ching-wei's faction: T'an Yen-k'ai, Ts'ai Yuan-p'ei, Li Shih-tseng, Li Tsung-jen, Ho Ying-ch'in, Sun Fo, Chang Ching-chiang, Li Chi-sen, Wu Ch'ao-shu, and Wu T'ieh-ch'eng, a very interesting combination. *KMWH*, 16. 2875–9 for Chiang's appeal to the conferees. *Ibid*. 17. 3122–4, for orders for a punitive campaign against Chang and Huang.
293 Wang's apologia and retirement statement is in *KMWH*, 17. 3134–5.

The Canton commune

The disastrous Canton uprising, engineered by a small group of daring Chinese communist leaders to carry out general instructions of the new Provisional Politburo in Shanghai, marked a low point in the Communist Party's long struggle for power. The last large-scale communist-led urban insurrection in China for two decades, it was a convincing failure of the insurrectionist policy mandated by the Comintern in July 1927. The international communist movement put on a brave face about the disaster, emphasizing the heroism of the participants and pronouncing the uprising a symbolic victory, but it was, nevertheless, a major miscalculation in itself, and another failure in the Comintern's effort to direct revolution in another country. The defeat and brutal suppression which followed struck a fearful blow to the radical labour movement in Canton, and had adverse effects in major cities elsewhere. Reports of the slaughter, burning and looting in Canton during the first two days, and assumed Russian involvement, turned Chinese public opinion against the Communist Party and Soviet Russia. The Nationalist government severed relations with Russia, and the Kuomintang terminated its tattered 'alliance' with the Comintern. Since there are many reportorial and analytic accounts of the uprising and its suppression, we present here only a factual sketch.[294]

294 Nearly all histories of the Chinese Communist Party describe the Canton uprising, which was well reported in the world press.
   The following are reports by observers: J. Calvin Huston, 'Peasants, workers, and soldiers revolt of December 11–13, 1927 at Canton, China.' Dispatch no. 699 to J.V.A. MacMurray, U.S. minister to Peking, 30 Dec. 1927, in Hoover Institution, Stanford, California, J. Calvin Huston Collection, package II, pt II, folder 5, item 20. (Item 12 is an original handbill in Chinese dated 11 Dec. 1927, announcing the Soviet and giving a list of officials.) The gist of Consul-General Huston's telegraphic reports may be read in *FRUS*, 1927, 2. 39–40; they are available in US National Archives microfilm. GBFO 405/256. Confidential. *Further correspondence respecting China*, 13583, no. 71, enclosure 1, James Brenan, Canton, to Miles Lampson, Peking, 15 Dec. 1927, a description; enclosure 3, a handbill distributed in Canton on Dec. 11 (trans.); and *ibid.* no. 80, enclosure 4, Cecil Clementi, governor of Hong Kong to Mr Amery, colonial secretary, London, 15 Dec., a description; and enclosure 5, translation from *Red flag* of 11 Dec., announcing the Canton Soviet and list of officials. GBFO 371/13199, contains many dispatches from Governor Clementi giving intelligence on conditions in Canton and Kwangtung from December to February 1928. A vivid eye-witness account by Earl Swisher, who went into Canton while the insurrection was underway and after it was crushed, is in Kenneth W. Rea, ed. *Canton in revolution: the collected papers of Earl Swisher, 1925–1928*, 89–125, including translations of documents and grim photographs. *Kung-fei huo-kuo shih-liao hui-pien*, 1. 510–65, reprints Chinese newspaper reports of 13–15 December, and a valuable document, a Resolution of the CCP Politburo of 3 January 1928 on 'The meaning and lessons of the Canton insurrection'.
   Scholarly and well-annotated analyses that use the extensive retrospective literature are S. Bernard Thomas, *'Proletarian hegemony' in the Chinese revolution*; Hsiao, *Chinese communism in 1927*, 134–56; and *TJK*, 794–9.

The Communist Party's Provisional Politburo held an enlarged meeting in Shanghai on 10 and 11 November to assess the recent defeats and develop plans to rebuild the party. To 'start on the path of true revolutionary bolshevik struggle', it laid down a general strategy for revolution,[295] after which plans for an insurrection in Kwangtung were worked out with Chang T'ai-lei, secretary of the Kwangtung Provincial Committee. News of Huang Ch'i-hsiang's coup against Huang Shao-hsiung in Canton on 17 November, made it seem likely there would soon be conflict between the armies of Chang Fa-k'uei and Li Chi-shen. To take advantage of this opportunity, the Politburo issued an 11-point programme on 18 November, which instructed the Kwangtung communists to unleash peasant insurrections in the countryside, worker uprisings in county centres, a general political strike in Canton, and military mutinies.[296] On 26 November the Kwangtung Provincial Committee resolved to stage an insurrection and appointed a five-man Revolutionary Military Council, with Chang T'ai-lei as chairman and Yeh T'ing as commander-in-chief. The council developed a political programme, began military preparations, selected officers for a soviet, mobilized workers in the remaining red unions, secretly recruited among the troops, and tried to establish contacts with nearby peasant movements. On 7 December the Kwangtung Provincial Committee secretly convened a meeting in Canton that was called a 'worker-peasant-soldier congress', and this adopted a soviet of 15 deputies, of whom nine were listed as workers and three each as peasants and soldiers, though the Provincial Committee later admitted that all were intellectuals. This meeting picked 13 December as the date for the Canton uprising.[297]

By then the Revolutionary Military Council had considerable resources. The cadet Training Regiment, which Chang Fa-k'uei had brought from Wuhan where its men had been under the influence of Yun Tai-ying, had some communist officers and Yeh Chien-ying was its deputy commander. The council had organized a Red Guard made up of about 500 former strike pickets from the Hong Kong–Canton strike organization and some 1,500 workers from unions still under communist leadership. There were also some communists among the cadets at the Whampoa Academy. The main difficulty was a shortage of arms. Canton was lightly protected in early December, since Chang Fa-k'uei had sent most of his troops out of the city to ward off the forces of Huang Shao-hsiung and

295 The plan appeared as 'Central announcement number 16', dated 18 Nov, in *Chung-yang t'ung-hsun*, 13, (30 Nov. 1927), 1–6.
296 Thomas, '*Proletarian hegemony' in the Chinese revolution*, 21–2.
297 *Ibid.* 23.

Li Chi-shen, leaving only small units to guard various headquarters and the arsenals. Li Fu-lin still controlled Honam Island, but with only a small guard since most of his troops were at Kongmoon. Canton had an efficient and well-armed police force. An intangible factor was the leftist sentiments of General Huang Ch'i-hsiang, commander of the Fourth Corps, who had been much influenced by Teng Yen-ta. Liao Shang-kuo, who was close to the communists, headed the political department of the Fourth Corps, and General Huang knew that communist leaders were slipping into Canton from Hong Kong; he even kept Yun Tai-ying in his home in Tung-shan.

News of communist activity in Canton and radical articles appearing in the journal published by the political department of the Fourth Corps apparently alarmed Wang Ching-wei in Shanghai, for on 9 and 10 December he telegraphed Ch'en Kung-po and Chang Fa-k'uei, directing them to take action against the communists. They should send troops to surround and search the Soviet consulate which, Wang charged, was the headquarters of a planned insurrection, and they should expel the Soviet consul. Huang Ch'i-hsiang should retire temporarily while the clean-up of communists was carried out.[298]

On 9 December the police discovered a cache of bombs. This, and news that Chang Fa-k'uei planned to disarm the Training Regiment, led the Revolutionary Military Council to advance the date of the uprising. They hastily called General Yeh T'ing to Canton from Hong Kong. Inauspiciously, he arrived to take command only a few hours before the revolt began. Also, advancing the date by two days may have made it impossible for some peasant units that had been recruited to reach the city. Reportedly only 500 came in from nearby suburbs to join the insurrection.

The insurrectionists had the advantage of surprise. At 3.30 a.m. Sunday, 11 December, workers' Red Guards attacked the Bureau of Public Safety – police headquarters – and were soon reinforced by most of the cadet Training Regiment, which had revolted and shot 15 of its officers. It was now commanded by Yeh Chien-ying. After subduing the Bureau of Public Safety, the attackers released some 700 prisoners who had been taken in raids during the past two days. These men, mostly from communist dominated labour unions, also joined the fight. By noon most police stations in Canton city had been taken, and several, though not all, the Canton headquarters of various military units in the field had been captured. The rebels controlled the railway stations, telegraph and post offices, and had taken over governmental offices and Kuomintang provincial headquarters. They captured the Central Bank but were unable to open the vault where silver and banknotes were stored. A fire soon gutted the building. They also looted other banks and money shops. The Bureau of Public Safety became the centre of the new soviet government. By nightfall there had been considerable private looting, burning of property, and shooting of suspected enemies, including about 300 of the police. However, Honam island escaped because it was protected by gunboats and Li Fu-lin's guards, and it was to Honam that Ch'en Kung-po, Chang Fa-k'uei, Huang Ch'i-hsiang and other Kuomintang loyalists fled early Sunday morning. Shameen remained a foreign sanctuary, and the British consul general assisted the loyalists by sending their telegrams to recall troops from the West River region.[299]

On the morning of the attack the soviet government proclaimed itself. The Kwangtung Provincial Committee of the Communist Party had printed several thousand leaflets announcing the formation of the Canton Soviet and its political programme, and appealing for mass support. *Red Flag* came out with a similar flier listing the officials of the new regime, which was to be headed by the popular leader of the Seamen's Union, Su Chao-cheng, who was at the moment away. His position was filled temporarily by Chang T'ai-lei. Nine other persons held the other 11 positions in the worker-peasant-soldier soviet, most of them, and possibly all, being communists. Four, in addition to Su Chao-sheng, were labour leaders.[300] Although some 3,000 workers, by police estimate, joined in the fighting or looting, they were a very small proportion of Canton's unionized work force, estimated at 290,000. Others had been so intimidated by the previous eight months of repression, or were already so hostile to the communist labour leadership, that they either remained passive or opposed the uprising. Very little popular support for the soviet emerged. Shopkeepers followed the classic tactic during a coup, shuttering their shops for fear of looting. Their apprentices and clerks remained passive. Few of the disarmed soldiers joined the revolt, and the populace simply stayed away from the two meetings that were called to show mass support.[301] Would a general strike called in advance of the

299 Stated in Consul-general Brenan's report of 15 Dec., in GBFO 405/256. Confidential . . . 13583, no. 71, enclosure 1, cited above f.n. 294.
300 Translations in *Ibid.* enclosure 3, and no. 80, enclosure 5. Photos and Swisher's translations in Rea, ed. *Canton in revolution*, 99–102. Biographies of Su, Chang, Ch'en Yü, P'eng P'ai (listed in absentia), Yang Yin, Yeh T'ing and Yün Tai-ying are in Klein and Clark, *Biographic dictionary*. The others listed were Chou Wen-yung, Huang P'ing, Ho Lai and Hsu Kuang-ying.
301 Yeh T'ing later described eloquently the hostility or apathy of the Cantonese towards the uprising; quoted in Hsiao, *Chinese communism in 1927*, 141–2.

uprising have made any difference? The Revolutionary Military Committee had decided against trying to call out a strike because the communist position with labour was too weak; but later the Politburo reproved them for this mistake.

On the second day, Chang T'ai-lei was killed in action at the age of 29. Chang had been one of the founders of the Socialist Youth Corps and an early member of the Chinese Communist Party. He was a central figure in both organizations, and particularly in relations with the Comintern. He was one of the organizers of the Hong Kong – Canton strike and boycott movement in 1925, had served as chief secretary in Borodin's Canton office, and later was Borodin's Chinese secretary in Wuhan. His death left General Yeh T'ing in command, but he had not been in Canton for 18 months, and was unfamilar with local conditions, party personnel, and sources of support. His hastily assembled military force soon faced overwhelming odds.

Generals Chang Fa-k'uei and Li Fu-lin recalled their troops from the West River region and they began arriving in Honam and on the outskirts of Canton on the night of December 12/13, as did a regiment of Hsueh Yueh's division and the independent regiment led by Mo Hsiung. On the morning of the 13th gunboats machine-gunned the bund to clear it for the landing of troops crossing from Honam. Other units closed in from west, north and east. Fighting squads from the Mechanics Union, eager to settle old scores, joined in the attack. The battle to recover the Public Security Office, the headquarters of the soviet, lasted four hours. By dusk all fighting had ceased. Many of the revolting workers and troops died at their posts, others went into hiding, and some escaped towards the north-west. Virtually all the planners and leaders of the revolt succeeded in escaping one way or another. Heinz Neumann, the resident Comintern agent, who helped in the planning and financing, also slipped away.

Two Russians were killed in the battle against Hsueh Yueh's troops and two others participating in the defence of the workers, peasants and soldiers soviet headquarters were captured. When Vice-consul M. Hassis, armed with grenades, attempted to reach the headquarters in a consulate car, he was seized. Searchers arrested two other Russians hiding near their consulate. All five men were marched through the streets and then shot. In a raid on the Russian consulate, Boris Pokvalisky, the consul-general, was arrested together with his wife and several Russian women and children, but the consular body intervened and persuaded the outraged authorities to spare their lives. A new regime in Canton deported them at the end of the year.[302] Documents found in the consulate allegedly implicated it in the conspiracy. The Russian Foreign Office denied any relationship between the consulate and the uprising.

Three days of fighting, incendiarism and looting devastated Canton. When the fighting ceased, the streets were littered with dead, and nearly 900 buildings on 46 streets were burned out, according to later police reports. The Communist Party's Kwangtung Provincial Committee estimated a few weeks after the event that more than 200 communist comrades and more than 2,000 Red Guards and Red Army men were killed, but that no more than 100 deaths were reported on the enemy side. Those killed during the uprising probably were fewer than those slaughtered after it had been put down. Execution squads rounded up several thousand suspects and dispatched them in an orgy of revenge. The American consulate estimated than between three and four thousand men and women, many of them innocent of any connection with the uprising, were executed, and the authorities admitted the killing of 2,000. Later communist sources reported even larger losses.[303]

The Nationalist government in Nanking ordered all Russian consulates and other facilities in nationalist areas to be closed and the personnel deported in consequence of the assumed responsibility of the Soviet consulate for the Canton uprising. In Hankow, Garrison Commander Hu Tsung-to ordered a raid on the Soviet consulate and all other institutions thought to harbour communists. On 16 December troops, police and plain-clothesmen raided and searched the consulate and other establishments, rounding up more than 200 suspected foreigners and Chinese in the French Concession and the three former concessions. Troops surrounded Sun Yat-sen University in Wuchang and other schools, and arrested hundreds of students. Then followed executions of labour leaders and students, many of them women. Two noted leftists were seized in the Japanese concession on 17 December and executed forthwith: Li Han-chün, one of the founders of the Chinese Communist Party, but no longer a member; and Chan Ta-pei, a noted anti-Manchu revolutionary,

---

302 Huston, 'Peasants, workers, and soldiers revolt', 36–8. Pictures of the slain men are in Hoover Institution, J. Calvin Huston Collection, package II, pt II. folder 3, no. 11. The collection also contains the personal papers of Vice-consul Hassis.

303 Hsiao, *Chinese communism in 1927*, 142, citing 'Resolution on the Canton Uprising', adopted by the Kwangtung Provincial Committee, 1–5 Jan. 1928; Huston, 'Peasant, workers and soldiers revolt', 28; and Thomas, '*Proletarian hegemony*' *in the Chinese revolution*, 27, citing *Bolshevik*, no. 12, Jan. 1928, in L. P. Deliusin, ed. *Kantonskaia Kommuna* (The Canton Commune), 207.

associate of Sun Yat-sen, and a member of the Kuomintang Central Executive Committee.[304]

In Canton, most of the members of the government set up by Wang Ching-wei, left in disgrace, some taking with them funds from the provincial treasury. Chang Fa-k'uei and Huang Ch'i-hsiang accepted pro-forma responsibility for the Canton uprising and resigned their commands. They sent their troops to the East River region, where they were defeated by forces under Ch'en Ming-shu. Li Chi-shen's troops retook Canton on 29 December and he returned in early January.

Thus by the end of the year, the Wang Ching-wei faction had lost its base of power, Wang was on his way to France and most of his important adherents were in eclipse. The Chinese Communist Party had been devastated by eight months of suppressions and abortive uprisings. A score of its best leaders and many thousands of its members and followers were slain. It would take many years of desperate struggle to rebuild the shattered party.

THE FINAL DRIVE – PEKING CAPTURED AND NANKING THE NEW CAPITAL

Preparations for a renewed drive on Peking

In order to complete the military unification of China, Chiang Kai-shek, now the most influential member of the Nationalist Party, had to secure adequate finances, regroup the widely scattered military forces, and attempt to reunite the party leadership. He persuaded T. V. Soong to resume the post of finance minister, in which he had been extraordinarily effective in the Canton days, and Soong planned in various ways to increase revenues, which were coming to the government only from Kiangsu and Chekiang. On taking his post on 7 January Soong announced that monthly income was less than three million yuan but expenses were 11 million. He hoped by March to increase income to 10 million a month.[305]

To rebuild a victorious military coalition could not be easy, for the

304 GBFO 405/256. Confidential . . . 13583, no. 144, enclosures 1–6, Acting Consul-General Harold Porter, Hankow, 21 Dec. 1927 to Miles Lampson in Peking, with extracts from the *Hankow Herald*, 17 to 21 Dec. 1927, describing the raids, reporting more than 700 Chinese suspects and 17 Russians arrested, and giving names of 20 persons executed, including five women students ranging in age from 20 to 26. Biographies of Li in Klein and Clark, *Biographic dictionary* and Chan in Boorman and Howard, *Biographical dictionary*.

Strangely, the raids apparently failed to apprehend any of the 39 communist leaders who attended a Hupei Provincial Party Congress in Hankow on 14 and 15 December, described in Hsiao Tso-liang, 'The dispute over a Wuhan insurrection in 1927', *CQ* 33 (Jan.–March 1968) 108–122, p. 133.

305 Kao, *Chronology*, 281.

original valiant Fourth Corps was now much reduced and its top commanders were in retirement; most of the old Eighth Corps had been driven back to Hunan and its commander was in Japan; and the Seventh Corps, now building its power base in Hupei, was led by Chiang's rivals, Li Tsung-jen and Pai Ch'ung-hsi, who, in turn, were linked to Huang Shao-hsiung and Li Chi-shen in the south. Chang Tso-lin's Manchurian Army and Chang Tsung-ch'ang's Shantungese were still formidable opponents for the conglomeration of forces Chiang could command; but there was hope that Feng Yü-hsiang and Yen Hsi-shan, the boss of Shansi, who had hoisted the Nationalist flag the previous June but maintained cautious relations with Chang Tso-lin until conflict between them erupted in October, might now cooperate in a drive on Peking. Chiang Kai-shek returned to Nanking on 4 January and announced resumption of his duties as commander-in-chief on the 9th. He also issued a preparatory call for the Fourth CEC Plenum.

It soon became evident that Chiang and his close supporters intended to reform and cleanse the Kuomintang as well as attempt to reunite a leadership body. The CEC Standing Committee of the moment issued instructions that provincial party headquarters in five provinces should cease activities pending reorganization, and that the Chekiang and Kiangsu party branches were being reorganized. It took from 13 January to 1 February for Chiang to get everything in place for the long-postponed Fourth Plenum of the Second Central Executive Committee. Besides getting agreement on the agenda and persuading certain factions not to bring up sensitive issues, an important question that Chiang had to get settled was: Who might be permitted to attend? Certainly none of the 13 communists elected two years earlier by the Second National Congress as members or alternates of the Central Executive Committee would be admitted to this plenum. But what of the Wang Ching-wei faction that many considered culpable, at least by negligence, for the communist devastation of Canton in December? Five members of the Central Supervisory Committee recommended that Wang and eight associates be excluded. In the end, however, only Wang, Ch'en Kung-po, Ku Meng-yü and Kan Nai-kuang were not permitted to attend. The others came. Hu Han-min, Sun Fo, and C. C. Wu, three opponents of Chiang Kai-shek, were conveniently persuaded to leave on a well-financed tour of inspection abroad, and there were some others who probably would not wish to attend.[306]

Twenty-nine members and alternates of the Central Executive and

---

306 *TJK*, 804–06, and Kao, *Chronology*, 281–84.

Central Supervisory Committees attended the opening ceremony of this joint plenum on 2 February. There were 77 living members and alternates of whom about 50 might have been available. Thereafter the numbers attending sessions fluctuated around 30.[307] The plenum had three main tasks: setting a new direction to party policy, putting old disputes to rest, and electing new governing bodies.

The participants listened to Chiang Kai-shek's policy proposals: to replace the communist-inspired ideology of class struggle, the Kuomintang should promote a spirit of mutual help and cooperation within the nation. All propaganda should be based upon the late leader's 'Plan for national reconstruction' – that is, on Dr Sun's ideas prior to direct Bolshevik influence – and all slogans used during the period of communist influence should be eliminated. The party's publications should be strictly supervised; no anti-party or anti-government propaganda should be permitted; and all publicity regarding foreign affairs must be in conformity with the government's policy. The Kuomintang should be cleansed by the dissolution of all provincial party bodies pending reregistration of members, and by the abolition of the departments for farmers, workers, merchants, women and youth at central headquarters and in party branches. There should be only three departments for the present: organization, propaganda and party-training. All mass movements must be brought under Kuomintang control, communist influence in them be eliminated, and armed corps of farmers' associations and workers' unions should be dealt with strictly. Education should emphasize science, and students should direct their attention to national reconstruction.[308] This conservative proposal won quick approval from the plenum, now shorn of all its radicals and all but a few of its leftist members. It foretold the direction in which the Nationalist Party would develop.

To paper over the earlier conflicts between the Wuhan and Nanking rivals, the plenum accepted a compromise formula: all previous resolutions related to the policies of allying with Russia and admitting communists should be annulled, while, on the other hand, all removals of persons from Kuomintang membership as part of Nanking's anti-communist drive would be set aside. However, there was to be a complete

---

307 Counting alternates, the total of the two committees was 80, but 3 were deceased, 15 were communists, 8 had been excluded or sent abroad, and 3 were in Russia. Names for the opening ceremony in *TJK*, 806. Eleven attenders were regular CEC members (total 36), 10 were alternates (total 24); 5 were CSC members (total 12), and 3 alternates (total 8).
308 *KMWH*, 17. 3138–52 presents in detail the proposals for reforming the Kuomintang as worked up by Ting Wei-fen, Ch'en Kuo-fu, and Chiang Kai-shek, and preserved in the Kuomintang Archives. For a brief account, GBFO 405/257. Confidential. *Further correspondence respecting China*, 13612, April–June 1928, no. 36, enclosure 3. Sidney Barton, Shanghai, to Miles Lampson, Peking, 16 Feb. 1928.

reregistration of party members; and this plenum specifically expelled all the communists from membership on the two central committees. It also expelled P'eng Tse-min and Teng Yen-ta on the grounds of being accessories to rebellion, and it suspended the rights of Hsu Ch'ien as a CEC member, and of two alternates of the CSC. To fill the empty slots, alternates were moved up systematically.[309]

The plenum considered and passed a number of bills. The Nationalist government should now be organized in a more elaborate way, with an Executive Yuan having seven ministries, a Supreme Court, an Examination Yuan and a Control Yuan, an Academy, an Auditing Yuan, a Legislative Drafting Office, and four Commissions, for Reconstruction, Military Affairs, Mongolian and Tibetan Affairs, and Overseas Chinese Affairs. It was not quite the five yuan system envisaged by Sun Yat-sen but tended in that direction, and most of it was still only a plan. The Kuomintang was to be reconstructed under the direct supervision of the new Central. A standard system of military organization, and reform of political work in the armed forces – an enterprise that had been deeply infiltrated by communists – were approved. (Chiang Kai-shek had chosen the anti-communist ideologist, Tai Chi-t'ao, who was also his close friend, to head the Political Training Department.) The plenum also held elections, but it is not clear what the process was in preparing the slates for voting. Elected to the Standing Committee of the Central Executive Committee were Chiang Kai-shek, Yü Yu-jen, Tai Chi-t'ao, Ting Wei-fen, and T'an Yen-k'ai, with four posts held open for leaders abroad. Forty-nine persons were named to the Government Council, with a Standing Committee consisting of T'an Yen-k'ai, chairman, Ts'ai Yuan-p'ei, Chang Ching-chiang, Li Lieh-chün, and Yü Yu-jen. The new Military Council named 73 persons, with a Standing Committee of 11, chaired by Chiang Kai-shek. Thus the new councils had room for all prominent Kuomintang figures and military leaders then in good repute, but the standing committees were stacked with conservative party veterans or military commanders with real power. Chiang was in charge of military matters and T'an Yen-k'ai seemed charged with supervising governmental affairs.[310]

With these political arrangements completed, Chiang Kai-shek began

---

309. *TJK*, 807; expulsions shown in *Chung-kuo Kuo-min-tang cheng-li tang-wu chih t'ung-chi pao-kao* (Statistical report on the work of party adjustment of the Chinese Nationalist Party), Organization Department of the CEC, March 1929.

310. Kao, *Chronology*, 285–86; GBFO 405/257. Confidential. *Further correspondence respecting China*, 13612, no. 36, cited, enclosures 1 and 2 (the latter lists the members of the Government Council). *KMWH*, 16. 2887–96 for the plenum's proclamation issued 8 February; and *KMWH*, 17. front plates and pp. 3153–5, for other documents.

preparations for a final military drive on Peking. Two months before, Feng Yü-hsiang had sent an army eastwards along the Lunghai Railway and Ho Ying-ch'in had sent part of the First Route Army north along the Tientsin-Pukow Railway. The two forces had met on 16 December at the strategic city of Hsuchow where the railways cross. On 9 February General Chiang left Nanking with his staff to review the troops at Hsuchow, and then went to Kaifeng for a conference with General Feng on 16 February to discuss a renewed offensive. Feng's Kuominchün was partly financed and provided with some military supplies by Nanking. Feng also had several associates in the Nanking government, Huang Fu as foreign minister, H.H. Kung as minister of industry, and Hsüeh Tu-pi as minister of interior. Hankow also provided Feng with some money and arms, perhaps as tribute, for the Kwangsi generals were busy campaigning in Hunan. They showed no interest in a northward campaign, nor did Li Chi-shen in Canton. On 28 February the newly established Central Military Council announced that Chiang Kai-shek would command the First Group Army, Feng Yü-hsiang the Second, and Yen Hsi-shan the Third. Ho Ying-ch'in, former commander of the First Route Army, had been appointed chief-of-staff of the combined Northern Expeditionary forces.[311]

It took about a month more to assemble troops, munitions, rations and the finances necessary for a resumed Northern Expedition. On paper General Chiang commanded a vast force in the First Group Army with more than 60 divisions grouped in 18 corps, and these into four principal armies commanded by Liu Chih, Ch'en T'iao-yuan, Ho Yao-tsu and Fang Chen-wu. The first of these armies had grown out of the original First Corps, officered by instructors and cadets from the Whampoa Academy, but it also had some other divisions and corps contributed by Chang Fa-k'uei and Chu P'ei-te. As usual, the First Army was the best equipped of the participating armies.[312] General Ch'en, a northerner and formerly military governor of Anhwei, had turned over to the Nationalist side in March 1927, opening the way for the drive on Nanking; but he

---

311 Kao, *Chronology*, 278–9, 286–7; *FRUS*, 1928, 2. 123–5.
312 According to the *History of the First Group Army*, a commission made a careful inspection of this army between 22 and 26 March 1928. Charts on pp. 10–14 show that the Headquarters and 1st, 2nd and 22nd Divisions of the First Corps had 2,681 officers and 30,269 troops equipped with 16,236 rifles, 502 machine guns and 93 cannon. The Ninth Corps, also made up of headquarters and three divisions, had 2,810 officers and 24,310 troops equipped with 12,436 rifles, 221 machine guns, and 77 cannon. However, the Tenth Corps from Kweichow with only two divisions had 1,437 officers and 8,263 troops with 2,953 rifles, 19 machine guns, and 29 cannon. Total combatants, 70,770, but only 31,625 rifles, plus 1,457 pistols for the officers. In addition there were 5,117 porters and 673 pack horses in the First and Ninth Corps. The average age of 22 commanding officers in the three corps was 33 years (the range was 24 to 43), or about a year less, if *sui* was meant.

was an old-time militarist still. General Ho had brought his Hunanese division into the National Revolutionary Army during the first phase of the Northern Expedition and had participated in the capture of Kiukiang and Nanking. His division had expanded into a corps, the Fortieth, and garrisoned the Nanking area. Fang Chen-wu's revolutionary credentials went back to the 1911 Revolution, and he had been associated with various opposition governments in Canton. More recently he had been a commander in Feng Yü-hsiang's Kuominchün, and participated in Feng's move out of Shensi into Honan in May 1927. He then enrolled his small force in the National Revolutionary Army. These four armies, some other miscellaneous units, and part of Feng Yü-hsiang's Second Group Army were responsible for the drive through Shantung. This motley force was a far cry from the highly indoctrinated and moderately well-trained five corps that had started north from Kwangtung nearly two years before.[313] Peking was about 500 miles distant.

Shortly before campaigning began, Foreign Minister Huang Fu and the American minister to China, J. V. A. MacMurray, negotiated a settlement of the Nanking Incident. This came after considerable effort on both sides, and after the Nanking government had issued two mandates on 16 March, one of which announced that a group of soldiers and others implicated in the Incident had been executed, while the other ordered that full protection must be given to foreigners and foreign property. The two representatives exchanged agreed upon notes, which offered regrets and explanations, and these were signed on 30 March, a little more than a year after the violence and shelling in Nanking. So far as the United States was concerned this ended the diplomatic difficulties with Nanking, although recognition came much later. To some Chinese officials, however, the settlement was far from satisfactory, for the American side only expressed regrets that 'circumstances beyond its control should have necessitated the adoption of such measures [that is, the naval bombardment] for the protection of its citizens at Nanking.' To many Chinese, the Nanking Incident *was* the American and British shelling of the city. The British minister, Miles Lampson, had also visited Nanking and held discussions with Huang Fu, but they had failed to find an acceptable formula.[314]

313 *PFCS*, 4. map facing p. 1170 shows the main thrusts of the campaign against Peking in four stages; order of battle following p. 1180. All this volume and the following items deal with the final campaign: *KMWH*, 18. 3169–271; 19. 3479–503; 20. 3671–773; 21. 3925–70. There are brief accounts in Jordan, *The Northern Expedition*, 151–68; Sheridan, *Chinese warlord: Feng Yü-hsiang*, 236–9; and Donald G. Gillin, *Warlord: Yen Hsi-shan in Shansi province, 1911–1949*, 108–9.

314 *FRUS*, 1928, 2. 323–69, for details of the long negotiations and the notes. Summarized in Borg, *American policy and the Chinese revolution*, 380–4. Lampson's difficulties are ex-

The final military campaign

Marshal Chang Tso-lin had overall command of the An-kuo Chün, a shaky alliance of his own Manchurian troops (the Fengtien Army), the remaining troops of Sun Ch'uan-fang, and the Chihli and Shantung provincial forces, under Ch'u Yü-p'u and Chang Tsung-ch'ang. The Manchurians were responsible for the defence of Peking and the railways leading south and west; Sun Ch'uan-fang and the Shantungese for defending the Tientsin-Pukow Railway on the east. But much of Chihli and western Shantung are open plains, making defence difficult, particularly against cavalry. Yen Hsi-shan on the western flank complicated the defence of the Peking-Hankow line.

Feng Yü-hsiang's Second Group Army commenced the Nationalists' spring campaign with a drive into south-western Shantung and a holding operation in the west against the Fengtien Army. The Nationalists' First Group Army joined the battle in Shantung about 9 April, advancing along the railway and sending another column northward near the coast to intercept the rail line leading from Tsinan, the provincial capital, to the port of Tsingtao. Chang Tsung-ch'ang's troops showed little fight, but Sun Ch'uan-fang attempted a counter attack. He was badly defeated, leaving the way open for the capture of Tsinan, which cavalry units of the Kuominchün under General Sun Liang-ch'eng entered on 30 April. On the western front, however, the Manchurians strongly resisted the Second Group Army, which had advanced only as far as Chang-te (An-yang), at the northern tip of Honan, still some 400 miles from Peking. During April the Manchurians had also engaged in preemptive attacks against Shansi along the Peking–Suiyuan Railway and the line leading from Shihchiachuang to Taiyuan, the provincial capital. At this point in the battle, during the first week in May, a bitter and bloody conflict broke out between advancing Nationalist troops and Japanese regular army units that had been sent to Tsinan to protect resident Japanese nationals.

The Tsinan Incident, 3–11 May 1928

The Tanaka government, while favourably impressed by the Nationalist movement under Chiang Kai-shek's leadership, remembered the Nanking

plained in Wilson, 'Britain and the Kuomintang', 644–9. Private letters of appreciation to Foreign Minister Huang Fu from Miles Lampson and J. V. A. MacMurray, both in very cordial terms, are reproduced in the reminiscences of Huang's widow, Shen I-yün, *I-yün hui-i*, 356–9.

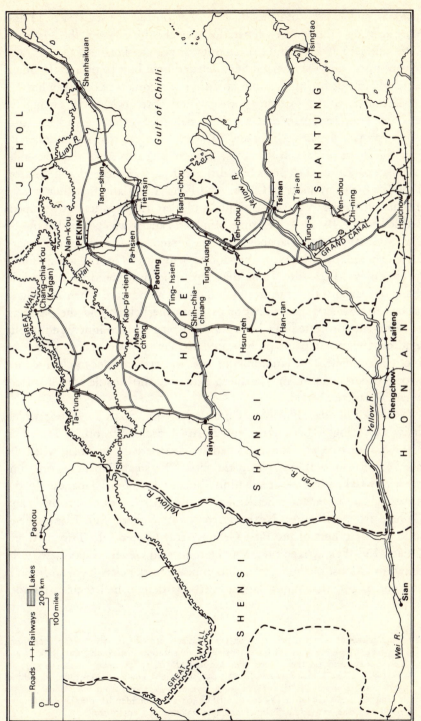

MAP 6.   North China about 1928

Incident and other anti-foreign disorders during earlier stages of the Northern Expedition. In preparation for the time when the National Revolutionary Army would resume its drive, the Japanese Cabinet, the War Ministry and the General Staff debated how best to protect Japanese nationals in north China: some favoured and some opposed sending an expeditionary force.[315] Chiang Kai-shek and Foreign Minister Huang Fu tried to reassure Japan that the Nationalist government and its army would protect Japanese lives and property in areas that came under its control. However, when it became evident in early April that the military campaign would probably drive through Tsinan despite Baron Tanaka's earlier request to Chiang and Feng Yü-hsiang that they bypass the city where 2,000 Japanese civilians resided, the Japanese government decided to act. By 18 April Prime Minister Tanaka was persuaded by the War Ministry, and the Japanese Cabinet agreed, to send an expeditionary force of 5,000 from the Sixth Division to Shantung. The public announcement sought to reassure China that Japan did not intend to interfere in the civil war and that the troops would be withdrawn when no longer needed to protect Japanese nationals. Both the Peking and the Nanking governments protested this intrusion on China's sovereignty, and public sentiment against Japan rapidly heated up. Yet the Nationalists wished to avoid a conflict. The Kuomintang and the commander-in-chief issued strong orders against anti-Japanese agitation and hostile acts in places where Japanese resided.

General Fukuda Hikosuke, commanding the Sixth Division, which arrived in Tsingtao between 25 and 27 April, ordered troops to Tsinan on his own initiative, and some 500 had arrived there by 30 April, when the northern forces withdrew from the city. The small Japanese force immediately staked out the area within Tsinan where most Japanese lived – it was called the Japanese Settlement – set up barricades, and forbade any Chinese troops to enter. Next day troops of General Sun Liang-ch'eng followed by others of the First Group Army poured into Tsinan. When Chiang Kai-shek arrived on 2 May he requested General Fukuda to withdraw his troops, pledging to maintain peace in the city. General Fukuda consented, and that night Japanese troops demolished their barricades

315 The following is based primarily on the scholarly account in Iriye, *After imperialism*, 193–205, which made use of the extensive documentation from both sides. Reports and other documents on the Chinese side are in *KMWH*, 19. 3504–657; 22. 4443–537; 23. 4783–815. *China Yearbook, 1929–30*, 878–93 for some documents from each side. Initial American reports in *FRUS*, 1928, 2. 136–9. Eye-witness reports from J. B. Affleck, British Acting Consul-General in Tsinan, in GBFO 405/257. Confidential. *Further correspondence respecting China*, 13612, April–June 1928, nos. 238 and 239, enclosures.

and seemed to be preparing to leave. A peaceful transition to Nationalist rule looked possible.

Unhappily, fighting broke out between small units on each side on the morning of 3 May. The origin of and responsibility for the fighting were in absolute dispute between the two sides. The local incident rapidly developed into fighting throughout the city between intensely nationalistic Japanese and Chinese troops, despite the efforts of Generals Chiang and Fukuda to stop it. Both sides committed atrocities which inflamed the conflict.[316] Finally a truce was worked out, with the Chinese side agreeing to withdraw all troops from the city except for a few thousand that would remain to keep order. Chiang Kai-shek obviously wished to avoid entrapment in a dangerous conflict that could only obstruct his drive on Peking.

General Fukuda, however, was determined to uphold the prestige of the Japanese Army by punishing the Chinese. He asked for reinforcements and Prime Minister Tanaka and the Cabinet decided on 4 May, to send additional troops from Korea and Manchuria. On 7 May, with Japanese reinforcements in Tsinan, the Japanese generals prepared for drastic action.[317] That afternoon, General Fukuda sent an ultimatum to the acting Chinese commissioner for foreign affairs with a 12-hour time limit. It demanded punishment of responsible high Chinese officers; the disarming of responsible Chinese troops before the Japanese army; evacuation of two military barracks near Tsinan; prohibition of all anti-Japanese propaganda; and withdrawal of all Chinese troops beyond 20 *li* (about seven miles) on both sides of the Tsinan-Tsingtao Railway. Such humiliating demands were more than any Chinese commander could accede to. That night, Chiang Kai-shek and his aides, who had left Tsinan, conferred on this new problem, and next morning General Chiang sent back a conciliatory reply that met only some of the demands. General Fukuda insisted that, since his ultimatum had not been accepted within twelve hours, he was forced to take action to uphold the prestige of the Japanese army.

---

316 The British Acting Consul-General, Mr Affleck reported that on 5 May he was taken to the Japanese hospital and shown the bodies of 12 Japanese, most of the males having been castrated. GBFO 405/257, cited, no. 238, 'Account of the Tsinan Incident', dated 7 May 1928. In a report dated 21 May Mr Affleck stated his belief that blame for beginning the incident on 3 May lay with Chinese troops, who were looting Japanese shops. GBFO 504/258. Confidential. *Further correspondence respecting China*, 13613, July–Sept., no. 37, enclosure. The American Vice-Consul, Ernest Price, blamed the poor discipline of the Chinese troops for the outbreak of the incident.

A Japanese atrocity was the blinding and then killing the Chinese Commissioner for Foreign Affairs, Ts'ai Kung-shih, and the murder of 16 of his staff. This happened on 4 May, according to Kao Yin-tsu, *Chronology*, 291.

317 Professor Iriye places the blame for renewed fighting squarely upon the Japanese. See *After imperialism*, 201.

On the afternoon of 8 May the Japanese attacked within the city and the surrounding area. By the 11th, after fierce fighting, the remaining Chinese troops had been overcome. There was great damage to the city and thousands of Chinese soldiers and civilians had been killed. Nothing could have done more to inflame Chinese hatred against Japan.[318]

The Tsinan Incident brought to an end the Chinese Nationalists' attempt at a *rapprochement* with Japan, but the government did what it could to prevent further trouble with its powerful neighbour. The Nationalist government requested the League of Nations to investigate and appealed to the American government for support, but these requests were of little effect – as was repeatedly to be the case thereafter. The arbitrary action by Japanese commanders in the field was the first of a series that led three years later to the Japanese Kwantung Army's seizure of Manchuria, then to an ever-spreading Sino-Japanese conflict, and ultimately to Japan's utter defeat in 1945.

Who shall have Peking?

In the spring of 1928 the major concern of the Japanese government with respect to China was to protect and enhance its special position in Manchuria. This might be done through cooperation with Chang Tso-lin or with the Nationalists. While attempting to present an appearance of impartiality between the contestants, Japan was determined to prevent the conflict from being carried into Manchuria. As early as January Prime Minister Tanaka had warned Chang Ch'ün, Chiang Kai-shek's special envoy in Tokyo, that Japan would not permit Nationalist troops to pursue the Fengtien Army beyond the Great Wall, but in return, Japan would assure the swift withdrawal of Chang Tso-lin to Mukden if he were defeated. By April the Japanese government had decided to maintain the peace in Manchuria by arranging a truce between the contestants if possible, and by the use of force if necessary.

To avoid embroilment with Japan, Chiang Kai-shek had pulled back most of the troops that had invaded Tsinan and sent them west for a crossing of the Yellow River and regroupment on the north bank. During the second week in May, even as the Japanese army was crushing Chinese forces in and around Tsinan, the Nationalists' three Group Armies began a general offensive, while the An-kuo Chün pulled back towards Peking and Tientsin. Yen Hsi-shan's troops pushed down on Shihchiachuang where, on 10 May, they met with a body of Feng Yü-hsiang's soldiers

---

318 Iriye, *After imperialism*, 207–8, based upon Japanese records.

following the retreating Manchurians on the Peking-Hankow Railway. Other units of Yen's army were recovering northern Shansi and moving along the Peking-Suiyuan Railway towards Peking's back door. The An-kuo Chün tried to establish a shorter line between Paoting on the west and Techow, at the northern tip of Shantung, on the east, reinforcing the Shantungese with Chihli provincial troops under Ch'u Yü-p'u, stiffened with some Manchurians. But the eastern end could not hold against Feng Yü-hsiang's attack; Techow fell on 12 May and its defenders fell back towards Tientsin. On 18 May Generals Chiang and Feng met at Chengchow to plan the advance on Tientsin, which, if taken and held, would cut the rail line that the Manchurian army would need should it retreat to its home base.

By this time it was becoming evident that the Manchurians were preparing to withdraw from North China. Officers were sending their families and valuables back home. Units of the Fengtien army on the Peking-Suiyuan Railway began to pull back on Kalgan and then beyond. At this late date the Kwangsi faction entered the campaign. General Pai Ch'ung-hsi, as field commander, led a force into Honan, which the Military Council designated the Fourth Group Army, with Li Tsung-jen its commander. General Pai met Commander-in-Chief Chiang at Chengchow on 20 May to receive his instructions. The troops were former elements of T'ang Sheng-chih's Hunanese Army.[319]

Japan and the Western powers were concerned for the safety of their nationals in Tientsin, with its five separate foreign concessions, and for the foreign community in Peking, should the cities be captured in battle. The experiences of Nanking and the more recent troubles in Tsinan made them wary of disorderly Chinese troops whether in defeat or in victory. The powers had kept contingents of troops in Tientsin for many years in accordance with the Boxer Protocol of 1901, and these garrisons had recently been reinforced so that there were thousands of foreign troops on hand. On 11 May the general commanding the Japanese force in Tientsin proposed excluding Chinese troops from a zone of 20 *li* around the city in accordance with the 1902 treaty between China and various powers. The United States had not been party to that treaty, nor did it have a concession in Tientsin. The American marine commander, Smedley Butler, devised his own plan for the protection of Americans, while the others drew up joint defence plans.

319 General Pai told the writer in 1962 that he had been urged by Commander-in-Chief Chiang to bring a force to the aid of the hard-pressed Feng and Yen. His three sub-commanders were Li P'in-hsien, Liao Lei and Yeh Ch'i. 'When the Fengtien Army saw the advance of such a large reinforcement, it hastily retreated outside the Great Wall', General Pai reminisced.

In Tokyo the Foreign Ministry was preparing the text of a warning that would be presented to both Chinese contestants, stating Japan's determination to prevent extension of the civil war into Manchuria. On 17 May Prime Minister Tanaka met with British, American, French and Italian representatives to explain the purpose of the memorandum that would be delivered next day to the Peking and Nanking governments. He said, in part:

Our policy was devised to prevent fighting at Peking, in order to keep disturbances from spreading into Manchuria. If Chang Tso-lin withdraws from Peking quietly, maintaining discipline among his soldiers, and if he is not pursued by the Southerners, we will permit him to enter Manchuria; but if he fights at Peking, and retreats towards Shanhaikuan, or to some other point which we may fix, fighting the Southerners as he goes, we will prevent him and the Southern army from passing into Manchuria. I believe this plan will have the effect of encouraging Chang Tso-lin to leave Peking quietly and without fighting. I think also that, if Chang Tso-lin retreats from Peking at the present moment, the Southerners will not molest him. I therefore look forward to Peking being evacuated and passing quietly into the hands of the Southerners.[320]

Baron Tanaka instructed his minister to Peking, Yoshizawa Kenkichi, to urge Chang Tso-lin to lose no time in withdrawing to Manchuria; and Consul-General Yada in Shanghai was instructed to let the Nationalists understand that once Chang Tso-lin had returned to his base, Japan would not permit him to interfere in affairs south of the Wall. Thus did Baron Tanaka and his government plan to divide China, and to protect Japan's special sphere in Manchuria. The War Ministry sent telegraphic instructions and explanations of Japan's policy to commanders in Manchuria, Korea and Formosa. Chang Tso-lin would not be advised to retire from public life and Fengtien soldiers need not be disarmed if they returned to Manchuria in good order, but the Japanese army would not permit the southern forces beyond the Wall. The Kwantung Army was to prepare itself to carry through this programme.

Minister Yoshizawa called on Marshal Chang on the night of 17/18 May and handed him the Japanese Memorandum. He told him that the northern army was on the verge of defeat, but that the Japanese government could save him and his army if he accepted the advice to return speedily to Manchuria. But Chang Tso-lin resisted. In Yoshizawa's opinion, he had expected assistance from Japan without having to give up Peking.[321]

---

320 GBFO 504/258. Confidential. *Further correspondence respecting China*, 13613, cited above f.n. 316, no. 2, enclosure. This is a memorandum on the meeting by Eugene Dooman of the U.S. Embassy. See also *FRUS*, 1928, 2. 224–5 and 229.
321 Iriye, *After imperialism*, 210–11, based upon Japanese records.

Next night, Marshal Chang sent an aide to tell the British minister, Miles Lampson, of Yoshizawa's midnight discussion and to seek Lampson's advice. Was it time to leave Peking and the foreigners to the forces of anarchy? he asked. Mr Lampson, who doubtless knew of Prime Minister Tanaka's explanation to the foreign diplomats the previous day, advised that Chang Tso-lin and his staff consider the matter carefully. He gave his opinion that Japan did not have aggressive designs, but that they would protect their interests in Manchuria. Chang should avoid at all costs a clash with Japan.[322]

Japanese representatives conveyed similar warnings against disturbing the peace of Manchuria to Feng Yü-hsiang, Yen Hsi-shan and Chiang Kai-shek, and probably encouraged all sides to negotiate a termination of the civil war. The American government would have no part in the Japanese *démarche*. Secretary of State Frank B. Kellogg telegraphed Minister MacMurray on 18 May and instructed: 'There will be no participation by the United States in joint action with the Japanese government or any other power to prevent the extension of Chinese hostilities to Manchuria or to interfere with the controlled military operation of Chinese armies, but solely for the protection of American citizens.'[323]

Events now moved very fast. The Fengtien Army had difficulty in holding its position at Paoting, and the line eastward of that strong point was very shaky. The Nationalists had agents in Peking attempting to negotiate defections. Chang Tso-lin and his generals had to consider the risks of holding on too long to north-eastern Chihli, which shielded Peking and Tientsin, for fear of being trapped therein. But if Chang Tso-lin and his army were to depart, who should be allowed to take over Peking? Feng Yü-hsiang was an old enemy of Chang Tso-lin. As early as mid April, the American minister had noted that the Peking regime hoped to defeat and drive off Feng's army, but to reach some compromise with Shansi and Nanking. Now, in May, Feng's army could certainly have captured the city, but a deal was worked out for the Fengtien Army to withdraw in such a way that Yen Hsi-shan's army would be first in the Peking-Tientsin area and Feng Yü-hsiang would be excluded from that rich prize.[324] By the end of May the Fengtien Army had given up Paoting

---

322 GBFO 504/258. Confidential. *Further correspondence respecting China*, 13613, no. 6, enclosure. Miles Lampson to Austen Chamberlain, Peking, 23 May 1928. 'Record of a conversation with Mr Ou Tching.' [Wu Chin].
323 FRUS, 1928, 2. 226, and Iriye, *After imperialism*, 321.
324 Sheridan, *Chinese warlord*, 238. GBFO 504/258. Confidential, *Further correspondence respecting China*, 13613, no. 40, Miles Lampson to Austen Chamberlain, Peking, 8 June 1928, a dispatch.

and was drawing back on Peking. Chang Tso-lin was preparing to depart from the capital.

On 1 June General Chiang, Feng and Yen met at Shihchiachuang to plan for the take-over of Peking and Tientsin and to settle on arrangements thereafter. Perhaps it was then – though it may have been earlier – that Feng Yü-hsiang learned he was not to get Peking; nor would Chiang, who returned to Nanking on the 3rd. Next day the Nationalist government appointed – that is, confirmed – Yen Hsi-shan as Peking's garrison commander.

Chang Tso-lin called in the diplomatic corps on 1 June for what turned out to be a valedictory address. He had already made arrangements to turn over governance of the city to a Peace Preservation Commission made up of Chinese elder statesmen, headed by Wang Shih-chen, once a close associate of Yuan Shih-k'ai and once a premier. Internal security was in the hands of Peking's efficient police and a brigade of Manchurian troops under General Pao Yü-lin, who would stay behind until the city passed to Yen Hsi-shan and then be permitted to return unmolested to Fengtien. Next day Marshal Chang issued a farewell telegram to the Chinese people, expressing regret that he had not successfully concluded the anti-Red campaign, and announcing his return to Manchuria in order to spare further bloodshed. He left Peking with pomp, accompanied by most of his cabinet and high ranking officers, on a special train on the night of 2/3 June, but the train was wrecked by bomb explosions early in the morning of 4 June as it neared Mukden. The Marshal died of his wounds within two hours. He had been assassinated by a group of officers of Japan's Kwantung Army, who plotted the deed on their own in opposition to Tanaka's policy.[325]

Chang Hsueh-liang, the Marshal's eldest son, and Yang Yü-t'ing his chief-of-staff, left together with Sun Ch'uan-fang on 4 June for Tientsin, which had to be held until the large Manchurian army had been evacuated toward Shanhaikuan. The Peace Preservation Commission then sent emissaries to Paoting to welcome Yen Hsi-shan to Peking. On 8 June a commander of the Third Army Group, General Shang Chen, led his Shansi troops into the capital, and on 11 June Yen Hsi-shan himself, accompanied by General Pai Ch'ung-hsi, entered the city. Another of his generals, Fu Tso-i, took over Tientsin by prearrangement on the 12th. The transition had been effected peacefully, except for one incident. General Han Fu-ch'ü, a subordinate of Feng Yü-hsiang, who had led the drive on Peking and whose troops were now barracked on the city's outskirts, surrounded and disarmed the departing Manchurian brigade that had been promised safe conduct. Peking's diplomatic corps had underwritten the safe passage, and protested to Nanking strenuously. Ultimately, the Manchurian troops were released and some of their arms returned.[326]

Launching on national reconstruction

The commanders of the Four Army Groups met in Peking on 6 July at a solemn ceremony before the coffin of their late Leader, Sun Yat-sen, in a temple in the Western Hills outside Peking. They reported that the long-cherished northern campaign had been accomplished with the capture of Peking and the elimination of its government. A few days later, the commanders and their staffs met in informal military conference to discuss the problem of troop disbandment. Ho Ying-ch'in had reported that the National Revolutionary Army now had about 300 divisions grouped in 84 corps, with troops numbering 2.2 million. (Apparently this counted all organized units as part of the NRA.) If properly paid, the normal cost of this vast army would be at least 60 million dollars a month. The commander-in-chief's office hoped to reduce the total to 80 divisions and 1.2 million men, which would consume only 60 per cent of the nation's revenues. Chiang Kai-shek presented his military colleagues with a memorandum prepared for the forthcoming meeting of the Central Executive Committee, which proposed a Military Rehabilitation Conference for the special purpose of formulating a disbandment scheme, fixing the number of troops and military expenses, and dividing the country into a definite number of military districts. He suggested 12, each having 40 to 50 thousand troops.[327] A disbandment conference was to be held in January 1929, but it achieved very little because, by then, the regional military factions had virtually divided the country. An indication of what was to come appeared in Peking at that July meeting of the commanders. Feng Yü-hsiang nursed a grievance at being cut out of the Peking and Tientsin spoils. When a Branch Political Council for Peking was established, with Yen Hsi-shan as chairman, General Feng would

326 *FRUS*, 1928, 2. 235–42; GBFO 504/258 confidential, *Further correspondence respecting China*, 13613, nos. 50 and 89, reports by Miles Lampson.
327 Kao Yin-tsu, *Chronology*, 300, 2 July 1928. (The figure for the victorious NRA in July 1928 was about 1.6 million.) *KMWH*, 21. 4067–71 for Chiang's preliminary disbandment plan. *Ibid.* 4076–85 for a list of divisions and corps counted as making up the NRA as of July 1928 (including many units that had no part in the Northern Expedition), and their commanders. GBFO 405/259. Confidential. *Further correspondence respecting China*, 13616, Oct.–Dec. 1928, no. 46, enclosure 7, 'Summary of military memorandum by Chiang Kai-shek' issued by Kuomin News Agency, Peiping, 15 July 1928.

not accept a position on it; ominously, he left Peking on 14 July to tend the graves of his ancestors, and thence to his military headquarters in Honan.[328]

The Fifth Plenum of the Kuomintang's Second Central Executive Committee met in Nanking from 8 to 14 August, to plan the nation's future. Generals Feng Yü-hsiang and Yen Hsi-shan, and Admiral Yang Shu-chuang were invited to attend as special guests.[329] The plenum faced important matters of national policy. The most contentious issue was how rapidly and rigorously to move towards centralization of political, financial and military power. Should the branch political councils, which, in effect, divided Nationalist China into satrapies, be abolished? After much wrangling between proponents of centralization and those who wished to retain local power – it almost ended the meeting – the plenum passed a resolution which affirmed that the Central Political Council should be appointed by the Central Executive Committee and pass its decisions through it to the national government to execute; branch political councils should be terminated by the end of the year, and in the meantime should not issue orders nor appoint and remove officials in their own names. Thus, the Political Council, originally created by Sun Yat-sen on Borodin's advice as his inner council, was not to be independent of and above the elected Central Executive Committee; and the recently created branch councils should be no more. However, when the list of Central Political Council members was announced, there were 46 persons, including nearly all regular members of the Central Executive and the Central Supervisory Committees, most major military figures, and some conservative veterans of the party who now were back in the fold.[330] It was very likely to be a figure-head organ, with decisions made by a small, inner group, as before. Another gesture toward centralization was passage of a resolution which stated, as a guiding principle, that all members of the party's Central Committees should reside at the capital and must not disperse to various places.

328 Kao Yin-tsu, *Chronology*, 300, 6 July 1928; GBFO 405/259. Confidential. *Further correspondence respecting China*, 13616, no. 9, Miles Lampson to Austen Chamberlain, Peking, 1 Aug. 1928.

329 *KMWH*, 21. 4092-100, for some documents on the Fifth Plenum. Kao Yin-tsu, *Chronology*, 305-7, for resolutions passed. Kao states that 24 regular members and one alternate, eight CSC members and one alternate, and Feng and Yang attended.

330 Beside Hu Han-min and Wang Ching-wei, who had missed the Plenum, two of Wang's followers who had been excluded from the Fourth and Fifth Plenums, Ch'en Kung-po and Ku Meng-yü, were included, as were Mme Sun Yat-sen and Eugene Chen. Important military men not members of either committee but included in the Central Political Council were Yen Hsi-shan, Feng Yü-hsiang, Yang Shu-chuang, Pai Ch'ung-hsi, and Ch'en Ming-shu. A list is in GBFO 405/259. Confidential. *Further correspondence respecting China*, 13616, no. 46, enclosure 3, from the Kuomin News Agency.

How might governmental finances be unified? T. V. Soong, the minister of finance, had convened two conferences, one on financial and one on economic reconstruction, drawing together leading private bankers, merchants and industrialists, provincial finance officers, representatives of the various armies, and financial experts. He described the nation's financial chaos and presented the plenum with detailed proposals coming from these conferences. They dealt with demarcation between national and provincial sources of revenue, abolition of internal transit taxes, recovery of tariff autonomy, liquidation of national indebtedness, unification of currency, promotion of commerce, stabilization of the money market, founding of a government central bank and regulating the private banking system, and issuance of public bonds to provide the cost of troop disbandment and reconstruction. Dr Soong insisted that unification of finance and adoption of a national budget were essential; it would be idle to talk of financial rehabilitation unless these two things were done. His plea was backed by a delegation of nearly 100 Shanghai bankers and merchants led by Yu Ya-ching (Yü Hsia-ch'ing), which threatened that no more loans could be exacted from them unless these reforms were carried out. They had had enough of extortion and blackmail by Chiang's agents. To Dr Soong, financial unification meant unified employment of financial personnel and centralized administration of the collection and expenditure of revenue. During the Northern Expedition, he complained, there was no budgeting at all; the minister of finance could only assemble funds and turn them over on command to the highest military authority for disposition. Now, he insisted, all revenues should be placed in the national treasury, while a powerful budget committee should decide on appropriations for all branches of government, and no deviations should be allowed without the committee's approval. 'Rehabilitation of finance and establishment of clean and efficient government cannot be realized unless a sound system of national budget is enforced', he concluded. The plenum considered his proposals 'proper and suitable' and turned them over to the Government Council for careful consideration and execution; and it agreed that establishment of a budget committee was imperative, and instructed the same council to organize the committee. A little later the Central Executive Committee's Standing Committee appointed a 13-man budget committee with a preponderance of the more powerful regional military men, but stipulated that the budget as drawn must be approved by the Government Council.[331]

---

331 On continued extortion of funds from Shanghai merchants and Soong's efforts to create a more orderly fiscal system, see Coble, 'The Kuomintang and the Shanghai capitalists,

The crucial problem in respect to centralization of power lay in the military sphere. So long as commanders had their independent bases and sources of revenue, there could be no real centralization. They might be persuaded to join the centre in reality, or they might be subdued by the centre. There seemed to be no other way. Chiang Kai-shek made an eloquent opening plea that those having military power should make a public vow that, despite differences in political views, they would never resort to arms and fight each other. The National Army hereafter should be used only for national defence and the suppression of bandits; it should never fight internal wars. 'If this principle is strictly adhered to, political differences among those in power will not develop into serious conflicts involving the entire country', he asserted.[332]

The plenum debated the problem of military reorganization and passed a resolution on fundamental principles: (a) military administration and military orders must be absolutely unified; (b) the army must quickly be reduced considerably in size, and annual military expenditures must not exceed half the national revenue; (c) military education must be unified and centralized and all military academies be established by the central government, no armies or local authorities being allowed to establish military academies or similar institutions; (d) all disbanded troops should be used as labourers for colonization and reconstruction purposes; and (e) in order to prepare for national defence, practical measures must be adopted to develop the navy and an airforce, and to strengthen forts and naval bases.

The last of these principles expressed the dream of 60 years; others sought to address problems that had grown out of China's protracted effort to protect itself from foreign aggression and internal disorder. Those problems could not be quickly solved. The plenum referred two other resolutions, one concerning party control of government and the army, and the other prohibiting military organs from interfering with mass movements, to the CEC Standing Committee and the highest military organ of the government, 'with instructions to formulate detailed measures based upon the principle of party supremacy in the state', and to carry them out.[333]

1927–29', 14–19. GBFO 405/259. Confidential. *Further correspondence respecting China*, 13616, no. 46, enclosure 6 for Soong's proposals, and no. 70, enclosure 1, Acting Consul-General Garstin, Shanghai, to Miles Lampson, 4 Sept. 1928. *KMWH*, 22. 4336–9 for the budget committee regulations and those appointed. They were Chiang Kai-shek, Yen Hsi-shan, Yang Shu-chuang, Wang Po-ch'ün, T'an Yen-k'ai, Ho Ying-ch'in, Feng Yü-hsiang. Li Tsung-jen, T.V. Soong, Yü Yu-jen, Li Chi-shen, Ts'ai Yuan-p'ei, and Chiang Tso-pin. Members unable to attend could send deputies.

332 GBFO, just cited, no. 46, enclosure 4, summary of a memorandum submitted by Chiang Kai-shek, from Kuomin News Agency, 9 Aug. 1928.

333 *Ibid.* enclosure 3.

Since the military campaigns were now thought to be over and the period of political tutelage was about to begin, the plenum resolved that a provisional constitution should be drawn up, adopted and enforced, and that the five-yuan system of government should come into effect. It also tried to legislate on a problem of conflicts between party and government, which, apparently, were more serious at lower levels than at the top, where the leaderships were fused. Should any party organ consider the action of a government organ at its same level as being improper, it should report the case upward to its superior party organ, which would then bring the matter to the attention of the governmental organ at its own level; that government organ would then discipline the offending lower organ according to law. The procedure was to be the same when a lower government organ had a complaint against a party organ at its level; it should report upward and after lateral consultation, the offending party organ would be disciplined by its superior.[334] But this regulation could not solve the problem inherent in two authorities – three, if the military be added – each with its own hierarchy and with separate lines of command.

The national revolution had been mounted to rid China of foreign domination. The 'unequal treaties', which gave extraordinary privileges to foreign nationals in China, outraged many patriotic Chinese. The Peking government had struggled to the last to revise such treaties as it could. On 7 July the Nationalist foreign minister, Wang Cheng-t'ing, had announced that all treaties that had expired, or were soon to do so, would be replaced by new ones, and that all other treaties would be abrogated and renegotiated. During a transition period, all foreign nationals in China, and their property, would be protected according to Chinese law, but foreigners must be subject to the laws of China and the jurisdiction of Chinese courts, and they must pay Chinese taxes and conventional tariffs. The ministry followed this order, which it lacked the power to enforce, with formal requests to a number of foreign governments to appoint negotiating delegates. The American minister, J. V. A. MacMurray, on instructions from Secretary of State Frank B. Kellogg, did negotiate a new tariff treaty with T. V. Soong, which they signed on 25 July. This accepted the principle of complete national autonomy for China and equal treatment of nationals of both countries in tariff matters. The new treaty would go into effect on 1 January of the next year, but this was contingent upon the 'most favoured nation' clause, which meant that it would not become operative until all other governments had acknowledged China's autonomous rights in respect of its tariffs. The

334 *Idem.*

negotiations and signing, with the approval of the secretary of state, seemed a form of *de facto* recognition of the Nanking government.[335] Furthermore, on 8 August Great Britain settled the Nanking Incident with the Nationalist government on terms similar to those of the United States.

It was in this nationalistic climate and mood of some elation that the Fifth Plenum had before it a memorandum on foreign policy prepared by T'an Yen-k'ai and Ts'ai Yuan-p'ei, which called for complete and unconditional abrogation of all the unequal treaties, set 1 January 1929 as the date for ending the treaties which imposed fixed tariffs upon China, demanded unconditional abolition of consular jurisdiction and the immediate retrocession of foreign concessions and settlements, and forbade the stationing of foreign troops and warships in China. No more than a year should be allowed for the process of negotiating new and reciprocal treaties.[336] This ambitious programme actually took 15 years to accomplish.[337]

The plenum ended on 15 August, leaving many proposals to the CEC Standing Committee to deal with. Then official Nanking busied itself preparing to establish a new government, both in form and in personnel. Hu Han-min returned from abroad on 3 September and, after some hesitation, agreed to participate together with Tai Chi-t'ao and Wang Ch'ung-hui in the drafting of an Organic Law of the National Government. Their work was completed on 3 October and the Kuomintang's Central Executive Committee promulgated the law on 8 October. It first promulgated 'The general principles governing the period of political tutelage', which made it quite clear that the Kuomintang, through its National Congresses and its Central Executive Committee, exercised sovereign power during the period in which the Chinese people were being prepared for democratic life. The Kuomintang's Political Council would guide and superintend the national government in the execution of important national affairs, and the Council might amend and interpret the Organic Law.[338]

On 10 October 1928, the seventeenth anniversary of the outbreak of the revolution which ended the Manchu dynasty, a refurbished Nationalist government was inaugurated at Nanking with pomp and fanfare. Its

335 Kao Yin-tsu, *Chronology*, 300–4; Borg, *American policy*, 400–2.
336 GBFO 405/259. Confidential. *Further correspondence respecting China*, 13616, no. 46, enclosure 5.
337 William L. Tung, *China and the foreign powers: the impact of and reaction to unequal treaties*, 249–57 for a systematic account of treaty revision before the 'Mukden Incident' of Sept. 1931.
338 *KMWH*, 22. 4356–63 for the Guiding Principles and the Organic Law; the former is translated in Shieh, *The Kuomintang*, 137–8.

structure was of Sun Yat-sen's conception: Five separate boards or yuan – executive, legislative, judicial, examination and control. The Standing Committee of the Kuomintang Central Executive Committee chose the five heads of these yuan, all prestigious veterans: T'an Yen-k'ai, Hu Han-min, Wang Ch'ung-hui, Tai Chi-t'ao, and Ts'ai Yuan-p'ei – although Ts'ai declined to accept the appointment, which was later given to Yü Yu-jen. Above these boards was a State Council made up of these men and 12 others, some powerful, some prestigious, and several far from Nanking: Feng Yü-hsiang, Sun Fo, Ch'en Kuo-fu, Yen Hsi-shan, Li Tsung-jen, Li Chi-shen, Ho Ying-ch'in, Chang Hsueh-liang, Lin Sen, Yang Shu-chuang and Chang Chi, with Chiang Kai-shek as its chairman, and hence the highest official of the government, its president. A few days later the Political Council appointed the ministers in the Executive Yuan.

The era of the Nanking government – ruled by the Kuomintang Political Council – had begun.

China's prospects in 1928

Seen from the perspective of late 1928, China's future seemed bright. It was a time of optimism that verged on jubilation. The Nationalists had destroyed the corrupt and bankrupt Peking government and a new government was in place, staffed by well educated and patriotic men who had long been concerned for the condition of the country, and who intended that the new government should solve the nation's many political, economic and social problems. The leaders of the Nationalist Party planned to control the government and to set its policies; they conceived their role as a stewardship during a period of tutelage. Theirs was a popular party in 1928. Few Chinese questioned its right to manage public affairs. It had a respected revolutionary history, and had just proved itself an effective organization for mobilizing and channelling power to achieve popular goals.

Four years of close Russian involvement with the Kuomintang had left upon it a Leninist stamp. It was very different from the loosely linked congeries of revolutionaries that had coalesced around Sun Yat-sen from time to time. Now it practised 'democratic centralism', with the inevitable emphasis on centralism and dictation by a very few. The party was better prepared to exercise tutelage than it had been before its reorganization in 1924. It had improved its propaganda techniques, though keeping nationalism as the central theme, and it had learned the utility of mobilizing 'the masses', as well as some of the risks involved. The Kuomintang had created a military force under its own leadership, which, through a

system of political training, had proved an effective instrument of revolution. Now the Kuomintang had a new leader, the 41-year-old Chiang
Kai-shek, respected and admired, who had shown determination and
ability at careful planning, intrigue and conciliation. He understood well
the ultimate power of the purse and the sword. The party's leadership
was now much more conservative in outlook than it had been during the
first two years after Sun Yat-sen's death, when Borodin's influence was
strongest. Most of the party's liberal-minded leaders were away, and communists had been driven out. The group which now intended to lead the
party was, as we have seen, riven by factionalism – entirely familiar in
the Chinese setting, yet an incubus.

The Chinese Communist Party, instead of being a temporary partner of
the Kuomintang and growing rapidly in numbers and influence, was now
in revolt against it, driven to that position long before it was ready for
the 'second stage' of revolution, the socialist stage. Reduced, probably,
to fewer than ten thousand members, if that many, the party's fortunes
were at a low ebb. Some 20 of its youthful leaders, idealistic activists
from the May Fourth student generation, had been executed, including the
two sons of Ch'en Tu-hsiu, and one of its most prestigious leaders, Li
Ta-chao. Hundreds of their members had died in battle or been killed in
ill-conceived uprisings; and thousands had simply withdrawn from the
dangerous party. The rest of its members lived furtively in cities, or in a
few remote rural areas trying to hold on to essential bases. Some of the
remaining leaders had journeyed secretly to Russia for the Sixth Congress
of the Chinese Communist Party, held during June and July 1928 in a
village outside Moscow. The Congress elected a 40-year-old proletarian,
Hsiang Chung-fa, as secretary-general, and vowed to drive imperialism
out of China, really unify the country, and abolish the landowning system
of the landlord class. It called upon the Chinese people to overthrow the
Kuomintang, establish soviets of workers', peasants', and soldiers' deputies, confiscate foreign enterprises, and carry out a variety of social
reforms, for this was still the epoch of bourgeois-democratic revolution.
Those leaders faced an enormously difficult task of rebuilding their party
in a hostile environment, and of emancipating themselves from Comintern direction.

Yet seven years since the party's founding had provided the leadership
with valuable experience on which to draw, and many lessons. It had
learned in a practical way how to organize a political movement directed
towards a nationalistic revolution, and how to recruit patriotic youth
through the party's subsidiary organization, the Communist Youth
League. Mostly people of education, the leaders had perfected the art of

propaganda through a variety of journals directed towards different groups in society; and they knew how to organize patriotic demonstrations in which they discovered activists, and how to manipulate such movements towards the party's other goals. They had gained experience in 'united front work', joining with a variety of other organizations in common patriotic efforts, usually anti-imperialist. Some of them had learned how to come 'close' to the real proletariat; how to organize workers into unions and federations that were controlled by the party, and in this process, how to mount and finance strikes, the importance of coercion, and the need to generate public support. Other leaders had been able to organize a vast number of poor farmers in South China, had learned what grievances and hopes would bring them into group action; but also, how fragile and weak such rapidly created organizations were in the face of established local power. Not a few of the remaining leaders had been involved in military work, either as cadets in Whampoa Academy and its branch at Wuhan, or as political instructors and combat officers. Starting from the school room, the workshop, or the farm, almost all the leaders had, by 1928, undergone their baptisms of violence. A screening process had removed the faint-hearted. In short, the Chinese Communist Party still had a vigorous young leadership with many talents, wide contacts, and much useful experience in revolutionary work, but the odds against them must have seemed enormous.

Enormous problems faced any group, party, or regime that hoped to remake China according to some more humane blueprint. In the field of foreign relations there was a 70-year legacy of treaties, many signed under duress, which restricted China's sovereignty and gave foreigners extraordinary privileges, which their governments enforced with gunboats and marines. Although Great Britain and the United States were moving towards negotiating the return of China's 'lost rights' step by step, a more determined imperialist power, Japan, was acting forcefully to protect and enhance its economic dominance of Manchuria.

Internally, warlordism had scarcely been ended, though a few militarists such as Wu P'ei-fu, Sun Ch'uan-fang, Chang Tsung-ch'ang, and Chang Tso-lin had been overthrown. They had been replaced by others out of the Northern Expedition. Now the country had five main agglomerations of regional military power – the group proclaiming itself the Nationalist government, based in the lower Yangtze valley; the Kwangsi faction holding much of Hupei, Hunan and Kwangsi; Feng Yü-hsiang's Kuominchün with its base in Shensi and populous Honan, and now stretching into Shantung and Hopei; Yen Hsi-shan of Shansi, with subordinates ensconced in the Peking-Tientsin area as well; and Chang Hsueh-liang and other Manchurian generals controlling domestic affairs in the North-east. Most of West and South-west China had scarcely been touched by the Northern Expedition; local commanders in Szechwan, Kweichow and Yunnan defended and exploited their territories as before. Even Kwangtung, the home of the nationalist revolution, was only loosely attached to the Nanking centre. This deeply rooted phenomenon of nearly autonomous regional power – a product of geography and history – must be a major obstacle to all efforts at centralization and nationwide rehabilitation.

Many other inheritances from the past created intractable problems – a chaotic monetary system; a taxation system characterized by exploitation of the poor and riddled with corruption; an inadequate transportation system for a modernizing nation; very little factory industry, and that concentrated in a few cities where the workers lived in slums and were overworked and underpaid. Most serious of all was the condition of rural life, with a dense population struggling with enormous industry to sustain itself on too little arable land and without benefit of scientific agricultural techniques. Education and public health needed great expansion because the vast populace was largely illiterate and was plagued by preventable diseases. Parts of the country were periodically ravaged by famine.

Thus, though the politically aware looked forward with hope in 1928, progress towards creating a modern nation-state was sure to be slow even under the most favourable conditions. And such were not to be.

BIBLIOGRAPHICAL ESSAY

For the activities of the Nationalist and Communist parties in cooperation and competition during the years 1923 to 1928, the Kuomintang Archives in Taiwan are fundamentally important. They contain minutes of party congresses and of weekly meetings and plenums of the Central Executive Committee; records of the Political Council and Military Council, and of the so-called Joint Council in Wuhan; a great variety of documents of the Kuomintang's central bureaux (such as those for Organization, Farmers, Workers, Youth, Women) as well as now rare publications, collections of news clippings arranged by subject, correspondence of important party personnel, field reports and the like. Thousands of documents from these archives are available in *Ko-ming wen-hsien* (Documents of the revolution), a multi-volume series published under the Kuomintang Central Executive Committee (vols. 8 through 22 especially pertain to the Nationalist Revolution). Two books based primarily on the Kuomintang Archives and written by staff members are Li Yun-han, *Ts'ung jung-Kung tao ch'ing-tang* (From admitting the communists to the purification of the Kuomintang), and Chiang Yung-ching, *Bo-lo-t'ing yü Wu-han cheng-ch'üan* (Borodin and the Wuhan regime). The National Historical Commission has published important collections such as the two volume chronological biography of Sun Yat-sen, entitled *Kuo-fu nien-p'u*, and a multi-volume collection of Dr Sun's writings, speeches, and correspondence, *Kuo-fu ch'üan-chi*. (There are at least 22 different collections of Dr Sun's works.)

Also in Taiwan are archives on the career of Chiang Kai-shek, not readily available to scholars at the time this was written. Mao Ssu-ch'eng compiled a chronological account of Chiang's life up to the end of 1926, which included excerpts of many documents, *Min-kuo shih-wu-nien i-ch'ien chih Chiang Chieh-shih hsien-sheng* (Mr Chiang Kai-shek up to 1926). The library of the National Government Ministry of Justice contains much archival material on the Chinese communist movement from about 1927, including the valuable intra-party journal, *Chung-yang t'ung-hsin* (Central newsletter). Many documents from this journal are translated in Hyobom Pak, *Documents of the Chinese Communist Party, 1927–1930*. Other important archival collections in Taiwan come from the various ministries of the Peking Government (including notably, the Foreign Office or Ministry of Foreign Affairs, held by the Institute of Modern History, Academia Sinica) and ministries of the Nationalist government.

The vast archives in the People's Republic of China are being energetically developed. Archives of the Communist International are preserved in Moscow and have been used by Soviet scholars. Books and articles cited in this volume have also used the records of the Russian aid missions in China and other valuable historical collections. Chinese police in Peking raided the Soviet military attaché's office on 6 April 1927 and carted off a great volume of documents generated by Soviet Russian activities in China in assisting the Nationalist Revolution, and some documents of the Chinese Communist Party. Many of these documents were translated and published; see the list of publications in C. Martin Wilbur and Julie Lien-ying How, eds. *Documents on communism, nationalism, and Soviet advisers in China, 1918–1927: papers seized in the 1927 Peking raid*, 565–68.

British archives in the Public Record Office in London have the correspondence with the Foreign Office and Colonial Office from China and Hong Kong. Particularly informative is the series of 'confidential print', FO 405, which contains important documents from and about China, printed for high-level circulation in the government and missions abroad, then cumulated and bound semi-annually or quarterly. (See Nathan, 69, for two guides to this series.)

American government archives concerning China, preserved in the National Archives in Washington, are also well arranged and open. Dispatches from the American legation in Peking and from consular officials in Canton, Changsha, Hankow, Nanking and Shanghai are useful for the period treated. The State Department's publication, *Papers relating to the foreign relations of the United States*, in annual volumes, gives excerpts, arranged by topic, from important correspondence between diplomatic and consular officials in China and the State Department. Most of the dispatches and telegrams are available on microfilms. (See Nathan, *Modern China, 1840–1972*, for series listing). The National Archives also contain information provided by military and naval intelligence, and from commercial attachés in China.

Two useful guides to Japanese collections that have been microfilmed are by Cecil H. Uyehara, and John Young, cited above.

Periodicals contemporary to the events are numerous and constitute important sources of historical information. Invaluable guides to Chinese periodicals are Contemporary China Institute, *A bibliography of Chinese newspapers and periodicals in European libraries*, and Library of Congress, *Chinese periodicals in the Library of Congress*. For the Nationalist Revolution the following are most important: *Tung-fang tsa-chih* (The eastern miscellany) and *Kuo-wen chou-pao* (The Kuowen weekly, illustrated) as non-party journals of news and opinion, which also published documents; *Hsiang-tao chou-pao* (The guide weekly) as an organ of the Chinese Communist Party; and *People's Tribune*, March to August 1927, as an organ of the Nationalist government in Hankow. Useful sources of foreign reporting are *North China Herald* (weekly edn of the British *North China Daily News*) and the American *China Weekly Review*, both published in Shanghai; *South China Morning Post*, Hong Kong; *The New York Times* and

The Times, London. A valuable series of translations from the Chinese press is
Léon Wieger, S.J., *Chine modérne*, particularly Tomes V-VII, covering the years
1924–27. Important collections which reprint materials from Chinese journals
and other sources of the day are: *Kung-fei huo-kuo shih-liao hui-pien* (A compilation of documents on the communist bandits' destruction of the nation), vols
1 and 4, published in Taipei; *Ti-i-tz'u kuo-nei ko-ming chan-cheng shih-ch'i ti kung-
jen yun-tung* (The labour movement during the first revolutionary civil war
period); and *Ti-i-tz'u . . . nung-min yun-tung* (The farmers' movement during
the first revolutionary civil war period), both published in the People's Republic
of China.

Other compilations reprint documents, such as *Chung-kuo Kuo-min-tang chung-
yao hsuan-yen hui-pien* (Collection of important proclamations of the Kuomintang
of China), and *Chung-kuo wu ta wei-jen shou-cha* (Letters of China's five great
leaders, i.e., Sun Yat-sen, Chiang Kai-shek, Wang Ching-wei, Hu Han-min
and Liao Chung-k'ai). Collected writings and speeches are numerous, for example, for Chang Chi, Chiang Kai-shek, Hu Han-min, Tai Chi-t'ao, Teng
Yen-ta, Wang Ching-wei and Wu Chih-hui, among others, on the Nationalist
side, and for Ch'en Tu-hsiu, Ch'ü Ch'iu-pai, Li Ta-chao and Mao Tse-tung
among those on the Communist side. Several documentary collections are
available in English, for example, Milton J. T. Shieh, *The Kuomintang: selected
historical documents, 1894–1969*, and Conrad Brandt, Benjamin Schwartz and John
K. Fairbank, *A documentary history of Chinese communism*, though each has only
a few documents from this period. For Soviet Russian and Comintern policies,
Soviet Russia and the East, 1920–1927: a documentary survey by Xenia Joukoff
Eudin and Robert C. North is most useful. The Wilbur and How collection has
been noted; see also *M. N. Roy's mission to China: the Kuomintang-Communist
split of 1927*, by Robert C. North and Xenia J. Eudin.

Many participants have left memoirs. Of particular interest is *The memoirs of
Li Tsung-jen*, with Dr Te-kong Tong as interviewer, research scholar, writer
and editor. General Li, who commanded the original Seventh Corps from
Kwangsi, gave an extended account of the battles and politics of the Northern
Expedition. For military organization and campaigns, the major compilations,
which remain invaluable sources for research, are: *Kuo-min ko-ming-chün chan-
shih* (A military history of the National Revolutionary Army); *Ti-ssu-chün chi-
shih* (Factual account of the Fourth Army), on the 'Ironsides' of Chang Fa-k'uei;
Pei-fa chan-shih (A battle history of the northern punitive expedition), 5 vols.,
comp. by the Ministry of National Defence, Historical Bureau, Taipei; *Kuo-
chün cheng-kung shih-kao* (Draft history of political work in the National Army),
2 vols., comp. by the Ministry of National Defence, Historical Bureau, Taipei.

Several Russians who assisted the Nationalist Revolution and who survived
the Stalin purges wrote their memoirs with the help of younger scholars, who
were given access to archives. The most extensive is a two volume account by
General A. I. Cherepanov. It is marred, however, by anachronistic biases. A

rough translation of volume one is *Notes of a military adviser in China*. Two other interesting and rather charming reminiscences have been translated into English: Vera Vladimirovna Vishnyakova-Akimova, *Two years in revolutionary China, 1925–1927*, translated by Steven I. Levine; and Marc Kasanin, *China in the twenties*, translated by his widow, Hilda Kasanina. An important source for information on the Russian military aid mission, as well as for recent Russian scholarship concerning it, is Dieter Heinzig, *Sowjetische militärberater bei der Kuomintang 1923–1927*. The posthumously published study by Lydia Holubnychy, *Michael Borodin and the Chinese revolution, 1923–1925* used and lists many recent works by Soviet scholars having access to Russian archives. The Russian sources have been used most recently by Dan Jacobs, *Borodin: Stalin's man in China*. The beginnings of cooperation between the two parties is detailed in Benjamin I. Schwartz, *Chinese communism and the rise of Mao*, a classic for its time of publication, and C. Martin Wilbur, *Sun Yat-sen: frustrated patriot*. Harold Isaacs, *The tragedy of the Chinese revolution*, first published in 1938, revised and reissued in 1951, has been very influential in its presentation of the 'under dog' communist and proletarian cause and for its anti-Stalin and anti-Chiang Kai-shek views. In similar vein is the path-breaking study by Jean Chesneaux, *The Chinese labor movement, 1919–1927*, translated from the French by H. M. Wright. In the field of foreign relations, two excellent works are Dorothy Borg, *American policy and the Chinese revolution, 1925–1928*, and Akira Iriye, *After imperialism: the search for a new order in the Far East, 1921–1931*.

BIBLIOGRAPHY

Andrews, Carol Corder, 'The policy of the Chinese Communist Party towards the peasant movement, 1921–1927: the impact of national on social revolution'. Columbia University, Ph.D. dissertation, 1978

Blackburn, V. 'Report on the situation in Shanghai', dispatch dated 15 April 1927 in Great Britain: Foreign Office 405/253. Confidential. *Further correspondence respecting China*, 13304 (April–June 1927) no. 156, enclosure 2

Boorman, Howard L. and Richard C. Howard, eds. *Biographical dictionary of Republican China*. New York: Columbia University Press, 4 vols. 1967–71 and index volume (vol. 5) 1979

Borg, Dorothy. *American policy and the Chinese revolution, 1925–1928*. New York: Macmillan, 1947

Brandt, Conrad, Schwartz, Benjamin and Fairbank, John K. *A documentary history of Chinese communism*. Cambridge, Mass.: Harvard University Press, 1952

Brenan, J. F. 'A report on results of translation of Russian documents seized in the Russian Consulate, December 14, 1927' in Great Britain: Foreign Office, 405/256. Confidential. *Further correspondence respecting China*, 13583, Jan.–March 1928

CCP: Chinese Communist Party

CEC: Central Executive Committee (of the KMT or the CCP)

Chan, Gilbert F. and Etzold, Thomas H., eds. *China in the 1920's: nationalism and revolution*. New York and London: New Viewpoints, 1976

Chang Chi 張繼. *Chang P'u-ch'üan hsien-sheng ch'üan-chi* 張溥泉先生全集 (A complete collection of works of Chang Chi), ed. by Chung-yang kai-tsao wei-yuan-hui tang-shih pien-tsuan wei-yuan-hui 中央改造委員會黨史編纂委員會 (Committee on party history, Central Committee of Reconstruction). Taipei: Chung-yang wen-wu kung-ying-she 中央文物供應社, 1951 ... *pu-pien* 補編 (supplement), 1952

Chang Kuo-t'ao. *The rise of the Chinese Communist Party, 1921–1927; ... 1928–1938*. 2 vols. Lawrence, Kansas: University Press of Kansas, 1971–2

Chang, T. C. *The farmers' movement in Kwangtung*, trans. by the Committee on Christianizing Economic Relations. Shanghai: National Christian Council of China, 1928

Chao Shih-yen 趙世炎 ('Shih-ying' 施英 pseud.), 'Record of the Shanghai general strike', *HTCP* 嚮導週報, 189 (28 Feb. 1927); reprinted in *Kung-jen*, 450–72, with documents

Chao Shih-yen ('Shih-ying', pseud.). 'A record of Shanghai workers' March insurrection'. *HTCP*, 193 (6 April 1927); reprinted with documents in *Kung-jen*, 473–90

Chapman, H. Owen. *The Chinese revolution 1926–27: a record of the period under communist control as seen from the Nationalist capital, Hankow*. London: Constable & Co., Ltd., 1928

Ch'en Hsun-cheng 陳訓正 (Ch'en Pu-lei 陳布雷?), *Kuo-min ko-ming-chün chan shih ch'u-kao* 國民革命軍戰史初稿 (A military history of the National Revolutionary Army). 4 vols. Taipei: Wen-hai, 1972

Ch'en Ta. *Chung-kuo lao-kung wen-t'i* 中國勞工問題 (Chinese labour problems). Shanghai: Commercial Press, 1929

Ch'en Tu-hsiu. 'Letter to Tai Chi-t'ao'. *HTCP* 129–30 (11 and 18 Sept. 1925) 1186–90, 1196–7

Ch'en Tu-hsiu. *Kao ch'üan-tang t'ung-chih shu* 告全黨同志書 (A letter to all comrades of the Party). Reprinted in *Kung-fei huo-kuo shih-liao hui-pien*, 427–44; trans. in *Chinese Studies in History*, 2.3 (Spring 1970) 224–50

Cheng Tien-fang. *A history of Sino-Russian relations*. Washington: Public Affairs Press, 1957

Cherepanov, A. I. *Severnyi pokhod Natsional'-no-Revoliutsionnoi Armii Kitaia (zapiski voennogo sovetnika 1926–1927)* (The Northern Expedition of the National Revolutionary Army of China – notes of a military adviser 1926–7). Moscow: Izdatel'stvo 'Nauka', 1968

Cherepanov, A. I. *Zapiski voennogo sovetnika v kitae: iz istorii pervoi grazdanskoi revolutsionnoi coiny, 1924–1927* (Notes of a military adviser in China; from the history of the first revolutionary civil war in China, 1924–1927). Moscow: Academy of Sciences of the USSR, Institut Narodov Azii, 'Nauka'. 2 vols., 1964, 1968. Draft trans. of vol. 1 by Alexandra O. Smith, edited by Harry H. Collier and Thomas M. Williamson, Taipei: (U. S. Army) Office of Military History, 1970

Chesneaux, Jean. *Le mouvement ouvrier chinois de 1919 à 1927*. Paris, La Hague: Mouton, 1962

Chesneaux, Jean. *The Chinese labor movement, 1919–1927*. Trans. from the French by H. M. Wright. Stanford: Stanford University Press, 1968

Ch'i Hsi-sheng. *Warlord politics in China 1916–1928*. Stanford: Stanford University Press, 1976

Chiang Kai-shek 蔣介石. 'A letter of reply to Wang Ching-wei', in Wen-hua yen-chiu she, comps. *Chung-kuo wu ta wei-jen shou cha* (q.v.), 246–53

Chiang Kai-shek. 'Military report' to the Second Kuomintang Congress (in Chinese), in *KMWH*, 11 (Dec. 1955) 1756–63

Chiang Kai-shek. *Chiang wei-yuan-chang ch'üan-chi* 蔣委員長全集 (Complete works of Generalissimo Chiang), ed. Shen Feng-kang 沈鳳崗. Taipei: Min-tsu ch'u-pan she 民族出版社, 1956

Chiang Yung-ching 蔣永敬. *Bo-lo-t'ing yü Wu-han cheng-ch'üan* 鮑羅廷與武漢政權 (Borodin and the Wuhan regime). Taipei: China Committee for Publication Aid and Prize Awards, 1964

Chiang Yung-ching. *Hu Han-min hsien-sheng nien-p'u* 胡漢民先生年譜 (Chronological biography of Mr Hu Han-min). Taipei: Chung-kuo Kuomintang Central Executive Committee, Party History Committee, 1978

Ch'ien I-chang 錢義璋, ed. 'Sha-chi t'ung shih' 沙基痛史 (The tragic history of Shakee). Canton?, n.p., 1925?; reprinted in *KMWH*, 18 (Sept. 1957), 3330–3419

China Quarterly. London, 1960–

China Weekly Review. Shanghai, 1917–

The China year book. H. G. W. Woodhead, ed. London: George Routledge & Sons, Ltd., 1912–21; Tientsin: The Tientsin Press, 1921–30; Shanghai: The North China Daily News & Herald, Ltd., 1931–9

Chinese Correspondence: weekly organ of the Central Executive Committee of the Kuomintang. Wuhan 2.6 (1 May 1927)

Chinese Studies in History: A Journal of Translation. White Plains, N.Y.: International Arts and Sciences Press, Inc., Fall 1967–

Ch'ü Ch'iu-pai 瞿秋白. *Ch'ü Ch'iu-pai hsuan-chi* 瞿秋白選集 (Selected writings of Ch'ü Ch'iu-pai). Peking: Jen-min, 1959

Chuan-chi wen-hsueh 傳記文學 (Biographical literature). Monthly. Taipei, 1962–

Chung-kuo Kuo-min-tang cheng-li tang-wu chih t'ung-chi pao-kao 中國國民黨整理黨務之統計報告 (Statistical report on the work of party adjustment of the Kuomintang of China). Nanking: KMT CEC Organization Department, March 1929

Chung-kuo Kuo-min-tang chou-k'an 中國國民黨週刊 (Kuomintang of China weekly). Canton, 1924

Chung-kuo Kuo-min-tang ch'üan-kuo tai-piao ta-hui hui-i-lu 中國國民黨全國代表大會會議錄 (Minutes of the national congress of the Kuomintang of China). Reprinted, Washington, D.C.: Center for Chinese Research Materials, 1971

Chung-kuo Kuo-min-tang chung-yao hsuan-yen hui-pien 中國國民黨重要宣言彙編 (Collection of important proclamations of the Kuomintang of China). n.p.: Tang-i yen-chiu hui 黨義研究會, May 1929

Chung-kuo Kuo-min-tang ti-erh-tz'u ch'üan-kuo tai-piao ta-hui hui-i chi-lu 中國國民黨第二次全國代表大會會議記錄 (Minutes of the Second National Congress of Kuomintang delegates). n.p.: Central Executive Committee of the Kuomintang of China, April 1926

Chung-kuo lao-kung yun-tung shih pien-tsuan wei-yuan-hui 中國勞工運動史編纂委員會, comp. *Chung-kuo lao-kung yun-tung shih* 中國勞工運動史 (A history of the Chinese labour movement). 5 vols. Taipei: Chinese Labour Welfare Publisher, 1959

Chung-kuo nung-min 中國農民 (The Chinese farmer). Canton: Farmers' Bureau of the Central Executive Committee of the Kuomintang of China, 1926. Photolithographic reprint edn, Tokyo: Daian, 1964

Chung-kuo wu ta wei-jen shou-cha. See Wen-hua yen-chiu she.

Chung-yang t'ung-hsin 中央通信 (Central newsletter). Organ of the Central Committee of the Chinese Communist Party, Aug. 1927–

Clifford, Nicholas R. *Shanghai, 1925: urban nationalism and the defense of foreign privilege*. Ann Arbor: Center for Chinese Studies, University of Michigan, 1979

Clubb, O. Edmund. *China and Russia: the 'great game'*. New York: Columbia University Press, 1971

Coble, Parks, Jr. 'The Shanghai capitalists and the Nationalist government 1927–1937', University of Illinois, Ph.D. dissertation, 1975. Published as a book by Harvard University Press, 1980

Coble, Parks M., Jr. 'The Kuomintang regime and the Shanghai capitalists, 1927–29'. *CQ*, 77 (March 1979) 1–24

Contemporary China Institute. *A bibliography of Chinese newspapers and periodicals in European libraries*. Cambridge: Cambridge University Press, 1975

CQ: See *China Quarterly, The*

Cressey, George Babcock. *China's geographic foundations: a survey of the land and its people*. New York and London: McGraw Hill Book Co., 1934

CSC: Central Supervisory Committee of the Kuomintang

CWR: China Weekly Review. Shanghai, 1917– (formerly *Millard's Review*)

CYB: The China Yearbook

Degras, Jane. *The Communist International, 1919–1943: documents selected and edited by Jane Degras*. 3 vols. London: Oxford University Press, 1956–65

Deliusin, L. P., ed. *Kantonskaia Kommuna* (The Canton Commune). Moscow: Akad. Nauk SSSR, Institut Dal'nego Vostoka, 'Nauka', 1967

Etō, Shinkichi 衛藤瀋吉. 'Hai-lu-feng – the first Chinese soviet government'. Pt I. *CQ*, 8 (Oct./Dec. 1961) 160–83; pt II (Jan./March 1962) 149–81

Eudin, Xenia Joukoff and North, Robert C. *Soviet Russia and the East, 1920–1927: a documentay survey*. Stanford: Stanford University Press, 1957

Evans, Lee and Block, Russell, eds. *Leon Trotsky on China: introduction by Peng Shu-tse*. New York: Monad Press, 1976

'First proclamation of the revolutionary government on the farmers' movement', in *Chung-kuo Kuo-min-tang chung-yao hsuan-yen hui-pien* (q.v.) 247–51

Fischer, Louis. *The soviets in world affairs: a history of the relations between the Soviet Union and the rest of the world*. 2 vols. London and New York: Jonathan Cape, 1930

Fischer, Louis. *Men and politics: an autobiography*. New York: Duell, Sloan and Pearce, 1941

Gauss, C. E. 'Labor, student and agitator movements in Shanghai during February, 1927'. Dispatch dated 9 April 1927, in U.S. Department of State. Records relating to the internal affairs of China, 1910–29. USNA 893.00/8822

Gauss, C. E. 'Political conditions in the Shanghai consular district'. Dispatch covering period 21 March to 20 April 1927, in U.S. Department of State. Records relating to the internal affairs of China, 1910–29. USNA 893.00/8906

Gillin, Donald G. *Warlord: Yen Hsi-shan in Shansi province 1911–1949*. Princeton: Princeton University Press, 1967

GLU: General Labour Union

Glunin, V. I. 'Komintern i stanovlenie kommunisticheskogo dvizheniia v Kitae (1920–1927)'. (The Comintern and the formation of the communist movement in China (1920–1927)). *Komintern i Vostok; bor'ba za Leninskuiu strategiiu i taktiku v natsional'no-osvoboditel'nom dvizhenii* (Comintern and the Orient; the struggle for the Leninist strategy and tactics in the national liberational movement). Moscow: Glav. Red. Vost. Lit., 1969, 242–99

Great Britain. Foreign Office. Archives, Public Record Office, London; cited as FO

Great Britain. Foreign Office. comd. 2636, China No. 1 (1926). *Papers respecting the first firing in the Shameen affair of June 23, 1925*. London: H. M. Stationery Office, 1926

Great Britain. Foreign Office. Comd. 2953. China No. 4 (1927). *Papers relating to the Nanking Incident of March 24 and 25, 1927*. London: H. M. Stationery Office, 1927

Great Britain. Foreign Office. 405/240–259. Confidential. *Further correspondence respecting China*. Jan.-June 1923–Oct.-Dec. 1928

Greene, Ruth Altman. *Hsiang-Ya journal*. Hamden, Conn.: Shoe String Press, 1977

Gruber, Helmut. *Soviet Russia masters the Comintern*. Garden City, N.Y.: Anchor Press/Doubleday, 1974

Guillermaz, Jacques. *A history of the Chinese Communist Party, 1921–1949*. New York: Random House, 1972. Trans. of *Histoire du parti communiste chinois 1921–49*. Paris: Payot, 1968

Hao, Yen-p'ing 郝延平. *The comprador in nineteenth century China: bridge between East and West*. Cambridge, Mass.: Harvard University Press, 1970

Harrison, James Pinckney. *The long march to power: a history of the Chinese Communist Party, 1921–72*. New York & Washington, D.C.: Praeger, 1972

Heinzig, Dieter. *Sowjetische militärberater bei der Kuomintang 1923–1927*. Baden-Baden: Momos Verlagsgesellschaft, 1978

History of the First Army Group. See *Kuo-min Ko-ming Chün Ti-i Chi-t'uan Chün . . .*

Ho Ping-ti and Tsou Tang 鄒讜, eds. *China in crisis*. 3 vols. Chicago: University of Chicago Press, 1968

Hobart, Alice Tisdale. *Within the walls of Nanking*. London: Jonathan Cape, 1928

Hofheinz, Roy, Jr. 'The Autumn Harvest uprising'. *CQ*, 32 (Oct.–Dec. 1967) 37–87

Hofheinz, Roy, Jr. *The broken wave: the Chinese communist peasant movement, 1922–1928*. Cambridge, Mass.: Harvard University Press, 1977

Holden, Reuben. *Yale in China: the mainland, 1901–1951.* New Haven: The Yale in China Association, 1964

Holoch, Donald, trans. *Seeds of peasant revolution: report on the Haifeng peasant movement by P'eng P'ai.* Ithaca: Cornell University China-Japan Program, 1973

Holubnychy, Lydia. *Michael Borodin and the Chinese revolution, 1923–1925.* Ann Arbor: University Microfilms International, 1979. Published for the East Asian Institute, Columbia University

Hsiang-tao chou-pao 嚮導週報 (The guide weekly). Shanghai and Canton: Chung-kuo Kung-ch'an-tang, Sept. 1923–July 1927

Hsiao Tso-liang. *Chinese communism in 1927: city vs. countryside.* Hong Kong: The Chinese University of Hong Kong, 1970

Hsieh Ping-ying. *Autobiography of a Chinese girl,* trans. by Tsui Chi. London: Allen & Unwin, 1943

HTCP: Hsiang-tao chou-pao

Hu Han-min 胡漢民. *Hu Han-min hsien-sheng yen-chiang chi* 胡漢民先生演講集 (Collection of Mr Hu Han-min's speeches). 4 vols. in 1. Shanghai: Min-chih shu-chü 民智書局, 1927

Hu Han-min. *Hu Han-min hsuan-chi* 胡漢民選集 (Selected writings of Hu Han-min). Taipei: P'a-mi-erh shu-tien 帕米爾書店, 1959

Huston, J. Calvin. 'Peasants, workers, and soldiers revolt of December 11–13, 1927 at Canton, China'. Dispatch no. 669 to J. V. A. MacMurray, U. S. Minister to Peking, 30 Dec. 1927. In Hoover Institution on War, Revolution, and Peace, Stanford, California, J. Calvin Huston Collection, Package II, Part II, Folder 5, Item 20.

'Important documents of the Western Hills Conference expelling communists from the Kuomintang, November 1925'. *Kuo-wen chou-pao,* 4.14 (17 April 1927) 14–16

Imprecor. See *International Press Correspondence*

International Commission of Judges, 1925. *A report of the proceedings of the International Commission of Judges.* Shanghai: reprinted from *Shanghai Mercury,* 1925

International Press Correspondence. Organ of the Executive Committee of the Communist International. English edn

Iriye, Akira. *After imperialism: the search for a new order in the Far East, 1921–1931.* Cambridge, Mass.: Harvard University Press, 1965

Isaacs, Harold R. *The tragedy of the Chinese revolution.* 1st edn, London: Secker and Warburg, 1938; rev. edn, Stanford; Stanford University Press, 1951

'Iz istorii severnogo pokhoda Natsional'no-Revolutskionnoi Armii' (From the history of the Northern Expedition of the National Revolutionary Army), *Istoricheskii Arkhiv,* 4 (1959) 113–26

Jacobs, Dan. *Borodin: Stalin's man in China.* Cambridge, Mass.: Harvard University Press, 1981

JAS: Journal of Asian Studies

Jordan, Donald A. *The Northern Expedition: China's national revolution of 1926–1928.* Honolulu: University Press of Hawaii, 1976

Journal of Asian Studies, 1956– (formerly *Far Eastern Quarterly,* 1941–56)

June Twenty-third: the report of the Commission for the Investigation of the Shakee Massacre June 23, 1925, Canton China. Canton: Wah On Printing Co., n.d.

Kao Yin-tsu 高蔭祖. *Chung-hua min-kuo ta-shih chi* 中華民國大事記 (Chronology of Republican China). Taipei: Shih-chieh she 世界社, 1957

Kartunova, A. I. 'Blucher's "grand plan" of 1926', trans. by Jan J. Solecki with notes by C. Martin Wilbur. *CQ,* 35 (July–Sept. 1968) 18–39

Kartunova, A. I. 'Vasilii Blyukher (1889–1938)', in *Vidnye Sovietskie kommunisty – uchastniki Kitaiskoi revolutsii* (The outstanding Soviet communists – participants in the Chinese revolution), 41–65. Moscow: Akad. Nauk SSSR, Institut Dal'nego Vostoka, 'Nauka' 1970

Kasanin, Marc. *China in the twenties.* Trans. from the Russian by Hilda Kasanina. Moscow: Central Department of Oriental Literature, 1973

KFNP: Kuo-fu nien-p'u

Khmeloff, A. 'Journey to Canton in October, 1925'. (A document from the Peking raid of 6 April 1927). Trans. in Jay Calvin Huston Collection, Hoover Institution on War, Revolution and Peace, Stanford, California

Klein, Donald W. and Clark, Ann B. *Biographic dictionary of Chinese communism, 1921–1965.* 2 vols. Cambridge, Mass.: Harvard University Press, 1965

KMT: Kuomintang

KMT Archives. Chung-kuo Kuo-min-tang chung-yang wei-yuan-hui tang-shih shih-liao pien-tsuan wei-yuan-hui

KMWH: Ko-ming wen-hsien

Ko-ming wen-hsien 革命文獻 (Documents of the revolution), comp. by Lo Chia-lun 羅家倫 and others. Taipei: Central Executive Committee of the Chung-kuo Kuomintang, many volumes, 1953–; cited as *KMWH; KMWH* printed in vols. 10–21 excerpts from Ch'en Hsün-cheng, *Kuo-min ko-ming-chün chan-shih ch'u-kao* (q.v.)

Komintern i Vostok: bor'ba za leninskuiu strategiiu i taktiku v natsional'no-osvo-boditel'nom dvizhenii (Comintern and the Orient: the struggle of the Leninist strategy and tactics in national liberation movements). Moscow: Glav. Red. Vost. Lit., 1969

Konchits, N. I. 'In the ranks of the National Revolutionary Army of China', (in Russian), in *Sovetskiie dobrovoltsy v pervoi grazhdanskoi revolutsionnoi voine v Kitae; vospominaniia* (Soviet volunteers in the First Revolutionary Civil War in China; reminiscences), 24–95. Moscow: Akademiia Nauk SSSR, Institut Narodov Azii, 1961

Kung-fei huo-kuo shih-liao hui-pien 共匪禍國史料彙編 (A compilation of documents on the communist bandits' destruction of the nation). 4 vols. Taipei: Committee for Compilation of Documents on the Fiftieth anniversary of the Founding of the Republic, 1964

Kung-jen. See *Ti-i-tz'u kuo-nei ko-ming chan-cheng shih-ch'i ti kung-jen yun-tung*.

Kuo-chün cheng-kung shih-kao. See Ministry of Defence

Kuo-fu ch'üan-chi. See Sun Yat-sen

Kuo-fu nien-p'u 國父年譜 (A chronological biography of the Father of the Country). 3rd edn, comp. by Lo Chia-lun 羅家倫 and Huang Chi-lu 黃季陸. 2 vols. Taipei: Central Executive Committee of the Chung-kuo Kuomintang, 1969; abbreviated as *KFNP*

Kuo-min-tang chou-k'an 國民黨週刊 (Kuomintang weekly). Canton, 23 Nov. 1923–13 Jan. 1924

Kuo-min Ko-ming-chün Ti-i Chi-t'uan-chün Ti-i Chün-t'uan li-shih 國民革命軍第一集團軍第一軍團歷史 (A history of the First Army Group of the First Group Army of the National Revolutionary Army), comp. by Chief of Staff, Office of the First Army Group. N.p., Sept. 1929

Kuo-min Ko-ming-chün Tung-lu-chün chan-shih chi-lueh 國民革命軍東路軍戰史紀略 (A brief record of the battle history of the Eastern Route Army of the National Revolutionary Army). Hankow, n.p., July 1930. Seen in the Kuomintang Archives

Kuo, Warren (Kuo Hua-lun). *Analytical history of the Chinese Communist Party*. Book One, Taipei: Institute of International Relations, 1966

Kuo-wen chou-pao 國聞週報 (Kuowen weekly, illustrated). Tientsin Kuowen Weekly Association, 1924–37

Kwang-tung nung-min yun-tung pao-kao 廣東農民運動報告 (A report on the farmers' movement in Kwangtung). Canton, 1926. (On microfilm, the Hoover Library, Stanford University)

Leong, Sow-theng. *Sino-Soviet diplomatic relations, 1917–1926*. Honolulu: University of Hawaii Press, 1976

'The letter from Shanghai'. See Nassanov

Levine, Steven I. See Vishnyakova-Akimova

Li Jui 李銳. *Mao Tse-tung t'ung-chih ti ch'u-ch'i ko-ming huo-tung* 毛澤東同志的初期革命活動 (Comrade Mao Tse-tung's early revolutionary activities). Peking: Chung-kuo ch'ing-nien ch'u-pan-she 中國青年出版社, 1957

Li Jui. *The early revolutionary activities of Comrade Mao Tse-tung*, trans. by Anthony W. Sariti, ed. by James C. Hsiung. White Plains, N.Y.: M. E. Sharpe, Inc., 1977

Li Ta-chao. *Shou-ch'ang wen-chi* 守常文集 (Collected essays of Li Ta-chao). Shanghai: Jen-min, 1952

Li Ta-chao. *Li Ta-chao hsuan-chi* 李大釗選集 (Selected writings of Li Ta-chao). Peking: Jen-min, 1959

Li Tsung-jen. See Tong, Te-kong

Li Yu-ning, Bernadette 李又寧. 'A biography of Ch'ü Ch'iu-pai: from youth to party leadership (1899–1928)'. Columbia University, Ph.D. dissertation, 1967

Li Yun-han 李雲漢. *Ts'ung jung-Kung tao ch'ing-tang* 從容共到清黨 (From admitting the communists to the purification of the Kuomintang). Taipei: China Committee on Publication Aid and Prize Awards, 1966; cited as *TJK*

Library of Congress. *Chinese periodicals in the Library of Congress*, comp. by Han Chu Huang. Washington: Library of Congress, 1977

Liu Li-k'ai 劉立凱 and Wang Chen 王真. *I-chiu i-chiu chih i-chiu erh-ch'i nien ti Chung-kuo kung-jen yun-tung* 一九一九至一九二七年的中國工人運動 (The Chinese labour movement from 1919 to 1927). Peking: Workers Publishing House, 1953

Liu Shao-ch'i 劉少奇. 'Report on the Chinese labour movement in the past year'. *Cheng-chih chou-pao* 政治週報 (Political weekly), 14 (5 June 1926). Canton. Available on U.S. National Archives microfilm 329, reel 56, 893.00/7980

Lo Ch'i-yuan 羅畸園. 'Short report on the work of this [Farmers] Bureau during the past year'. *Chung-kuo nung-min*, 2 (1 Feb. 1926) 147–207

Lo Ch'i-yuan. 'Hui-wu tsung pao-kao' 會務總報告 (General report of the [Farmers'] Association work). *Chung-kuo nung-min*, 6/7 (July 1926) 639–87

Lo I-nung 羅亦農. 'Chung-kuo ti-erh-tz'u ch'üan-kuo lao-tung ta-hui chih shih-mo' 中國第二次全國勞動大會之始末 (A complete account of the Second National Labour Congress). *HTCP*, 115 (17 May 1925) 1063–4

Lo-sheng 樂生 (pseud.). 'Ti-san-tz'u ch'üan-kuo lao-tung ta-hui chih ching-kuo chi ch'i chieh-kuo' 第三次全國勞動大會之經過及其結果 (Experiences and results of the Third National Labour Congress). *HTCP*, 155 (5 May 1926). Reprinted in *Ti-i-tz'u kuo-nei ko-ming chan-cheng shih-ch'i ti kung-jen yun-tung*, 219–24. 3rd edn, Peking: Jen-min ch'u-pan she, April 1963

Lutz, Jessie G. 'Chinese nationalism and the anti-Christian campaigns of the 1920s'. *Modern Asian Studies*, 10.3 (July 1976) 395–416

Malone, Col. C. L'Estrange. *New China: report of an investigation. Part II. Labour conditions and labour organizations 1926*. London: Independent Labour Party Publication Department, 1927

Malraux, André. *Man's fate*. Trans. by Haakon M. Chevalier from the French *La condition humaine*. New York: Smith and Haas, 1934

Mann, Tom. *What I saw in China*. London: National Minority Movement, 1927?

Mao I-heng 毛以亨. *O Meng hui-i-lu* 俄蒙回憶錄 (Recollections of Russia and Mongolia). Hong Kong: Asia Book Co., 1954

Mao, *CKSHS*. See next item Mao Ssu-ch'eng.

Mao Ssu-ch'eng 毛思誠. *Min-kuo shih-wu-nien i-ch'ien chih Chiang Chieh-shih hsien-sheng* 民國十五年以前之蔣介石先生 (Mr Chiang Kai-shek up to 1926). N.p. (1936); Taipei edn (1948?) Often referred to as 'Chiang's Diary'.

Mao Tse-tung. *Selected works of Mao Tse-tung*. Vol. 1. London: Lawrence & Wishart, 1954. Abbrev. *SW*

Mao Tse-tung. *Mao Tse-tung on art and literature*. Peking: Foreign Languages Press, 1967

(Mao) Tse-tung (毛) 澤東. 'Pei-ching cheng-pien yü shang-jen' 北京政變與商人 (The Peking coup d'etat and the merchants). *HTCP*, 31–32 (11 July 1923)

Mao Tse-tung. *Mao Tse-tung chi* 毛澤東集 (Collected writings of Mao Tse-tung), ed. by Takeuchi Minoru 竹內実 10 vols. Tokyo: Hokubōsha 北望社, 1970–2. Cited as Takeuchi edn

McDonald, Angus W., Jr. *The urban origins of rural revolution: elites and masses in Hunan province, China, 1911–1927*. Berkeley, Los Angeles and London: University of California Press, 1978

McDonald, Angus W., Jr. 'The Hunan peasant movement: its urban origins'. *Modern China,* 1.2 (April 1975) 180–203

McGuire, Catherine M. 'The union movement in Hunan in 1926–1927 and its effect on the American community'. Columbia University, M.A. essay in History, 1977

Mif, Pavel. *Heroic China: fifteen years of the Communist Party of China*. New York: Workers Library Publisher, 1937

Mikami Taichō 三上諦聽, Ishikawa Tadao 石川忠雄 and Shibata Minoru 芝田稔. *Kohoku shūshū bōdō keika no hōkoku* 湖北秋収暴動経過の報告 (A report on the Autumn Harvest uprising in Hupei). *Kansai daigaku tōzai gakujutsu kenkyūjo shiryō shūkan* 関西大学東西学術研究所資料集刊 (Sources of the Kansai University Institute of Oriental and Occidental Studies), no. 1. Osaka: Kansai Daigaku Tōzai Gakujutsu Kenkyūjo, 1961. This is a translation of the whole text of the *Chung-yang t'ung-hsun* 中央通訊 (Central Committee circular), no. 11: *Hu-pei ch'iu-shou pao-tung chuan-hao* 湖北秋収暴動專號 (Special issue on the Autumn Harvest uprising in Hupei), which was probably published on 24 or 25 November, 1927

Min-kuo jih-pao 民國日報 (National daily). Shanghai and Canton, *ca.* 1914–

Ministry of Defence. Kuo-fang-pu shih-cheng-chü 國防部史政局. *Pei-fa chan-shih* 北伐戰史 (A battle history of the northern punitive expedition). 4 vols. Taipei, 1959; another set bound in 10 *ts'e*; another edn published at Yang-ming-shan: Chung-hua ta-tien pien-yin hui, 5 vols., 1967; our citations are to the 4 vols. 1959 edn.

Ministry of Defence. General Political Department. *Kuo-chün cheng-kung shih-kao* 國軍政工史稿 (Draft history of political work in the National Army). 2 vols. Taipei: General Political Department of the Ministry of Defence, 1960

Ministry of Defence. *Pei-fa chien-shih* 北伐簡史 (A brief history of the northern punitive expedition). Taipei: Ministry of Defence, 1961

'Minutes of the Military Section on... 1927', in *Soviet plot in China,* 143–8; also in *Chinese Social and Political Science Review*, 7 (1927) 232–9. (A document seized in the Peking raid of 6 April 1927.)

Mirovitskaia, R. A. 'Pervoe destiatiletie' (The first decade), in *Leninskaia politika SSSR v otnoshenii Kitaia* (The Leninist policy of the USSR with regard to China). Moscow: 'Nauka', 1968

Mirovitskaia, R. A. 'Mikhail Borodin (1884–1951)', in *Vidnye sovietskie kommunisty – uchastniki kitaiskoi revolutsii*, 22–40

Misselwitz, Henry Francis. *The dragon stirs: an intimate sketchbook of China's Kuomintang revolution, 1927–1929*. New York: Harbinger House, 1941

Mitarevsky, N. *World-wide soviet plots, as disclosed by hitherto unpublished documents seized in the USSR embassy in Peking*. Tientsin: Tientsin Press, Ltd., 1927

Nassanov, N., Fokine, N. and Albrecht, A. 'The letter from Shanghai', 17 March 1927. Trans. from the French in Leon Trotsky. *Problems of the Chinese revolution*, 397–432

Nathan, Andrew J. *Modern China, 1840–1972: an introduction to sources and research aids.* Ann Arbor: University of Michigan, 1971

'The National Revolutionary Army. A short history of its origin, development and organization', Trans. from a document seized in the Soviet Military Attache's office in Peking, 6 April 1927. In British Foreign Office Archives, FO 371: 12440/9156

NCH. North China Herald

North China Daily News. Shanghai, 1864–

The North China Herald and Supreme Court and Consular Gazette. Weekly. Shanghai, 1850–

North, Robert C. *Moscow and Chinese communists.* Stanford: Stanford University Press, 1952

North, Robert C. and Eudin, Xenia J. *M. N. Roy's mission to China: the Communist-Kuomintang split of 1927.* Berkeley and Los Angeles: University of California Press, 1963

Pai Ch'ung-hsi 白崇禧. *Shih-liu nien ch'ing-tang yun-tung ti hui-i* 十六年清黨運動的回憶 (Recollections of the party purification movement of 1927). Kuomintang Kwangsi Party Reconstruction Committee, Propaganda Department, 1932

Pak, Hyobom. *Documents of the Chinese Communist Party, 1927–1930.* Hong Kong: Union Research Institute, 1971

Pei-fa chan-shih. See Ministry of Defence

Pei-fa chien-shih. See Ministry of Defence

People's Tribune. Organ of the National Government in Hankow. March–Aug. 1927

PFCS: Pei-fa chan-shih. See Ministry of Defence

Rea, Kenneth W. See Swisher, Earl.

'Report of the communistic movement of youth of China'. *China Illustrated Review*, Peking (28 Jan. 1928) 14–16

Report of the trial of the Chinese arrested during the riots of May 30, 1925. Shanghai: North China Daily News and Herald, Ltd., 1925

'Report of the Young Communist International at the Sixth World Congress of the Communist International'. *Lieh-ning ch'ing-nien* 列寧青年 (Leninist youth), 1.10 (15 Feb. 1929) 69–94

'Resolution on the Chinese question of the Sixth ECCI Plenum', in *International press correspondence*, 6.40 (6 May 1926) as quoted in Gruber, *Soviet Russia masters the Comintern*, 475–61

Schram, Stuart R. 'On the nature of Mao Tse-tung's "deviation" in 1927'. *CQ*, 18 (April–June 1964) 55–66

Schram, Stuart R. *Political leaders in the twentieth century: Mao Tse-tung.* Harmondsworth, England: Penguin Books, Ltd., 1966

Schram, Stuart R. *The political thought of Mao Tse-tung*. Rev. edn, New York: Praeger, 1969

Schwartz, Benjamin I. *Chinese communism and the rise of Mao*. Cambridge, Mass. Harvard University Press, 1951; paperback edn with new introduction, 1980

Sheean, Vincent. *Personal history*. Garden City, N.Y.: Doubleday, Doran & Co., 1935

Shen I-yun 沈亦雲. *I-yun hui-i* 亦雲回憶 (Reminiscences of Shen I-yun). Taipei: Chuan-chi wen-hsueh, 1968

Sheridan, James E. *Chinese warlord: the career of Feng Yü-hsiang*. Stanford: Stanford University Press, 1966

Shieh, Milton J. T. *The Kuomintang: selected historical documents, 1894–1969*. Jamaica, N.Y.: St. John's University Press, 1970

Smedley, Agnes. *The great road: the life and times of Chu Teh*. New York: Monthly Review Press, 1956

Snow, Edgar. *Red star over China*. New York: Random House, 1938; 1st rev. and enlarged edn, Grove Press, 1968

South China Morning Post. Hong Kong, 1903–

Strong, Anna Louise. *China's millions*. New York: Coward McCann, 1928

Su-ch'ing 肅清 (pseud.). *Kung-ch'an-tang chih yin-mou ta pao-lu* 共產黨之陰謀大暴露 (The plots of the Communist Party exposed). Canton: San Min Chü-lo-pu, 1924

Sun Yat-sen. *Kuo-fu ch'üan-chi* 國父全集 (The collected works of the national father Sun Yat-sen). 6 vols. Rev. edn, Taipei: Chung-kuo Kuomintang Central Executive Committee, 1961

Swisher, Earl. *Canton in revolution: the collected papers of Earl Swisher, 1925–1928*, ed. by Kenneth W. Rea. Boulder, Colorado: Westview Press, 1977

Tai Chi-t'ao. *Tai Chi-t'ao hsien-sheng wen-ts'un* 戴季陶先生文存 (Collected writings of Mr Tai Chi-t'ao), ed by Ch'en T'ien-hsi 陳天錫. 4 vols. Central Executive Committee of the Kuomintang, 1959

T'an-ho Kung-ch'an-tang liang ta yao-an 彈劾共產黨兩大要案 (Two important cases of impeachment of the Communist Party). n.p.: Kuomintang Central Supervisory Committee, Sept. 1927; reprinted in *KMWH*, 9 (June 1955) 1271–3

Teng Chung-hsia 鄧中夏. *Chung-kuo chih-kung yun-tung chien-shih* 中國職工運動簡史 (A brief history of the Chinese labour movement). Original edn, Moscow, 1930; Central China: New China Bookstore, 1949

Teng Yen-ta 鄧演達. *Teng Yen-ta hsien-sheng i-chu* 鄧演達先生遺著 (A posthumous collection of Mr Teng Yen-ta's writings). Preface (1949) by Yang I-t'ang 楊逸棠. Hong Kong: n.p., n.d.

TFTC. See *Tung-fang tsa-chih*

Thomas, S. Bernard. *'Proletarian hegemony' in the Chinese revolution and the Canton Commune of 1927*. Ann Arbor: University of Michigan Center for Chinese Studies, 1975

'Three Shanghai uprisings'. *Problemi Kitaii*, Moscow, 2 (1930); mimeographed

Ti-i-tz'u kuo-nei ko-ming chan-cheng shih-ch'i ti kung-jen yun-tung 第一次國內革命戰爭時期的工人運動 (The labour movement during the first revolutionary civil war period). 3rd edn, Peking: Jen-min, 1963; cited as *Kung-jen*

Ti-i-tz'u kuo-nei ko-ming chan-cheng shih-ch'i ti nung-min yun-tung 第一次國內革命戰爭時期的農民運動 (The farmers' movement during the first revolutionary civil war period). Peking: Jen-min, 1953; cited as *Nung-min*

Ti-ssu-chün chi-shih 第四軍紀實 (Factual account of the Fourth Army), comp. by Compilation Committee on the Factual Account of the Fourth Army. Canton: Huai-yuan wen-hua shih-yeh fu-wu-she 懷遠文化事業服務社, 1949

TJK: See Li Yun-han, *Ts'ung jung-Kung tao ch'ing-tang*

Tong, Hollington K. (Tung Hsien-kuang 董顯光). *Chiang Kai-shek*. Rev. edn, Taipei: China Publishing Co., 1953

Tong Te-kong and Li Tsung-jen. *The memoirs of Li Tsung-jen*. Boulder & Folkestone: Westview Press and Wm. Dawson and Sons, Studies of the East Asian Institute, Columbia University, 1979

Trotsky, Leon. *Problems of the Chinese revolution*. 2nd edn, reprint, New York: Paragon Book Gallery, 1962

Trotsky, Leon. *Leon Trotsky on China: introduction by Peng Shu-tse*, eds. Les Evans and Russell Block. New York: Monad Press, 1976

Ts'ai Ho-sen. 'The Kwangtung farmers' movement on May First this year'. *HTCP*, 112 (1 May 1925) 1030–6

Tsou Lu 鄒魯. *Chung-kuo Kuo-min-tang shih kao* 中國國民黨史稿 (A draft history of the Kuomintang of China). 2nd edn. Chungking: Commercial Press, 1944; Taipei: Commercial Press, 1970

Tsou Lu. *Hui-ku-lu* 回顧錄 (Reminiscences). 2 vols. Nanking: Tu-li 獨立, 1946; reprint 1947

Tung, William L. *China and the foreign powers: the impact of and reaction to unequal treaties*. Dobbs Ferry, N.Y.: Oceania Publications, Inc., 1970

Tung-fang tsa-chih 東方雜誌 (The eastern miscellany). Shanghai, 1904–48; cited as *TFTC*

U.S. Department of State. *Papers relating to the foreign relations of the United States*. Washington, D.C.: U.S. Government Printing Office, annual volumes.

U.S. Department of State. 'Records relating to the internal affairs of China, 1910–1929'. Washington, D.C.: U.S. National Archives, Microcopy 329

USFR. See U.S. Department of State, *Papers relating to. . . .*

USNA. United States National Archives

Uyehara, Cecil H., comp. *Checklist of archives in the Japanese Ministry of Foreign Affairs, Tokyo, Japan, 1868–1945, microfilmed for the Library of Congress, 1949–1951*. Washington, D.C.: Library of Congress, 1954

Vishnyakova-Akimova, Vera Vladimirovna. *Dva goda v vosstavshem Kitae, 1925–1927: vospominania*. Moscow: Akad. Nauk SSSR, Institute of the Peoples of

Asia, Izd-vo 'Nauka', 1965. Trans. by Steven I. Levine, *Two years in revolutionary China, 1925–1927*. Cambridge, Mass.: Harvard University Press, 1971

Wang Chien-min 王健民. *Chung-kuo Kung-ch'an-tang shih kao* 中國共產黨史稿 (A draft history of the Chinese Communist Party). 3 vols. Taipei: published by the author, 1965

Wang Ching-wei 汪精衛. 'Political report' to the Second Kuomintang Congress, in *KMWH*, 20 (March 1958) 3851–70

Wang Ching-wei. *Wang Ching-wei hsien-sheng tsui-chin yen-shuo chi* 汪精衛先生最近演説集 (Mr Wang Ching-wei's most recent speeches collected). N.p., n.d. (1928?)

Wang, Y. C. 'Tu Yueh-sheng (1888–1951): a tentative political biography'. *JAS*, 26.3 (May 1967) 433–55

Wen-hua yen-chiu she 文化研究社, comps. *Chung-kuo wu ta wei-jen shou-cha* 中國五大偉人手札 (Letters of China's five great leaders). Shanghai: Ta-fang 大方, 1939

Wieger, Léon, S.J. *Chine moderne*. Hien-hien (Hsien hsien, Shantung). 7 vols. 1921–7

Wilbur, C. Martin and How, Julie Lien-ying 夏連蔭, eds. *Documents on communism, nationalism, and Soviet advisers in China, 1918–1927: papers seized in the 1927 Peking raid*. New York: Columbia University Press, 1956

Wilbur, C. Martin. *Forging the weapons: Sun Yat-sen and the Kuomintang in Canton, 1924*. New York: East Asian Institute of Columbia University, 1966 (mimeograph)

Wilbur, C. Martin. 'The ashes of defeat'. *CQ*, 18 (April–June 1964) 3–54

Wilbur, C. Martin. 'Military separatism and the process of reunification under the Nationalist regime, 1922–1937', in Ho Ping-ti and Tsou Tang, eds. *China in crisis*, 1.203–63. Chicago: University of Chicago Press, 1968

Wilbur, C. Martin. 'Problems of starting a revolutionary base: Sun Yat-sen in Canton, 1923'. *Bulletin of the Institute of Modern History*, Academia Sinica (Taipei), 4.2 (1974) 665–727

Wilbur, C. Martin. *Sun Yat-sen: frustrated patriot*. New York: Columbia University Press, 1976

Wilson, David Clive. 'Britain and the Kuomintang, 1924–28: a study of the interaction of official policies and perceptions in Britain and China'. University of London, School of Oriental and African Studies, Ph.D. dissertation, 1973

Woo, T. C. *The Kuomintang and the future of the Chinese revolution*. London: George Allen & Unwin Ltd., 1928

Wou, Odoric Y. K. *Militarism in modern China: the career of Wu P'ei-fu, 1916–1939*. Studies of the East Asian Institute, Columbia University. Folkestone, Kent: Wm. Dawson and Sons; Canberra: Australian National University, 1978

Wu Chih-hui. *Chih-hui wen-ts'un* 稚暉文存 (Wu Chih-hui's writings). 1st collection. Shanghai: Hsin-hsin Book Store, 1927

Wu Chih-hui. 'Shu Wang Ching-wei hsien-sheng hsien tien hou' 書汪精衛先生銑電後 (Written after Mr Wang Ching-wei's telegram of the 16th [April 1927]). *Chih-hui wen-ts'un*, 1–14

Wu Tien-wei. 'Chiang Kai-shek's March twentieth coup d'état of 1926'. *JAS*, 27 (May 1968) 585–602

Wu Tien-wei. 'A review of the Wuhan debacle: the Kuomintang-Communist split of 1927'. *JAS*, 29 (Nov. 1969) 125–43

Wu Tien-wei. 'Chiang Kai-shek's April 12 coup of 1927', in Gilbert F. Chan and Thomas H. Etzold, eds. *China in the 1920s*, 146–59

Yip, Ka-che. 'The anti-Christian movement in China, 1922–1927'. Columbia University, Ph.D. dissertation, 1970

Yokoyama, Suguru. 'The peasant movement in Hunan'. *Modern China*, 1.2 (April 1975) 204–38

Young, John, comp. *Checklist of microfilm reproductions of selected archives of the Japanese Army, Navy, and other government agencies, 1868–1945.* Washington, D.C.: Georgetown University Press, 1959

INDEX

All China General Labour Union 64,
129
Amoy 107, 112
An-kuo chün 176, 180
An T'i-ch'eng 100
An-yang (near Chang-te) 176
An-yuan 63, 153
Anfu (Anfu Clique) 1
Anhwei 52; KMT drive into 125
Anking 88
anti-Christian movement 70-2
anti-foreign demonstrations 23
anti-imperialism: of Sun Yat-sen 10;
of Nationalist Revolution 68–73;
movement for 68–73; question of
restraining 77; centred on Great
Britain 82; Third Plenum on 87;
attacks on foreigners in capture of
Nanking 91–3; in Shanghai 94–9;
and Wuchang government 115
Arcos raid 114
armies: Kwangtung 3, 20, 27; Kwangsi
20, 24; Party 20, 26; Yunnan 20, 24;
National Revolutionary 25, 29–30,
52–3; Hunan 26; Eastern Route 61;
Fengtien 125, 176; Shantung 125;
regrouping of, for Eastern
Campaign 138; Red 148; before
drive on Peking 171; of Northern
Expeditionary forces 176; An-kuo
chün 176, 180; see also National
Revolutionary Army, Kuo-min
chün

arms: Russian, for KMT 14, 40–1
Autumn Harvest Uprisings 150–5

Bank of China (Chung-kuo yin-hang):
loans to Chiang Kai-shek 85
Blyukher, Gen. Vasilii K. (Galen) 14,
24, 45; financial data of 40; plans
for Northern Expedition 49–50; on
Northern Expedition 57, 60, 62;
strategy of towards Shanghai 78;
on Yangtze campaign 83; after split
of parties 147
Borodin, Michael 127, 141, 168, 186;
adviser to KMT 5, 192;
rejuvenating of KMT 7–13; on rift
between CCP and KMT 18–19; on
reorganization at Canton 25, and
special committee of three 27;
declared ousted 31–2; on financial
backing 40–1; after coup of Chiang
Kai-shek 48–9; on anti-British
agitation 73; role in Provisional
Joint Council 78; breach with
Chiang 79, 80, 83; on Nanking
Incident 93; expulsion urged 97,
100, 103, 139, 143; on move to
Nanking 106; denounced by
Nanking 113; on 'tactical retreat'
115; report on foreign policy 116;
on rural unrest 119, 121, 122; on
Changsha coup 129, 130, 135, 136;
Eastern campaign urged by 137; on
social revolution 138; departure of
142, 144, 145–6

Borodin, Mme 142, 144
bourgeoisie: place of in revolutionary
  strategy 6; communists on 82
Boxer Protocol: on access to sea 44;
  cited in Tientsin 181
boycotts 160; of Shameen 15; of
  Canton–Hong Kong (1925–6) 23,
  69; see also strikes
British–American Tobacco Co.: loans
  to Chiang Kai-shek 85
Bubnov, A.S. 43
Budget committee, Nationalist
  government 187
Bukharin, Nikolai Ivanovich 130
Butler, Smedley 181

Canton: Sun Yat-sen's presidency in
  1, 2; revolutionary army organized
  in 2–3; Sun's government in 3–4;
  customs crisis in 10; KMT's
  Central Headquarters at 12; strikes
  in 15, 23, 69; merchant corps of 19-
  20; as southern revolutionary base
  20–7; clash of revolutionaries in
  107; communist purge in 110–11;
  Wang Ching-wei's headquarters
  159; coup in 161–2; communist
  uprising in 164–70; Canton
  Commune 164–70; preparations for
  165–6; events of 166–9; aftermath
  169–70
Canton–Hong Kong strike 15, 25–7
Central Bank of China: branch at
  Canton 111
Central Executive Committee (KMT)
  8, 12, 15, 25, 48, 64; composition
  of 1926 committee 32; standing
  committee of 33, 173; on party
  purge 98; Chiang Kai-shek expelled
  by 113; manifesto to farmers 116;
  replaced 157; plans for Fourth
  Plenum 171
Central Land Commission 118; report
  of 122

Central Military Political Academy
  (Whampoa) 55
Central Political Council (KMT):
  establishment of government at
  Nanking by 112–13; no longer
  independent 186
centralization: topic at Fifth Plenum
  186; impediments to 194
Chamberlain, Austen 72, 77
Chan Ta-pei 169
Chang Chao-yuan 115
Chang Chi; 18; on Special Central
  Committee 157; on State Council
  191
Chang Chia-ao, see Chang Kia-ngau
Chang Ching-chiang (Chang Jen-
  chieh) 48, 78; denounced by
  communists 80, 87; on expulsion of
  communists 96, 98; in Nanking
  government 113; on Chiang's
  retirement 156; on Special Central
  Committee 157–8; and Canton
  coup 162; on Standing Committee
  of CEC 173
Chang-chou: capture of 588
Chang Ch'ün 180
Chang Fa-k'uei 55, 137, 174; of
  Fourth Corps 82, 83; in Wuhan
  drive 125, 136; in Eastern
  campaign 138, 141; to Kiangsi 145;
  object of CCP campaign 147; and
  Nanchang Uprising 148, 152;
  support of Wang Ching-wei 159,
  161; in Canton labour movement
  160; in Canton coup 161–2, 163;
  and Canton Commune 165, 166,
  167, 168, 170
Chang Hsueh-liang 125, 184, 191,
  193–4
Chang Hui-tsan 92
Chang I-p'eng 133
Chang Jen-chieh, see Chang Ching-
  chiang
Chang Kia-ngau (Chang Chia-ao;

Chang Kung-ch'üan) 84 (*cont.*)
Chang Kuo-t'ao 147, 148; labour
　organizer 64, 126; in Stalin's
　telegram 131
Chang Shu-shih: report on Nanking
　106; escape from Nanking 107
Chang T'ai-lei 147; in command in
　Kwangtung 150; and the Canton
　Commune 165, 167; death of 168
Chang Tso-lin 2, 171, 193; supported
　by Japan 43, 181; enemy of Russia
　43; Russian proposals concerning
　45–6; coalition of 51; favoured by
　Western powers 80; negotiations
　with Chiang 83, 137, 159; menace
　to Wuhan government 113; in
　campaign north 125, 176; Japan's
　memorandum to 182–3; departure
　and assassination 184
Chang Tsung-ch'ang 83, 171, 176,
　193; in campaign for Shanghai 85,
　90; in northward push 125, 137;
　Hsu-chow captured by 156
Changsha: in Northern Expedition
　55, 71; labour organization in 66;
　missionaries in 71–2; Communist
　purge in 112; rural unrest around
　119; provincial court in 120; battle
　for 127–8; in Autumn Harvest
　revolts 152–3
Chao Shih-yen 91
Ch'ao-chow (Chao-chou) 51, 149
Chekiang 30, 52; purge of leftists in
　112; KMT branch reorganized in
　171
Chen, Eugene, *see* Ch'en Yu-jen
Ch'en Ch'i-mei 52
Ch'en Ch'i-yuan 117, 135
Ch'en Chiung-ming: in Canton 2, 3,
　9, 18; First Eastern Expedition
　against 20; Second Eastern
　Expedition against 29
Ch'en Ch'ün 104
Ch'en Chung-fu, *see* Ch'en Tu-hsiu

Ch'en I (General) 62, 148
Ch'en K'o-yü 57
Ch'en Kung-po 80, 129, 138; on CEC
　standing committee 33; head of
　Political Training Department 34,
　50; on Northern Expedition 57; in
　Changsha 135; in Canton 159, 161,
　166, 167; excluded from Fourth
　Plenum 171
Ch'en Kuo-fu 49, 87, 96, 191
Ch'en Ming-shu 55, 82, 97, 170
Ch'en T'iao-yuan 83, 88, 174
Ch'en Tsan-hsien 88
Ch'en Tu-hsiu (Ch'en Chung-fu) 192;
　Sun Yat-sen warned against 10; on
　break with KMT 19, 31, 97–8, 108;
　joint statement with Wang 98;
　denounced by Nanking 113; on
　telegram from Stalin 131;
　resignation of 144; censured for
　opportunism 150; sons of 192
Ch'en Yi, *see* Ch'en I
Ch'en Yu-jen (Eugene Chen) 48;
　foreign minister 49, 69; talks with
　Lampson 73; negotiations on
　Hankow 75, 76–7; on Nanking
　Incident 93; relations with foreign
　business 115–16, 117; departure of
　145, 148; sons of 145; omitted from
　Special Central Committee 158
Ch'en Yü 167
Chengchow 83, 125, 138, 139, 181;
　Borodin in 145–6
Ch'eng Ch'ien 29, 53, 98, 106; on
　Northern Expedition 59–60; in
　campaign for Nanking 88, 91–2;
　anti-communist 197; on Fourth
　Plenum 158; campaign against
　T'ang Sheng-chih 159
Ch'eng T'ien-fang 134
Cherepanov, A. I. 29, 83
Chiang Chieh-shih, *see* Chiang Kai-
　shek
Chiang Kai-shek (Chiang Chieh-shih):

commandant at Whampoa 14, 19, (cont.)
52; in First Eastern Expedition 20;
in battle for Canton 24; on special
committee of three 27; and
Western Hills group 33; on CEC
33; and the Russians 45, 47; coup
of 47–9; as commander-in-chief 55,
56; in the field 57, 59, 60, 61; on
Hong Kong strike 69;
proclamation on Northern
Expedition 71; circle of 78–9;
breach with Borodin 79; alliance
against 82–3; demoted 87–8, 156;
capture of Shanghai and Nanking
88–94; in struggle for control 94–9;
and Feng Yü-hsiang 136, 139, 143;
break with communists 143–5;
retirement of 156, 160–1; on
Special Central Committee 158; in
talks with Wang Ching-wei 160,
162; resumption as commander
163, 171; drive for military
unification 170–1; and the Fourth
Plenum 171–3; in Tsinan 178; in
drive on Peking 180–5; on national
reconstruction 185–91; see also
Kuomintang; Nationalist
government; Nationalist
Revolution
Chiang Kai-shek, Madame, see Sung
Mei-Ling
Chiang Tso-pin 75
Chicherin, Gregorii 7
Ch'ien Ta-chün 110
China: prospects as of 1928 191–4; see
also imperialism; nationalism
China Merchants' Steam Navigation
Co. (Chao-shang chü) 114
Chinese Communist Party (Chung-
kuo kung-ch'an tang) (CCP):
relationship with KMT 5, 10;
infiltration tactics 10, 18; May 30th
Incident 21–3; moves to expel from
KMT 31–2; penetration of

Nationalist Revolutionary Army
33–7; leadership of mass
movements by 37–40; relations
with Russians 40–7; after Chiang's
coup 48–9; labour organization by
63–8; Wuhan leftists supported by
79; on rightist KMT 80–2; in
Shanghai campaign 85–6; at Third
Plenum 87; in growing violence
94–108; spreading purge of 108–12;
struggle to survive 113–17; and the
rural revolution 117–24; on land
distribution 123–4; dilemma of
Russian instructions 138 143; terms
of Feng Yü-hsiang to 139, 141–2;
split with KMT 144–6; beginning
of communist revolt 147–9;
Autumn Harvest revolts 150–5;
Canton Commune 164–70; state of
in 1928 192–3; see also Borodin;
Ch'en Tu-hsiu; Li Ta-chao; Mao
Tse-tung; Russia
Chinese Eastern Railway 103; and
Russia 5, 45; transport of troops on
43
Ching-kang-shan 154
Ch'ing-pang (Green Gang) 104, 109
Chou En-lai 34, 91; escape from
Shanghai 109; and Nanchang
Uprising 148
Chou Feng-ch'i 85, 97, 107; in
Shanghai communist purge 108
Chou I-ch'ün (Y. T. Tsur) 147
Chou Lan 132, 159
Chou Shih-ti 149
Chou Yin-jen 62
'Christian General', see Feng Yü-
hsiang
Christianity: CCP on 71–2; see also
missionaries
Christmas Memorandum 72–3, 74
Chu P'ei-te 3, 13, 159, 174;
commander of Third Corps 29, 52,
82; on Northern Expedition 50;

governor of Kiangsi 102; in (*cont.*)
Changsha 134, 135, 137, 138; and
Nanchang Uprising 148
Chu Te 102, 148, 149
Ch'u Yü-p'u 176, 181
Ch'ü Ch'iu-pai: CCP secretary-general
144, 150; plan for uprising 147;
retreat to Shanghai 155
Ch'üan-chou (Zayton): capture of 62
Ch'üan-kuo tsung-kung hui (National
General Labour Union) 21, 38–9
Chung-kuo kuo-min-tang *see* Kuo-
min-tang, Chinese Nationalist Party
Chung-shan (gunboat; name taken by
Sun Yat-sen) 47
Chung-shan (University) 111
Chungking: revolutionary conflict in
100–1
cliques: in KMT 11–12, 18–21, 27;
Western Hills group 31–2; in CCP
32
Communist International (Comintern;
CI): Second Congress 6; on
organizing peasantry 15; advice
from on united front 42; on clashes
with KMT 108; on rural revolution
117, 121; on Changsha coup 129;
order on communist withdrawal
from government 144; on
Nanchang uprising 147; and the
Canton Commune 164–70
Communist Youth Corps 37, 192
copper currency, urged by Borodin
116
counter-revolution, aborted 27–30
Creation Society 51
currency: copper 116
customs, *see* Maritime Customs
Service

Dalbank 103
Dalin 7
democratic centralism: mark of KMT
189–90

Eastern Campaign 20, 24, 137–8
Eastern Route Army 61; in capture of
Hangchow 85
economy: and the Wuhan
government 113–17
Egorov (Russian attaché) 40, 44
Eighth Corps, National
Revolutionary Army 30, 52, 53; in
Northern Expedition 57, 59; in
alliance against Chiang 82; changes
in 171
Eighth Plenum (Executive
Committee, Comintern) 130
Eleventh Corps, National
Revolutionary Army 136; in
alliance against Chiang 82; at
Wuchang 126; and Nanchang
Uprising 148
Everson, Inspector 22
Executive Committee, Comintern
(ECCI), Chinese directives of 6, 7–
8
extraterritoriality: proposals in
Christmas Memorandum 72–3; *see
also* imperialism; treaty system

Fan Chung-hsiu 13
Fang Chen-wu 174
Farmers' Bureau (KMT) 15; peasant
committee of 16
farmers' movement 39, 65–8, 193;
and self-government of villages
117–24; smashed in Changsha 128;
see also mass mobilization
Farmers' Movement Training
Institute 16, 39, 66
Feng Yü-hsiang 146, 159, 163, 193;
coup of 20; supported by Soviets
41–2, 78, 114; army trained and
equipped by Russia 41–2, 43, 44,
78: war with Chang Tso-lin 43, 51;
to join Chiang 83; and Wuhan
government 114, 135; drive along
Lunghai Railway 125; agreement

with KMT Political Council 136; defection to Nanking 139, 143, 156, 171; on Special Central Committee 158; on Peking offensive 174, 176, 178, 185; and Japanese Memorandum 183–4; at Fifth Plenum 186; on State Council 191

Fengtien Army 83, 125, 176, 180; Japan's restriction of 181; retreat of 183

feudalism: farmers' struggles against 118

Fifteenth Corps, National Revolutionary Army 59

Fifth Congress, CCP (1927): land policy stated at 6, 124

Fifth Corps, National Revolutionary Army 29, 53

Fifth Plenum (KMT–CEC) 186–91; on centralization *v.* local power 186; on government finance 187; on military centralization 188; on constitution 189; on re-negotiation of treaties 189–90

finances: Sun Yat-sen 3–4; Russian support of revolutionary activities 41; T. V. Soong on reconstruction of 187

First Corps, National Revolutionary Army 29, 49, 52; communists in 36; in Northern Expedition 56, 59–60, 62; in Nanking 107, 143, 157; changes in 138, 174

First Eastern Expedition 20

First Group Army: in drive on Peking 174, 176; in Tsinan 178

Fischer, Louis 40

Foochow: capture of 62; revolutionary conflict in 102–3

Fourteenth Corps, National Revolutionary Army 55, 59

Fourth Congress, CI (1922) 15

Fourth Corps, National

Revolutionary Army 29, 50, 53, 136; in Northern Expedition 55, 59, 62; in alliance against Chiang 82; at Canton 166; changes in 171

Fourth Group Army 138, 181

Fourth Plenum (KMT–CEC): proposed 158; called by Wang Ching-wei 160; discussions in Shanghai on 162–3; summoned by Chiang 171; attendance at 171–2; tasks of 172–3

France: and Canton–Hong Kong strike 26; in anti-imperialist movement 68, 86; attacks on citizens of 93

French Concession, Shanghai 95, 104

French Settlement, Shanghai, *see* French Concession

Fu Tso-i 184

Fukien: campaign in 61–2

Fukuda Hikosuke, Gen. 178–80

Galen, *see* Blyukher, V. K.

General Labour Unions: Hunan 64; Hupei 64, 116, 138; All China 64, 129; in 'Shanghai uprising' 86, 88, 90; after fall of Shanghai 94, 104, 105, 108; Hangchow 100; Chungking 100–1; Nanking 107; Changsha 127–8; 134; Fourth Congress of 140–1; *see also* labour unions; mass mobilization

Gobi Desert 146

Goffe, Herbert 75

Great Britain: and May 30th Incident 23; and Canton–Hong Kong strike 26; and Japan 45–7; target of anti-imperialism 68–73, 82; Christmas Memorandum 72–3; Lampson-Chen talks 73; seizure of Concession at Hankow 73–7; and capture of Shanghai 86; attacks on in Nanking 91–2, 175, 190

Green Gang (Ch'ing-pang) 104

Hai-feng 16, 39, 154
Hainan (Island) 30
Han Fu-ch'ü 184
Han Lin-fu 111n
Hangchow: captured by First Corps 85, 88; revolutionary conflict in 100
Hankow: KMT office in 12; anti-foreign riots in 23; in Northern Expedition 59; mass mobilization in 64; seizure of British Concession in 73–7, 86; meeting of Third Plenum in 86–7; Japanese incident in 94, 114; foreign exodus from 114; meeting of labour congress in 140–1; aftermath of Canton Commune in 169
Hanyang; mass mobilization in 64
Hanyang Arsenal 137
Harbin: KMT office in 12
Hassis, M., shot in Canton 168
Heilungkiang 569
Hengyang 55
Ho Chien 127–8, 132, 159; on communists 141, 143; in attack on Nanking 157
Ho Hsiang-ning (Mme Liao Chung-k'ai) 148, 159
Ho Lai 167n
Ho Lung 138, 148, 149, 160
Ho-sheng (bridge) 57
Ho Yao-tsu 60, 97, 174
Ho Ying ch'in 52, 85, 156, 163; in Fukien campaign 60, 62; commander of Eastern Route Army 61, 85; in campaign for Shanghai 90; anti-communist 97, 103; in Nanking 107; in northern campaign 126; in defence of Nanking 157; on Special Central Committee 158; and Peking campaign 174, 185; on State Council 191
Honam Island 166; refuge of KMT

loyalists 167, 168
Honan: Wu P'ei-fu in 51; Wuhan group's moves into 124–5 135–6; Feng Yü-hsiang in control of 136, 186
Hong Kong: strike in 25–6, 69, 149, 160, 168
Hou Shao-ch'iu 106, 107
Hsia Hsi 120
Hsia Tou-yin 126, 128, 152
Hsiang River 55, 66, 152
Hsiang Chung-fa 135, 192
Hsiang Fu-i 101
Hsiang-ya (Yale-in-China hospital and medical college) 71
Hsiang Ying 64
Hsiao Ch'u-nü 111
Hsiao K'o 148
Hsieh Ch'ih 18, 31; expelled from KMT 32
Hsieh Ping-ying 121
Hsin-tien 152
Hsu Ch'ien 75, 78, 79, 87, 103, 113; denounced by Nanking 113; on land commission 122; in Honan 136; and break between parties 143; suspended as CEC member 173
Hsu Ch'ung-chih, General 13; in First Eastern Expedition 20; on Political Council 25; on special committee of three 27; expelled from army post 27
Hsu K'o-hsiang 127, at Changsha 129, 132, 134
Hsu Kuang-ying 167n
Hsu Pai-hao 64
Hsuan Chung-hua 100
Hsuchow 125, 139, 156, 174
Hsueh Tu-pi 174
Hsueh Yueh 85, 91, 94, 108; in Canton coup 161; and Canton commune 168
Hsun-tzu 9
Hu Han-min 14, 97; on Political

Council 25; to Russia 27, 33; on CEC 33; and Chiang's coup 48–9; in Nanking government 113; on Chiang's retirement 156; on Special Central Committee 157–8; on Canton coup 162; not at Fourth Plenum 171; drafting of Organic Law by 190; on Standing Committee 191

Hu Shu-wu 109

Hu Tsung-to 169

Huang Ch'i-hsiang 57; coup by 161–2, 165; and Canton Commune 166, 167, 170

Huang Chin-jung 84

Huang Fu 84, 93, 96; in Nanking government 174; settlement of Nanking Incident 175; as foreign minister 178

Huang Jih-k'uei 53

Huang Shao-hsiung (Shao-hung) 30, 50, 52, 97, 137; in communist purge 112; in Kwangsi clique 160; at Canton 161, 163, 165, 171

Hui-chow (Waichow) 29

Hunan: target of Northern Expedition 50, 55, 62; Wu P'ei-fu in 51; and Second Corps 52; labour organization in 64; farmers' movement in 65–7, 117–19; anti-foreign movement in 71–2; agrarian disorder in 114, 132–3; Mao Tse-tung in charge of rural revolt in 151, 152–3

Hunan Army 26, 181; in National Revolutionary Army 29

Hupei: Wu P'ei-fu in 51; under Nationalist government 59, 62, 64; farmers' movement in 65, 68, 114, 117–18; rioting in 128, 137; autumn riots in 150, 151–2

Ichang 126

imperialism: Leninist theory of 6; attacked by Nationalist Party 11; see also anti-imperialism

International Settlement Shanghai: in May 30th Incident 22; in capture of Shanghai by Nationalists 88; in purge of communists 108; see also Shanghai

Ivanov, A. N. 43

Izvestia 41

Japan: Russian proposal to 45–6; and anti-imperialism movement 68; Chiang's negotiations with 84, 160–1; and the Nanking Incident 91–2; and Hankow Incident 91–3, 114; and Tsinan Incident 176–80; nationals in Tientsin 181; Manchuria 181; memorandum on Manchuria 182

Joffe, Adolf 7

Juan Hsiao-hsien 17

Kaifeng 174; Russian advisers in 43

Kalgan: Kuominchün base at 43, 49, 51; Fengtien Army in 181

Kan Nai-kuang 33, 159; excluded from Fourth Plenum 171

Kan River 59

Kanchow 88

Karakhan, Lev M. 6, 43, 44

Kashing 85

Kellogg, Frank B. 183, 189

Kiangsi: Northern campaign in 59–60, 62; farmers' movement in 65, 68, 117–18; actions against communists in 87–8; communist activity in 102; flight of communists to 145

Kiangsu: purge of leftists in 112; KMT moves into 125; party reorganization in 171

Kiukiang: anti-foreign riots in 23; in Northern Expedition 59; capture of 60; seizure of British enclave in 75,

77; suppression of communists in
88, 149
Ko-lao hui 133
Ku Meng-yü 122, 123, 136, 159;
excluded from Fourth Plenum 171
Ku Shun-chang 109
Ku Ying-fen 96, 111
Kung Ch'u 147n
Kung, H. H., see K'ung Hsiang-hsi
K'ung Hsiang-hsi (H. H. Kung) 160,
174
Kuo Liang 64
Kuo-min chün (Kuominchün;
National People's Army) 125, 193;
Russian contacts with 43; in drive
to Peking 174
Kuo-min-tang (Chung-kuo Kuo-min-
tang; KMT; Chinese Nationalist
Party) 2; position under Sun Yat-
sen 2–5; membership in 4; entrance
of CCP into 6; Borodin's work in
7–13; military force for 13–14;
rivalry with CCP 15–18; conflict in
Shanghai and Canton 18–27;
polarization of 30–3; party
representatives in NRA 35; on
Russian relations 40–1, 44–5;
readjusted power relations of 47–9;
split with Wuhan 82–5; purge of
leftists from 108–12; government at
Nanking 112–13; continued
military drives 124–35; split with
CCP 144–6; attempts to unify
leadership 155–63; drive for Peking
170–6; Chiang's reorganization of
171–3; as continued power in
Nationalist government 190;
condition of (1928) 191–2; see also
Chiang Kai-shek; Nationalist
government; Nationalist
Revolution
Kuo Mo-jo: head of Propaganda
Department 50–1; and Nanchang
Uprising 148

Kuo P'in-po 112
Kuo Sung-ling 43
Kuybyshev, N. V. ('Kisan'ka') 44–
5, 47
Kwangsi: army units of 3, 53;
farmers' associations in 18; allied
with Canton 30, 50; Nationalists in
62; anti-Christian riots in 70; purge
of communists in 112
Kwangsi Clique 137; v. Whampoa
group 156; weakness of 160; in
drive on Peking 181
Kwangtung: peasant organization in
16–17; under Nationalist control
24–30; farmers' movement in 39;
purge of leftists in 112; autumn
harvest revolts in 150, 154–5
Kwangtung Army 3, 20, 182; in
National Revolutionary Army 29,
52
Kwangtung Provincial Committee:
and the Canton Commune 165; and
Canton Soviet 167
Kweichow: army of 52; Nationalists
in 62

labour: and May 30th Incident 21–3;
organizers of 63–4; see also
peasants; proletariat; working class
labour unions 193; KMT work with
15; national organization 21, 38–9;
revived after military victories 63–
4; violence connected with 80; after
capture of Shanghai 95, 99; CCP
work with 99; in Nanking 106;
purge of communist leaders in 112;
in Canton 160; see also General
Labour Union; mass mobilization
Lai Shih-huang 55, 59, 61
Lampson, Miles 72–3, 76, 175; on
Japanese Memorandum 183
land: Borodin's advice on 9, 11;
demands for redistribution 66, 118;
report of commission of 122–3,

and the Autumn Harvest revolts
151
land taxes: Sun Yat-sen on 9
landlords, and farmers' organizations
17, 118
landowners: and farmers' associations
39
Lazovskii, Aleksandr 140
League of Military Youth 20, 37
League of Nations 180
leftists: in KMT organization 32; as
party representatives in NRA 36; in
General Political Department 51;
on Provisional Joint Council 78–9;
at Third Plenum 87; in Chungking
100–1; separating communists from
135–46; Shanghai faction 155–63;
absent from Fourth Plenum 172–3
Lenin, Nikolai: on capitalist countries
and colonies 6; Sun Yat-sen's
interest in 7; death of 11
li (Chinese mile; one-third English
mile) 179, 181
Li Chi-shen 29, 53, 97; and the
Northern Expedition 50, 53; anti-
communist 97, 107; in Canton
purge 110–11; in Kwangtung 136,
154; on Special Central Committee
158; in new Canton group 159,
160, 161, 171; on Canton coup 162,
165; recapture of Canton by 170;
and Northern campaign 174; on
State Council 191
Li Ch'i-han (Li Sen) 111
Li Chih-lung 47
Li Feng-hsiang 60
Li Fu-ch'un 52; in Nanking 105, 106
Li Fu-lin 29; in Canton coup 161,
163; and Canton Commune 166,
168
Li Han-chün 169
Li Hsien-p'ei 121n
Li Li-san 38, 64, 120; in anti-British
agitation 73; in labour organization

141; and Nanchang Uprising 148
Li Lieh chün: in Nanchang 102; on
new Standing Committee 158, 173
Li Pao-chang, Gen. 85, 86
Li P'ei-t'ung 102–3
Li P'in-hsien 159
Li Sen, *see* Li Ch'i-han
Li Shih-chang 92n
Li Shih-tseng (Li Yü-ying): on
communists 96, 97, 99; in Nanking
government 113; on Chiang's
retirement 156; on Canton coup
162
Li Ta-chao: on united front 12, 18;
warrant for arrest 44; arrest of 103;
execution of 104, 192
Li Tsung-jen 137, 139, 159; in KMT
30, 50; and Kwangsi forces 50, 52,
53; in Northern Expedition 57; and
Seventh Corps 82, 171; in
campaign for Shanghai 88; on
expulsion of communists 97; in
northern campaign 126; and the
Kwangsi Clique 156; in defence of
Nanking 157; on Fourth Plenum
158; Canton coup 162; in
command of Fourth Army 181; on
State Council 191
Li Wei-han (pseudonym Lo Mai) 130,
147
Liao Chung-k'ai 9, 14; head of
Labour Bureau 12, 15; on Political
Council 25; assassination of 27
Liao Chung-k'ai, Mme, *see* Ho
Hsiang-ning
Liao Lei 181n
Liao Shang-kuo 166
Lien River 55
lien-tso fa (law of collective
responsibility) 20
Lin Piao 148
Lin Po-ch'ü, *see* Lin Tsu-han
Lin Sen 27, 191
Lin Tsu-han (Lin Po-ch'ü) 12; on

CEC standing committee 33; in Sixth Corps, 53, 105; denounced by Nanking 113; on new foreign policy 117; on Land Commission report 124
Ling Ping 120
Liu Chen-huan, Gen. 3, 13, 24
Liu Chih, Gen. 104, 108, 174
Liu Chih-hsun 67
Liu Erh-sung 15; executed 111
Liu Hsiang 101
Liu Hsing 157, 159
Liu Po-ch'eng 101, 148
Liu Shao-ch'i 38, 64
Liu Tso-lung 57
Liu Wen-tao 53
Liu-yang 130, 153, 154
Lo Ch'i-yuan 16, 17
Lo I-nung 91, 151
Lo Jui-ch'ing 148
Lo Mai, see Li Wei-han
loans, foreign: to Chiang Kai-shek 84
Locarno treaties 45
Lominadze, Besso 147; conference called by 150
Loyang 83
Lu-chün chün-kuan hsueh-hsiao (Army Officers' Academy) 14
Lu Chung-lin 136n
Lu-feng 18, 39, 149, 154
Lu River 55
Lu-shan 148, 156
Lu Shih-ti 13
Lu Shih-ying 112
Lu Ti-p'ing 52, 159
Lü Ch'ao 101
Lung-t'an battle 157
Lunghai (railway) 83, 114, 125, 146, 174

Ma K'e-fu 152, 153
Ma Shih-ts'ai 102–3
Ma Soo 41
MacMurray, J. V. A. 175, 183; treaty

negotiated by 189
Mai Huan-chang 53
Manchuria: Russian proposals on 45–6; special concern of Japan 180–5
Mandalian, A. 108
Mao I-heng 139
Mao Tse-tung: work with farmers 16, 66, 67; on break with KMT 19; on agrarian revolution 67, 119, 120; on violence as necessary phase 81; on Land Commission 122; and disturbances in Hunan 133, 149, 151, 152–3, 154
Maring, see Sneevliet, H.
Maritime China, see individual cities by name
Maritime Customs Service: Sun's attempt to keep revenue 4, 10
mass mobilization: rivalry of CCP and KMT in 17; communist 37–40, 100–1; farmers' movement 39, 152; labour unions 40, 63; and success of Northern Expedition 63–8; violence connected with 80–1; advised by Stalin 130; under KMT control 172; communist skills in 193; see also farmers' movement; labour unions; peasants
May Thirtieth movement 21–3, 68
Mei-foo see Standard Oil of New York
Meng Chao-yueh 83
Merchants' Corps, Canton 19–20
Military Council (KMT) 33–7, 49–50, 87
military forces: Nationalist 2–3; KMT 13–14; proposed unification of 185–6, 188; see also armies
Military Youth, League of 20, 37
Milo River 57
Min-kuo jih-pao (National daily) 31
Min River 62
min t'uan (militia) 18, 40, 154
missionaries: Nationalist campaign

against 70; evacuated from interior
75; *see also* Christianity
Mo Hsiung 166
Morioka Shōhei 92
Moscow: in tariff re-negotiation 189;
see also anti-imperialism

Nan-k'ou 51
Nanchang: objective of Northern
Expedition 57, 59–60; capture of
60, 68; seat of NRA 78, 88, 102;
revolutionary conflict in 101–2, 155
Nanchang uprising 147–9
Nanking: site of government 78, 105;
campaign for 88, 91; Chiang Kai-
shek's take-over of 105–7;
government established at 112–13;
attacked by Sun Ch'uan-fang 157
Nanking government: attempts at
reconciliation with Wuhan 155–6;
conflicts within 156; on a northern
campaign 174; re-inaugurated
(1928) 190 *see also* Nationalist
government
Nanking Incident 91–2, 114;
attribution of blame for 92, 95;
U.S. settlement of 175; British
settlement of 190
National Congress of Kuomintang
Delegates 11
National General Labour Union 21;
communist expansion of 38–9;
Fourth Congress of 140
National Peasant Conference 17
National People's Army, *see* Kuo-min
chün
National Revolutionary Army 14;
formation of 25; reorganization of
29–30; campaigns of 29;
politicization of 33–5; communist
penetration of 35–7; on plans for
Northern Expedition 50, 51; make-
up of corps of 52–5; growth of 52;
campaign against Wuchang 57, 59;

Kiangsi offensive 59–60, 62; losses
of 59, 60; Fukien campaign 61–2;
basis of victories 62; treatment of
populace by 63; in capture of
Shanghai 90; anti-communist
generals of 97; after fall of Peking
185
nationalism, Chinese: as incentive of
NRA 62; *v.* social revolution 99; *see
also* imperialism
Nationalist government: organization
of 25; drive for military unification
171; reorganized by Fourth Plenum
172–3; reconstruction launched by
185–91; Organic Law promulgated
190; prospects for (1928) 190, 191–
4; region of 193–4; *see also* Nanking
government; Nationalist
Revolution
Nationalist Party, *see* Kuo-min-tang
Nationalist Revolution: background
of 1–2; position of Sun Yat-sen 2–
5; Soviet interest in KMT 5–8;
Borodin's rejuvenation of KMT 8–
13; Nationalist Congress (1924) 11;
military force 13–14; efforts
towards mass movement 15–18;
conflict between CCP and KMT
18–23; southern base at Canton 24–
7; aborted counter-revolution 27–
30; polarization of KMT 30–3;
penetration of NRA 33–7;
organization of mass movements
37–40; Russian role in 40–7;
planning for Northern Expedition
49–55; Northern Expedition 55–63;
mass mobilization 63–8; anti-
imperialist movement 68–73;
seizure of British concession in
Hankow 73–7; conflict over
revolutionary goals 77–82; growing
split 82–5; capture of Shanghai and
Nanking 85–94; struggle for
control 94–9; mounting violence

99–105; anti-communist purge 108–12; rural revolution 117–24; military moves 124–35; separation of leftists from communists 135–46

naval groups, menace to Northern Expedition 51, 62

Neumann, Heinz 168

Nieh Jung-chen 148

nihilists, European 51

Nilov, *see* Sakanovsky

Ningpo 84; clashes of revolutionaries at 107, 112

Ninth Corps, NRA 57

Niu Yung-chien 90

North China Daily News 96, 105

Northern Expedition 20; Russian attitude towards 46–7; planning for 49–55; coalitions in path of 51–2; beginning of 55–63; resumption of 115, 121, 124, 159, 174–6; culmination at Peking 185; limits of 194

nung-min hsieh-hui (farmers' associations) 16

O'Malley, Owen 76

Organic Law of the National Government 190

Outer Mongolia: Russia and China rivals in 5

Pai Ch'ung-hsi 30, 137, 139, 156; and Northern Expedition 50, 52, 57; in capture of Hangchow 85, 90; in campaign for Shanghai 90–1, 105; anti-communist 97, 105, 107; in Communist purge 108; in northern campaign 126; in defence of Nanking 157; on Special Central Committee 158; on Canton coup 162; and Seventh Corps 171; in drive on Peking 181, 184

Pamiat Lenina 142

Pao Yü-lin 184

Paoting 181, 183

Paoting Military Academy 14, 50

Party Army: in First Eastern Expedition 20; Chiang commander of 25; at Shameen 26

Pavlov, Gen. P. A. 14

peasants: and the KMT 11; and the Comintern 15–16, 42; in farmers' organizations 17, 67, 118; and the CCP 37; violence of 81; in rural uprisings 151–2; in Canton commune 165; *see also* labour; land

Peking: KMT office in 12; goal of Nationalists 78–9; raid on Soviet Embassy in 103–4; preparations for drive on 170–5; military campaign 176, 180–5

Peking–Hankow railway 64; in campaigns 79, 83, 125, 176, 181

Peking–Suiyan railway 176, 181

P'eng Han-chang 57

P'eng Kung-ta 151

P'eng P'ai: peasants organized by 16, 17, 39, 149; and Nanchang Uprising 154

P'eng Tse-hsiang 129

P'eng Tse-min 173

People's Tribune 116

Pi Shu-ch'eng 83, 88; defeat and execution 90

P'ing-chiang: objective on Northern Expedition 57; goal in Hunan rural uprising 153, 154

P'ing-Han railway 137

P'ing-hsiang Chu-chou Railway 55, 133

Po Wen-wei 97

Pokvalisky, Boris 168

Politburo 129, 140; resolution on China 45

Political Council, KMT 19; at Wuhan 93; on Eastern Campaign 137

political parties: Chinese Communist Party 155–63; *see also individual parties by name*

Political Training Department (NRA) 33–5, 50, 173
Political Work, newspaper of Political Training Department 34
Po-yang Lake 59
Preparatory Conference before CEC 4th Plenum 162–3
Profintern: support of Chinese strikes by 41; at Congress of National Labour Union 140
proletariat: CCP to organize 37; see also working class
'Protecting the Party' (Canton coup) 162
Provisional Central Political Council, at Nanchang 79
Provisional Executive Committee (KMT) 8
Provisional Joint Council 78–9

Red Army 5, 33; founding of 148
Red Flag 167
revolution: rural 18, 117–24, 131
Revolution of 1911: anniversary of 190
rice: shortage in Wuhan 114
Roy, M. N. 137; on rural revolution 121; at Wuchang 126–7; on Changsha coup 129, 132, 135; and telegram from Stalin 131, 135; departure from China 143
Russia: and the Kuomintang 5–8; Borodin sent by 7–13; influence on Whampoa 14; army advisers from 14, 20; role in China (1926) 40–7, 62–3; on Japan and Chang Tso-lin 45–6; on anti-imperialism 68; right-wing opposition to 80; raid on Peking Embassy of 103–4; advice on land question 122; dilemma of instructions from 129, 138, 143; exodus of advisers from 143; CCP leaders' departure for 146; relations after Canton commune 164, 168–9,

172; see also Communist International; Stalin; and individual advisers by name

Sakanovsky, V. A. ('Nilov') 17, 36
San-min chu-i (Three principles of the people) 35
Second Corps, National Revolutionary Army 52, 56; in Nanking 105–6
Second Eastern Expedition 29
Second Group Army 174, 176
Second National Congress (KMT) 31, 70, 96
Seventeenth Corps, National Revolutionary Army 61
Seventh Corps, National Revolutionary Army 30, 52, 53; in Northern Expedition 55, 57, 59, 60; in alliance against Chiang 82; to Kiangsi 143; in defence of Nanking 157; changes in 171
'Shakee massacre' 25
Shameen 23; blockade of 15; strike in 25–6; and the Canton commune 167
Shang Chen 184
Shanghai: Nationalist Party in 4, 9, 12; strike in 21–2; May Thirtieth Incident 22–3; Western Hills faction in 31; workers in 38; goal of Northern Expedition 50; naval concentration at 51–2; International Settlement endangered 75; as buffer zone 79; Chiang's campaign to take 84, 88–94; 'second uprising' in 86; 'third uprising' in 90–1; struggle for control of 94–9, 104–5; action against Soviet consulate 104; communist purge in 108–12; CCP proposal for general strike 110, 140; secret CCP headquarters in 155; Chiang-Wang discussions in 161

Shanghai–Nanking line 88
Shanghai University 21
'Shanghai uprising' 86
Shanghai Volunteer Corps 23
Shanhaikuan 182, 184
Shantung: armies in, on drive to
    Peking 175, 176; Japanese troops
    sent to 176, 178
Shao-kuan 55, 59
Shen Hung-ying 3
Shen Ting-i 30
Shidehara Kijūrō 93
Shih Ch'ing-yang 101
Shihchiachuang 176, 180, 184
silver: embargo on 114
Sixth Congress (CCP) 192
Sixth Corps, National Revolutionary
    Army 29, 53; on Northern
    Expedition 56, 59–60; in Nanking
    105–6
Sneevliet, Hendricus (Maring) 6, 7
social revolution: v. nationalism 99;
    goals of 99; CCP v. KMT 137;
    issue of in party split 144–5
Socialist Youth Corps 15, 18, 42, 168
Society for the Study of Sun Yat-
    sen's Doctrines 21, 37; and the
    First Corps 52
Sokolsky, George 85
Soong, see Sung
Soong, T.V., see Sung Tzu-wen
Special Central Committee 157–8;
    Government Council of 158; coup
    supposedly against 162
Stalin, Josef 46; China policy attacked
    130; telegram of instructions 131,
    135, 136, 137, 138, 143, 144
Standard Oil Co. of New York 116;
    in Nanking 91
strikes: Canton–Hong Kong 15, 23,
    25, 39, 41, 69; Shanghai 21–3, 38–
    9; Russian support for 41; Peking–
    Hankow railway 64; in Wuhan 65;
    disruptive power of 80; in the

'Shanghai uprisings' 86, 90; in
    Hankow 94; in communist purges
    110, 111; Canton 165; see also
    boycotts; labour unions
Strong, Anna Louise 145
students: in Youth Corps 38
Su Chao-cheng 140, 144; head of
    Canton soviet 167
Sun Ch'uan-fang 50, 80, 90, 125, 137,
    193; in Alliance of five provinces
    51; and the Northern Expedition
    56, 59, 60, 62, 125; losses of 59–60;
    possible European assistance to 80;
    Chiang's shift away from 83, 85;
    Shanghai uprising against 86; in
    drive towards Yangtze 156; attack
    on Nanking 157; secret intrigues of
    159; in Peking drive 176, 184
Sun Chung-shan, see Sun Yat-sen
Sun Fo (Sun K'o) 4, 116, 148; on
    party unification 157; not at Fourth
    Plenum 171; on State Council 191
Sun K'o, see Sun Fo
Sun Liang-ch'eng, Gen. 176; in
    Tsinan Incident 178
Sun Yat-sen (Sun Wen, Sun Chung-
    shan) 18, 143, 173, 186; alliance
    with Chang Tso-lin 1–2; position
    in 1923 2–5; and Borodin 7–13;
    military force of 13–14; and Canton
    Merchants' Corps 19–20; death of
    20, 21; finances of 40–1; and CCP
    98; Chiang on Russian influence on
    155, 156, 169; meeting at grave of
    185; ideas of in Nationalist
    government 191
Sun Yat-sen, Madame (Sung Ch'ing-
    ling), departure for Russia 145,
    148; omitted from Special Central
    Committee 158; marriage of sister
    160
Sun Yat-sen University 169
Sun Yat-senism 52
Sung Ch'ing-ling (Soong Ch'ing-ling)

see Sun Yat-sen, Madame
Sung Mei-ling (Soong Mei-ling)
  (Madame Chiang Kai-shek):
  marriage of 160
Sung Tzu-wen (T. V. Soong) 97, 143,
  160; omitted from Special Central
  Committee 158; in negotiations
  with Wang Ching-wei 161; finance
  minister 170; on unification of
  finance 187; tariff treaty with U.S.
  189
Swatow 29, 149, 155; repression of
  communists in 112
Szechwan 194; KMT office in 12;
  army corps from 29; purge of
  communists in 101
Szechwan Daily 101

Ta-yeh 64
Tai Chi-t'ao 191; on KMT Standing
  Committee 12, 191; at Whampoa
  14; on communist participation 30,
  32; on Special Central Committee
  157; head of Political Training
  Department 173; drafting of
  Organic Law by 190
T'an P'ing-shan 129, 135; in KMT
  party organization 12, 32, 33; in
  Foochow 103; on Land
  Commission 122; in hiding 144;
  and Nanchang Uprising 148-9;
  censured for opportunism 150
T'an Yen-k'ai, Gen. 13, 25, 139;
  commander of Second Corps 29,
  52; on CEC 33; at Nanchang 78; in
  talks on party unification 157; on
  Standing Committee 158, 161, 173,
  191; on abrogation of treaties 190
Tanaka Giichi, Baron 160; and the
  Tsinan Incident 176-80; on
  Manchuria 182
tang-t'uan ('party fractions') 9
T'ang Sheng-chih 30, 52, 151; in
  Northern Expedition 53, 55, 55-6,

57; on Shanghai campaign 78; in
  alliance against Chiang 82, 87; in
  Honan campaign 125, 128, 132; to
  restore order in Hunan 133-4, 137,
  141, 181; and Eastern Campaign
  137, 138; and Nanchang Uprising
  148; and attack on Nanking 157;
  on Special Central Committee 158;
  Nanking denounced by 159;
  campaign against 162
tariff autonomy 189
tariffs: U.S. treaty on 189
Techow 181
Teichman, Eric 76, 93, 115
tenants: commission report on 123
Teng Chung-hsia 148
Teng Pen-yin 29
Teng Tse-ju 113
Teng Yen-ta 50, 57, 78, 87, 166; in
  Foochow 103; in Political
  Department 112; denounced by
  Nanking 113; on Central Land
  Commission 122, 124; departure
  for Russia 145, 148; expelled by
  KMT 173
Tenth Corps, National Revolutionary
  Army 57
Third Army Group 184
Third Corps, National Revolutionary
  Army 29, 52-3; on Northern
  Expedition 56, 60; in alliance
  against Chiang Kai-shek 82
Third Group Army 174, 184
Third Plenum of KMT Central
  Executive Committee 80, 86-7;
  manifesto to farmers 118; validity
  questioned 158
Three People's Principles 2, 30, 35,
  48; explained in Moscow 143
Tientsin: arrest of KMT members in
  74; search of Soviet establishments
  in 104; and drive on Peking 181;
  protection of foreigners in 181-5;
  taken over by Nationalists 184

Tientsin–Pukow Railway Agreement (1908) 88
Tientsin–Pukow line 125, 157, 174, 176
Ting-chou: missionary hospital at 149
Ting-ssu (bridge) 57
Ting Wei-fen 173
Trans-Siberian Railway 5
treaty system: and May Thirtieth Incident 22; and Canton–Hong Kong strike 26–7; and Peking incident 44; target of Nationalist movement 68–73, 189; transition to revision 190, 193; see also anti-imperialism; foreign network; nationalism
Treint, Albert 130
Trotsky, Leon: and resolution on China 45; on China policy 130
Ts'ai Ho-sen: on break with KMT 19; on Eastern Campaign 137
Ts'ai Kung-shih 179n
Ts'ai T'ing-k'ai 149
Ts'ai Yuan-p'ei: on expulsion of communists 96, 97; in Nanking government 113; on Chiang's retirement 156; on Standing Committee 158, 173, 191; on Canton coup 162; on abrogation of treaties 190
Ts'ao Wan-shun 60
Tsinan 90; Japanese troops in 125, 176
Tsinan Incident 176–80
Tsingtao (Ch'ing-tao) 90, 176; Japanese troops in 125
Tsou Lu 27, 31; expelled from KMT 32
Tsur, Y.T., see Chou I-chün
Tu Ch'i-yun 61
Tu Yueh-sheng 104, 108
Tuan Ch'i-jui 1; and 18 March incident 44

Tung Pi-wu (Tung Yung-wei) 119, 120
Tung Yung-wei, see Tung Pi-wu
Twentieth Corps, National Revolutionary Army 126, 138

Ulan-Bator 146
unions, see labour unions
United States: in the anti-foreign campaign 72; and Shanghai campaign 86; attacks on citizens of 91–2; settlement of Nanking Incident 175; and Japanese memorandum 183; new tariff treaty with 189
U.S.S.R., see Russia
University of the Toilers of the East 53
urban elite, see elite

Vladivostock 14, 40, 44, 142
Voitinsky, G. 7; in China 19

Waichow 29
Wan-hsien 126; incident at 69
Wang Chen (Wang I-t'ing) 96
Wang Cheng-t'ing (C. T. Wang) 189
Wang Ching-wei 14, 21, 116; on Political Council 25; on special committee of three 27; declared suspended 31, 155; on expulsion of Western Hills dissidents 32; on CEC 33; and Chiang Kai-shek 47–8, 79; advanced by Third Plenum 87; return to China 97–9, 106; to Wuhan 98; in Shanghai 108; failure to go to Nanking 112; on Stalin's telegram 131, 135–6; on Changsha 133, 135; on Eastern Campaign 137; Feng Yü-hsiang's terms to 139; in split with Nanking 143; farewell to Borodin 145–6; and Nanchang Uprising 148; in talks on

party unification 157; on Special
Central Committee 157; resignation
of 158; headquarters in Canton 159,
160; negotiations with Chiang 161–
3; and the Canton Coup 163, 170;
and Canton commune 166;
excluded from Fourth Plenum 171;
on Standing Committee 191
Wang Chün 102
Wang Ch'ung-hui 190
Wang Fa-ch'in 78n, 136n
Wang I-t'ing, see Wang Chen
Wang Ling-chi 101
Wang Po-ch'ün 188n
Wang P'u 83, 88, 97
Wang Shih-chen 184
Wang Shou-hua 91, 95, 104, 108;
death of 109
Wang Ssu-tseng 110n
Wang T'ien-p'ei 57
warlords: a persistent problem 193–4
Wei I-san 83
Wei Pang-p'ing 29
Western Hills: meeting of KMT CEC
in 31, 101, 155
Whampoa Cadets Association 100,
102, 103, 105
Whampoa Military Academy 27, 156;
communist groups at 193;
establishment of 14, 50; Chiang
Kai-shek commandant 14, 20, 24;
and political training 33–4; Russian
financial backing of 40; regiments
from in First Corps 52; and
communist purge 111
working class: included in national
revolution 6; see also labour;
proletariat
Wu Ch'ao-shu (C. C. Wu) 25, 96;
expelled from KMT 49; not at
Fourth Plenum 171
Wu Chih-hui: on communists 96, 97,
99; in Nanking government 113;
on Chiang's retirement 156; on

Special Central Committee 157–8;
on Canton coup 162
Wu P'ei-fu 20, 193; at Canton 2, 3;
coup against 42; enemy of Russia
43, 46; coalition of 51; in Northern
Expedition 56, 57, 59, 125
Wu T'ieh-ch'eng 4; imprisonment of
49
Wu Yü-chang 87, 101, 133;
denounced by Nanking 113; on
Land Commission report 124; in
hiding 144
Wuchang: objective of Northern
Expedition 57, 59, 63; battle for
126–7; CCP headquarters in 141
Wuhan: in Northern Expedition 50;
labour unions in 64; Nationalist
government set up in 78–9;
vulnerability of 136
Wuhan government: on Nanking
Incident 93; Chiang's plots against
95; struggle to survive 103–17;
executions by 112; attempt to
control rural revolution 117–24;
military moves of 125–6 and
Changsha coup 128–9, 134–5;
Stalin's telegram to 131; and the
party split 144–6; attempted
reconciliation with Nanking 155–6

Yada Shichitarō 93, 96, 182
Yale-in-China (Ya-li) 67, 70, 71
Yang Chieh 92
Yang Hsi-min, Gen. 2, 13, 24
Yang Hu 104; in Nanking 106; in
Shanghai 108; in Ningpo 112
Yang Pao-an 33
Yang Sen 125, 138; in northern
campaign 126
Yang Shu-chuang, Admiral 83; shift
to Nationalists 90; on Special
Central Committee 158; at Fifth
Plenum 186; on State Council 191
Yang Yin 167n

Yang Yü-t'ing 184
Yangtze River: and Northern
  Expedition 50, 59; campaign in
  lower area 83, 87, 88–94
Yeh Ch'i 159
Yeh Chien-ying 165, 166
Yeh K'ai-hsin 55
Yeh Te-hui 112
Yeh T'ing 53, 55; in Northern
  Expedition 59, 63; at Wuchang
  126–7; and Nanchang uprising 148;
  in Kwangtung 160; and Canton
  Commune 165, 166
Yen Hsi-shan 137, 163, 171; on
  Special Central Committee 158; and
  Peking drive 174, 176, 180; and
  Japanese memorandum 183; to take
  over Peking 184; at Fifth Plenum
  186; on State Council 191; warlord

role of 193
Yoshizawa Kenkichi 182
Youth Corps: and mass organization
  37
Yü Fei-p'eng 85
Yü Hsia-ch'ing (Yü Ho-te, Yü Ya-
  ching) 84, 96, 187
Yü Shu-te 78n, 136n
Yueh Wei-chün 43
Yü Ya-ching, see Yü Hsia-ch'ing
Yü Yu-jen 136, 173, 191
Yuan Tsu-ming 56
Yuan Tzu-ying 112
Yueh Wei-chün 43
Yun Tai-ying 165, 166; at Wuchang
  126; and Nanchang uprising 148–9
Yunnan 194; revolutionary armies of
  2–3, 13, 24, 52–3
Yunnan military academy 14, 52